T0180615

Lecture Notes in Computer Science

Lecture Notes in Artificial Intelligence   14392

Founding Editor

Jörg Siekmann

Series Editors

Randy Goebel, *University of Alberta, Edmonton, Canada*
Wolfgang Wahlster, *DFKI, Berlin, Germany*
Zhi-Hua Zhou, *Nanjing University, Nanjing, China*

The series Lecture Notes in Artificial Intelligence (LNAI) was established in 1988 as a topical subseries of LNCS devoted to artificial intelligence.

The series publishes state-of-the-art research results at a high level. As with the LNCS mother series, the mission of the series is to serve the international R & D community by providing an invaluable service, mainly focused on the publication of conference and workshop proceedings and postproceedings.

Hiram Calvo · Lourdes Martínez-Villaseñor ·
Hiram Ponce
Editors

Advances in Soft Computing

22nd Mexican International Conference
on Artificial Intelligence, MICAI 2023
Yucatán, Mexico, November 13–18, 2023
Proceedings, Part II

 Springer

Editors
Hiram Calvo ⓘ
Center for Computing Research
Instituto Politécnico Nacional
Ciudad de México, Distrito Federal, Mexico

Lourdes Martínez-Villaseñor ⓘ
Facultad de Ingeniería
Universidad Panamericana
Ciudad de México, Mexico

Hiram Ponce ⓘ
Facultad de Ingeniería
Universidad Panamericana
Ciudad de México, Mexico

ISSN 0302-9743   ISSN 1611-3349 (electronic)
Lecture Notes in Artificial Intelligence
ISBN 978-3-031-47639-6   ISBN 978-3-031-47640-2 (eBook)
https://doi.org/10.1007/978-3-031-47640-2

LNCS Sublibrary: SL7 – Artificial Intelligence

This Springer imprint is published by the registered company Springer Nature Switzerland AG
The registered company address is: Gewerbestrasse 11, 6330 Cham, Switzerland

Paper in this product is recyclable.

Preface

The Mexican International Conference on Artificial Intelligence (MICAI) is a yearly international conference series that has been organized by the Mexican Society for Artificial Intelligence (SMIA) since 2000. MICAI is a major international artificial intelligence (AI) forum and the main event in the academic life of the country's growing AI community.

This year, MICAI 2023 was graciously hosted by the Instituto de Investigaciones en Matemáticas Aplicadas y en Sistemas (IIMAS) and the Universidad Autónoma del Estado de Yucatán (UAEY). The conference presented a cornucopia of scientific endeavors. From incisive keynote lectures and detailed paper presentations to hands-on tutorials, thought-provoking panels, and niche workshops, the spectrum of activities aimed to cater to a wide audience. Moreover, we continued the legacy of announcing the José Negrete Award, the SMIA Best Thesis in Artificial Intelligence Contest's results. This year, the historic and culturally rich city of Mérida, Yucatán was our chosen rendezvous.

MICAI conferences publish high-quality papers in all areas of AI and its applications. The proceedings of the previous MICAI events have been published by Springer in its Lecture Notes in Artificial Intelligence (LNAI) series (volumes: 1793, 2313, 2972, 3789, 4293, 4827, 5317, 5845, 6437, 6438, 7094, 7095, 7629, 7630, 8265, 8266, 8856, 8857, 9413, 9414, 10061, 10062, 10632, 10633, 11288, 11289, 11835, 12468, 12469, 13067, 13068, 13612, and 13613). Since its foundation in 2000, the conference has grown in popularity and improved in quality.

The proceedings of MICAI 2023 are published in two volumes. The first volume, *Advances in Computational Intelligence*, contains 24 papers structured into three sections:

- Machine Learning
- Computer Vision and Image Processing
- Intelligent Systems

The second volume, *Advances in Soft Computing*, contains 25 papers structured into three sections:

- Natural Language Processing
- Bioinformatics and Medical Applications
- Robotics and Applications

The two-volume set will be of interest for researchers in all fields of artificial intelligence, students specializing in related topics, and the general public interested in recent developments in AI.

The conference received for evaluation 115 submissions from 17 countries: Bolivia, Brazil, Colombia, Cuba, Denmark, Ecuador, Spain, USA, France, The Netherlands, Italy, Kazakhstan, Mexico, Peru, UK, Russia, and Sweden. Gender representation also echoed with 90 male authors and 21 female authors adding their voice. From these submissions, 49 papers were selected for publication in these two volumes after 3 reviews per submission in a double-blind peer-reviewing process carried out by the international Program Committee. The acceptance rate was 43%.

The international Program Committee consisted of 80 experts from 10 countries: Australia, Brazil, France, Germany, Japan, Kazakhstan, Mexico, Russia, Spain, and UK.

Three workshops were held jointly with the conference:

- WILE 2023: 16th Workshop on Intelligent Learning Environments
- HIS 2023: 16th Workshop of Hybrid Intelligent Systems
- CIAPP 2023: 5th Workshop on New Trends in Computational Intelligence and Applications

We want to thank all the people involved in the organization of this conference: the authors of the papers published in these two volumes –it is their research work that gives value to the proceedings– and the organizers for their work. We thank the reviewers for their great effort spent on reviewing the submissions and the Program and Organizing Committee members.

A special acknowledgment goes to the local committee led by Antonio Neme, whose meticulous coordination has been instrumental in realizing MICAI 2023 in Mérida, Yucatán, Mexico. Our thanks extend to IIMAS's director, Ramsés Mena, and its academic secretary, Katya Rodríguez. We are also indebted to Anabel Martín from the Faculty of Mathematics at the UADY for her invaluable assistance in securing the university facilities.

The entire submission, reviewing, and selection process, as well as preparation of the proceedings, was supported by Microsoft's Conference Management Toolkit (https://cmt3.research.microsoft.com/). Last but not least, we are grateful to Springer for their patience and help in the preparation of these volumes.

In conclusion, MICAI 2023 is more than just a conference. It is a confluence of minds, a testament to the indefatigable spirit of the AI community, and a beacon for the future of Artificial Intelligence. As you navigate through these proceedings, may you find inspiration, knowledge, and connections that propel you forward in your journey.

The MICAI series website is www.MICAI.org. The website of the Mexican Society for Artificial Intelligence, SMIA, is www.SMIA.mx. Contact options and additional information can be found on these websites.

November 2023

Hiram Calvo
Lourdes Martínez-Villaseñor
Hiram Ponce

Organization

Conference Committee

General Chair

Hiram Calvo   Instituto Politécnico Nacional, Mexico

Program Chairs

Hiram Calvo   Instituto Politécnico Nacional, Mexico
Lourdes Martínez-Villaseñor   Universidad Panamericana, Mexico
Hiram Ponce   Universidad Panamericana, Mexico

Workshop Chair

Hiram Ponce   Universidad Panamericana, Mexico

Tutorials Chair

Roberto Antonio Vázquez   Universidad La Salle, Mexico
   Espinoza de los Monteros

Doctoral Consortium Chairs

Miguel González Mendoza   Tecnológico de Monterrey, Mexico
Juan Martínez Miranda   Centro de Investigación Científica y de Educación
                                       Superior de Ensenada, Mexico

Keynote Talks Chairs

Gilberto Ochoa Ruiz   Tecnológico de Monterrey, Mexico
Iris Méndez   Universidad Autónoma de Ciudad Juárez, Mexico

Publication Chair

Hiram Ponce   Universidad Panamericana, Mexico

Financial Chairs

Hiram Calvo   Instituto Politécnico Nacional, Mexico
Lourdes Martínez-Villaseñor   Universidad Panamericana, Mexico

Grant Chair

Leobardo Morales   IBM, Mexico

Local Organizing Committee

Abigail Uribe Martínez   Universidad Autónoma del Estado de Yucatán, Mexico

Abraham Mandariaga Mazón   Universidad Autónoma del Estado de Yucatán, Mexico

Ali Bassam   Universidad Autónoma del Estado de Yucatán, Mexico

Anabel Martin   Universidad Autónoma del Estado de Yucatán, Mexico

Antonio Aguileta   Universidad Autónoma del Estado de Yucatán, Mexico

Antonio Neme   Universidad Autónoma del Estado de Yucatán, Mexico

Blanca Vázquez   Universidad Autónoma del Estado de Yucatán, Mexico

Joel Antonio Trejo Sánchez   Universidad Autónoma del Estado de Yucatán, Mexico

Jorge Perez-Gonzalez   Universidad Autónoma del Estado de Yucatán, Mexico

Julián Bravo Castillero   Universidad Autónoma del Estado de Yucatán, Mexico

Karina Martínez   Universidad Autónoma del Estado de Yucatán, Mexico

Mauricio Orozco del Castillo   Universidad Autónoma del Estado de Yucatán, Mexico

Nidiyare Hevia Montiel   Universidad Autónoma del Estado de Yucatán, Mexico

Nora Cuevas Cuevas   Universidad Autónoma del Estado de Yucatán, Mexico

Nora Pérez Quezadas   Universidad Autónoma del Estado de Yucatán, Mexico

Candy Sansores	Universidad Autónoma del Estado de Yucatán, Mexico
Carlos Bermejo Sabbagh	Universidad Autónoma del Estado de Yucatán, Mexico
Eric Ávila Vales	Universidad Autónoma del Estado de Yucatán, Mexico
Erik Molino Minero Re	Universidad Autónoma del Estado de Yucatán, Mexico
Fernando Arámbula Cosío	Universidad Autónoma del Estado de Yucatán, Mexico
Helena Gomez Adorno	Universidad Autónoma del Estado de Yucatán, Mexico
Israel Sánchez Domínguez	Universidad Autónoma del Estado de Yucatán, Mexico
Norberto Sánchez	Universidad Autónoma del Estado de Yucatán, Mexico
Paul Erick Méndez Monroy	Universidad Autónoma del Estado de Yucatán, Mexico
Ramón Aranda	Universidad Autónoma del Estado de Yucatán, Mexico
Vicente Carrión	Universidad Autónoma del Estado de Yucatán, Mexico
Victor Manuel Lomas Barrie	Universidad Autónoma del Estado de Yucatán, Mexico
Víctor Sandoval Curmina	Universidad Autónoma del Estado de Yucatán, Mexico
Victor Uc Cetina	Universidad Autónoma del Estado de Yucatán, Mexico
Yuriria Cortés Poza	Universidad Autónoma del Estado de Yucatán, Mexico

Program Committee

Alberto Ochoa-Zezzatti	Universidad Autónoma de Ciudad Juárez, Mexico
Aldo Marquez-Grajales	Instituto Tecnológico Superior de Xalapa, Mexico
Alexander Bozhenyuk	Southern Federal University, Russia
Andrés Espinal	Universidad de Guanajuato, Mexico
Angel Sánchez García	Universidad Veracruzana, Mexico
Anilu Franco	Universidad Autónoma del Estado de Hidalgo, Mexico
Antonieta Martinez	Universidad Panamericana, Mexico
Antonio Neme	UNAM, Mexico

Jaime Cerda	Universidad Michoacana de San Nicolás de Hidalgo, Mexico
Jerusa Marchi	Federal University of Santa Catarina, Brazil
Joanna Alvarado Uribe	Tecnológico de Monterrey, Mexico
Jorge Perez Gonzalez	UNAM, Mexico
José Alanis	Universidad Tecnológica de Puebla, Mexico
José Martínez-Carranza	INAOE, Mexico
Jose Alberto Hernandez-Aguilar	Universidad Autónoma del Estado de Morelos, Mexico
José Carlos Ortiz-Bayliss	Tecnológico de Monterrey, Mexico
Juan Villegas-Cortez	UAM - Azcapotzalco, Mexico
Juan Carlos Olivares Rojas	Tecnológico Nacional de México - ITM, Mexico
Karina Perez-Daniel	Universidad Panamericana, Mexico
Karina Figueroa Mora	Universidad Michoacana de San Nicolás de Hidalgo, Mexico
Leticia Flores Pulido	Universidad Autónoma de Tlaxcala, Mexico
Lourdes Martinez-Villaseñor	Universidad Panamericana, Mexico
Luis Torres-Treviño	Universidad Autónoma de Nuevo León, Mexico
Luis Luevano	Institut National de Recherche en Informatique et en Automatique, France
Mansoor Ali Teevno	Tecnológico de Monterrey, Mexico
Masaki Murata	Tottori University, Japan
Miguel Gonzalez-Mendoza	Tecnológico de Monterrey, Mexico
Miguel Mora-Gonzalez	Universidad de Guadalajara, Mexico
Mukesh Prasad	University of Technology Sydney, Australia
Omar López-Ortega	Universidad Autónoma del Estado de Hidalgo, Mexico
Rafael Guzman-Cabrera	Universidad de Guanajuato, Mexico
Rafael Batres	Tecnológico de Monterrey, Mexico
Ramon Brena	Instituto Tecnológico de Sonora, Mexico
Ramón Zatarain Cabada	Tec Culiacán, Mexico
Ramón Iván Barraza-Castillo	Universidad Autónoma de Ciudad Juárez, Mexico
Roberto Antonio Vasquez	Universidad La Salle, Mexico
Rocio Ochoa-Montiel	Universidad Autónoma de Tlaxcala, Mexico
Ruben Carino-Escobar	Instituto Nacional de Rehabilitación - Luis Guillermo Ibarra Ibarra, Mexico
Sabino Miranda	INFOTEC-CONACyT, Mexico
Saturnino Job Morales	Universidad Autónoma del Estado de México, Mexico
Segun Aroyehun	University of Konstanz, Germany
Sofía Galicia Haro	Sistema Nacional de Investigadoras e Investigadores, Mexico
Tania Ramirez-delReal	CentroGEO-CONACyT, Mexico

Vadim Borisov

Valery Solovyev
Vicenc Puig
Vicente Garcia Jimenez
Victor Lomas-Barrie

Branch of National Research University "Moscow
    Power Engineering Institute" in Smolensk,
    Russia
Kazan Federal University, Russia
Universitat Politècnica de Catalunya, Spain
Universidad Autónoma de Ciudad Juárez, Mexico
IIMAS-UNAM, Mexico

Contents – Part II

Bioinformatics and Medical Applications

Robotics and Applications

Contents – Part I

Computer Vision and Image Processing

Intelligent Systems

Natural Language Processing

Visualizing the Cosmos: A Novel Method for Text Recombination with Space News

Zhalgas Zhiyenbekov[1]([⊠]) [iD], Zhanar Omirbekova[2] [iD], Galymkair Mutanov[3] [iD], and Madiyar Tasbolatov[3] [iD]

[1] School of Information Technology and Engineering, Kazakh-British Technical University, Almaty 050000, Kazakhstan
z_zhiyenbekov@kbtu.kz
[2] Affiliation Department of Computer Science, Al-Farabi Kazakh National University, Almaty 050000, Kazakhstan
zh.omirbekova@ipic.kz
[3] Affiliation Institute of Informational and Computational Technologies, Almaty 050000, Kazakhstan
https://kbtu.edu.kz/en/faculties/faculty-of-information-technology-eng,
https://www.kaznu.kz/en

Abstract. As the volume of data continues to surge, researchers are confronted with the challenge of extracting meaningful insights from this wealth of information. Despite rapid advancements in Natural Language Processing (NLP) techniques in the AI industry, there remain gaps and opportunities for further exploration, particularly in the realm of data recombination techniques and methods. This paper proposes a novel text recombination method to facilitate the generation of recombined words from a given text. The process commences with a 'stanza' model, which identifies and compiles Named Entity Recognitions (NERs) into a list. These NERs are then cross-referenced with Wikipedia pages to retrieve relevant information, thereby enhancing entity understanding and analysis. The ensuing step involves preprocessing the output text from the previous stage, generating a list of unique words while eliminating stop words. This preprocessing stage serves to remove noise and focus on meaningful words, laying the groundwork for more effective clustering. To enable clustering, we employ vector embeddings, representing words in a 2-dimensional space, rendering them suitable for clustering techniques. Notably, the proposed method further enhances results by re-clustering words after applying K-Means, thereby identifying the most fitting candidate words for recombination. Comparatively, this method outperforms large language models (LLMs) due to its incorporation of NER information, utilization of Wikipedia pages, and effective preprocessing techniques. Unlike LLMs, which operate as resource-intensive black boxes on static data, this method benefits from real-time information access and knowledge base updates. Furthermore, each stage of the process is visualized to control the progress correctly. Thus, due to the plots of word clusterization, the proposed text recombination approach showed positive results.

H. Calvo et al. (Eds.): MICAI 2023, LNAI 14392, pp. 3–15, 2024.
https://doi.org/10.1007/978-3-031-47640-2_1

Keywords: Named Entity Recognition · word embeddings · Principal Component Analysis · Natural Language Processing

1   Introduction

Data recombination is a novel framework for injecting prior knowledge into a model. It uses a high-precision generative model that expands the empirical distribution by allowing fragments of different examples to be combined in particular ways. Samples from this generative model are then used to train a domain-general model. Data recombination can capture important conditional independence properties commonly found in semantic parsing [3]. In comparison to data augmentation, data recombination refers to the process of combining or manipulating existing data to create new data samples.

The field of data recombination techniques in natural language processing (NLP) has evolved significantly over time, and tracing back to the very first attempts can be challenging. However, we can discuss some early approaches that laid the foundation for data recombination in NLP. One of the earliest attempts at data recombination in NLP involved the use of n-grams. The n-grams approach provides a straightforward way to generate variations of text while preserving the original context. Another previous approach in natural language processing is word substitution methods that replace words in a sentence with their synonyms or similar words [6,7]. Word substitution is achieved through different approaches, including lexical databases, word embeddings, and lexical resources. These resources provide information about words and their relatedness, allowing for the identification of suitable substitutes. One commonly used resource for word substitution is a lexical database or thesaurus, such as Word-Net.

In recent years, several data recombination approaches have emerged in the field of natural language processing (NLP). The field of NLP is rapidly evolving, and new approaches for data recombination continue to emerge [13]. The latest research papers, conferences, and advancements in deep learning and generative models often introduce novel techniques and architectures for data recombination. There are some recent approaches to list: Meta-Learning for Data Recombination, Unsupervised Data Recombination, Neural Architecture Search, Contrastive Learning, and Multi-Task Learning and Transfer Learning [3,9]. In this paper, we use recursive text clustering to achieve appropriate text clustering. To do text clustering for data recombination was used Fast Text embedding after considering all possible embedding models. The output of the word embedding is a multidimensional vector, we perform a dimensionality reduction technique with a principal analysis component (further PCA) by identifying linear combinations of the original variables, that capture the maximum variance in the data [10]. PCA allows for simplified analysis and visualization while retaining the most important information. The pipeline of our study ends up with the K-means clustering technique by providing the vocabulary of old words and new words which allows us to create a new text in result. Our proposed clustering approach works recursively until it gets the single word to cluster [8].

It is important to note that, one of the challenges during the study was finding the relevant pages through Wikipedia. The experiments show that not all word entities can be found in Wikipedia. Also, there were ambiguous ideas about defining the best group segment. The question in that was is the best segment with more cluster points or not? For further analysis of the work was created a table at the end and each column saved the results of every iteration of the pipeline [12].

To evaluate the result, we leveraged the power of Bidirectional Encoder Representations from Transformers (BERT), a popular pre-trained transformer-based model, to compute the text similarity score. By comparing the generated text with a reference text, we obtained a similarity score that reflects the semantic closeness between the two texts. To increase the accuracy rate in a fair comparison it was additionally and reasonably added the human and multi check each text. To derive the overall evaluation score, we combined the assessments from the Chat GPT model, human experts, and the text similarity score from BERT. Each method's contribution to the final score was weighted appropriately, ensuring a comprehensive evaluation of the generated text [11–13].

2   Dataset

Texts are the main resource in the data recombination process and provide a more complex and informative representation than just single words. The choice of text as the basic unit for recombination is due to several factors. Firstly, texts retain context and semantics, which allows more accurate transmission of information and relationships between words. As a result, recombination at the text level contributes to the preservation of semantic integrity and allows to obtain better and more interpretable results. Second, the texts provide additional information about the context and area of expertise that may be relevant to the study. In some cases, words in a passage of text may have different meanings depending on the context, and only the use of the text allows these meanings to be correctly interpreted. This opens up opportunities for creating unique and flexible datasets tailored to specific needs.

For a total of 13.7 million tokens (words), the dataset of the research covers the title, URL, text content, author, publication date, and post excerpts of more than 18,000 English news stories relevant to the space sector. This makes it the ideal dataset to train language models tailored to the ecosystem of the space industry.

It is important to note that all articles in the dataset are publicly available from the news aggregator website. The dataset is freely accessible for research purposes and does not contain any personally identifiable information. As such, no ethical approval was required for the utilization of this dataset.

3   Data Recombination Method

The study of data recombination consists of several stages starting from identifying NER to word replacement to get a new text. The study proposed the method of text clustering to generate a combination of words.(see Fig. 1). The process starts with identifying the named entity recognized words through neural models and all words to be replaced in the text will be specified. It was imperative to identify a pertinent data source to augment these words and conduct word substitution.

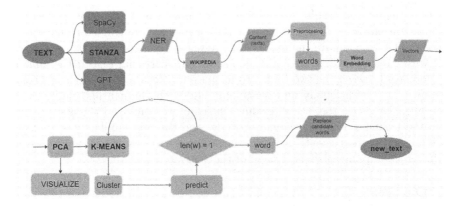

Fig. 1. The pipeline of the data recombination method

The present study employed the Wikipedia library, which affords admission to an extensive repository of Wikipedia articles. Through systematic library research, we were able to programmatically retrieve all pages that were associated with the designated target words. This procedure ensured the acquisition of a comprehensive scope of data pertaining to the selected terms. The textual content for each page was extracted from the retrieved Wikipedia pages. The present discourse features a comprehensive overview of the information pertaining to the designated page candidate for a given Named Entity Recognition (NER) task [10]. The STANZA model detected "NASA" as an organizational entity, as illustrated by the findings. Subsequently, the aforementioned terminology is transferred onto Wikipedia's platform in order to identify the utmost pertinent web pages that may be deemed suitable. Many recent researchers have leveraged the utility of Wikipedia in order to construct named entity recognition (NER) systems that demonstrate a high degree of accuracy in identifying and categorizing entities such as individuals, organizations, and geographic locales. Gathered word candidates from Wikipedia transfer to word embedding process. The process of word embedding holds significant importance in the realm of natural language processing (NLP) tasks and is especially pertinent in the context of a lexical inventory [1]. The process of word embedding is regarded as a robust approach to representing words through a numerical format that successfully captures their contextual information and semantic relationships. In this study, word embedding is utilized to bolster the analysis and comprehension of the fundamental structure and significance present within the collection of individual words (see Fig. 2).

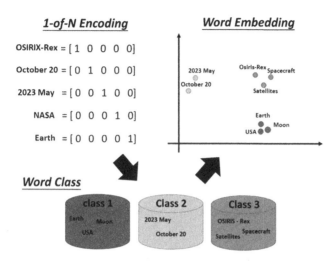

Fig. 2. Word embedding process

The simple reason why we use Fast Text is that it handles out-of-vocabulary (OOV) words more effectively than Word2Vec. Word2Vec treats each word as a single entity and does not have representations for OOV words. In contrast, FastText represents words as bags of character n-grams. This allows Fast-Text to generate embeddings for OOV words based on their character-level subword information, making it more robust for handling rare or unseen words. Since the output of this stage is a multidimensional vector, we perform the PCA process by identifying linear combinations of the original variables, that capture the maximum variance in the data. By selecting a smaller number of principal components that capture most of the variance in the data, PCA allows for simplified analysis and visualization while retaining the most important information (see Fig. 3). This process follows with word clustering, the K-means algorithm segments word vectors to several clusters and predicts the best closest segment to the initial text [17].

This study employs the K-Means clustering algorithm to merge embedded words within textual data with the aim of capitalizing on its efficacy. Through the application of K-Means clustering methodology to embedded words, our objective is to unveil latent structures and patterns within the textual content, thereby establishing a fundamental basis for sophisticated analysis and profound insights [19]. The text clustering approach works recursively and stops once it gets the single word to be clustered. One challenge of recursive clustering was to find the best approach for transmitting the segment of words to the next iteration. Thus, the first idea was to select a group of segments with many points,

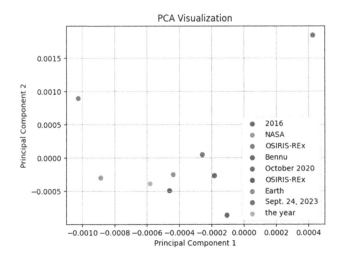

Fig. 3. Word vectors in two-dimensional distance

but the experiments prove that it is not a reasonable approach. Ultimately, after a number of experiments, the best segment of words is selected by calculating the closest distance between initial text words and the candidate segments. The result of recursive clustering is a single word that is considered the best candidate for recombination. In each stage, we saved the output results and recorded them in separate columns. The results of the experiments were assessed by three different methods. First, we checked the augmented text with the results of Concept Net and Chat GPT. Then analyzed it with our own database table where we collected all word - vectors that are similar in Euclidean space [17].

4   Experiments

In this study, we have tested two optimal NER models, namely Spacy and Stanza from Stanford NLP. The objective was to ascertain the merits and demerits of each model and ascertain the optimal option. To ensure an impartial and exhaustive assessment, a meticulous selection process was undertaken to procure a heterogeneous dataset that encompasses various domains and languages. The corpus encompassed a collection of textual data from diversified sources, such as journalistic pieces, social media entries, and scholarly publications [5].

A sequence of experiments was undertaken utilizing both Spacy and Stanza models. Various NLP tasks were assessed on each model which encompassed part-of-speech tagging, named entity recognition, dependency parsing, and sentiment analysis. The assessment criteria comprised various quantitative measures to evaluate the performance of the system, namely, accuracy, F1-score, precision, recall, and processing time of the two models. For illustration, we see in the Table 1 the differences between identified entities by two models. The Spacy

Table 1. Named entity recognition by STANZA model

Words	Entity by Spacy	Entity by STANZA
2016	DATE	DATE
NASA	ORG	ORG
OSIRIS-REx	*ORG*	PRODUCT
Bennu	*Person*	GPE
October 2020	DATE	DATE
OSIRIS-REx	ORG	ORG
Earth	LOC	LOC
Sept. 24, 2023	DATE	DATE
the year	DATE	DATE

model exhibited a lower degree of entity recognition and exhibited inaccurate labelling in a majority of instances.

In this work, we have also observed quite interesting results which are considered as mistakes of the Wikipedia request. Some words from Wikipedia are generated not correctly than assumed. Due to these words, the recombination results are extremely changed in meaning.

Table 2. Detection of error candidate words

№	Initial word	Candidate word
1	Earth	Death
2	NASA	GAS
3	Lemur	Lemon
4	DoD	Dog
5	Enveil	Meizu M8

Also important to note that the above achievements are general observations based on the utilization and impact of the Wikipedia library in the text processing and NLP domain. The example of some error words is demonstrated in Table 2. For more specific and up-to-date information, I recommend referring to research papers, academic resources, or the Wikimedia Foundation website, which provides detailed information on the contributions and initiatives of the Wikipedia library in NLP and text processing.

In the step of word classification, determining the optimal number of clusters, k, for a given dataset stands as a significant challenge in the application of K-Means. There exists a multitude of techniques and standards for selecting the parameter k, contingent upon the distinctive attributes and aims of the given data investigation. In the study, determining the optimal value of k entails

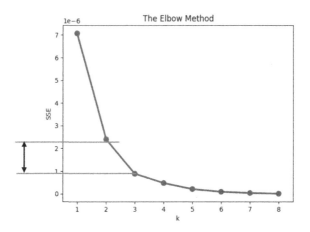

Fig. 4. Identifying the k-number in text clustering

employing the elbow method, a graphical approach that contrasts the within-cluster sum of squares (WCSS) with varying values of k. The Within-Cluster Sum of Squares (WCSS) metric quantifies the degree of compactness or uniformity within a given cluster [4].

The elbow method seeks to identify a value for k such that the addition of further clusters does not yield a substantial decrease in WCSS, signifying that the clusters are amply distinct and unambiguous. The value of k corresponds to a significant point of inflexion in the plotted data, commonly referred to as an elbow or bend within the graph(see Fig. 4).

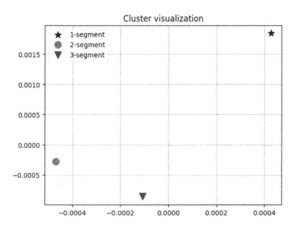

Fig. 5. Visualizing the K-means results

Visualizing the results of K-Means at each iteration of clustering is of paramount importance as it offers valuable insights into the algorithm's behaviour and convergence. By observing the visualizations, researchers can better understand how the data points are grouped, dispersed, and refined throughout the clustering process. This helps in validating the effectiveness of the proposed text recombination method and identifying potential issues (see Fig. 5). Visualizations play a key role in fine-tuning clustering parameters, as they allow researchers to iteratively adjust settings and observe the impact on the clustering outcome. This iterative exploration enhances the method's performance and ensures the generation of meaningful clusters [18]. Moreover, visualizing the clustering process enables the identification of optimal cluster numbers, avoiding underfitting or overfitting scenarios. Researchers can detect the elbow point in the plot, indicating the number of clusters that best capture the underlying structure of the data.

In the context of text recombination, visualizations offer a tangible way to evaluate the quality of the generated clusters. Clear visual representations of how news articles or documents are grouped together can provide meaningful insights into the underlying themes and topics present in the space news dataset.

5   Evaluation and Results

The proposed pipeline of data recombination has demonstrated quite satisfactory results. To assess our work, we have used three assessment methods, AI, Human, and similarity model. First, the large language model checked the provided two texts for their similarity and scored from 0 to 1. The score 1 was put if the meaning of the text did not change and 0 otherwise. In the experiment, I used 100 texts for recombination. 87 of them successfully recombination based on the similarity score. 30 text was identified as correct by AI and 23 text were identified as incorrect both by AI and Human evaluation [17].

Table 3. Statistics of result

Metrics	Value
count_all_text	489
count_successful_texts	415
min_score	0.87
max_score	1.0
(AI=1) & (H=1)	409
(AI=0) & (H=0)	27
(AI=0) & (H=1)	41
(AI=1) & (H=0)	12

To calculate the accuracy score and find the golden mean between the Human and AI scores, it was reasonably used text similarity model of BERT. In the figure below we can that the minimum score for Human value 0 was 0.87 and the

Table 4. Table of results

№	Text	Newtext	Similarity Score	AI Score	Human Score
1	*The U.S. Space* Systems Command signed an agreement with Blue Origin that "paves the way" for the company's New Glenn rocket to compete for national security launch contracts	Structure of *the United States Space* Force signed an agreement with Blue Origin that "paves the way" for the company's New Glenn rocket to compete for national security launch contracts	0,9626	0	1
2	Over the last year, Microsoft and Xplore worked with the *National Oceanic and Atmospheric Administration* to show how commercial services could support operations of polar-orbiting weather satellites	Over the last year, Microsoft and XploRe worked with *Office of Oceanic and Atmospheric Research* to show how commercial services could support operations of polar-orbiting weather satellites	0,9914	0	1
3	*U.S. Space Command's* Lt. Gen. John Shaw said 'one of the challenges that we will have as a nation is understanding the lunar environment'	*U.S. Route 1 Sassuolo Calcio Space Command's* Lt. Gen. John Shaw said 'one of the challenges that we will have as a nation is understanding the lunar environment'	0,9615	0	1
4	*The European Space Agency* has awarded funds to develop a demonstrator for Skimsat, a small satellite platform designed to operate in very low *Earth* orbit (VLEO)	*UK Space Agency* has awarded funds to develop a demonstrator for Skimsat, a small satellite platform designed to operate in very low *Death* orbit (VLEO)	0,9792	0	1
5	Leaders of *the House space* subcommittee have asked the Federal Aviation Administration for more details on its investigation	Leaders of *the House of Commons* Canada space subcommittee have asked Federal Aviation Administration for more details	0,9120	0	1
6	The unclassified version of the *U.S.* national defense strategy released by the *Defense Department* Oct. 27 forecasts a decades-long competition with *China*	The unclassified version of the Georgia *(U.S. Route 1 state)* national defense strategy released by *Department of National Defense* (Philippines) Oct. 27 forecasts a decades-long competition with *Taiwan*	0,9283	0	1

maximum was 0.99, while for Human score 1 displayed 0.90 and 1 minimum and maximum score respectively (see the Table 3). We have calculated the mean value from them and decided to take that value as a threshold. If the text similarity score is above or equal to the threshold then we can say that recombination was successful.

Thus, the last stage provides the best candidate that suits the initial text given. As shown in the Table 4, results were quite satisfactory with an assessment of AI, Human verifications, and BERT transformer. Data recombination is considered successful due to the following cases:

1. Accuracy: Most of the text, ideally a high percentage, is correctly recombined without errors. In our example, 415 out of 489 texts were correct which indicates a relatively high success rate.
2. Preservation of Meaning: The recombined text maintains the intended meaning and context of the original data.
3. Contextual Coherence: The recombined text flows smoothly and maintains coherence in terms of grammar, syntax, and semantic relationships between words and phrases.
4. Task-Specific Evaluation: Depending on the specific task or objective of the data recombination, success can be determined by evaluating the performance or output against specific metrics or benchmarks. In this study, as metrics we have used AI score, Human evaluation and BERT score of sentence similarity
5. User Acceptance: The recombined text is deemed satisfactory and acceptable by the intended users and human judgment.

It is noteworthy to acknowledge that attaining a level of precision of 100% in data amalgamation poses significant difficulties, particularly in intricate natural language processing exercises. It is possible that a degree of errors or alterations in the intended connotation may be inescapable. The assessment of the efficacy of data recombination frequently hinges on the task at hand, the dataset under consideration, and the requisite quality standards. Therefore, it is my conviction that perpetual evaluation, iteration, and improvement are essential for the augmentation of the precision and quality of the recombination procedure.

6   Conclusion

In this research, data recombination has been done as proposed at the beginning of the study. We have successfully implemented a recursive clustering method for finding the best candidates for data recombination. The research clearly showed that it is possible to get word candidates through Wikipedia by giving the named entity recognized words. However, the study revealed the fact that Wikipedia can provide the wrong title for the topic which can highly influence the results [15].

In specific cases of the experiment, some words were not found in Wikipedia and iteration went through. In the clusterization process, we came to the decision to make a recursive algorithm for k-means. Thus, the last stage provides the best candidate that suits the initial text given. As shown in previous slides, results were quite satisfactory with an assessment of AI, Human verifications and BERT transformer. With regard to limitations or improvements, our algorithms are not capable of keeping the linguistic rules. For instance, prepositions and articles will remain after the changes. The best way it should be modified depends according to neighbour words which is the next step of our research.

Acknowledgments. This research is funded by the Aerospace Committee of the Ministry of Digital Development, Innovations and Aerospace Industry of the Republic of Kazakhstan (BR11265420)

References

1. Ramos, F.O., Pinto, D.: Proposal for named entities recognition and classification (NERC) and the automatic generation of rules on Mexican news. Computación y Sistemas **24**(2), 533–538 (2020)
2. Mi, C., Xie, L., Zhang, Y.: Improving data augmentation for low resource speech-to-text translation with diverse paraphrasing. Neural Netw., 194–205 (2022)
3. Zhou, X., Huang, L., Zhang, Y., Yu, M.: A hybrid approach to detecting technological recombination based on text mining and patent network analysis. Scientometrics **121**(2), 699–737 (2019). https://doi.org/10.1007/s11192-019-03218-5
4. Gallardo, G.R., Beltrán, B., Vilariño, D., Zepeda, C., Martínez, R.: Comparison of clustering algorithms in text clustering tasks. Computación y Sistemas **24**(2), 429–437 (2020)
5. Butt, S., Ashraf, N., Siddiqui, M.H.F., Sidorov, G., Gelbukh, A.: Transformer-based extractive social media question answering on TweetQA. Computación y Sistemas **25**(1), 23–32 (2021)
6. Qiu, L., Shaw, P., Pasupat, P., Nowak, P., Linzen, T., Sha, F., Toutanova, K.: Improving compositional generalization with latent structure and data augmentation. In: Proceedings of the 2022 Conference of the North American Chapter of the Association for Computational Linguistics: Human Language Technologies, pp. 4341–4362 (2022)
7. Zhang, L., Yang, Z., Yang, D.: Compositional constituency-based data augmentation for natural language understanding. In: Proceedings of the 2022 Conference of the North American Chapter of the Association for Computational Linguistics, pp. 5243–5258 (2022)
8. Fang, F., Luo, F., Zhang, H.-P., Zhou, H.-J., Chow, A.L.H., Xiao, C.-X.: A comprehensive pipeline for complex text-to-image synthesis. J. Comput. Sci. Technol. **35**(3), 522–537 (2020). https://doi.org/10.1007/s11390-020-0305-9
9. Lam, T.K., Schamoni, S., Riezler, S.: Leveraging audio alignments for data augmentation in end-to-end speech translation. In: Proceedings of the 60th Annual Meeting of the Association for Computational Linguistics, pp. 245–254 (2022)
10. Zhai J., Guo Y., Zhang H., Ding J.: TextRank keyword extraction method weighted by multivariate quantitative indexes. In: 2022 4th International Conference on Applied Machine Learning (ICAML), pp. 151–155. IEEE (2022). https://doi.org/10.1109/ICAML57167.2022.00036
11. Li, H: Multi-publisher news corpus construction via text recombination. In: Proceedings of the 28th International Joint Conference on Artificial Intelligence (IJCAI), vol. 12156, pp. 110–118 (2021). https://doi.org/10.1117/12.2626538
12. Liu, L., Ding, B., Bing, L., Joty, S., Si, L., Miao, C.: A multilingual data augmentation framework for low-resource cross-lingual NER. In: Proceedings of the 59th Annual Meeting of the Association for Computational Linguistics and the 11th International Joint Conference on Natural Language Processing, vol. 1: Long Papers, pp. 5834–5846 (2021). https://doi.org/10.18653/v1/2021.acl-long.453
13. Beguš, G.: CiwGAN and fiwGAN: encoding information in acoustic data to model lexical learning with generative adversarial networks. Neural Netw. **139**, 305–325 (2021). https://doi.org/10.1016/j.neunet.2021.03.017

14. Zhang, X., Shi, S., Guo, Z., Chen, G., Wei, H., Tang, Y., Yu, L.: Controlled text style transfer via noise enhancement of deep learning transformer. In: International Conference on Neural Networks, Information, and Communication Engineering (NNICE), vol. 12258, pp. 63–69 (2022). https://doi.org/10.1117/12.2639492
15. Liu, S.-T., Hsu, S.-C., Huang, Y.-H.: Data paradigm shift in cross-media IoT system. In: Yamamoto, S., Mori, H. (eds.) HCII 2020. LNCS, vol. 12185, pp. 479–490. Springer, Cham (2020). https://doi.org/10.1007/978-3-030-50017-7_36
16. Sohn H., Park B.: Robust and informative text augmentation (RITA) via constrained worst-case transformations for low-resource named entity recognition. In: Proceedings of the 28th ACM SIGKDD Conference on Knowledge Discovery and Data Mining, pp. 1616–1624 (2022)
17. Gimaletdinova, G., Khalitova, L., Solovyev, V., Bochkarev, V.: Lexicographic study of synonymy: clarifying semantic similarity between words. Computación y Sistemas 25(3), 667–675 (2021)
18. Pichardo-Lagunas, O., Martinez-Seis, B., Basurto-Carrillo, F.D.J.: Fernández-Flores D: data integration for the evaluation of cancer evolution in Mexico through data visualization. Computación y Sistemas 26(2), 1557–1567 (2022)
19. Sagingaliyev, B., Aitakhunova, Z., Shaimerdenova, A., Akhmetov, I., Pak, A., Jaxylykova, A: A bibliometric review of methods and algorithms for generating corpora for learning vector word embeddings. In: Mexican International Conference on Artificial Intelligence, pp. 148–162 (2022)

Propitter: A Twitter Corpus for Computational Propaganda Detection

Marco Casavantes[1(✉)], Manuel Montes-y-Gómez[1],
Luis Carlos González[2], and Alberto Barrón-Cedeño[3]

[1] Instituto Nacional de Astrofísica, Óptica y Electrónica, Puebla, Mexico
{mcasavantes,mmontesg}@inaoep.mx
[2] Universidad Autónoma de Chihuahua, Chihuahua, Mexico
lcgonzalez@uach.mx
[3] Università di Bologna, Forlì, Italy
a.barron@unibo.it

Abstract. Social networks have become one of the most popular ways for people to communicate with others and get informed. For this reason, these platforms are being widely used to spread propaganda and thereby influence the beliefs, opinions and actions of their users. Despite its relevance, current computational approaches to detect propaganda are mainly focused on analyzing its presence in news articles, and have not been equally developed for other sources of information, such as Twitter. In this paper, we introduce *Propitter*, a new corpus for propaganda detection with over 385K tweets. Its construction was based on a novel methodology that refines what is obtained by distant supervision through a cross-domain filtering and a subsequent in-domain expansion. We provide baseline results for this corpus, using both traditional and transformer-based methods, and also present an experiment that points to the need for methods that go beyond topics and allow for capturing the propaganda styles.

Keywords: Propaganda detection · Propaganda corpus · Twitter

1 Introduction

In 2016, in the middle of the US presidential campaign, it was seen the use of social networks to disclose large amounts of information for the purpose of tarnishing the reputation of specific candidates. More recently, a large amount of misinformation was spread on social media about COVID-19, which was disguised as reliable news, and that prevented various health and safety measures from being properly applied [9]. These are just two examples of how information shared in social networks can be exploited to misinform through propaganda mechanisms [5].

Propaganda is defined as the action to disseminate "expressions of opinions or actions by individuals or groups, deliberately designed to influence opinions or actions of other individuals or groups with reference to predetermined ends" [15]. Unfortunately, propagandist agents have found in social networks an excelent medium to achieve their goals. This given the size, ubiquity and diversity of social networks, but also, because it lacks effective mechanisms to automatically detect this behavior.

Generally, propaganda is linked to news and political campaigns driven in mainstream media, such as newspapers or websites that feature news as their main content. However, as some research indicates, the use of social networks has changed over time, moving from entertainment to serving as main source of news for many people [14,17,25]. Despite this situation, the detection of propaganda in these media is still very incipient; this work aims to contribute in this direction.

Related research demonstrates that there have been some initial attempts to identify propaganda on social media, however, most have focused on automated or bot-generated content [6], while others have reused previous data collections assuming that, by default, they include propaganda [23]. In this study, we follow a different path. We focus on investigating the propaganda spread on Twitter by media outlets that have been deemed unreliable or questionable due to their promotion of propaganda. Thus, our main contribution is a new Twitter corpus for computational propaganda detection. This corpus, which we named as *Propitter*, to the best of our knowledge is the largest of its kind, containing more than 385 thousand tweets from more than 240 news sources accounts.

For the construction of this corpus, we propose a novel methodology that refines what is obtained by distant-supervision through the application of a cross-domain filtering and a subsequent in-domain expansion. The key idea of this refinement approach is to take advantage of an existing corpus of manually annotated news articles to remove some noisy tweets, that, although coming from suspicious sources, do not appear to be propaganda.

We carried out the experimental section with two main objectives: *i*) to establish some benchmark results for *Propitter*, using both traditional classification methods and state-of-the-art approaches; and, *ii*) to study the suitability of the current propaganda detection methods, analyzing their dependence on thematic information and their difficulties in modeling the propaganda styles.

The remainder of this paper is organized as follows: Sect. 2 provides an overview of related work; Sect. 3 describes the methodology followed for the construction of *Propitter*; Sect. 4 explains our experimental settings and shows the obtained benchmark results; finally, Sect. 5 presents our conclusions.

2   Related Work

Examples of computational propaganda were included for the first time in the *TSHP-17* collection to analyze news media language in the context of political fact checking and fake news detection [19]. To create this corpus, the authors picked typical trusted news items from the English Gigaword corpus[1], and

---

[1] https://catalog.ldc.upenn.edu/LDC2003T05.

crawled articles from distinct unreliable news sites of various categories (such as satire and hoax), including two sites for propaganda. Motivated by the difficulty of conducting further research using the *TSHP-17* corpus, particularly due to the small number of propagandist sources and lack of information from individual articles, [4] built an enhanced corpus called *QProp*. This time, they looked at ten different sources of propaganda. The criteria for labeling news articles were derived from the website MediaBias/FactCheck (MBFC)[2], a resource that categorizes media based on the bias they exhibit. Subsequently, [10] introduced a new dataset, smaller than the previous ones but manually annotated. In addition, it was annotated at the span level, which means that individual text fragments were labeled rather than full articles.

As described above, most of the current resources for the computational study of propaganda have focused primarily on news articles. To date, very few efforts have been made to analyze it in other sources of information. For example, [23] investigated propaganda across multiple sources, including public speeches, news articles, and a combination of two datasets of tweets. In particular, they used the 8,963 tweets from the *Twitter Russian Internet Research Agency* (IRA) [12] as examples of propaganda, and an equal number of tweets extracted from *twitter7* [24] as examples of non-propaganda. They conducted cross-domain studies emphasizing the strong challenges related to the scarcity of labeled data. Similarly, propaganda on Reddit has been thoroughly investigated by [2]. They collected and studied six political forums in the US and UK, and found that minority parties are more likely to spread propaganda, that the US and UK forums tend to use different propaganda techniques, and that posts containing more propaganda usually got more comments and votes. All these findings highlight the need to carry out specific studies for social network content, whose form and purpose are different from that of conventional news media.

At this point, it is important to mention that most of the previous research employed data collected using the "distant supervision" approach. This approach, initially conceived for relation extraction purposes [16], relies on an external database to provide the labeled sources of information to promptly create instances for training data. Only one earlier study by [10] produced labels by manual annotation. This type of corpora is considered to be of higher quality compared to those obtained through distance supervision; however, they are much more expensive to build and therefore usually end up being relatively small. This has motivated authors such as [21] to suggest that future work should explore semi-supervised models or active learning techniques to annotate and prepare larger corpora. In a similar direction, [3] gathered nearly 35K hyperpartisan news articles by distance supervision, and analyzed their differences with regard to their manual labels, finding that for nearly 96% of the articles, distance-supervised and manual labels were identical. Supported on these last observations, in this paper we propose a combination of both labeling schemes,

---

taking advantage of the best of both approaches to create a new corpus for propaganda detection focused on a less explored media for this problem, Twitter.

3   The Construction of Propitter

Our proposal, *Propitter*, stands out from previous collections in its focus on social media content, and in having data sampled from a large number of information sources, which were selected through an external knowledge source about media bias. Figure 1 illustrates the three steps involved in its construction, which are detailed in the following subsection.

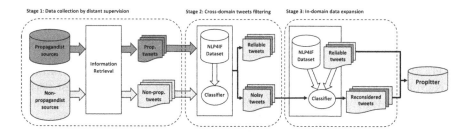

Fig. 1. General diagram of the three-step methodology used for the construction of *Propitter*.

3.1   Construction Methodology

Stage 1: Data Collection by Distant Supervision. *Propitter* was built by first analyzing the *QProp* dataset [4]. This corpus includes news articles from 10 propagandist and 122 non-propagandist sources. We used these 132 sources as the core of our corpus, but we added additional information sources in order to enrich it and reduce the strong imbalance present in *QProp*. Basically, we took the MBFC web resource, and identified all information sources marked as non-reliable due to posting propaganda content. After that, we identified the subset of sources that had a Twitter account and retrieved their tweets using the Twitter API[3]. We collected 550K tweets from 244 different sources[4] published between January and August 2021[5]. As a first preprocessing step, we only kept English tweets[6], and then, following the suggestions described in [14],

---

[3] https://developer.twitter.com/en/docs/twitter-api.

[4] The complete list of considered sources is shown at https://github.com/mcasav/Propitter.

[5] With the intention of later being able to carry out cross-domain experiments, we also gathered an extra set of tweets corresponding to the same period as the articles in the *QProp* collection.

[6] We removed non English posts using Polyglot (version 16.7.4) https://polyglot.readthedocs.io/en/latest/.

we discarded retweets and removed tweets that had three or more trending topics on the day they were posted in order to minimize spam[7].

Stage 2: Cross-Domain Tweets Filtering. As expected, the collected corpus is not free of errors, since it was built automatically using the distance supervision approach. Thus, in order to reduce the number of noisy tweets and improve the quality of the corpus, we applied a filtering process that leverages an already available collection of manually labeled propaganda news articles by [10], hereinafter referred to as the *NLP4IF Dataset*.

Basically, the filtering process is as follows: the categories given by distance supervision are used as pseudo-labels [1], and the NLP4IF Dataset is used to train a classifier to make new predictions about the category of the collected tweets. The tweets for which both labels match are considered as "reliable tweets", while those that get different labels are marked as "noisy tweets" and temporarily discarded.

For the classifier we used the "base-uncased" model of BERT [11]. Initially, we considered using the same approach as the team that achieved the best performance in the development set of the NLP4IF workshop [8], which implemented an ensemble of three classifiers [13], two based on BERT and one based on Google's Universal Sentence Encoder [7], however, when reproducing its results, we observed better performance using only the uncased BERT model.

Stage 3: In-Domain Data Expansion. In the previous stage of the methodology, we identified a set of "possibly" mislabeled tweets based on the discrepancy between their labels assigned by the initial distance supervision process and the news-based classifier; however, this discrepancy could be due to the fact that propaganda and non-propaganda content are manifested differently in tweets and news articles. Thus, with the intention of recovering some of these tweets, perhaps improperly discarded, we carried out an expansion process. This process is as follows: first, the set of reliable tweets is incorporated into the training set, that is, it is combined with the news articles from the NLP4IF Dataset; then, using this assembled collection, a new classifier is trained, now more closer to the tweets domain; finally, all tweets previously marked as noise are classified for a second time, and those whose classification coincided with the pseudo-labels given by distance supervision are re-inserted into the *Propitter* corpus. As in the previous stage, the classifier used was based on the "base-uncased" model of BERT.

As a final note, it is important to mention that after the filtering and expansion processes, the number of tweets in our collection decreased from 550K to around 385K, which indicates that approximately 30% of the tweets in the initial collection were considered noisy examples. The numbers in Table 1 are provided to help illustrate the role that each stage had in the process of building our

---

[7] This was determined according to the Trend Calendar, https://us.trend-calendar.com/.

dataset, along with the average length of tweets per stage and token richness expressed by Mass index [22], which indicates the relation between number of different tokens and total number of tokens, not sensitive to text-length. Table 1 further shows that the tweets recovered in the third stage are somewhat longer and richer in token diversity than the tweets retrieved in the prior two stages. Summing up, Stage 2 marks 208,842 as "noisy tweets". Stage 3 starts with these noisy tweets and reconsiders the label of 48,236 cases. Therefore, 337,155 reliable tweets + 48,236 reconsidered tweets add up to 385,391 tweets as the final volume of Propitter.

3.2   Propitter Statistics

Table 2 presents some statistics about *Propitter*. In total, it includes 385,391 tweets, of which 101,175 correspond to the propaganda category, that is, 26% of instances. These tweets were extracted from 244 different information sources, and most of them were published in a short period, between January and August 2021, to ensure some thematic cohesion. As mentioned above, we also gathered a small fraction of tweets for the same period as the articles in the QProp collection, our idea is to allow future cross-domain experiments and exploration of the problems caused by temporal concept drift.

Given our interest in sharing this collection[8], and thereby encouraging the study of propaganda on Twitter, we define three reference partitions: Train ('17-'18 &'21), Development and Test, in proportions of 80%, 10% and 10%, respectively. To give a glimpse of this corpus, Table 3 shows some examples of tweets from propaganda and non-propaganda categories. As can be seen, these examples vary greatly in length, style, and subjects. There are very simple statements and comments, as well as posts expounding more developed concepts, on topics as diverse as politics, economics, and sports. In the particular case of the first three examples, the presence of propagandist techniques such as *reductio ad hitlerum*, doubt, and exaggeration are evident.

Table 1. Number of tweets with which each filter stage begins and ends. The average tokens per tweet and Mass indices were calculated based on the number of ending tweets per stage. The lexical or token richness increases as the Mass index value decreases.

Stage	Starting tweets	Ending tweets	Avg. tokens/tweet	Mass index
Stage 1	635,934	545,997	23	0.0148
Stage 2	545,997	337,155	23	0.0148
Stage 3	208,842	48,236	26	0.0144

---

[8] *Propitter* will be available to other researchers upon request in the form of tweet IDs and their respective class, following Twitter's Content Redistribution Guidelines.

Table 2. General statistics of *Propitter*. Volume indicates the amount of tweets in each partition, and Propaganda shows the number of tweets corresponding to the propaganda category (i.e., positive examples).

Partition	Volume	Propaganda
Train ('17-'18)	14,899	10,509
Train ('21)	293,480	77,167
Development	38,511	6,454
Test	38,501	7,045
Total	385,391	101,175

Table 3. Examples of tweets from *Propitter*. At first they were considered noisy samples by the classifier who solely trained on news articles. These instances now have correct predictions after the classifier was retrained using tweets.

Tweet	Label
Cancel culture is based in communism.	Propaganda
Do you think the Trump impeachment is constitutional?	Propaganda
Hussein Zaki is considered one of the most prominent legends in the history of #Egyptian handball, with his career with Zamalek, the Egyptian national team and some #European clubs. #Tokyo2020 #TokyoOlympics Read more: URL	Propaganda
Upset workers changed a Burger King sign to read "We all quit". CNN's Jeanne Moos reports on the mutiny at a Nebraska fast food joint. URL	Non-propaganda
Diminutive track cyclist Azizulhasni Awang is heading to the Tokyo Games with big dreams of becoming the first Malaysian to win an Olympic gold medal. URL	Non-propaganda
Minnesota's yellowing grass and drier-than-normal weather may soon force cattle farmers to make tough decisions about how to feed their herds. URL	Non-propaganda

4 Experiments and Results

In this section, we present some first results on the *Propitter* collection, which are intended to serve as a baseline for future works using this corpus. In addition, we show the results of an exploratory experiment aimed to know the characteristics and difficulties of *Propitter* as well as the capacity of the baseline methods to unmask the propaganda.

4.1 Baseline Results

As baseline methods we are considering the following two:

Traditional Method: As representation, it uses a bag of word n-grams, with $n = \{1, 2, 3\}$ and *tf-idf* weights; for classification, it employs a SVM classifier[9], with linear kernel and default hyperparameters as defined in the scikit-learn 1.2.0 library [18].

---

[9] https://scikit-learn.org/stable/modules/generated/sklearn.svm.LinearSVC.

Transformer-Based Method: It is based on the DistilBERT model [20]; for its implementation we used the same parameters as the uncased BERT classifier from [13], such as a learning rate of 1e-3 and a batch size of 128. All models were trained on Google Colaboratory[10].

Table 4 reports our benchmark results, corresponding to the two classification methods. In both cases the classifiers were trained with the "Train 21" partition and evaluated on the "Test" partition. The table reports precision, recall and F_1 values on the propaganda class. As can be noticed, the results of DistilBERT are considerably higher than those of the linear SVM, showing the difficulty of the task to be addressed by methods based solely on the presence of short sequences of words, and pointing to the convenience of employing approaches that allow a global (semantic) interpretation of the posts.

Table 4. Baselines results for *Propitter*. Evaluation measures are reported on the propaganda category.

Classifier	Precision	Recall	F_1
DistilBERT	0.9159	0.8676	0.8158
Linear-SVM	0.6805	0.7268	0.7029

4.2   On the Challenges of Propitter

The following experiments were designed to observe the impact that the volume of training data as well as its temporal dispersion have on the detection of propaganda tweets.

These experiments consisted of dividing the 2021 training set into several folds, in order to carry out the classification on the test set by gradually increasing the training data, fold by fold, and measuring the corresponding increase in performance in each case. Two types of data divisions were employed. The first considered folds of 60K tweets arranged chronologically, each covering approximately a month and a half[11]. On the other hand, the second partition considered folds of 60K tweets randomly selected without replacement, which means that they included tweets from different time slots.

The results of these experiments are shown in Table 5. From them we can observe the following:

First, these new results confirm our previous ones (refer to Sect. 4.1), showing that DistilBERT was better than the linear SVM in all cases.

Second, there is a clear impact on the results due to the size of the training set; the more data, the better performance. However, it is important to note that, when using the random partitions, this impact was relatively small for

---

[10] https://colab.research.google.com/.
[11] Given the size of the training set, the last fold had slightly fewer tweets.

both classifiers, as their differences in F_1 using 60K and 293K to train the model were about 3.3 and 6.2 points, respectively. In a way, this suggests that the size of *Propitter* is not an issue of particular concern.

Third, when comparing the results of the two classifiers for the chronological and random orderings, we observe a notable difference in the results, which suggests that tweets' topics are playing an important role in the detection of propaganda.

Table 5. F_1 scores over the propaganda category of the experiments with incremental training, using chronological and random selections.

	DistilBERT	
Train Vol.	F_1-**Chrono.**	F_1-**Random**
60k	0.6897	0.7659
120k	0.7284	0.7878
180k	0.7524	0.7789
240k	0.7709	0.7820
Full	0.8158	0.8018
	Linear SVM	
Train Vol.	F_1-**Chrono.**	F_1-**Random**
60k	0.5427	0.6372
120k	0.6076	0.6749
180k	0.6192	0.6897
240k	0.6550	0.6934
Full	0.7029	0.7035

To confirm the above intuition, we carried out an additional experiment in order to assess the lexical similarity between the different folds of the chronological partition and the test set. Particularly, we used the Dice coefficient to measure the overlap between the vocabularies of the different sets. Table 6 shows the obtained values. From this we can notice that the Dice coefficient grows for the partitions temporarily closer to the test set, when considering both categories and just the propaganda class. Furthermore, when measuring the Pearson correlation between the Dice similarity values and the results of the two classifiers, reported in Table 5, we found that they are greater than 0.93, suggesting that these variables are significantly connected. That is, the greater the temporal proximity, the greater the thematic similarity and, consequently, a better detection of propaganda content.

In summary, taking into account that the differences in performance using only 60k tweets vs. the full training set were much smaller for the random partition than for the chronologically ordered one, and having the lexical overlap results as reference, we can conclude that propaganda detection using *Propitter* was not affected as much by the amount of training data as by the topics covered in the tweets, which are directly related to their publication dates. This opens

Table 6. Lexical overlap, measured by the Dice coefficient, between each training fold of the chronological ordered partition and the test set. Fold 1 is the most distant from the test set, while fold 5 is the closest.

Fold	Overlap (both classes)	Overlap (only prop)
1	0.442	0.399
2	0.473	0.451
3	0.492	0.476
4	0.503	0.489
5	0.513	0.500

the possibility of using *Propitter* to study the concept drift in the detection of propaganda and with it to develop methods focused on capturing the style and not only the topics of propaganda.

5   Conclusions

Propaganda is pernicious and takes advantages of the widespread use of social networks. Our research addresses the challenge of identifying propaganda on Twitter by employing a construction process that leverages on pre-existing resources from the news article domain to clean a collection of data gathered under a distant supervision scheme. This allowed us to create a corpus in which we evaluated classification approaches as baselines. As a consequence, we discovered that a state-of-the-art transformer-based classifier is, as expected, more resilient than other alternatives (such as SVM with Bags-of-Words) in terms of being less affected by variables like temporal placement and volume of training data. Considering these two variables, we were able to observe that the chronological order of data affects more than the amount of data (volume) while training a classifier. However, we must emphasize that these approaches do not detect the root of propaganda, which is found in dissemination techniques rather than topics. We consider that there is a need to further study this issue and develop detection systems that adequately handle the problem of propaganda. We expect our corpus to be a useful resource for this purpose in the area of computational propaganda detection, since it would be the first collection of tweets in English specifically built for this task. A limitation of *Propitter* is that it only includes data from Twitter and in English, which implies that the conclusions drawn from it, in this work and in future studies, will not necessarily be transferable to other social networks or languages. As future work, we intend to incorporate multiple contextual and content variables as new features, as well as propaganda detection tests aligned to other datasets (including *QProp* using our Train set from 2017 and 2018) to allow more experimentation over cross-domain scenarios.

References

1. ALRashdi, R., O'Keefe, S.: Robust domain adaptation approach for tweet classification for crisis response. In: Serrhini, M., Silva, C., Aljahdali, S. (eds.) EMENA-ISTL 2019. LAIS, vol. 7, pp. 124–134. Springer, Cham (2020). https://doi.org/10.1007/978-3-030-36778-7_14
2. Balalau, O., Horincar, R.: From the stage to the audience: propaganda on reddit. In: EACL 2021–16th Conference of the European Chapter of the Association for Computational Linguistics, Proceedings of the Conference, pp. 3540–3550 (2021). https://doi.org/10.18653/v1/2021.eacl-main.309
3. Baly, R., Da San Martino, G., Glass, J., Nakov, P.: We can detect your bias: predicting the political ideology of news articles. In: Proceedings of the 2020 Conference on Empirical Methods in Natural Language Processing (EMNLP), pp. 4982–4991. Association for Computational Linguistics, Online (2020). https://doi.org/10.18653/v1/2020.emnlp-main.404
4. Barrón-Cedeño, A., Jaradat, I., Da San Martino, G., Nakov, P.: Proppy: organizing the news based on their propagandistic content. Info. Process. Manage. 56 (2019). https://doi.org/10.1016/j.ipm.2019.03.005
5. Bolsover, G., Howard, P.: Computational propaganda and political big data: moving toward a more critical research agenda. Big Data 5(4), 273–276 (2017)
6. Bolsover, G., Howard, P.: Chinese computational propaganda: automation, algorithms and the manipulation of information about Chinese politics on Twitter and Weibo. Inf. Commun. Soc. 22(14), 2063–2080 (2019). https://doi.org/10.1080/1369118X.2018.1476576
7. Cer, D., et al.: Universal sentence encoder for English. In: Proceedings of the 2018 Conference on Empirical Methods in Natural Language Processing: System Demonstrations, pp. 169–174. Association for Computational Linguistics, Brussels, Belgium (2018). https://doi.org/10.18653/v1/D18-2029
8. Da San Martino, G., Barrón-Cedeño, A., Nakov, P.: Findings of the NLP4IF-2019 shared task on fine-grained propaganda detection. In: Proceedings of the Second Workshop on Natural Language Processing for Internet Freedom: Censorship, Disinformation, and Propaganda, pp. 162–170. Association for Computational Linguistics, Hong Kong, China (2019). https://doi.org/10.18653/v1/D19-5024
9. Da San Martino, G., Cresci, S., Barrón-Cedeño, A., Yu, S., Pietro, R.D., Nakov, P.: A survey on computational propaganda detection. In: IJCAI (2020)
10. Da San Martino, G., Yu, S., Barrón-Cedeño, A., Petrov, R., Nakov, P.: Fine-grained analysis of propaganda in news article. In: Proceedings of the 2019 Conference on Empirical Methods in Natural Language Processing and the 9th International Joint Conference on Natural Language Processing (EMNLP-IJCNLP), pp. 5636–5646. Association for Computational Linguistics, Hong Kong, China (2019). https://doi.org/10.18653/v1/D19-1565
11. Devlin, J., Chang, M.W., Lee, K., Toutanova, K.: BERT: pre-training of deep bidirectional transformers for language understanding. In: Proceedings of the 2019 Conference of the North American Chapter of the Association for Computational Linguistics: Human Language Technologies, Volume 1 (Long and Short Papers), pp. 4171–4186. Association for Computational Linguistics, Minneapolis, Minnesota (2019). https://doi.org/10.18653/v1/N19-1423
12. Edgett, S.: Testimony of sean j. Edgett to the United States Senate Committee on the Judiciary, Subcommittee on Crime and Terrorism. Hearing Before the United States Senate Committee on the Judiciary Subcommittee on Crime and Terrorism (2017)

13. Fadel, A., Tuffaha, I., Al-Ayyoub, M.: Pretrained ensemble learning for fine-grained propaganda detection. In: Proceedings of the Second Workshop on Natural Language Processing for Internet Freedom: Censorship, Disinformation, and Propaganda, pp. 139–142. Association for Computational Linguistics, Hong Kong, China (2019). https://doi.org/10.18653/v1/D19-5020

14. Kwak, H., Lee, C., Park, H., Moon, S.: What is twitter, a social network or a news media? In: Proceedings of the 19th International Conference on World Wide Web, pp. 591–600. WWW '10, Association for Computing Machinery, New York, NY, USA (2010). https://doi.org/10.1145/1772690.1772751

15. Miller, C.: How to detect and analyze propaganda ...: an address delivered at town hall, Monday, February 20, 1939. A Town Hall pamphlet, Town Hall, Incorporated (1939). https://books.google.com.mx/books?id=UAc4AAAAMAAJ

16. Mintz, M., Bills, S., Snow, R., Jurafsky, D.: Distant supervision for relation extraction without labeled data. In: Proceedings of the Joint Conference of the 47th Annual Meeting of the ACL and the 4th International Joint Conference on Natural Language Processing of the AFNLP, pp. 1003–1011. Association for Computational Linguistics, Suntec, Singapore (2009). https://aclanthology.org/P09-1113

17. Newman, N., Dutton, W., Blank, G.: Social media and the news, pp. 135–148 (2014). https://doi.org/10.1093/acprof:oso/9780199661992.003.0009

18. Pedregosa, F., et al.: Scikit-Learn: machine learning in Python. J. Mach. Learn. Res. **12**, 2825–2830 (2011)

19. Rashkin, H., Choi, E., Jang, J.Y., Volkova, S., Choi, Y.: Truth of varying shades: analyzing language in fake news and political fact-checking. In: Proceedings of the 2017 Conference on Empirical Methods in Natural Language Processing, pp. 2931–2937. Association for Computational Linguistics, Copenhagen, Denmark (2017). https://doi.org/10.18653/v1/D17-1317

20. Sanh, V., Debut, L., Chaumond, J., Wolf, T.: Distilbert, a distilled version of BERT: smaller, faster, cheaper and lighter. arXiv preprint arXiv:1910.01108 (2019)

21. Sinno, B.M., Oviedo, B., Atwell, K., Alikhani, M., Li, J.J.: Political ideology and polarization of policy positions: a multi-dimensional approach. ArXiv abs/2106.14387 (2021)

22. Torruella, J., Capsada, R.: Lexical statistics and tipological structures: a measure of lexical richness. Procedia - Soc. Behav. Sci. **95**, 447–454 (2013). https://doi.org/10.1016/j.sbspro.2013.10.668, https://www.sciencedirect.com/science/article/pii/S1877042813041888, corpus Resources for Descriptive and Applied Studies. Current Challenges and Future Directions: Selected Papers from the 5th International Conference on Corpus Linguistics (CILC2013)

23. Wang, L., Shen, X., de Melo, G., Weikum, G.: Cross-domain learning for classifying propaganda in online contents. In: Truth and Trust Online Conference, pp. 21–31. Hacks Hackers (2020)

24. Yang, J., Leskovec, J.: Patterns of temporal variation in online media. In: Proceedings of the Fourth ACM International Conference on Web Search and Data Mining, pp. 177–186. WSDM '11, Association for Computing Machinery, New York, NY, USA (2011). https://doi.org/10.1145/1935826.1935863

25. Zubiaga, A., Liakata, M., Procter, R., Wong Sak Hoi, G., Tolmie, P.: Analysing how people orient to and spread rumours in social media by looking at conversational threads. PLOS ONE **11**(3), 1–29 (2016). https://doi.org/10.1371/journal.pone.0150989

Data Mining and Analysis of NLP Methods in Students Evaluation of Teaching

Diego Acosta-Ugalde[✉], Santiago Enrique Conant-Pablos,
Claudia Camacho-Zuñiga, and Andrés Eduardo Gutiérrez-Rodríguez

Tecnologico de Monterrey, Escuela de Ingeniería y Ciencias, Monterrey, Nuevo León, Mexico
{a01367987,sconant,claudia.camacho}@tec.mx

Abstract. Student evaluations of teachings (SETs) are essential for determining the quality of the educational process. Natural Language Processing (NLP) techniques may produce informative insights into these surveys. This study aims to provide an overview of the various approaches used in NLP and sentiment analysis, focusing on identifying the top outcomes, models, and text representations used. Furthermore, we investigate NLP methods applied to a Spanish corpus of SETs, which is relatively uncommon, and discuss the application of less well-known tools in this scenario. In general, by showing the top models and text representations, especially in the case of a Spanish corpus, this study contributes to NLP and sentiment analysis. Additionally, it promotes research and interest in other languages that receive little attention.

Keywords: NLP · Data Mining · Student Evaluation of Teaching · Education Rating · Machine Learning · Educational Innovation

1 Introduction

The applicability of Natural Language Processing (NLP) has completely changed how we evaluate and extract meaningful observations from unstructured data like text, allowing us to discover a wealth of insightful information like sentiments, patterns, opinions, preferences and other aspects that were previously locked away in the text because the amount of information surpassed the human capability to analyze it [4,22,26]. Artificial Intelligence and, specifically, NLP boost our capacities to analyze information and open new and exciting opportunities to use information already gathered and create value from there [16,22].

Sentiment analysis, a sub-field of natural language processing, is an effective tool for understanding the core thoughts, feelings, and opinions expressed in survey responses [10,14]. Machine learning algorithms can recognize sentiments with incredibly high accuracy through sentiment analysis models, enabling organizations to assess customer satisfaction, understand overall and specific sentiments, and reach well-informed decisions [22]. Even though sentiment analysis has been a popular research area recently, most experiments and studies have been done in English. The dataset used in this study offers a new valuable corpus reasonably large for experimentation using diverse machine learning and deep learning techniques.

In NLP, text representations have significance because they enable us to transform unstructured text into practical numerical representations [9]. The word importance within a document in relation to a corpus is captured by the traditional text representation technique known as TF-IDF (Term Frequency-Inverse Document Frequency). We may analyze document similarities, find significant features for further NLP tasks, and discover relevant terms by applying it [10].

SETs are a common practice in higher education institutions for enhancing the academic structure of the program, gathering valuable data about the performance of the professors, and getting the student's perspective on matters like the learning experience, their interactions with the professors, the classroom environment, and their satisfaction with the education that they received [1,11,16,22,23]. Most institutions of higher learning structure their course offerings on the use of intellectually demanding teaching strategies, and the SETs are a helpful tool to validate this characteristic [1,2,16,23].

The effectiveness of instruction in educational institutions is largely evaluated by student evaluations of teaching [4,25]. These surveys gather valuable student feedback and provide perspectives on multiple aspects of instructional efficacy, course material, and overall learning experiences [26]. Such surveys have traditionally been reviewed by statistical analysis [2,16,23,27]. That type of analysis can be laborious and inconsistent. Nowadays, it is possible to use NLP methods to analyze large amounts of unstructured data present in these surveys to extract valuable data [9,17,18].

Employing NLP to analyze student surveys on their educational experiences has various benefits. It allows educational institutions to efficiently analyze vast amounts of text data, enabling them to spot patterns and trends that might have been difficult to notice manually. Additionally, automatic data mining using NLP techniques can provide a more profound knowledge of students' thoughts and perspectives toward education by identifying sentiments and aspects that human analysis cannot perceive [6].

The use of NLP and text mining techniques to analyze student evaluation of teaching surveys still needs to be explored in Spanish despite their broad use across many different fields [9,15]. Most previous research in this field has also concentrated on SETs conducted in English, leaving a gap in surveys on other languages. Some authors have made a similar approach to the SETs in Spanish but with much smaller datasets (about 3% of the size of the corpus presented in this research) [8]. For instance, due to linguistic characteristics and the availability of NLP tools and libraries designed explicitly for English, the analysis of student evaluation of teaching surveys in Spanish offers an opportunity [17].

This research aims to give a general overview of some of the classic approaches used in NLP and sentiment analysis and identify the top models tested for the analysis of SETs using TF-IDF representation. Additionally, by emphasizing the analysis of SETs conducted in Spanish, which received limited attention in the literature, this paper aims to contribute to the research gap [8]. The usage of less-known libraries, like the Stanza library, is also pursued, revealing their application and potential for a broader audience. With an emphasis on the Spanish language, this study intends to demonstrate the applicability of NLP approaches for different linguistic scenarios and extend its techniques in interpreting SETs.

2   Related Work

The educational process's effectiveness is largely evaluated by student evaluations of teaching (SETs). Natural language processing techniques have recently attracted much attention for their use in evaluating these surveys and giving insightful information about students' opinions. With an emphasis on identifying the most significant outcomes or models used in this field, this section evaluates the research that has been published on NLP techniques and sentiment analysis in the context of student evaluations of teaching [7].

Textual data from student evaluations has been processed and analyzed using a variety of NLP approaches. Researchers have also experimented with several text representations, including Word2Vec, Term Frequency-Inverse Document Frequency (TF-IDF), and Bag-of-Words (BoW). These methods have been shown to be successful at extracting semantic data from student feedback.

In addition, sentiment analysis, a branch of NLP, has been widely used to analyze instruction assessments by students. Researchers have used both machine learning-based approaches, which use supervised learning algorithms to categorize sentiments, and lexicon-based techniques, where sentiment scores are given to words based on predefined sentiment dictionaries [19,23,24].

While earlier research has mainly focused on English corpora of student evaluations, this work differs by looking at NLP techniques utilized on a Spanish corpus of SETs. By comparing the predicted label for the review-such as sentiment polarity or topic-with the actual label provided by the student or determined by a human expert analysis of the review, the accuracy is determined [12,24]. In the particular case of this study, it is compared with the overall average score that the student determined previously to the comments. Similar experiments by other authors resulted in accuracy in the 67–89% [22]. Other authors employed lexicon to predict the sentiment polarity in SETs. The accuracy range was 63–78%, but it increased to 76–85% when employing similarity of word embedding [12,20,22]. LSTM neural network approaches have shown accuracy greater than 90% when predicting the sentiment as positive or negative [10,22].

In order to gain a better understanding of the difficulties and potential in sentiment analysis for non-English languages, the use of less well-known tools with a Spanish corpus is examined. This study advances sentiment analysis and

NLP by spotlighting some of the most influential models, particularly in the context of a Spanish corpus. It increases the body of knowledge already known and sparks interest in other languages that have received less attention [9].

3   Methodology

3.1   Data Sampling and Participants

The dataset provided by one of the top private universities in Mexico consists of 100,000 evaluations of the ECOA, which is the SET that the Tecnologico of Monterrey (ITESM) uses every semester. This system was developed to gather data on the students' course evaluations. For this study, we used the quantitative data from the ECOA and the comments the students submitted in response to the question, "Would you recommend or not recommend the professor?".

The ECOA aims to gather comments from the students expressing their feedback and take appropriate action to improve the course and ensure its requirements are met. This study tries to improve the analysis done to the ECOA because this purpose is not completely accomplished. Comments are impossible to read by humans due to the number of submissions the SET receives, even though it is not the ideal participation [12]. All students are encouraged to submit the SET, and although the submission is optional, some professors may reward with extra points to those who complete it. Factors involved in the participation of the SET diminish the value of the data [7,11]. Comments are entirely optional and not a requirement to finish the SET. For this reason, this study aims to obtain valuable data that has received minor consideration using artificial intelligence techniques [7].

The dataset includes detailed information on each student who reviewed the course, but due to the students' privacy guarantees, the student's name is kept anonymous. The course structure, teaching strategies, and recommendation questions were all based on an 11-point Likert scale with a range of "0" to "10" [13,16]. The choice "I do not have the elements to evaluate" was also offered on each of the eight quantitative questions. "0" on this scale means "totally unsatisfied", while "10" means "completely satisfied".

It was necessary to clean the data to use the dataset. Negative and positive comments were separated. For that reason, it was considered adequate to merge those comments and add a new column with the comments' label to keep the sentiment information that the student attributes to their own comment.

The SET does not constrain the student to write a comment to finish the SET; therefore, all columns that did not contain comments or additional relevant information for the evaluation required to carry out the tests were removed for analysis purposes. The experiments used the columns containing the student and professor's genders, the course ID, and eight numerically evaluated aspects graded on the 11-point scale that serve to evaluate the professor in the methodology used, comprehension of concepts, the interaction with the professor, the evaluation, intellectual challenge, learning guidance and the domain of the area of knowledge. The text of the comments was preprocessed using some of the conventional techniques for cleaning text data, including tokenization, stop word removal, *lemmatization*, lowercasing, and removal of special characters and symbols [4,21]. The TF-IDF method was used to represent the text utilized in the tests, and the *sklearn* library was chosen to produce this vector representation after the comments went through the proper preprocessing.

Since the used SET allows another choice for the student that considers that *they do not have elements to evaluate*, those responses were not considered either. It was necessary to perform a correlation analysis using the Pearson Correlation Coefficient to analyze the relation between the aspects the student evaluated since the initial tests showed poor results in the attempt to predict each aspect separately. According to the 'halo effect,' students may rationalize disregarding or faking other variables by considering some variables to be so important [3,7]. In order to diminish these effects, those aspects that resulted in correlations lower than 0.7 were removed. Only two of the eight aspects were removed: DOM, which refers to the professor's domain of the topics, and MEJ, which responded to the question, "Would you recommend this professor as one of the best you have had?". For the analysis of the dichotomous variables like MEJ, it was used the point biserial correlation. Results of the two lowest aspects are shown in the Table 1.

Table 1. Correlation between MEJ and DOM aspects with the other aspects in the SET.

	APR	DOM	EVA	MEJ	MET	PRA	REC	RET
MEJ	0.520	0.386	0.431	1.0	0.554	0.485	0.585	0.476
DOM	0.702	1.0	0.620	0.386	0.675	0.675	0.645	0.674

Only six elements were left after removing those two: APR, EVA, MET, PRA, REC, and RET. These six factors evaluate aspects of the course structure, like the methodology and learning activities, understanding concepts, intellectual challenge, the professor's performance as a learning guide, the domain expertise, and the student-professor relationship. These aspects were averaged to generate a new column (AVG), which was used to create a global score of the student's evaluation and then use the comments to predict that score. The Table 2 shows an example of the dataset structure. Real comment examples are not shown due to the privacy of the dataset. Nonetheless, comments concatenate both negative (the answer to 'Why would you not recommend this professor?') and positive (the answer to 'Why would you recommend this professor?'). The 'Lemmatized' column contains the list of words from the comments in their root form. Since both negative and positives comments were concatenated, the 'Type' column was necessary to classify the comment with the student label.

Table 2. Example of the dataset used.

	APR	EVA	MET	PRA	REC	RET	AVG	Type	Comment	Lemmatized
0	0.0	0.0	0.0	1.0	0.0	1.0	0.0	1	...	...
1	1	0.0	0.0	0.0	0.0	0.0	0.0	0	...	...

4   Results

4.1   Data Exploration

The dataset contained 98,427 rows with comments and the six aspects scored by the student with the average. The distribution of the submitted scores with a comment, shown in Fig. 1, displayed a significant imbalance in the quantitative data. Submissions with an average score of 10 represent 39% of the total submissions, and 65.5% of the average scores were greater than 9.1.

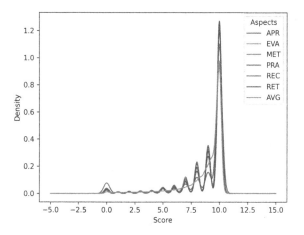

Fig. 1. Density of the scores for each aspect evaluated

On the other hand, the type of comment labeled by the students themselves, shown in Fig. 2, follows a different unbalance. The students that wrote their comments in the positive section were 56.3%, while only 9.3% wrote a negative review, and 34.4% used both text fields to write both a negative and a positive comment of their professor performance.

Our attempt to estimate if a comment would be below or above 9.0 in the average score of the ECOA using the comments and NLP techniques is motivated by the inconsistent relationship between the type of comment and the overall average score seen in the quantitative section of the SET. This score was chosen to delimit if a comment was negative or positive because it helped to divide the submissions more unbalanced and therefore, was more effective for prediction.

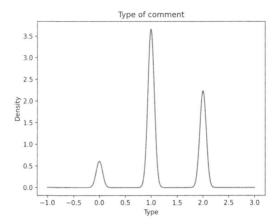

Fig. 2. Type of comment

The generation of the WordCloud in the Fig. 3 was also performed to visualize the dataset and have a different perspective of the frequency of terms now that the data has been preprocessed [9,10]. It is interesting to see that the word "buen" (good) and the word "no" (not) are almost the same size, but the combination of these two words or the usage of only "buen" can change completely the meaning of the phrase. The word "malo" (bad) is not even present in the figure.

Fig. 3. Word Cloud of the dataset using TF-IDF vector

4.2   Results with TF-IDF Vectors

We chose to employ conventional models that did not demand a lot of computing resources or long training times since the idea of this study was to explore and therefore, time between each iteration of experiments was required to be performed more effectively. Additionally, TF-IDF vector representation was selected for this study because it is one of the most popular methods and offers an acceptable introduction to text analysis using such classic models [8, 22]. Our research revealed that the key terms and semantic data available in the SET submissions were successfully caught by the models using TF-IDF, enabling the models to train successfully and deliver acceptable performance.

Table 3. Metrics obtained using TF-IDF text representation in three different models

Model	Accuracy	Weighted F1 Score	Balanced Accuracy
Decision Tree	0.74	0.73	0.68
Random Forest	0.74	0.71	0.65
SVM	0.79	0.79	0.74

In Table 3, we presented the report of the metrics obtained for the three different methods used here: Decision Tree, Random Forest, and SVM. The results presented using the TF-IDF representation of the text are Accuracy, Balanced Accuracy, and Weighted F1 Score. We decided to use those performance metrics since it allowed our study to serve as a pivot for reference to the performance with other studies [8]. It is observed that the Support Vector Machine Classifier obtained the best performance metrics in the prediction of the comment.

5   Discussion and Conclusion

In terms of using NLP techniques to analyze student evaluations of teaching (SETs) in a Spanish corpus, the analysis suggested in this work is a pioneering effort. We have shown that NLP approaches may successfully collect significant information from SET comments. The experiments carried out in this study required small computational resources, highlighting the accessibility and usefulness of using NLP for survey analysis [21]. It may be premature to affirm that the results shown are enough in the case of the ECOA to show the incapacity of the quantitative part of the SET to capture the student opinion for each aspect and the type of comment, as well as the ability of the survey to score the aspects and measure the professors teaching performance.

The results provide a solid starting point for analyzing comments in Spanish SETs and open the discussion to new teaching performance validation approaches. The gathered information demonstrates the efficacy of sentiment analysis and text representations like TF-IDF, offering insightful interpretations of student comments that can help us understand educational success more in-depth [21].

Additionally, the dataset's characteristics present promising opportunities for using more computationally intensive approaches, like LSTM, Transformers, and other Deep Learning techniques [5,10]. These cutting-edge methods have shown an exceptional ability to capture intricate linguistic patterns and contextual complexity, and they offer enormous potential to enhance the data mining process of SETs further [4,28]. In the case of the ECOA, the mentioned techniques could help us compare the aspects evaluation using, for example, Aspect Based Sentiment Analysis techniques and obtain a better contrast with the current results shown by the 11-point scale questions of the SET. The use of artificial intelligence may impact the potential implication on educational institutions and how students and teachers interact and create an exciting space for innovation in education [24].

Finally, integrating NLP on educational evaluation in SETs offers motivating possibilities for significant shifts in the educational environment [12]. In order to fully realize NLP's potential for improving quality in teaching and learning, it is necessary for additional research, interest, and experimentation as we explore the potential of AI in education [16,18,25].

Acknowledgments. The authors would like to acknowledge the financial support and the supply of the data set to the iClassroom, a project of the Institute for the Future of Education of the Tecnologico de Monterrey.

Data Availability Statement. The dataset used in this work may be available on request to the Institute for the Future of Education Data Hub.

References

1. Bedggood, R.E., Donovan, J.D.: University performance evaluations: what are we really measuring? Stud. High. Educ. **37**(7), 825–842 (2012)
2. Cheng, M., Taylor, J., Williams, J., Tong, K.: Student satisfaction and perceptions of quality: testing the linkages for PhD students. High. Educ. Res. Dev. **35**(6), 1153–1166 (2016)
3. Clayson, D.E., Haley, D.A.: Are students telling us the truth? a critical look at the student evaluation of teaching. Mark. Educ. Rev. **21**(2), 101–112 (2011)
4. Cook, J., Chen, C., Griffin, A.: Using text mining and data mining techniques for applied learning assessment. J. Effect. Teach. High. Educ. **2**(1), 60–79 (2019)
5. Devlin, J., Chang, M.W., Lee, K., Toutanova, K.: BERT: pre-training of deep bidirectional transformers for language understanding. arXiv preprint arXiv:1810.04805 (2018)
6. Hoang, M., Bihorac, O.A., Rouces, J.: Aspect-based sentiment analysis using BERT. In: Proceedings of the 22nd nordic conference on computational linguistics, pp. 187–196 (2019)
7. Hoel, A., Dahl, T.I.: Why bother? student motivation to participate in student evaluations of teaching. Assess. Eval. High. Educ. **44**(3), 361–378 (2019)

8. Ikauniece, I.: Sentiment analysis of student evaluation of teaching (2018)
9. Jojoa, M., et al.: Analysis of the effects of lockdown on staff and students at universities in Spain and Colombia using natural language processing techniques. Int. J. Environ. Res. Public Health **19**(9), 5705 (2022)
10. Kandhro, I.A., Wasi, S., Kumar, K., Rind, M., Ameen, M.: Sentiment analysis of students' comment using long-short term model. Indian J. Sci. Technol. **12**(8), 1–16 (2019)
11. Kite, M.E., Subedi, P.C., Bryant-Lees, K.B.: Students' perceptions of the teaching evaluation process. Teach. Psychol. **42**(4), 307–314 (2015)
12. Kučak, D., Juričić, V., Đambić, G.: Machine learning in education-a survey of current research trends. Annals of DAAAM & Proceedings 29 (2018)
13. Leung, S.O.: A comparison of psychometric properties and normality in 4-, 5-, 6-, and 11-point likert scales. J. Soc. Serv. Res. **37**(4), 412–421 (2011)
14. Litman, D., Forbes-Riley, K.: Predicting student emotions in computer-human tutoring dialogues. In: Proceedings of the 42nd Annual Meeting of the Association for Computational Linguistics (ACL-04), pp. 351–358 (2004)
15. Miranda, C.H., Buelvas, E.: AspectSA: unsupervised system for aspect based sentiment analysis in Spanish. Prospectiva **17**(1), 87–95 (2019)
16. Okoye, K., et al.: Impact of students evaluation of teaching: a text analysis of the teachers qualities by gender. Int. J. Educ. Technol. High. Educ. **17**(1), 1–27 (2020)
17. Pandey, S., Pandey, S.K.: Applying natural language processing capabilities in computerized textual analysis to measure organizational culture. Organ. Res. Methods **22**(3), 765–797 (2019)
18. Pedro, F., Subosa, M., Rivas, A., Valverde, P.: Artificial intelligence in education: challenges and opportunities for sustainable development (2019)
19. Rajput, Q., Haider, S., Ghani, S., et al.: Lexicon-based sentiment analysis of teachers' evaluation. Appl. Comput. Intell. Soft Comput. 2016 (2016)
20. Ren, P., Yang, L., Luo, F.: Automatic scoring of student feedback for teaching evaluation based on aspect-level sentiment analysis. Educ. Inf. Technol. **28**(1), 797–814 (2023)
21. Rybinski, K.: Are rankings and accreditation related? examining the dynamics of higher education in Poland. Qual. Assur. Educ. **28**(3), 193–204 (2020)
22. Rybinski, K., Kopciuszewska, E.: Will artificial intelligence revolutionise the student evaluation of teaching? A big data study of 1.6 million student reviews. Assess. Eval. High. Educ. **46**(7), 1127–1139 (2021)
23. Santhanam, E., Lynch, B., Jones, J.: Making sense of student feedback using text analysis-adapting and expanding a common lexicon. Qual. Assur. Educ. **26**(1), 60–69 (2018)
24. Santos, C.L., Rita, P., Guerreiro, J.: Improving international attractiveness of higher education institutions based on text mining and sentiment analysis. Int. J. Educ. Manag. **32**(3), 431–447 (2018)
25. Schuck, S., Gordon, S., Buchanan, J.: What are we missing here? problematising wisdoms on teaching quality and professionalism in higher education. Teach. High. Educ. **13**(5), 537–547 (2008)
26. Sindhu, I., Daudpota, S.M., Badar, K., Bakhtyar, M., Baber, J., Nurunnabi, M.: Aspect-based opinion mining on student's feedback for faculty teaching performance evaluation. IEEE Access **7**, 108729–108741 (2019)

27. Stupans, I., McGuren, T., Babey, A.M.: Student evaluation of teaching: a study exploring student rating instrument free-form text comments. Innov. High. Educ. **41**, 33–42 (2016)
28. Wolf, T., et al.: Transformers: state-of-the-art natural language processing. In: Proceedings of the 2020 Conference on Empirical Methods in Natural Language Processing: System Demonstrations, pp. 38–45 (2020)

Data Imputation with Adversarial Neural Networks for Causal Discovery from Subsampled Time Series

Julio Muñoz-Benítez[✉] and L. Enrique Sucar

Instituto Nacional de Astrofísica Óptica y Electrónica, Coordinación de Ciencias Computacionales, Puebla, Mexico
{jcmunoz,esucar}@inaoep.mx

Abstract. A relevant and challenging problem is causal discovery from time series data. This helps to understand dynamics events present in real world scenarios. However, causal interactions may occur at a timescale faster than the measurement frequency, resulting in a subsampled time series. This can lead to significant errors during causal discovery. We propose an approach based on imputing the missing data using adversarial neural networks to try to recover the true causal structure. The trained model is fed with the subsampled time series in order to generate data that behaves similarly to the original time series, so that the original causal structure can be recovered. The completed data series is then fed to a causal discovery algorithm. Experimental results on several synthetic dynamic models show that the imputed data time series is close to the original one, and that the causal structure derived from this data resembles the correct causal structure.

Keywords: Causal Discovery · Time Series · Subsampling

1 Introduction

Inferring causal relations from time series have served as the basis for causal discovery in various fields of science such as climate systems, ecological networks, effective connectivity in the brain, and finance [5,8,14,17]. Data collected can provide precise measurements at regular points of time [1]. One of the main advantages of using observational data from time series is that the temporal order of the information can simplify causal analysis [9,14]. That is, the causal driver can be identified as the variable that occurred first, as the future can't affect the past [1,15,16]. However, the study of causal relations in time series is still a challenging issue, which is partly due to the complexity and dynamism of real world systems and, in many cases, the time series data may contain erroneous measurements, inconsistent data, or even missing data.

One of the main challenges of causal discovery from time series is that causal interactions may occur on a timescale faster than the frequency of measurement

H. Calvo et al. (Eds.): MICAI 2023, LNAI 14392, pp. 39–51, 2024.
https://doi.org/10.1007/978-3-031-47640-2_4

[8,9], this phenomena is known as *subsampling*. This can lead to a loss of valuable information to determine the true causal relationships between events. Subsampling could lead to significant errors in the obtained causal structure, as shown in previous work [2]. Causal discovery in subsampled time series is relatively under explored [3]; it is a challenge that must be addressed in order to avoid learning incorrect causal relations from time series data. Previous work that considers the subsampling problem has focused on obtaining an *equivalence class* of causal structures consistent with the subsampled data measurements [2,8,15]. However, they can not determine the *true* causal structure in the equivalence class.

We present a novel approach to obtain a unique causal structure given under sampled time series data. Our approach is based on imputing the missing data using generative adversarial neural networks (GANs). We assume that the rate of subsampling is known, and we estimate the missing data between the data samples provided. We train a GAN to estimate the missing samples based on several time series, and then, given new data and the subsampling rate, we estimate the missing samples. Once the time series is completed, we obtain the causal structure using a method for causal discovery from time series [13]. We have evaluated the proposed approach in different scenarios of increasing complexity. The results show that the imputed data is close to the original data, and that the discovered causal structure is also very close the correct one.

2   Background

2.1   Causal Graphical Models for Time Series

In order to model dynamical systems, one may use graphical models such as *Directed Acyclic Graphs (DAGs)* [10]. The nodes in the DAG represent the variables, and the links indicate the causal relationships between these variables. In particular, in the case of dynamic systems, this representation is known as a *dynamic causal Bayesian network* [12]. In this work, it is assumed that there is causal sufficiency, that is, that there are no hidden variables that affect the observed variables [2,14]. In addition, it is also assumed that the causal relationships are invariant over time [2,15]. An example of the representation of a causal structure from a time series can be seen in Fig. 1a where the interaction between nodes in discrete time stages is shown.

2.2   Subsampling in Time Series

One of the main challenges of using data from time series is that causal interactions may occur on a timescale faster than the frequency of measurement [8,9]. This can lead to a loss of valuable information to determine the true causal relationships between events. An example of this can be seen in Fig. 1, where the original causal structure of the time series is shown (Fig. 1a); and the causal structure of the same process under subsampling, obtained by making observations every two time steps (Fig. 1b). If it is assumed that the structure of Fig. 1b is correct, valuable information about the true causal relationships between the variables is lost. This may lead to believe that variable Z can be intervened to control Y, but the true influence of Z on Y is mediated by X. Thus, an intervention in X would be more effective. Similarly, if the structure of Fig. 1b is used, the predictions of the behavior of the variables can be completely different from those obtained if the true causal structure of the time series is used [8].

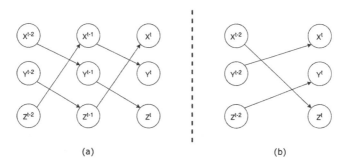

(a)   (b)

Fig. 1. Causal structures for a time series with variables$\{X, Y, Z\}$. (a) Original structure. (b) Structure obtained from subsampled data (every two time steps).

3   Related Work

Most causal discovery methods are designed to analyze identically distributed and independent data (IID). Causal discovery from time series requires a different approach [2,9,10,15]. Next we present a summary of related work, including the causal discovery algorithm we use in this work; the application of deep learning for causal discovery; and causal discovery for the case of subsampling.

3.1   PCMCI Algorithm

The PCMI algorithm is focused on causal discovery in time series [14], solving some limitations of the PC algorithm [17]; in particular the processing time in data sets with high dimensionality, and eliminating irrelevant variables that could lead to the appearance of inconsistent causal relationships. The PCMI algorithm aims to solve these problems through the selection of conditions to eliminate irrelevant variables and a test of conditional independence for the discovery of causal relationships between variables [13].

This is achieved in two stages. The first being the condition selection in order to identify the most relevant conditions for all the variables in the time series; that is, only those variables with the largest associations are selected rather than selecting all possible combinations. Subsequently, momentary conditional independence (MCI) is used as an estimator of causal strength, based on auto correlation, and as an identifier of false positives by means of a conditional independence test. In this way, the causal relationships with the highest probability are established, estimating the causal strength as well as the type of correlation between them. However, the PCMCI algorithm, as most causal discovery algorithms from time series, assumes that the data is sampled at the appropriate timescale; so if it is presented with subsampled data it will produce, in general, an incorrect causal structure.

3.2   Deep Learning in Causal Discovery

One of the novel approaches for causal discovery is the use of deep learning techniques, such as learning the causal structure from observational data taking advantage of continuous optimization [18]. The use of neural networks allows data to be analyzed to infer causal relationships [4,6]; likewise, the use of adversarial neural networks has been a promising approach for generating missing samples. In [19], a deep learning framework is used to impute data on an incomplete observational data set. Synthetic data generated by this approach helps in causal discovery. However, this data is invariant over time, this means that the observational data set is not part of a time series. The work proposed in [7] reflects the versatility of the use of neural networks for causal discovery of observational data in time series, obtaining good results in the inference of causal relationships, including their direction and intensity, although it is assumed that the time series is complete and is not affected by subsampling.

3.3   Causal Discovery in Subsampled Time Series

Danks et al. [2] developed an algorithm that allows learning a set of causal structures even if the level of subsampling is unknown. This is performed through a graphical representation of the causal structure of the time series which is known or inferred. Subsequently, all the possible causal structures are obtained, comparing them with the initial causal structure, which may be affected by some degree of sub-sampling. In this way, if the new structures are consistent with the original structure they are considered as a possible causal structures, obtaining an *equivalence class* of causal structures.

The use of this approach presents computational challenges that limits its use to *small* models. Furthermore, since the causal structure is obtained from limited time series data, statistical errors may occur that imply that some structures are not consistent with the original causal structure or that structures that are actually consistent are not taken into account. [8] extends the previous approach by proposing a constraint satisfaction procedure which is computationally more efficient, and can also recover from conflicts due to statistical errors. Recent work [15] extends this approach to obtain an equivalence class of causal structures with multiple measurement timescales. In this way, it is possible to indicate how many structures are part of the subset of possible causal structures given an initial one. This allows to quantify the resolution, or gain, of the size of the equivalence class and to evaluate whether or not a causal structure belongs to the subset of possible causal structures.

The previous developments can find the set of possible causal structures that are consistent with the under-sampled data given a known or even unknown subsampling rate, but can not select among these the *correct* one. The present work proposes an approach to impute the missing data due to subsampling, in order to obtain a **single causal structure** that corresponds to the time series without subsampling, or is close to it.

4   Data Imputation for Causal Discovery of Time Series

The proposed approach aims to minimize subsampling in time-series, by imputing data generated in an artificial way, to obtain the original causal structure. A conceptual diagram of the proposed model is shown in Fig. 2.

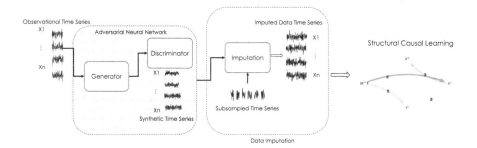

Fig. 2. A block diagram of the proposed method. The gray block at the left represents the training stage and the white block at the right the imputation phase. The generator model generates samples until the discriminator model accepts the synthetic time series as valid. This synthetic time series complements the missing values so that the output is a time series with imputed data that resembles the original time series. The completed data is fed to a causal structure learning algorithm to obtain the causal structure. (Color figure online)

4.1   Representation and Assumptions

In this work, the time series data is composed of a set of variables $V^t = \{X_1^t, X_2^t, X_3^t, ...\}$ that may take discrete or continuous values in discrete points of time. This means that the time series can be represented as a dynamic Bayesian network. The following assumptions are considered: (i) Time invariant; that is, the causal links between variables are repeated through time. (ii) Causal sufficiency; that is, V^{t-1} includes all common causes of V^t and there are no causal links of the form $X_i^t \rightarrow X_j^t$ [8].

4.2   Data Imputation

Imputation methods aim to make use of the available information and estimate missing data to obtain a complete data set. For data generation and imputation a generative adversarial neural network (GAN) [20] was used. This type of model learns regular patterns from the input data in such a way that the model can generate output data that may have a similar behavior, such that the generated data may be considered as part of the original data set. In this sense, we may capture the original distribution by making the distribution of the outputs (synthetic data) approximate the original data distribution. This is achieved by two models: the *generator* that is trained to generate data based on the original data set, and the *discriminator* that aims to classify the received data as real or fake. These two models work together until the discriminator model accepts the generated data as if these data belong to the original data set.

4.3   Generative Adversarial Model Architecture

Figure 3 shows the architecture of the generator and discriminator. The Generator receives the input data and outputs a synthetic sample $G(z)$. The Discriminator takes either a training sample x or a synthetic sample $G(z)$ as input. The output is a scalar indicating the probability that x or $G(z)$ follows the original data behavior. The generator performs 1-D fractional convolutions (deconvolutions), using rectified linear units (ReLU). The discriminator is an inverse of the generator. The features of the time series are extracted using 1-D kernel layers based on convolutions with stride 1 which outputs a scalar. For imputation we use the generator based loss as the loss function; we employ back-propagation to find the closest latent value of input data and then use the samples generated by the generator to impute the missing values. The batch size used in the model is 32. The learning rate was set to a value of 0.01, while the model was trained with a limit of 50 epochs.

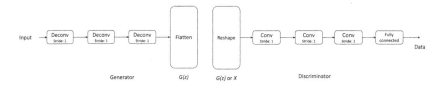

Fig. 3. Architecture of the generator and discriminator, which contain three fractional convolution layers (Deconv) and three strided convolution layers (Conv), respectively.

Training. The discriminator was trained to minimize the classification loss, and the generator was trained to maximize the discriminator's miss classification rate. Considering the data input $\mathbf{X}$, the main objective is to generate data that approaches the data distribution, $P(\mathbf{X})$. **Testing.** In the test phase, the input to the ANN is a time series data affected by the subsampling. Assuming a subsampling rate of two, the input consists of an incomplete time series, $\mathbf{X_1, X_3, X_5, ...X_{N-1}}$; and the output is the completed time series generated by the ANN: $\mathbf{X_1, X_2, X_3, X_4, ...X_{N-1}, X_N}$. The data that complements the subsampled time series are data that has the highest probability for the missing values of the time series.

4.4 Causal Structure Learning

Once the data generated complements the time series, the PCMCI algorithm [14] is used to reconstruct its causal structure[1]. This algorithm was used due to its good performance in the causal discovery of time series, which have not been affected by subsampling. Likewise, the causal links between the variables are reconstructed, specifying both causal strength of the relationships between them and the time step in which these relationships arise. In this way, this algorithm serves to analyze and compare the original causal structure and the structure resulting from the imputed data. Thus, we can verify if the data generated by the GAN maintains the causal relationships.

5 Experimental Results

5.1 Experimental Setup

To perform an analysis of the imputation of data on the time series and compare the resulting causal structure, artificially generated time series were used. In this way, the resulting causal structure of the time series is known beforehand to be compared with the structure obtained from the subsampled time series, and the resulting structure of the time series with the imputed data.

To generate the data, the structure and parameters of the time series are specified, and the tool developed in [9] was used to generate N data points. A detailed description of the dataset can be found in [11][2]. A fraction of this data points is deleted to simulate subsampling ($N/2$ for a subsampling rate of two); we apply the proposed method to this data. The time series generated are based on a structural causal model that assumes that the child nodes in a causal graph have a functional dependence on their parents. That is, given a set of variables $\{X_1, X_2, ..., X_n\}$ each variable X_i can be represented in terms of a function of its parents $Pa(X_i)$, as $X_i = F_i(Pa(X_i), N_i)$ where F_i are linear models and N_i are noise terms with a given distribution (Gaussian, Student's t, Laplace, Uniform).

We performed a series of experiments. First, a simple example with four variables in which the training and testing time series have the same noise distribution. Next, more complex scenarios with four variables and causal links at different time steps, in which the training and test time series have different

---

[1] The PCMCI implementation in the Python module Tigramite [14] was used.
[2] The data set and the program to generate the data are available at the following link: https://github.com/juliocmunoz/synthetic_time_series_causal_discovery.

distributions. In each experiment we compare: (i) the reconstruction of the time series, comparing the original data with the imputed data; (ii) the causal structures learned from the subsampled and imputed data vs. the correct structure.

5.2 Experiment 1: Subsampled Time Series with the Same Noise Distributions

For an initial experiment we consider a simple time series with four variables, X_1, X_2, X_3, and Y_1. A time series composed of 1,000 observations was generated for each one of the variables. This same time series was affected by a subsampling rate of two, that is, the observed data comprise values of the variables every two time steps. Figure 4a depicts the causal structure of the original time series where there is a causal link from $X1$ to $X2$ every two time steps. However, when analyzing the causal structure of the time series affected by subsampling, Fig. 4b, the resulting causal link, although it is specified in a correct way from $X1$ to $X2$, it is represented in a single time step. Similarly, for the links from $X3$ to $X1$ and $X3$ to $Y1$. These represent errors in the causal structure.

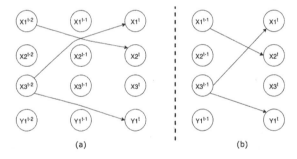

(a)   (b)

Fig. 4. Causal structure of the time series used in the first experiment: (a) The original causal structure shows a link from X_1 to X_2, a link from X_3 to X_1 and X_3 to Y_1 at two time steps. (b) The causal structure of the subsampled time series shows a link from X_1 to X_2 at one time step, as well for the links from X_3 to X_1 and to Y_1. This demonstrates how subsampling affects the causal relationships between variables.

The time series was completed with imputed data for each one of the observed variables: X_1, X_2, X_3 and Y_1. A comparison is depicted in Fig. 5, where it can be seen that the generated data is very close to real data, presenting a similar behavior over time. The mean absolute error, which is the measure of the difference between both sets of values, allows us to quantify the precision of the generated values compared to the original values, resulting in a value of 0.0209 (approx. 2%).

A comparison of the causal structures of the three scenarios was made, that is, the causal structure of the time-series obtained with the imputed data compared with the original causal structure and the one obtained from the subsampled

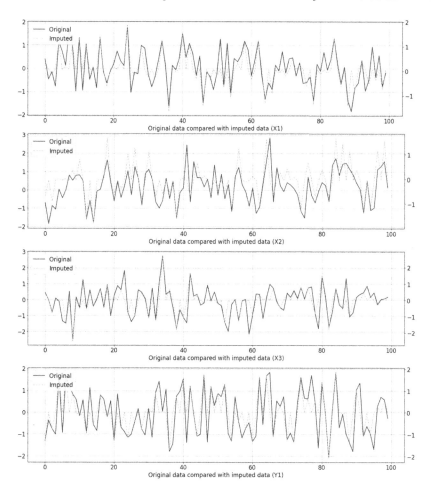

Fig. 5. Experiment 1: graphs of the original (blue) and generated (orange) data for variables (from top to bottom) X_1, X_2, X_3 and Y_1. The generated data for each one of the variables resembles the behavior of of the original values. (Best seen in color.) (Color figure online)

data. This comparison is shown in Fig. 6. In Fig. 6c it can be seen that the causal structure obtained from the subsampled data has a causal link from X_1 to X_2 at the incorrect time step compared to the original causal structure (Fig. 6a); while the structure from the imputed data, Fig. 6b, has this link at a correct time step. However, the appearance of a causal link from X_1 to Y_1 is appreciated in 6c, although this link has a minimal causal strength. The links from X_3 to Y_1 and from X_3 to X_1 appear at the correct time step in the imputed data (6b). The causal structure of the imputed data time series is very close to the original causal structure even though it is obtained from a subsampled time series.

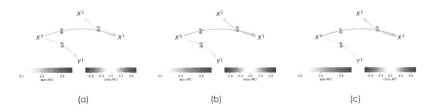

Fig. 6. Experiment 1: causal structure for (a) the original time series, (b) the time series with imputed data and (c) the subsampled time series. Each graph represents the causal structure via a compact representation (*rolled graph*), indicating the time delay (number associated to the link) and strength (color code) of each causal link. (Best seen in color.) (Color figure online)

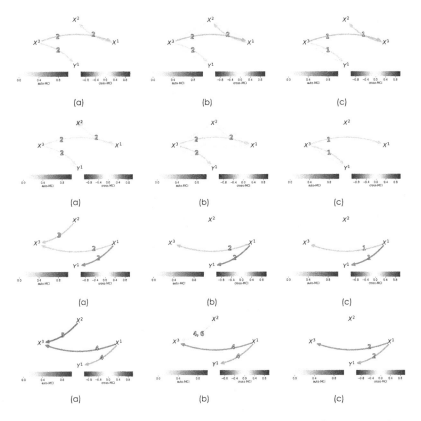

Fig. 7. Causal structure of the times series for experiments 2–5 (from top to bottom): (a) original causal structures, (b) causal structures of imputed data, and (c) causal structures of subsampled time series.

5.3   Experiments 2–5: Subsampled Time Series with Different Noise Distributions and Time Steps

Next we present four more challenging scenarios, using the same number of variables but changing the maximum lag in which causal links may appear and considering different noise distributions for the training and test time series. Subsequently, these time series were affected by subsampling. For each of the time series the proposed approach was used, where imputed data complemented the time series, and their causal structure was obtained. This causal structure was compared versus the original causal structure of the time series and the causal structure of the time series affected by subsampling for each scenario. Figure 7 shows the comparison for the four different scenarios: of the original causal structure (a); the causal structure of the time series with imputed data (b); and the causal structure of the time series affected by subsampling (c).

Table 1. Summary of the characteristics and results for Experiments 2–5. MAE: *Mean Average Error.*

	Number of Variables	Maximum Lag	MAE Subsampled Time Series	MAE Imputed Time Series
Scenario 2	4	2	0.1875	0
Scenario 3	4	2	0.156	0
Scenario 4	4	3	0.1041	0.0208
Scenario 5	4	5	0.052	0.0312

Table 1 summarizes the results for the four experiments. The *Mean Average Error* (MAE) is used to evaluate the causal structures obtained, by comparing the adjacency matrices of the learned structure and the ground truth[3]. In the first two experiments, the causal structure of the imputed data is the same as the original structure, while the one of the subsampled time series presents some errors. However, as we increased the maximum lag the errors in the causal structure of the imputed data started to increase, this is, there were differences with the original causal structure. Although this error increased, the differences of the subsampled causal structure were significantly higher. This highlights the impact of subsampling in the discovery of causal relations in time series. Although the causal structure of scenarios 4 and 5 were not completely recovered, the causal structure of the imputed data tend to recover the *strong* causal relations and at the appropriate delay, see Fig. 7.

---

[3] We use the adjacency matrix to evaluate the difference between the causal structures. The difference between the matrices divided by the number of elements gives the MAE.

5.4   Discussion

The following conclusions can be reached from these experiments: (i) The imputed data is in general very close to the original data. (ii) The causal structure obtained from the imputed data tends to maintain the *strong* causal links in the original model with the correct timescale. In contrast, the structure derived from the subsampled data tends to have causal links at an incorrect timescale. (iii) Some *weak* causal links may be deleted or added in the structure derived from the imputed data.

6   Conclusions and Future Work

We have proposed a way to minimize the effect of subsampling in causal discovery of time series by using a GAN to estimate the missing data. In this way, the imputed time series presents a similar behavior to the original one, so causal discovery algorithms can produce a causal structure close to the true one. Experiments with synthetic data show promising results, as the imputed data is very close to the original and the recovered causal structure is in general the correct one or very similar, maintaining at least the strong causal relations. To our knowledge, this is the first attempt to recover a single causal structure from subsampled time series, as previous works obtain a set of possible structures.

Future work includes applying the proposed approach to real scenarios, such as neuro images, where the sampling frequency is lower than the causal mechanisms in the brain; and climate data, as some monitoring stations could have a low sampling frequency.

References

1. Danks, D.: Causal search, causal modeling, and the folk. In: A Companion to Experimental Philosophy, pp. 463–471 (2016)
2. Danks, D., Plis, S.: Learning causal structure from undersampled time series. JMLR: Workshop and Conference Proceedings (2014)
3. Gain, A., Shpitser, I.: Structure learning under missing data. In: International Conference on Probabilistic Graphical Models, pp. 121–132. PMLR (2018)
4. Goudet, O., Kalainathan, D., Caillou, P., Guyon, I., Lopez-Paz, D., Sebag, M.: Learning functional causal models with generative neural networks. In: Escalante, H.J., et al. (eds.) Learning functional causal models with generative neural networks. TSSCML, pp. 39–80. Springer, Cham (2018). https://doi.org/10.1007/978-3-319-98131-4_3
5. Granger, C.: Investigating causal relations by econometric models and cross-spectral methods. Econometrica **37**(3), 424–438 (1969)
6. Grover, A., Zweig, A., Ermon, S.: Graphite: iterative generative modeling of graphs. In: International Conference on Machine Learning, pp. 2434–2444. PMLR (2019)
7. Huang, Y., Fu, Z., Franzke, C.L.: Detecting causality from time series in a machine learning framework. Chaos Interdisc. J. Nonlinear Sci. **30**(6), 063116 (2020)

8. Hyttinen, A., Plis, S., Järvisalo, M., Eberhardt, F., Danks, D.: A constraint optimization approach to causal discovery from subsampled time series data. Int. J. Approximate Reason. **90**, 208–225 (2017)

9. Lawrence, A., Kaiser, M., Sampaio, R., Sipos, M.: Data generating process to evaluate causal discovery techniques for time series data. In: Causal Discovery & Causality-Inspired Machine Learning Workshop at NeurIPS (2020)

10. Malinsky, D., Danks, D.: Causal discovery algorithms: a practical guide. Philos Compass **13**(1), e12470 (2018)

11. Munoz-Benítez, J., Sucar, L.E.: Synthetic time series: a dataset for causal discovery. CLeaR 2023 Datasets Track (2023). https://www.cclear.cc/2023/AcceptedDatasets/munozbenitez23a.pdf

12. Murphy, K.P.: Dynamic Bayesian Networks: Representation, Inference and Learning. University of California, Berkeley (2002)

13. Runge, J.: Causal network reconstruction from time series: from theoretical assumptions to practical estimation. Chaos Interdisc. J. Nonlinear Sci. **28**(7), 075310 (2018)

14. Runge, J., Nowack, P., Kretschmer, M., Flaxman, S., Sejdinovic, D.: Detecting and quantifying causal associations in large nonlinear time series datasets. Sci. Adv. **5**(11) (2019)

15. Solovyeva, K., Danks, D., Abavisani, M., Plis, S.: Causal learning through deliberate undersampling. In: 2nd Conference on Causal Learning and Reasoning (2023)

16. Spirtes, P.: Introduction to causal inference. JMLR **11**(5) (2010)

17. Spirtes, P., Glymour, C., Scheines, R.: Causation, Prediction, and Search, vol. 81 (2001). https://doi.org/10.1007/978-1-4612-2748-9

18. Vowels, M.J., Camgoz, N.C., Bowden, R.: D'ya like dags? A survey on structure learning and causal discovery. arXiv preprint arXiv:2103.02582 (2021)

19. Wang, Y., Menkovski, V., Wang, H., Du, X., Pechenizkiy, M.: Causal discovery from incomplete data: a deep learning approach. arXiv:2001.05343 (2020)

20. Yoon, J., Jarrett, D., Van der Schaar, M.: Time-series generative adversarial networks (2019)

Exploring the Challenges and Limitations of Unsupervised Machine Learning Approaches in Legal Concepts Discovery

Philippe Prince-Tritto[1]([⊠])(iD) and Hiram Ponce[2]([⊠])(iD)

[1] Universidad Panamericana, Facultad de Derecho, Augusto Rodin 498,
Ciudad de México 03920, México
pprince@up.edu.mx
[2] Universidad Panamericana, Facultad de Ingeniería, Augusto Rodin 498,
Ciudad de México 03920, México
hponce@up.edu.mx

Abstract. The utilization of machine learning methods for the analysis and interpretation of legal documents has been growing over the years, yet their potential and limitations remain under-explored. This study aims to address this gap, using unsupervised machine learning techniques to discover legal concepts from a corpus of Spanish legal documents. In addition to striving for optimal results, our research also embarks on an exploration of the challenges and limitations of unsupervised machine learning, investigating its capabilities and limitations in legal text analysis. We demonstrate that even relatively simplistic methodologies can yield noteworthy insights, with the highest identification rate of 70% achieved by Topic Modeling with Latent Dirichlet Allocation (LDA). However, challenges were encountered with the identification of some concepts, suggesting potential improvements in the corpus preprocessing and tokenization stages or the techniques to be used. The findings underscore the potential of unsupervised learning algorithms in legal text analysis, offering an intriguing path for future research. While acknowledging the need for higher accuracy in practical applications, this study emphasizes the remarkable feat achieved and proposes a way forward for a hybrid or adaptable approach.

Keywords: Legal NLP · Legal Concept Discovery · Unsupervised Machine Learning · Military Law · Topic Modeling with LDA

1 Introduction

The application of Natural Language Processing (NLP) techniques, such as Named Entity Recognition (NER), to the legal domain has the potential to improve the efficiency and effectiveness of legal practice [21,31,35]. NER can enables the identification and standardization of legal entities [9], such as elements of policy, reason and logic, authority, process or obligation [43], which can enable automatic legal reasoning from text.

© The Author(s), under exclusive license to Springer Nature Switzerland AG 2024
H. Calvo et al. (Eds.): MICAI 2023, LNAI 14392, pp. 52–67, 2024.
https://doi.org/10.1007/978-3-031-47640-2_5

In classic cases, i.e., NLP uses that do not deal with law, these entities are surrounded by dollar amounts, places, locations, numbers, time, etc. Grammatical concepts and categories are also part of the elements that are identified. This problem, however, has been solved to a greater extent by some of the famous NLP tools such as Google Cloud Natural Language [37], Stanford CoreNLP [41], spaCy [42], AllenNLP [36], and Apache NLTK [40], among others, and can be used with Python. However, the use of AI for legal entity recognition is not without challenges [29,35].

NER tools are tailor-made to detect the most commonly used entities in common language [23]. But using NER for legal texts presupposes that the entities to be identified are normalized, and can serve a defined purpose. In this respect, most of the tools are limited to very restricted lists of legal concepts [38,39], without orienting the NER exercise towards the achievement of a particular objective for legal practice. Indeed, there are some markup languages for representing legal documents and rules in a machine-readable format [44], but those are not classification systems or standards for normalizing legal concepts. Thus, the coverage and suitability of these standards for the legal domain may be limited, and alternative approaches may be necessary if we want to achieve automatic legal reasoning tasks [29].

NER techniques generally rely on supervised training, which requires a large amount of training data with labeled entities. However, legal databases are generally not labeled. This is a difficult problem to solve, since each legal system has its own concepts, references, and the law is always codified in the official language used in the target country. Thus, before any concept identification on unstructured legal text, simply determining which legal concepts should be identified requires expertise. It is therefore a costly operation since data pre-processing or determining the relevant parameters for the use of AI algorithms in legal NLP is not the legal expert's primary function.

However, in order to effectively harness these tools for such complex tasks, it is vital not only to strive for optimal results but also to explore the challenges and limitations of what these technologies can achieve, especially when they are working unsupervised and without the benefit of a human perspective.

This study seeks to contribute to that exploration, employing a range of unsupervised machine learning techniques to discover legal concepts from a corpus of Spanish non-annotated legal corpus in Military Law. We compared three classics unsupervised methods (K-Means, Fuzzy C-Means and Hierarchichal Clustering), and one method that is especially suited for NLP (Topic modelling with Latent Dirichlet Allocation) to discover potential legal concepts in the corpus. The concepts were then compared one by one with a ground truth in Word2Vec's vector space using a cosine similarity measure.

Our research does not aim only at finding the most accurate methodologies but also seeks to expose the capabilities and limitations of these techniques. By doing so, we aim to uncover not only what these algorithms can accomplish today but also where they might lead us in the future, offering an intriguing path for subsequent research in the field.

2   Theoretical Framework

The state of the art in unsupervised concept extraction from text corpora is characterized by a variety of innovative approaches. Concepts are more abstract than entities and can be characterized as:

> a sequence of words that may represent real or imaginary ideas or entities expressed in plain text. [15]

Krishnan et al. [19] have developed an unsupervised, domain-independent algorithm that extracts key concept mentions from scientific literature, showing significant improvements over previous methods. Similarly, Dalvi et al. [12] have proposed an open-domain information extraction method that clusters terms found in HTML tables and assigns concept names to these clusters, thereby extracting concept-instance pairs. Anoop et al. [16] have introduced a novel approach that identifies relevant concepts from plain text and learns a hierarchy of concepts by exploiting subsumption relations, without the need for a domain-specific training corpus. Furthermore, to enrich the field of concept-aware unsupervised user embedding, Huang et al. [32] have proposed a novel technique that harnesses both text documents and medical concepts from clinical corpora. Their work demonstrates the effectiveness of this embedding in various tasks. Lastly, Khademi et al. [18] have proposed a hybrid approach that clusters the concepts of Persian texts using deep learning and traditional statistical methods, achieving state-of-the-art results in text summarizing.

Some researchers have attempted to use unsupervised learning methods for legal entity or concept recognition, but the results have been mixed, and the challenges of applying these methods to the legal domain are significant [25, 26, 34]. The potential of unsupervised learning methods for legal entity recognition has been discussed [4, 27, 30], since unsupervised learning methods do not require a labeled training dataset, but for NER they may be less effective and reliable than supervised learning methods [28].

These methods do not require a labeled training dataset, and instead rely on statistical or linguistic techniques, such as clustering or n-gram analysis, in order to identify and classify the concepts in the documents [4]. A challenge is that the concepts may not be mapped to a standardized representation, which can hinder the ability to search and compare the concepts across different documents and data sources.

In order to overcome this challenge, some researchers have proposed the use of self-supervised learning approaches, which combine the strengths of supervised and unsupervised learning methods [34]. Some approaches known as fine tuning can provide the benefits of transfer learning. The idea it to use a pre-trained supervised large language model (LLM), such as the Bidirectional Encoder Representations from Transformers (BERT) [22], and then adapt the model to a specific legal domain, using a small, domain-specific dataset [25, 26]. However, this method suppose using a lot of resources and can be costly depending on the specific LLM at use. Additionally, they depend entirely on the quality of the underlying model for the specific domain at stake, which must be based on a large number of domain-specific parameters.

Another approach is to combine supervised and unsupervised learning [34]. The supervised learning model aims to provide a high-quality, domain-specific labeling of a small subset of the dataset. The unsupervised learning model is then used to label the remaining, unlabeled documents, based on the learned patterns and features. The approach is similar to CycleNER [33], a method for performing NER in an unsupervised manner. It utilizes two functions, called sentence-to-entity (S2E) and entity-to-sentence (E2S), and relies on cycle-consistency training to align the representation spaces of these functions. This allows CycleNER to be trained without the need for annotations, using only a set of sentences with no entity labels and another independent set of entity examples. Evaluation of CycleNER on various domains has shown that it can achieve competitive performance compared to both supervised and unsupervised competitors, reaching 73% of the performance of supervised models on the CoNLL03 dataset without the need for annotations and significantly outperforming unsupervised approaches. However, in both of these cases, intervention is required as the entity determination continues to rely on prior expertise.

Finally, we can mention the Lbl2Vec approach [34], an algorithm for unsupervised text classification. The idea is to first create a joint embedding of document and word vectors, where similar documents and words are located close to each other in the vector space. Next, the algorithm defines keywords for each classification category of interest and computes the cosine similarity between the documents and these keywords. Documents that are similar to the keywords are assigned to a set of candidate documents for the respective category. Finally, the algorithm removes outlier documents from each set of candidate documents and returns the documents that are most similar to the keywords as the final classification results. This method is promising for our case, but it should be emphasized that it aims at the classification of documents and not at the pure and simple discovery of concepts.

3   Methodology

3.1   Data Source

We chose to work on legal data made available by the Mexican government [45]. The database consists of a corpus of legal and regulatory documents related to the military field, in DOC and TXT format. It has a total of 81 documents written in Spanish language.

3.2   Data Preprocessing

In order to be able to import *Microsoft Word* data with the *python-docx* library, we first manually converted the documents that were in DOC format into DOCX format. Because of the *Non-ISO extended-ASCII text, with CRLF line termina-tors* encoding of the TXT files, we then combined regex techniques and the use of the *Unidecode* Python library to normalize the text data to UTF-8 format.

In order to keep only the most relevant tokens for the rest of the experiment, we also removed double spaces, numbers in Roman numerals, numbers from one to ten written in full, single characters and two-letter-words, and recurrent non-relevant words 'articulo' and 'capitulo' that do not necessarily help for getting relevant legal concepts.

Finally, Natural Language Toolkit (NLTK) [8] was used to remove stop-words in Spanish, tokenize each document, and we also used a stemming algorithm in Spanish to normalize the shape of words with the same root. We then used several unsupervised approaches, described in the following sections, to classify the text into 200 word clusters on the text corpus. To maintain consistency between the methods that needed a determined number of words in the hyperparameter, such as fuzzy c-means, and the other methods, when a cluster contained over 50 words, it was reduced to keep only the 50 top words.

3.3   Topic Modelling Approach

After building a document-term matrix using gensim [11], we use a Latent Dirich-let Allocation (LDA) [7] to define observation sets defined by data similarities. To get the best results, we varied the parameters by trial and error following a grid search algorithm [5] for the LDA model such as the number of requested latent topics to be extracted from the training corpus and the number of passes through the corpus. This classification algorithm can be seen as a comparative state-of-the-art method, due to its specificity for language processing, unlike the other unsupervised learning methods we will describe later.

3.4   Word Embedding Approach

We loaded the corpus as a list of sentences to train a Word2Vec [14] model to learn word embeddings. In each following methods, we varied the number and size of clusters to obtain the best results.

KMeans Clustering. We used KMeans clustering [13] to cluster similar word vectors clusters. We execute the centroids search following:

$$S_i = x_p : ||x_p - \mu_i|| \leq ||x_p - \mu_j|| \ \forall \ 1 \leq j \leq k \tag{1}$$

where S_i is the set of data that belongs to group i, x_p is a particular data point from the data set that is being grouped, μ_i is the centroid of group i, $||x_p - \mu_i||$ is the Euclidean distance between the data point x_p and the centroid μ_i and $||x_p - \mu_j||$ is the Euclidean distance between the data point x_p and the centroid μ_j.

We used t-distributed Stochastic Neighbor Embedding (t-SNE) [6] to visu-alize the clusters in two dimensions with Scikit-learn [10] and extracted the top words in each cluster.

Hierarchical Clustering. We computed pairwise cosine similarities between embeddings as:

$$cosine similarity = \frac{\mathbf{a} \cdot \mathbf{b}}{\|\mathbf{a}\|\|\mathbf{b}\|} \tag{2}$$

where $\mathbf{a}$ and $\mathbf{b}$ are two vectors being compared. We used hierarchical clustering [17] to group similar items into clusters based on a tree-like structure. We did not present the results in dendrograms due to the number of clusters.

Fuzzy Clustering. We use Fuzzy c-means [3], which assigns a membership degree to each point for all clusters, thus managing uncertainty and possible overlaps between clusters, which is especially useful in the context of legal texts, where terms and concepts may often be related. We use the objective function:

$$J_m = \sum_{i=1}^{k} \sum_{j=1}^{n} (\mu_{ij})^m \, ||x_i - v_j||^2, \tag{3}$$

where k is the number of points, n is the number of groups, m is the fuzzy exponent, μ_{ij} is the membership of point i to group j, x_i is the feature vector of point i, and v_j is the center of group j.

To reduce noise, we filtered the words by retaining only those with the highest score μ_{ij} relative to the clusters generated by Fuzzy c-means. To balance noise reduction and retaining relevant information, we set a threshold of $\mu_{ij} = 0.95$.

3.5   Clusters Appraisal

Qualitative measure were used manually inspecting the clusters and seeing if they made sense. We looked for clusters that contained words that are semantically related and belong to the same topic or category.

We then compared the clustering results produced by different unsupervised machine learning algorithms with expert responses that had been categorized according to distinct legal concepts. These responses represented a ground truth and were collected with a preliminary questionnaire to an expert in military law in Mexico in order to recover the key concepts of military law. These responses were categorized into groups and are represented in Table 1.

We acknowledged that the dataset used is imbalanced in terms of the number of concepts in each category. This imbalance in the dataset is addressed by computing the percentage of correctly identified concepts within each category and relative to the total number of concepts as indicated by expert responses as:

$$Identification Rate (IR) = \frac{N}{T} \times 100 \tag{4}$$

where:

- N is the number of expert-identified concepts also identified by the method,
- T is the total number of expert-identified concepts.

Table 1. Categorization of Expert Responses

Category	Description	Number of Responses
principles	General principles of military law	6
differences	Differences between military and civil law	5
sources	Sources of military law	117
legal_concepts	Legal concepts in military law	52
institutions_actors	Institutions and actors in military law	13
emerging_issues	Emerging issues in military law	7
total	**Total number of responses constituting the ground truth**	**200**

Each unsupervised machine learning method produced a number of clusters, where each cluster contained a subset of the dataset. These clusters were then compared to the expert responses in a pairwise manner using cosine similarity in the vector space, generating a measure of similarity between each cluster and each expert response. To do this, each word list were converted into a feature vector using a Word2vec model pre-trained on a large and diverse corpus that covers a very wide range of the Spanish language [24]. Then, the cosine similarity between these two vectors is calculated and used as a measure of how similar a cluster is to an expert response.

In order to ensure that the matched pairs were meaningful and robust, we established a similarity threshold of 0.8. Only those pairs with a similarity score equal to or above this threshold were considered valid matches.

Given that several clusters identified several expert's response, we implemented the Hungarian algorithm [1] to solve this assignment problem, also known as the Kuhn-Munkres algorithm [2], to find the optimal one-to-one mapping of clusters to expert responses. Each cluster was assigned to exactly one response, and each response was assigned to exactly one cluster. The final output included the maximum possible similarity between the clusters and the expert responses under these constraints.

The end result was a dataset for each machine learning method, listing the optimally matched pairs of clusters and expert responses, along with their associated similarity scores. These dataset were saved to tabular files for further analysis and interpretation.

Our main objective is to explore the latent structures of legal texts. As a result, the clusters generated are not categorized. It is important to note that the approach used in this study is fundamentally unsupervised, aiming to discover inherent groupings in legal texts without using predefined categories. Although we compare the resulting clusters to expert-defined categories as a form of qualitative validation, class-based evaluation measures for supervised learning such as precision, recall, and category-balanced accuracy are not directly applicable.

While our approach may not capture nuanced differences between categories or provide insights into how well the algorithm performs for specific types of legal concepts, it enabled a quantitative comparison of machine learning derived clusters to expert responses, offering a measure of how well the machine learning models have captured the expert's understanding of the legal concepts.

4   Results and Discussion

Using t-SNE for data points and PCA for centroids, we visualized how KMeans clustering evolves over selected iterations (Fig. 1). The visualization revealed that the data points are mostly closely clustered, indicating high similarity among them. However, as iterations progress, the centroids undergo subtle adjustments, refining the data's underlying cluster structure. This demonstrates the algorithm's ability to converge to stable solutions that capture the inherent patterns in the data.

The Topic modelling approach with LDA and Fuzzy clustering showed encouraging result when performing manual inspection, although coherence had to be compared with the expert's responses to avoid bias. This result was expected, given that LDA is an algorithm specifically designed for language processing. It should be noted that these clusters were all 50 words long, so we represent a sample of the top 10 words for 5 random clusters for Topic modelling approach in Table 2 and for Fuzzy clustering in Table 3.

Table 2. Sample of Top 10 Words for 5 Random LDA Clusters

LDA Cluster 1	LDA Cluster 2	LDA Cluster 3	LDA Cluster 4	LDA Cluster 5
personal	personal	militar	militar	personal
militar	plantel	nacional	personal	militar
plantel	instruccion	defensa	militares	servicio
servicio	militar	secretaria	servicio	general
escuela	director	academias	general	plantel
jefe	aerea	tipo	secretaria	militares
instruccion	seccion	particulares	ley	jefe
comandante	escuela	retirar	plantel	seccion
mayor	fuerza	diferencias	fuerza	comandante
general	coordinar	instruccion	aerea	instruccion

With a hierarchical clustering, we were also able to find a number of clusters that seemed to have a common thread linking them. Table 4 shows some examples of these clusters and their corresponding keywords. In order to show interpretable results, we randomly selected clusters of 10 words or less to display samples that are easily readable by humans.

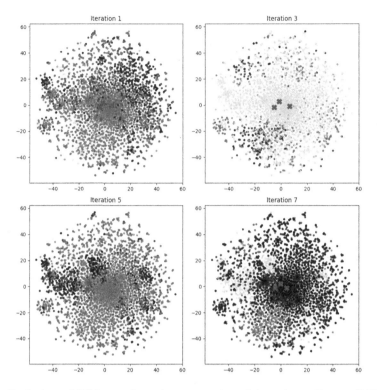

Fig. 1. Evolution of KMeans clustering over selected iterations. For readbility, the number of cluster have been reduced to 3, but our method it is 200. Each subplot shows the state of the clusters at iterations 1, 3, 5, and 7. Points are colored according to their cluster assignments, and red 'X' markers indicate the position of cluster centroids. Dimensionality reduction for visualization is done using t-SNE for the data points and PCA for the centroids. (Color figure online)

Table 3. Sample of Top 10 Words for 5 Random Fuzzy Clusters

Fuzzy Cluster 1	Fuzzy Cluster 2	Fuzzy Cluster 3	Fuzzy Cluster 4	Fuzzy Cluster 5
servicio	paracaidismo	servicio	personal	personal
personal	cursante	comandante	instruccion	militar
militar	paracaidista	guardia	unidadescuela	jefe
fuerza	salto	jefe	militar	servicio
comandante	maestro	tropa	comandante	instruccion
secretaria	caida	armas	director	plantel
militares	libre	oficiales	curso	fuerza
aerea	acordar	ordenes	escuela	aerea
caso	saltos	superior	jefe	nacional
tropa	fase	parte	supervisar	general

The KMeans clustering also produced interesting results, showing a clear separation between some clusters that appeared to be related to specific legal concepts. Some of these clusters are shown in Table 5.

Table 4. Sample of 5 ramdom Hierarchical Clusters of 10 words or less

Hierarchical Cluster 1	Hierarchical Cluster 2	Hierarchical Cluster 3	Hierarchical Cluster 4	Hierarchical Cluster 5
momento	primera	muerte	resultado	respectivamente
arresto	segunda	probada	sujeto	grados
sancion	tercera	rinda	fuero	nombrados
impondra	trastornos	embarcaciones	encontrarse	patentes
prevista	tablas	levante	comun	expidan
comunique	funcionales	buque	haberse	fungira
restriccion	inutilidad	mar	aceptada	expediran
amonestacion	categorias	perdido	encontrado	actuales
comuniquen	anexas	ocurrida	ponga	
impuso			absuelto	

Table 5. Sample of 5 random KMeans Clusters of 10 words or less

KMeans Cluster 1	KMeans Cluster 2	KMeans Cluster 3	KMeans Cluster 4	KMeans Cluster 5
requisitos	archivo	fondo	junta	republica
sargentos	expedientes	adquisicion	ausencias	unidos
promocion	correspondencia	creditos	tecnicaconsultiva	politica
ascenso	oficinas	vivienda	consultiva	constitucion
seleccion	expediente	construccion	suplidos	dispuesto
participantes	archivos	casas	tecnicoconsultiva	dip
concurso		habitaciones		sen
promociones		habitacionales		rubricas

Each method's performance was evaluated by calculating the percentage of correctly identified concepts within each category, relative to the total number of concepts as indicated by expert responses. Cluster evaluation comparing them to the ground truth collected from the expert is shown Fig. 2. We broke the results by category in Table 6.

Table 6. Percentage of Correctly Identified Concepts per Method

Category	Fuzzy C-Means	Hierarchical Clustering	K-Means	LDA
Principles	83.33%	33.33%	33.33%	100%
Differences	80%	60%	20%	80%
Sources	37.61%	14.53%	10.26%	73.50%
Legal Concepts	65.38%	23.08%	13.46%	75%
Institutions/Actors	0%	0%	15.38%	15.38%
Emerging Issues	14.29%	0%	0%	42.86%
All Categories	44%	17%	12%	70%

Observing the results, it is evident that the performance of the methods varied significantly across different categories. For instance, the LDA method achieved 100% in identifying Principles, while Fuzzy C-Means attained 83.33%

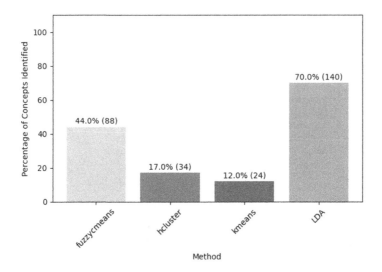

Fig. 2. Percentage of Concepts Identified per Method for All Categories

of Identification Rate (IR) in the same category. In contrast, the category 'Institutions/Actors' posed challenges for all methods. While K-Means and LDA managed to correctly identify 15.38% of the concepts, the other methods had a success rate of 0%.

Moreover, when considering the overall performance of each method across all categories, LDA exhibited the highest IR at 70%, followed by Fuzzy C-Means at 44%, Hierarchical Clustering at 17%, and K-Means at 12%. The differences observed suggest that the choice of method significantly impacts the concept identification rate within specific categories.

Relative to LDA, despite the latter demonstrated superior effectiveness, the performance of Fuzzy C-Means clustering was still found to be commendably favorable. Moreover, empirical examination of the corpus underscores the observation that the performance of this algorithm tends to excel within expansive textual environments. Indeed, analyzing the 'Principles', 'Differences' and 'Legal Concepts' categories, there appears to be a direct correlation between the comprehensive length of ground truth, measured in terms of word count, and the successful identification of conceptual meaning.

This leads to a compelling conjecture that the intrinsic nature of the legal concept, specifically its level of specificity or its abstract quality, may adversely affect the efficiency of concept detection with unsupervised methods.

Another no less important point is that a manual review of the cluster-concept pairs does not confirm the cosine similarity to the extent desired, and this can be attributed to at least two reasons:

Firstly, clusters represent groups of words, and thus, the words within them do not form easily understandable phrases that can be readily identified in the original text. They merely suggest that a particular concept might be present in a given corpus, which complicates the interpretability of the final results.

Secondly, certain concepts highlighted by the domain expert consist of very few words, making it difficult to conclusively determine if they have been accurately identified (e.g., concept: 'Reglamento - Reglamento del Heroico Colegio Militar').

In other words, while the mathematical aspects of the results may appear satisfactory, the difficulty for interpretability suggests a potential limitation within the field of machine learning concept discovery, an area meriting further, in-depth exploration.

However, a high threshold of concept identification is useful for various applications in the legal field, for example, to monitor the pragmatic nature of a given legal text in relation to another corpus of legal texts of higher value, or to find patterns that would be invisible to the human eye. Similarly, these results give an indication of the expectations that the legal professional may have when using unsupervised algorithms on a legal corpus. As Cathy O'Neil [20] has wrote, 'Sometimes the job of a data scientist is to know when you don't know enough'.

On the other hand, the achieved results, once validated against the ground truth, demonstrate successful identification of certain concepts, with the highest identification rate reaching 70% in the case of the LDA method. However, without a comparison to this ground truth, it was not possible to ascertain with certainty which clusters or topics were truly relevant and which were not.

Future research efforts should focus on enhancing relevance rates to ensure that a given method can accurately identify relevant concepts in a corpus of texts with a significantly high level (>90%), thereby allowing for the exploitation of these findings. However, it's important to point out once again that the methodology we've developed discovers legal concepts in a corpus of text without ever having been pre-trained on a larger corpus, either with supervised or unsupervised methods. No context has been provided and, even so, it is notable that the overall result is 70%.

It is also vital to emphasize that our research was not solely aimed at achieving optimal results, but also at exploring the boundaries of unsupervised learning in the absence of human intervention. In this light, even with relatively simple methodologies requiring minimal resources and computational time, the results obtained pave an intriguing avenue for future investigations. As machines lack a human-equivalent worldview, the achievement of a 70% identification rate is a significant accomplishment, highlighting the potential of unsupervised learning algorithms in legal text analysis.

5   Conclusion and Future Work

This study has explored the challenges and limitations of unsupervised machine learning approaches in extracting and categorizing relevant legal concepts from a corpus of legal documents in Spanish. Our methodology employed several techniques, namely Topic Modeling with LDA, Fuzzy C-Means, Hierarchical Clustering, and K-Means, unveiling their capabilities and limitations when tasked with the semantic clustering of a legal corpus.

The Topic Modelling approach with LDA achieved the highest identification rate among different techniques in discovering legal concepts in legal documents, achieving up to 70% overall and 100% in the 'Principles' category, with Fuzzy C-Means also showing effectiveness in large contexts. However, the research identified challenges such as the inability of any method to correctly identify concepts in the 'Institutions/Actors' category, potentially due to their complexity and abstract nature, which suggests an opportunity for enhancement in context retrieval.

While the 70% identification rate achieved by the best-performing model is encouraging, it may fall short of practical application needs, particularly in high-stakes legal scenarios necessitating high precision. Further improvements could be made in semantic mapping between clusters and legal concepts. Future endeavors could examine alternative measures of semantic similarity or leverage semantic graph-based algorithms, such as causal discovery techniques, to better depict relationships among words in a cluster. Even so, despite the absence of contextual information or pre-trained method, the achieved outcome for discovering concepts is particularly noteworthy.

Finally, it would be worthwhile to extend these methodologies to other types of legal documents and legal systems. While our study was centered on Mexican military law documents, the methodologies and lessons learned could have potential applicability to other types of legal documents and jurisdictions. Our unsupervised machine learning approaches could be leveraged for semantic clustering of legal concepts in other languages, given the provision of relevant stop-words and stemming algorithms. Furthermore, the nature of legal language, characterized by precise terminology and structured syntax, may offer a favourable environment for the application of these techniques. The applicability could extend to international law documents, contracts, or court case decisions, among others. However, the intricacies of each legal system, language nuances, and the specificity of legal terminology pose challenges that need to be addressed. Future research could explore these possibilities, contributing to the development of versatile, language-agnostic tools for legal text analysis.

Acknowledgments. We are especially grateful to Frida Angelica Castillo Zuñiga, Master in Constitutional Law and Human Rights, for her invaluable expertise and participation. Her expert responses, categorized according to distinct legal concepts, have been crucial to our work and have constituted the ground truth that permitted our unsupervised clusters appraisal. Her insightful contributions significantly improved the quality and rigor of this research.

We would also like to acknowledge the assistance provided by ChatGPT, developed by OpenAI. ChatGPT was used to enhance the syntax and wording of this paper, particularly in the editing and refinement of the manuscript. While ChatGPT offered suggestions and improvements, the responsibility for the scientific content and ideas presented in this paper remains solely with the authors.

References

1. Kuhn, H.W.: The Hungarian method for the assignment problem. Naval Res. Logist. Q. 2.1-2, 83–97 (1955)
2. Munkres, J.: Algorithms for the assignment and transportation problems. J. Soc. Ind. Appl. Math. 5.1, 32–38 (1957). https://doi.org/10.1137/0105003
3. Peizhuang, W.: Pattern recognition with fuzzy objective function algorithms (James C. Bezdek). Siam Rev. 25.3, 442 (1983). https://doi.org/10.1137/1025116
4. Barlow, H.B.: Unsupervised learning. Neural Comput 1.3, 295–311 (1989)
5. Bengio, Y.: Gradient-based optimization of hyperparameters. Neural Comput. 12.8, 1889–1900 (2000). https://doi.org/10.1162/089976600300015187
6. Hinton, G.E., Roweis, S.: Stochastic neighbor embedding. In: Becker, S., Thrun, S., Obermayer, K., Ed. 15 (2002). https://proceedings.neurips.cc/paper_files/paper/2002/file/6150ccc6069bea6b5716254057a194ef-Paper.pdf
7. Blei, D.M,. Ng, A.Y., Jordan, M.I.: Latent dirichlet allocation. J. Mach. Learn. Res. 3 Jan, 993–1022 (2003)
8. Bird, S., Klein, E., Loper, E.: Natural language processing with Python: analyzing text with the natural language toolkit. O'Reilly Media, Inc., (2009). https://doi.org/10.3115/1627306.1627317
9. Dozier, C., Kondadadi, R., Light, M., Vachher, A., Veeramachaneni, S., Wudali, R.: Named entity recognition and resolution in legal text. In: Francesconi, E., Montemagni, S., Peters, W., Tiscornia, D. (eds.) Semantic Processing of Legal Texts. LNCS (LNAI), vol. 6036, pp. 27–43. Springer, Heidelberg (2010). https://doi.org/10.1007/978-3-642-12837-0_2
10. Pedregosa, F., et al.: Scikit-Learn: machine learning in Python. J. Mach. Learn. Res. **12**, 2825–2830 (2011)
11. Rehurek, R., Sojka, P.: Gensim-Python framework for vector space modelling. In: NLP Centre, Faculty of Informatics, Masaryk University, Brno, Czech Republic 3.2 (2011)
12. Dalvi, B.B., Cohen, W.W., Callan, J.: Websets: extracting sets of entities from the web using unsupervised information extraction. In: Proceedings of the Fifth ACM International Conference on Web Search and Data Mining, pp. 243–252 (2012). https://doi.org/10.1145/2124295.2124327
13. Junjie, W.: Advances in K-means clustering: a data mining thinking. Springer Sci. Bus. Media (2012). https://doi.org/10.1007/978-3-642-29807-3
14. Mikolov, T., et al.: Efficient estimation of word representations in vector space. In: arXiv preprint arXiv:1301.3781 (2013)
15. Anoop, V.S., Asharaf, S., Deepak, P.: Unsupervised concept hierarchy learning: a topic modeling guided approach. Procedia Comput. Sci. **89**, 386–394 (2016)
16. Anoop, V.S., Asharaf, S., Deepak, P.: Learning concept hierarchies through probabilistic topic modeling. arXiv preprint arXiv:1611.09573 (2016)
17. Nielsen, F.: Hierarchical clustering. In: Introduction to HPC with MPI for Data Science, pp. 195–211 (2016). https://doi.org/10.1007/978-3-319-21903-5_8
18. Khademi, M.E., Fakhredanesh, M., Hoseini, S.M.: Conceptual text summarizer: a new model in continuous vector space. arXiv preprint arXiv:1710.10994 (2017)
19. Krishnan, A., et al.: Unsupervised concept categorization and extraction from scientific document titles. In: CIKM '17 (2017), pp. 1339–1348. https://doi.org/10.1145/3132847.3133023
20. O'neil, C.: Weapons of math destruction: how big data increases inequality and threatens democracy. Crown (2017)

21. Badji, I.: Legal entity extraction with NER systems. PhD thesis. ETSI Informatica (2018)
22. Devlin, J., et al.: BERT: pre-training of deep bidirectional transformers for language understanding. arXiv preprint arXiv:1810.04805 (2018)
23. Tran, Q.H., et al.: The context-dependent additive recurrent neural net. In: Proceedings of the 2018 Conference of the North American Chapter of the Association for Computational Linguistics: Human Language Technologies, Volume 1 (Long Papers), pp. 1274–1283 (2018). https://doi.org/10.18653/v1/n18-1115
24. Cardellino, C.: Spanish Billion Words Corpus and Embeddings (2019). https://crscardellino.github.io/SBWCE/
25. Elwany, E., Moore, D., Oberoi, G.: Bert goes to law school: quantifying the competitive advantage of access to large legal corpora in contract understanding. arXiv preprint arXiv:1911.00473 (2019)
26. Chalkidis, I., et al.: LEGAL-BERT: the muppets straight out of law school. arXiv preprint arXiv:2010.02559 (2020)
27. Mahesh, B.: Machine learning algorithms-a review. Int. J. Sci. Res. (IJSR) **9**, 381–386 (2020)
28. Bose, P., et al.: A survey on recent named entity recognition and relationship extraction techniques on clinical texts. Appl. Sci. 11.18 (2021). ISSN: 2076–3417. https://doi.org/10.3390/app11188319
29. Prince-Tritto, P.: La clasificación del lenguaje jurídico: barrera de entrada de la inteligencia artificial en el campo del derecho. In: Economia, empresa y justicia. Nuevos retos para el futuro. Dykinson, pp. 411–429 (2021)
30. Çetindağ, C., Yazıcıoğlu, B., Koç, A.: Named-entity recognition in Turkish legal texts. Nat. Lang. Eng., pp. 1–28 (2022). https://doi.org/10.1017/s1351324922000304
31. Csáki, C., et al.: NLP in the legal profession: how about small languages? In: EGOV-CeDEM-ePart 2022, p. 203 (2022)
32. Huang, X., Dernoncourt, F., Dredze, M.: Enriching unsupervised user embedding via medical concepts. In: Proceedings of the Conference on Health, Inference, and Learning. Ed. by Gerardo Flores et al., vol. 174. Proceedings of Machine Learning Research. PMLR, pp. 63–78 (2022). https://proceedings.mlr.press/v174/huang22a.html
33. Iovine, A., et al.: CycleNER: an unsupervised training approach for named entity recognition. In: Proceedings of the ACM Web Conference 2022, pp. 2916–2924 (2022). https://doi.org/10.1145/3485447.3512012
34. Schopf, T., Braun, D., Matthes, F.: Lbl2Vec: an embeddingbased approach for unsupervised document retrieval on predefined topics. arXiv preprint arXiv:2210.06023 (2022). https://doi.org/10.5220/0010710300003058
35. Shi, J., et al.: A named entity recognition method based on deep learning for Chinese legal documents. In: 2022 7th International Conference on Image, Vision and Computing (ICIVC), pp. 65–68. IEEE (2022). https://doi.org/10.1109/icivc55077.2022.9887060
36. AllenNLP — Allen Institute for AI — allenai.org. https://allenai.org/allennlp. Accessed 15 Dec 2022
37. Cloud Natural Language — Google Cloud — cloud.google.com. https://cloud.google.com/natural-language. Accessed 15 Dec 2022
38. GitHub - openlegaldata/legal-ner: named entity recognition for the legal domain — github.com. https://github.com/openlegaldata/legal-ner. Accessed 15 Dec 2022
39. Legal Zero-shot NER — nlp.johnsnowlabs.com. https://nlp.johnsnowlabs.com/2022/09/02/legner_roberta_zeroshot_en.html. Accessed 15-Dec-2022

40. NLTK : Natural Language Toolkit — nltk.org. https://www.nltk.org/. Accessed 15 Dec 2022
41. Overview — stanfordnlp.github.io. https://stanfordnlp.github.io/CoreNLP/. Accessed 15 Dec 2022
42. spaCy · Industrial-strength Natural Language Processing in Python — spacy.io. https://spacy.io/. Accessed 15 Dec 2022
43. The Legal Elements - a Law Dictionary Classification System — clearpointlaw.com. http://www.clearpointlaw.com/legal-elements.php. Accessed 15 Dec 2022
44. Use cases — Akoma Ntoso — akomantoso.org. http://www.akomantoso.org/?page_id=275. Accessed 15 Dec 2022
45. SEDENA: Leyes y reglamentos militares 2023 (2023). https://datos.gob.mx/busca/dataset/leyes-y-reglamentos-militares. Accessed 23 Feb 2023

Large Sentiment Dictionary of Russian Words

Vladimir V. Bochkarev[1]([✉])(iD), Andrey A. Achkeev[2](iD), Andrey V. Savinkov[1](iD), Anna V. Shevlyakova[1](iD), and Valery D. Solovyev[1](iD)

[1] Kazan Federal University, Kazan, Russia
Vladimir.Bochkarev@kpfu.ru
[2] TGT Diagnostics, Kazan, Russia

Abstract. Sentiment analysis is a widely studied area of computational linguistics. The main tool for sentiment analysis of texts are dictionaries with positive/negative ratings of words. Hundreds of such dictionaries have been compiled for dozens of world languages. The largest English dictionary contains up to 500 thousand words. By contrast, the largest dictionary of the Russian language contains less than 50 thousand words. We compiled a large Russian dictionary with positive/negative ratings of approximately 2 million word forms. To do this, we applied the technique of machine extrapolation of valence ratings contained in 6 existing dictionaries obtained by the survey method. Pretrained fasttext vectors were used as input to the neural network sentiment predictor. Multiple trained models allowed us for cross–validation of sentiment estimations. The obtained Spearmen's correlation coefficient between the human ratings and their machine estimates is up to 0.835.

Keywords: Sentiment analysis · Sentiment dictionary · Word valence ratings · Word embeddings · Neural networks

1 Introduction

Sentiment analysis is an important and widely used technique in computational linguistics [23]. It is conventionally applied to textual data to monitor customer feedback on products and services. Also, sentiment analysis can be employed for other purposes. For example, [38] uses sentiment analysis to predict behaviour of stocks in the stock markets. The main sentiment analysis tool is dictionaries that contain words with positive/negative sentiment.

Hundreds of sentiment dictionaries have been created for dozens of world languages. An overview of the English dictionaries is presented in [21,33]. The dictionaries were compiled for various purposes, some of them are highly specialized, others are universal and designed to be employed in various fields. Various tasks require great number of estimated words. The SenticNet_en English dictionary [11] contains 100 thousand items and Sentiment140–Lexicon [29] includes more than 500 thousand English words. By contrast, the largest Russian sentiment dictionary contains less than 50 thousand words. Therefore, there is a

H. Calvo et al. (Eds.): MICAI 2023, LNAI 14392, pp. 68–82, 2024.
https://doi.org/10.1007/978-3-031-47640-2_6

need to create a large Russian dictionary including words with sentiment (positive/negative) ratings.

There is another important problem considered in this paper. Currently, there are no methods developed to determine which sentiment dictionary is "correct". Six English dictionaries were compared in [33] showing a large discrepancy in the analysed data. For example, average positivity rating in the Society section of New York Times of LIWC and MPQA dictionaries differs by 0.48 (with a scale from -1, 0 to +1), i.e. almost by a quarter of the scale.

A significant discrepancy between the balance of positive and negative vocabulary in different dictionaries created by the method of interviewing respondents was also revealed in [7]. This was especially evident when calculating the average valence of Russian texts in the Google Books Ngram diachronic corpus (https://books.google.com/ngrams/). It was shown in [7] that the compared dictionaries can be divided into two clusters according to the behaviour of the time series of the average valence of words. This raises important questions about the choice of a dictionary, reliability of estimates contained in the dictionary, and the possibility of obtaining balanced estimates from multiple independent dictionaries. It should be noted that a simple averaging of ratings over all dictionaries will not work because dictionaries contain different sets of words.

The work objective is to extrapolate human valence ratings of words from several dictionaries (created by interviewing respondents) to the widest possible range of Russian lexicon to create large sentiment dictionary.

2   Related Works

Currently, there are more than 10 Russian language dictionaries with positivity/negativity ratings [21]. Some of them are specialized. For example, the dictionary by E. Tutubalina [37] was compiled based on customer feedback on cars. In this study, we use 6 most popular non–specialized dictionaries. Below is a brief description of the selected dictionaries.

1. LinisCrowd Dictionary (http://www.linis-crowd.org) [20] was created by crowdsourcing. Words were estimated on a scale -2, -1, 0, 1, 2. Each word received at least 3 estimates. More than 7.5 thousand words were estimated, however, only 4.5 thousand received estimations other than 0.
2. RuSentiLex (https://www.labinform.ru/pub/rusentilex) [25] was created in a complex hybrid semiautomatic way. Experts have developed several patterns for text fragments that are characteristic of positive and negative entities. For example, *to worry about X, to increase X* clearly characterize some positive X. By contrast, the constructions *to protect from Y, to counteract Y* characterize some negative Y. In total, 19 templates for positive words and 35 for negative ones were created. Further, words that satisfy these templates were automatically extracted from the corpus of news texts. Words were marked as positive, negative, and neutral; some words may possess several marks.

The results were checked by experts. A detailed description of this procedure is given in the article cited above. The dictionary contains more than 12 thousand words and expressions.

3. KartaSlovSent (https://kartaslov.ru) [22] is currently the largest Russian sentiment dictionary that contains more than 46 thousand words. It was compiled using a survey method with at least 25 estimates for each word on a scale {-1, 0, +1}. According to the author, only the commonly understood words was selected. A number of words with positive ratings prevail over words with positive ones 4 times.

4. KFU sentiment (https://kpfu.ru/tehnologiya-sozdaniya-semanticheskih-elek tronnyh.html) contains 1000 words. It was obtained by a survey method via the Yandex.Toloka service with at least 50 estimates on a 9-point scale for each word. The dictionary is compiled using the most frequent words from the dictionary of O. Lyashevskaya, S. Sharova (http://dict.ruslang.ru/freq. php) (nouns, adjectives, and verbs in equal proportions).

5. Hedonometer (Russian) [12], containing 10,000 words, was also crowdsourced via Amazon's Mechanical Turk service with estimates on a 9–point scale. The most frequent words were selected from various sources (Google Books, New York Times articles, Music Lyrics, Twitter messages) and translated into Russian. For each word, 50 estimates were obtained. The dictionary is available at https://hedonometer.org/words/labMT-en-v2/.

6. NRC VAD (Russian) [28] contains estimates of 20 thousand words. The estimates were obtained by Best–Worst Scaling [26] with 6 estimates per word. The characteristic feature of the method is that the respondents do not estimate the word on some absolute scale, but give relative estimates, which word is the most positive and which is the most negative of the 4 given words for consideration. As a result, after processing the data, estimates are obtained on a continuous interval from 0 to 1. The words are taken from various sources with a focus on emotive–evaluative vocabulary. Original English words are translated into Russian using Google Translate (http://saifmohammad.com/WebPages/NRC-Emotion-Lexicon.htm).

Thus, the dictionaries we have considered differ significantly by many parameters: the number of words, the method of selecting vocabulary, the range of estimates, the method of obtaining ratings (expert assessment, semi–automatic, translation), the number of estimates for one word. Not to mention the fact that they differ by the respondents (experts) who participated in the surveys and the time of estimation.

The lexicon size of approximately 50 thousand words is apparently the practical limit for the method of interviewing respondents. To compile large dictionaries, automatic methods are used. The essence of all automatic methods is to extrapolate already available human estimates of a certain number of words to other words for which it is required to have sentiment estimates. Extrapolation can be performed in different ways. In [24], the set of estimated words is expanded with synonyms. Galinsky R.B. et.al. [14] demonstrated an increase in the accuracy of sentiment analysis in Russian when applying this idea, which is recommended for under–resourced languages. Various variants of machine learning make it possible to train a classifier on the initial marked up set, which is then applied to other words [15]. A similar approach, including more modern deep learning neural networks, has been applied to different dictionaries but not sentiment ones [3–5].

A set of words can be turned into a graph in which the length of the rib between the words corresponds to the semantic distance between them according to some metric. In this case, label propagation algorithms on graphs, such as label propagation and others, are used to propagate estimates [18]. In [29] estimates are extrapolated based on the degree of co-occurrence of the analyzed word and words from the initial set, which is quantitatively characterized by pointwise mutual information (PMI) values.

3   Data and Method

To estimate valence of a word, we use vector representations of words developed within the framework of distributive semantics. The hypothesis suggests that distributional similarity and meaning similarity correlate [13, 19, 34]. Therefore, word meaning can be estimated by its distribution. There are various algorithms of distributional meaning acquisition. Word representations based on co–occurrence vectors were predominantly used in earlier works [9, 17, 30, 39]. Later, it was proposed in [10] to employ vectors obtained from the Point Mutual Information (PMI) values. Various techniques for reducing dimension of vector representations, such as those that use SVD, were also considered in the related works [10, 36]. An improved word embeddings technique proposed in 2013 [8, 27] gave rise to studies. An overview of the current state of research on low–dimensional word embeddings can be found in [31, 32, 35, 40].

Methods based on vector neural network models are currently the most widely used ones. However, simpler representations based on explicit word vectors are also employed in computational linguistics to study the evolution of a language, reveal new meanings of words, and solve other related problems. The advantage of explicit word vectors is the ease of interpretation of the results [1], as well as the simplicity of building diachronic models [4]. These two types of vector representations show different efficiency when used to estimate certain properties of words [3–5]. Therefore, in this paper, we will compare the accuracy of models based on neural network embeddings of words and on explicit word vectors.

Firstly, we use a set of pre–trained fasttext vectors [16]. Vector sets for 157 languages, trained on the Common Crawl corpus using the most advanced word embedding algorithms at the time, were made publicly available in 2018. The great advantage of this dataset in terms of the tasks set in our work is the large size of the dictionary, for which the pre–trained vectors are presented. The set includes vectors for 2 million Russian words.

Secondly, we use the method of co–occurrence with the most frequent words (CFW). A detailed description of the method is presented in [5, 41]. This approach suggests that a word is represented using information about the frequency of 2–grams that include this word. We extract the N most frequent words (hereinafter, we will call them context words) from the corpus. At the next stage we characterize the target word W. To do it, we extract N frequencies of 2–grams of the Wx type (where 'x' is some context word) and the same number of 2–grams of the xW type. Some of these word combinations do not exist in the language and the corpus; in these cases, there will be zeros at the corresponding positions in the frequency vector. In this paper, as well as in [3,5], 20,000 most frequent words are used as context ones. Thus, the word is described by a vector of 40,000 dimensions. Analogous to [3,5], a vector that represents the target word is composed of pointwise mutual information values of word combinations of the Wx and xW types, where the target word W co–occurs with each of the context words x. The word and word combinations frequency data required to build the vectors were extracted from the Google Books Ngram corpus and averaged over the period 1920–2019.

To obtain word valence estimates, multilayer feed–forward neural networks were used. Several experiments were carried out to select the optimal network architecture and parameters of the learning algorithms. The number of layers and the number of neurons in a layer varied; various activation functions (ReLU, ELU, sigmoid function) and optimization algorithms (adadelta, adagrad, adam, sgd), with different learning rate parameters were tested. L1– and L2–regularization were employed, as well as Dropout. Based on the results of the experiments, the following parameters were chosen:

- 4–5 hidden layers of 512 neurons each (ReLU activation), linear activation is used for the output layer;
- Metrics for the MSE early stopping (no improvement higher than $1 \cdot 10^{-6}$ during 10 epochs), loss function — MSE;
- Optimization algorithm — ADAM, learning rate from $1 \cdot 10^{-5}$ to $5 \cdot 10^{-5}$ for different dictionaries;
- L2–regularization with a coefficient from $1 \cdot 10^{-4}$ to $5 \cdot 10^{-4}$ for different dictionaries.

To increase reliability of the results, it is advisable to carry out cross–checking. For this purpose, the lexicon of each of the dictionaries was divided into 6 groups. The division was performed in such a way that all lemmas of the word belong only to one of the groups. Four of the six word groups were used to train the model, and the remaining two groups were used as a test set. There are 15 different ways to select 4 groups out of 6, therefore, we obtained 15 independently trained models for each dictionary. At the same time, there are 5 models for any word, for which this word was in the test sample not in the training one. The presence of several models makes it possible to further increase the accuracy by averaging the estimates, as well as to determine the standard deviation of the obtained valence estimate.

In total, the six dictionaries include 65,340 different word forms and word combinations. Among these words, there are some misspelled words and even words in foreign languages (words in foreign languages are found in the NRC

VAD and Hedonometer dictionaries). All such words and word combinations were removed from the lists.

As stated in [21], most dictionaries have a certain percentage of stop words (Hedonometer includes the largest number of stop words). In our opinion, interpretation of the sentiment ratings of prepositions, conjunctions and other functional words is not clear. Therefore, the lists included only content words such nouns, adjectives, verbs, adverbs etc. Parts of speech a word belonged to was determined using the electronic morphological dictionary OpenCorpora (http://opencorpora.org/dict.php) [2]. It should also be noted that words can duplicate in some cases. For example, this can be due to the fact that the same Russian word was used to translate different English words when compiling dictionaries (those that were obtained by translation). In such cases, we averaged the ratings using different entries of the word.

The number of words from each dictionary after the filtering is shown in the 2nd column of Table 1. To train the models from these lists, word forms were selected for which there are pretrained vectors [16]. The number of such words for each of the dictionaries is given in the 3rd column of Table 1.

Table 1. The number of words used in the dictionaries

	The number of content words	The number of words possessing pre–trained fasttext vectors
Hedonometer	8,238	8,227
KFU Sentiment	991	991
NRC VAD	13,694	13,557
RuSentiLex	9,566	8,278
LinisCrowd	6,705	6,646
KartaSlovSent	42,559	28,426
total	54,504	49,782

Thus, 6 groups of models were trained, 15 models for each dictionary independently trained on different subsets of words. When testing, we calculated estimates for each word using those 5 models from each group for which this word was not presented to the neural network at the training stage. The estimates were also calculated for all words that were not included in the given dictionary.

4   Results

The results of testing of the models using pre–trained fasttext vectors are shown in Table 2. Each column of the table corresponds to the models trained using the data from a particular dictionary. The table shows the values of the Spearman correlation coefficient between human ratings for a particular dictionary and their estimates obtained by averaging over 5 independently trained models. The use of averaging increases the values of the Spearman correlation coefficient by 0.0065 — 0.0168. For example, for the KartaSlovSent dictionary, the increase is 0.0116.

Table 2. Spearman's correlation coefficient between human word valence ratings and their estimates (machine ratings) according to models based on the corresponding dictionaries

		Machine ratings					
		Hedonometer	KFU Sentiment	NRC VAD	RuSentiLex	LinisCrowd	KartaSlovSent
Human ratings	Hedonometer	**0.780**	0.649	0.687	0.496	0.473	0.675
	KFU Sentiment	0.730	**0.724**	0.667	0.523	0.568	0.692
	NRC VAD	0.698	0.622	**0.758**	0.666	0.638	0.726
	RuSentiLex	0.723	0.681	0.759	**0.779**	0.751	0.784
	LinisCrowd	0.700	0.636	0.738	0.727	**0.776**	0.768
	KartaSlovSent	0.688	0.636	0.747	0.720	0.694	**0.835**

As mentioned above, the methods used to obtain human ratings for the dictionaries are different. Therefore, it can be expected that for a model, trained on the data of a certain dictionary, the highest accuracy will be achieved when predicting a rating from this dictionary; and using ratings from other dictionaries, the correlation of the estimate with the rating will be lower. Indeed, we see that the numbers on the main diagonal of the table are in all cases the largest in their column. The dependence of the Spearman's correlation coefficient on the size of the dictionary is shown in Fig. 1. As it was expected the highest accuracy is achieved for the KartaSlovSent dictionary, which includes the largest number of words. Only the point for the NRC VAD dictionary falls out of the general trend in the figure. Apparently, this is due to the fact that this Russian dictionary is the only one of the six considered that was created by the translation of the English dictionary.

You should also pay attention to the column for the KartaSlovSent dictionary in Table 1. It can be seen that the model trained for this dictionary predicts human rat-ings from the LinisCrowd and NRC VAD dictionaries only slightly worse, and even slightly better for the RuSentiLex dictionary (0.784 vs. 0.779) than the models trained on the data of these dictionaries. In turn, the model trained on the data of the Hedonometer dictionary predicts human ratings well for the KFU Sentiment dictionary but decreases accuracy for the other four dictionaries. Thus, according to the degree of correspondence between human and machine ratings, dictionaries can be conditionally divided into two groups: KartaSlovSent, RuSentiLex, LinisCrowd, NRC VAD are in the first group and Hedonometer, KFU Sentiment are in the second one. This coincides with the division of the dictionaries into two groups (specified in [7]) according to the behaviour of the average valence time series.

Similarly, models based on explicit word vectors (the CFW–algorithm) were trained and tested. For the Hedonometer dictionary, the Spearman's correlation

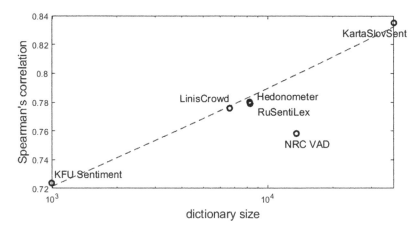

Fig. 1. Spearman's correlation coefficient between the human valence ratings of words and their estimates for the considered dictionaries depending on the size of the dictionary

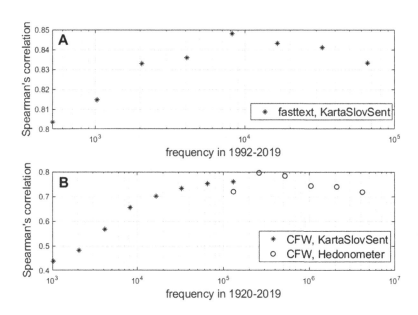

Fig. 2. Spearman's correlation coefficient between the valence rating of a word and its estimate depending on the word frequency, A — based on pre–trained fasttext vectors for the KartaSlovSent dictionary; B — using the CFW method for the KartaSlovSent and Hedonometer dictionaries

coefficient between the valence rating averaged over 5 independently trained models and the human rating was 0.731 (without averaging — 0.701), for the KartaSlovSent dictionary it was 0.661 (without averaging — 0.638). Thus, in terms of accuracy, the CFW model is significantly inferior to the accuracy of the model using fasttext vectors (see Table 2). However, these models can be used to obtain diachronic word valence models, as well as to study semantic change.

Figure 2 shows the dependence of the Spearman's correlation coefficient between the valence rating and its estimate depending on the word frequency. Figure 2A shows the results for an algorithm that uses pre–trained fasttext vectors for words from the KartaSlovSent dictionary. The frequency of the words was estimated using the Google Books Ngram corpus for the period 1992–2019 (the post–Soviet period, the total size of the corpus for these years is 38.4 billion words). All words were divided into frequency classes, the threshold value for each next class was twice as large than that for the previous one (for example, 32–65, 64–127, 128–255, etc.). Correlation coefficients were then calculated separately for each frequency class containing at least 2000 words. We see, firstly, a slow drop in the accuracy of the estimate with decreasing frequency. It was shown in [6] that the variance of estimates of the vectors representing words when using neural network word embeddings algorithms [8, 27] increases with frequency decrease, but rather slowly. Our result obviously agrees with this observation.

We also observe a slight decrease in the correlation coefficient for the most frequent words. It can be assumed that this is due to the presence of a certain number of stop words among the most frequent words in the dictionary, the human ratings of which are less accurately predicted by the algorithm.

Figure 2B shows the results obtained using the CFW algorithm for words from the KartaSlovSent and Hedonometer dictionaries. In this case, the frequency of the words was estimated employing the Google Books Ngram corpus data for the period 1920–2019, according to which vectors were built (the total size of the corpus for this period is 86.7 billion words). As in the previous graph, we observe a drop in accuracy with decreasing frequency, however, in this case this effect is much more pronounced. One can see that the points for both dictionaries fall on a common curve (within the expected error of the sample correlation coefficients). Based on this, it can be assumed that the difference in accuracy for the models trained for the KartaSlovSent and Hedonometer dictionaries is associated with a higher frequency of the lexicon presented in the second dictionary.

5   Discussion

Valence rating estimates were calculated for each of the trained models for all two million Russian word forms for which pre–trained fasttext vectors are available (see [16]). The resulting large sentiment Russian dictionary is placed in the public domain on the laboratory website https://kpfu.ru/tehnologiya-sozdaniya-semanticheskih-elektronnyh.html. Parts of speech of these word forms can be determined using the electronic morpho-logical dictionary OpenCorpora. Out of a total amount of 2 million word forms, OpenCorpora describes 582,579 word forms relating to 135,176 lemmas. The "core" of the resulting large sentiment dictionary is those 50,000 words for which we can match machine valence ratings with human ratings in at least one of the six dictionaries.

To assess the quality of the resulting model, we can also compare the values of the correlation coefficients of human and machine ratings with the values of the correlation coefficients of human ratings in different dictionaries. Table 3 shows the values of the correlation coefficients of the valence ratings of words from various dictionaries according to [7]. These values seem to set an upper limit on the achievable accuracy of the model. It can be seen that in many cases the obtained values of the correlation coefficients of human and machine ratings approach this threshold.

Table 3. Spearman's correlation coefficient between human word valence ratings in different dictionaries [7]

	Hedonometer	KFU Sent.	NRC VAD	RuSentiLex	LinisCrowd	KartaSlovSent
Hedonometer	1.000	0.855	0.773	0.875	0.614	0.797
KFU Sentiment	0.855	1.000	0.720	0.808	0.526	0.752
NRC VAD	0.773	0.720	1.000	0.762	0.706	0.746
RuSentiLex	0.875	0.808	0.762	1.000	0.762	0.797
LinisCrowd	0.614	0.526	0.706	0.762	1.000	0.779
KartaSlovSent	0.797	0.752	0.746	0.797	0.779	1.000

Table 4 shows the values of the correlation coefficients of machine ratings for the models trained on the data of different dictionaries. As one can see, the level of correlation is quite high (at least within each of the two groups of dictionaries distinguished above). It is interesting that the values of the correlation coefficient of machine ratings in most cases (within the first group of four dictionaries — in all cases) are higher than between the corresponding human ratings. It can be assumed that, due to the generalizing ability, the neural network could partially

Table 4. Spearman's correlation coefficient between machine word valence estimates using different models

	Hedonometer	KFU Sent.	NRC VAD	RuSentiLex	LinisCrowd	KartaSlovSent
Hedonometer	1.000	0.854	0.889	0.776	0.768	0.812
KFU Sentiment	0.854	1.000	0.814	0.727	0.731	0.746
NRC VAD	0.889	0.814	1.000	0.848	0.820	0.867
RuSentiLex	0.776	0.727	0.848	1.000	0.825	0.831
LinisCrowd	0.768	0.731	0.820	0.825	1.000	0.808
KartaSlovSent	0.812	0.746	0.867	0.831	0.808	1.000

correct errors in determining the valence ratings of certain words. First of all, this concerns extreme human estimates, which are often "smoothed out" by machine learning methods.

Now we discuss the results of the manual analysis of words rated by humans and the machine based on the KartaSlovSent dictionary. All 38,426 words in this dictionary were sorted in descending order of the absolute value of the difference between a human rating and their estimate. The words for which human and machine ratings differ the most are of great interest to us and will be discussed first. The first 445 words (1.16% of the total number) show the highest discrepancy between the ratings (the ratings differ for more than 1/3 of the range). This group of words includes nouns, verbs and adjectives. Meaning and connotation of most of them are contextually and sometimes culturally dependent. For example, the word *gluten* is originally a term with neutral connotation and dictionary rating of 0,090 (the scale ranges from −1 to 1). However, this term has gained a negative connotation when it was popularized as a protein that may negatively influence one's health and gluten free products appeared on the market. The machine captured this tendency; and the automatically obtained rating equals −0.890. The human rating of the word *prostitelnij* is 0.520. The machine rating is −0.674 which seems to be more precise since the word is usually used with words with negative connotation. The word *znakharstvo* is also an interesting example. Its dictionary rating is 0.430 this can be explained that curing people is something positive. However, development of official medicine doubted the methods of untraditional medicine and it could naturally change its rating (the machine rating is negative and equals −0.498). Some more examples include words that denote people of particular social status or with certain traits of character (such as *shkodnik, sozhitel', bogachka, svyatosha, pain'ka*), abstract nouns (*khladnokrovie, poshada, samouspokoennost', derznpovenie*), polysemantic words (*rediska, zaigrivat', pobolet'*). Thus, in most of the 445 cases examined, the deviation of a machine rating from a human one can hardly be considered an error. It can be assumed that experts, when compiling a dictionary estimated words using the basic meaning of the word. However, these words can be often used with another connotation in modern Russian texts.

The bottom of the ordered list includes words which human and machine rating are almost similar. Among them are a lot of terms and professional words with neutral connotation (such as *korneplod, fol'kloristika, morfemnij*), words denoting profession (*taksist, lodochnik, shkiper, fizik*), words denoting animals and flowers (*meduza, ryba, oduvanchik*), words denoting nationality or peoples' place of living (*nizhe–gorodets, portugalets, ukrainka, anglichanka*), words with undoubtful positive or negative connotation (*blagoslovenie, kapriznost', podlizivat'sja*).

The analysis showed that there are not so many words that show significant discrepancy between human and machine ratings; most of them determined by word context of use and meaning change with time.

6   Conclusion

The main practical result of this work is the compilation of an extra–large Russian dictionary with sentiment ratings for 2 million word forms with a carefully checked core of 50 thousand words. This dictionary can be used in applied sentiment analysis systems, which ensures greater accuracy of the results.

An important theoretical result is the proposed methodology. In particular, we combined data from several dictionaries obtained by the survey method and used extrapolation of estimates by machine learning methods together with cross–validation of the results. Application of several methods for obtaining human dictionaries allows one to significantly reduce possible systematic errors, which may appear when only one method is used. The proposed technique of co–use of several dictionaries provides balanced estimates of words in the resulting dictionary.

It is shown that the consistency (considering correlation coefficients) of the machine versions of the dictionaries is even higher than that of human dictionaries. A possible explanation is that neural networks, fasttext, and other similar methods trained on extra–large corpora consider a greater number of word contexts, including metaphorical ones, that simply may not be regarded by respondents during the survey. Clarification of this issue requires further research.

Acknowledgements. This research was financially supported by Russian Science Foundation, grant №20–18–00206.

References

1. Basile, P., McGillivray, B.: Exploiting the web for semantic change detection. In: Soldatova, L., Vanschoren, J., Papadopoulos, G., Ceci, M. (eds.) DS 2018. LNCS (LNAI), vol. 11198, pp. 194–208. Springer, Cham (2018). https://doi.org/10.1007/978-3-030-01771-2_13

2. Bocharov, V., Alexeeva, S., Granovsky, D., Protopopova, E., Stepanova, M., Surikov, A.: Crowdsourcing morphological annotation. In: Computational Linguistics and Intellectual Technologies. Papers from the Annual International Conference "Dialogue", vol. 12, pp. 109–115. RGGU (2013)

3. Bochkarev, V., Achkeev, A., Shevlyakova, A., Khristoforov, S.: Diachronic neural network predictor of word animacy. In: Pichardo Lagunas, O., Martínez-Miranda, J., Martínez Seis, B. (eds.) Advances in Computational Intelligence, pp. 215–226. MICAI 2022. LNCS, vol. 13613. Springer, Cham (2022). https://doi.org/10.1007/978-3-031-19496-2_16

4. Bochkarev, V.V., Khristoforov, S.V., Shevlyakova, A.V., Solovyev, V.D.: Neural network algorithm for detection of new word meanings denoting named entities. IEEE Access **10**, 68499–68512 (2022). https://doi.org/10.1109/ACCESS.2022.3186681

5. Bochkarev, V., Khristoforov, S., Shevlyakova, A., Solovyev, V.: Comparison of the three algorithms for concreteness rating estimation of English words. Acta Polytechnica Hungarica **19**(10), 99–121 (2022). https://doi.org/10.12700/APH.19.10.2022.10.7

6. Bochkarev, V., Maslennikova, Y., Shevlyakova, A.: Testing of statistical significance of semantic changes detected by diachronic word embedding. J. Intell. Fuzzy Syst. **43**(6), 6965–6977 (2022). https://doi.org/10.3233/JIFS-212179

7. Bochkarev, V., Solovyev, V., Nestik, T., Shevlyakova, A.: Variations in average word valence of Russian books over a century and social change. LNAI (2023, in press)

8. Bojanowski, P., Grave, E., Joulin, A., Mikolov, T.: Enriching word vectors with subword information. Trans. Assoc. Computat. Linguist. **5**, 135–146 (2017)

9. Bullinaria, J., Levy, J.: Extracting semantic representations from word co-occurrence statistics: a computational study. Behav. Res. Methods **39**(3), 510–526 (2007)

10. Bullinaria, J.A., Levy, J.P.: Extracting semantic representations from word co-occurrence statistics: stop-lists, stemming, and SVD. Behav. Res. Methods **44**(3), 890–907 (2012). https://doi.org/10.3758/s13428-011-0183-8

11. Cambria, E., Poria, S., Hazarika, D., Kwok, K.: SenticNet 5: discovering conceptual primitives for sentiment analysis by means of context embeddings. In: Proceedings of the AAAI Conference on Artificial Intelligence, pp. 1795–1802 (2018). https://doi.org/10.1609/aaai.v32i1.11559

12. Dodds, P., et al.: Human language reveals a universal positivity bias. Proc. Natl. Acad. Sci. **112**(8), 2389–2394 (2015)

13. Firth, J.: Studies in linguistic analysis, chap. A synopsis of linguistic theory, 1930–1955, pp. 1–32. Blackwell, Oxford (1957)

14. Galinsky, R., Alekseev, A., Nikolenko, S.: Improving neural models for natural language processing in Russian with synonyms. J. Math. Sci. **273**, 583–594 (2023). https://doi.org/10.1007/s10958-023-06520-z

15. Gatti, L., Guerini, M., Turchi, M.: Sentiwords: deriving a high precision and high coverage lexicon for sentiment analysis. IEEE Trans. Affect. Comput. **7**(4), 409–421 (2016). https://doi.org/10.1109/TAFFC.2015.2476456

16. Grave, E., Bojanowski, P., Gupta, P., Joulin, A., Mikolov, T.: Learning word vectors for 157 languages. In: Proceedings of the Eleventh International Conference on Language Resources and Evaluation (LREC 2018). European Language Resources Association (ELRA), Miyazaki, Japan (2018)

17. Gulordava, K., Baroni, M.: A distributional similarity approach to the detection of semantic change in the Google Books Ngram corpus. In: Proceedings of the GEMS 2011 Workshop on GEometrical Models of Natural Language Semantics, pp. 67–71. Association for Computational Linguistics, Edinburgh, UK (2011)

18. Hamilton, W.L., Clark, K., Leskovec, J., Jurafsky, D.: Inducing domain-specific sentiment lexicons from unlabeled corpora. In: Proceedings of the 2016 Conference on Empirical Methods in Natural Language Processing, pp. 595–605. Association for Computational Linguistics, Austin, Texas (2016). https://doi.org/10.18653/v1/D16-1057

19. Harris, Z.: Papers in structural and transformational Linguistics. Reidel, Dordrecht (1970)

20. Koltsova, O., Alexeeva, S., Kolcov, S.: An opinion word lexicon and a training dataset for Russian sentiment analysis of social media. In: Komp'yuternaia Lingvistika i Intellektual'nye Tekhnologii: Trudy Mezhdunarodnoj Konferentsii "Dialog", pp. 277–287 (2016)

21. Kotel'nikov, E., Razova, E., Kotel'nikova, A., Vychegzhanin, S.: Sovremennye slovari ocenochnoj leksiki dlya analiza mnenij na russkom i anglijskom yazykah (analitich-eskij obzor). Nauchno-tekhnicheskaya informaciya. Seriya 2: Informacionnye processy i sistemy **12**, 16–33 (2020). https://doi.org/10.36535/0548-0027-2020-12-3, in Russian

22. Kulagin, D.: Publicly available sentiment dictionary for the Russian language KartaSlovSent. In: Computational Linguistics and Intellectual Technologies. Papers from the Annual International Conference "Dialogue", Suppl. volume, vol. 20, pp. 1106–1119 (2021)

23. Liu, B.: Sentiment analysis: mining opinions, sentiments, and emotions. Cambridge University Press, Cambridge (2015). https://doi.org/10.1017/CBO9781139084789

24. Loughran, T., Mcdonald, B.: When is a liability not a liability? Textual analysis, dictionaries, and 10-ks. J. Financ. **66**(1), 35–65 (2011). https://doi.org/10.1111/j.1540-6261.2010.01625.x

25. Loukachevitch, N., Levchik, A.: Creating a general Russian sentiment lexicon. In: Proceedings of the Tenth International Conference on Language Resources and Evaluation (LREC2016), pp. 1171–1176. European Language Resources Association (ELRA), Portorož, Slovenia (2016)

26. Louviere, J., Flynn, T., Marley, A.A.J.: Best-Worst Scaling: Theory. Cambridge University Press, Methods and Applications (2015)

27. Mikolov, T., Sutskever, I., Chen, K., Corrado, G., Dean, J.: Distributed representations of words and phrases and their compositionality. In: Advances in Neural Information Processing Systems, pp. 3111–3119. Curran Associates, Inc (2013)

28. Mohammad, S.: Obtaining reliable human ratings of valence, arousal, and dominance for 20,000 English words. In: Proceedings of the 56th Annual Meeting of the Association for Computational Linguistics (Volume 1: Long Papers), pp. 174–184. Association for Computational Linguistics, Melbourne, Australia (2018). https://doi.org/10.18653/v1/P18-1017

29. Mohammad, S., Kiritchenko, S., Zhu, X.: NRC-Canada: building the state-of-the-art in sentiment analysis of tweets. In: Second Joint Conference on Lexical and Computational Semantics (*SEM). Volume 2: Proceedings of the Seventh International Workshop on Semantic Evaluation (SemEval 2013), pp. 321–327. Association for Computational Linguistics, Atlanta, Georgia, USA (2013)

30. Pantel, P.: Inducing ontological co-occurrence vectors. In: Proceedings of the 43rd Annual Meeting of the Association for Computational Linguistics (ACL2005), pp. 125–132. Association for Computational Linguistics, Ann Arbor, Michigan (2005). https://doi.org/10.3115/1219840.1219856

31. Pilehvar, M., Camacho-Collados, J.: Embeddings in natural language processing: theory and advances in vector representations of meaning. Morgan and Claypool Publishers (2020)

32. Qiu, X., Sun, T., Xu, Y., Shao, Y., Dai, N., Huang, X.: Pre-trained models for natural language processing: a survey. SCIENCE CHINA Technol. Sci. **63**, 1872–1897 (2020). https://doi.org/10.1007/s11431-020-1647-3

33. Reagan, A.J., Danforth, C.M., Tivnan, B., Williams, J.R., Dodds, P.S.: Sentiment analysis methods for understanding large-scale texts: a case for using continuum-scored words and word shift graphs. EPJ Data Sci. **6**(1), 28 (2017). https://doi.org/10.1140/epjds/s13688-017-0121-9

34. Rubenstein, H., Goodenough, J.: Contextual correlates of synonymy. Commun. ACM **8**(10), 627–633 (1965)

35. Tang, X.: A state-of-the-art of semantic change computation. Nat. Lang. Eng. **24**(5), 649–676 (2018). https://doi.org/10.1017/S1351324918000220

36. Turney, P., Pantel, P.: From frequency to meaning: vector space models of semantics. J. Artif. Intell. Res. **37**(1), 141–188 (2010). https://doi.org/10.1613/jair.2934
37. Tutubalina, E.: Metody izvlechenija i rezjumirovanija kriticheskih otzyvov pol'zovatelej o produkcii: PhD dissertation (2016, in Russian)
38. Vo, D.T., Zhang, Y.: Don't count, predict! an automatic approach to learning sentiment lexicons for short text. In: Proceedings of the 54th Annual Meeting of the Association for Computational Linguistics (Volume 2: Short Papers), pp. 219–224. Association for Computational Linguistics, Berlin, Germany (2016). https://doi.org/10.18653/v1/P16-2036. https://aclanthology.org/P16-2036
39. Weeds, J., Weir, D., McCarthy, D.: Characterising measures of lexical distributional similarity. In: COLING 2004: Proceedings of the 20th International Conference on Computational Linguistics, pp. 1015–1021. COLING, Geneva, Switzerland (2004)
40. Worth, P.: Word embeddings and semantic spaces in natural language processing. Int. J. Intell. Sci. **13**, 1–21 (2023). https://doi.org/10.4236/ijis.2023.131001
41. Xu, Y., Kemp, C.: A computational evaluation of two laws of semantic change. In: Proceedings of the 37th Annual Meeting of the Cognitive Science Society, CogSci 2015. Pasadena, California, USA (2015)

An Interpretable Authorship Attribution Algorithm Based on Distance-Related Characterizations of Tokens

Victor Lomas[1] , Michelle Reyes[2], and Antonio Neme[1(✉)]

[1] Instituto de Investigaciones en Matemáticas Aplicadas y en Sistemas (IIMAS), Universidad Nacional Autónoma de México, Ciudad Universitaria, CDMX, Mexico
[2] Postgraduation Program in Computer Science, Universidad Nacional Autónoma de México, Mexico City, Mexico
{victor.lomas,antonio.neme}@iimas.unam.mx

Abstract. Natural Language Processing has focused its efforts in sentiment analysis, token categorization, topic identification, translation, authorship attribution and many other relevant and useful tasks. In this contribution, we describe an algorithm able to characterize texts in a feature space from which, among other tasks, the authorship attribution problem can be tackled. Although several deep learning architectures have shown good results, the solution they offer is usually hard to interpret and the explanation about the attribution is opaque. In our algorithm, each token is characterized in terms of both, the number of tokens that separate it from its previous appearance within the text, and the number of words that separate it from the last novel token. A novel token is an element that appears for the first time in the context of the analyzed writing. Following the proposed approach, we analyzed hundreds of texts from dozens of writers. The embeddings created by our proposal allows classifiers to correctly attribute the authorship of a novel text, as shown by several tests. Our proposal achieves identification metrics similar, and in some cases, better than state-of-the-art models. Equally relevant, our method is interpretable and shows a far lower computational complexity than deep learning architectures as Large Language Models.

Keywords: authorship attribution · unsupervised learning · embeddings

1 Introduction

Texts can be studied from a wide range of perspectives. Literary critics, biographers, and art historians focused in specific writers, periods or genres are interested in detecting patterns of writing in texts created by that author, and how those patterns change over time [1–3]. Of particular relevance is the study of stylistics, which is focused in the analysis of language and style in texts. The style usually refers to some features that are maintained along the majority of

H. Calvo et al. (Eds.): MICAI 2023, LNAI 14392, pp. 83–94, 2024.
https://doi.org/10.1007/978-3-031-47640-2_7

texts from a given author. Stylistics has two legs to identify those features that distinguish a writer or genre from the rest. One of such paths is qualitative, whose aim is to understand the message of the writer in her/his social context, taking into account the reader state of mind [4]. The second foundation of stylistics is quantitative, heavily based on the identification of explicit or implicit mathematical descriptions derived from the texts. In a computational perspective of stylistics, algorithms are applied to raw texts in order to find certain patterns in which some structures are overrepresented [1,5]. Strongly associated to stylistics is a relevant problem known as authorship attribution [6,7].

The authorship attribution problem (AA) can be stated as follows. Given a previously unseen text, known to be authored by one of several candidate writers, a system should select, or offer a rank of, the most likely author of the text. Although the AA has several applications in forensic informatics [8], in software disputes [9], medicine [10], among other fields, we are interested in the AA problem for literary reasons. The relevance of AA is wide within literary studies, as for example, it can help to settle disputes concerning authorship [11]. Besides, the structures or characterizations in which AA algorithms are usually based on to achieve a decision may offer literary specialists new insights into the stylistics or patterns of the studied texts and authors [1].

From a computational perspective, AA is a special case of classification. A system learns or approximates a function between two sets. The first set is defined by the feature space, in which each text occupies a certain position. The second set is the label or author of the text. In the AA case, the text to be attributed can be thought of as a validation instance previously unseen. The feature space can be derived by experts or by algorithms. Within the Natural Language Processing and Computational Linguistics community, the feature space that describes texts is usually known as an embedding. Neural networks have been applied in the construction of the classification function [12], and more recently, in the generation of the embedding [13,14].

The algorithm we present in this contribution is a useful tool in NLP in two directions. The first one is a practical one. Our proposal is able to solve the AA problem, at least in the studied datasets, as good as state-of-the-art algorithms. The advantage is that our approach is interpretable. An algorithm should be able to provide elements to answer the question of why a text was attributed to the selected author. This is as important as presenting good metrics. It is common in deep learning AA algorithms to be opaque or at least, hard to interpret. It is in this regard that we consider our contribution to be a good choice for AA.

The second contribution of our proposal is related to the embedding. Since it provides an interpretable embedding, it offers specialists to look into the texts with a new perspective. The AA task can be achieved by several classifiers based on the constructed embeddings.

Positional information of tokens within a text refers to the order of appearance of tokens. A token is any word, number or punctuation mark. By considering the positional information, a temporal-like structure is added to the analysis [15]. Based on this structure, the concept of distance can be induced. The distance between a token in position i and a token in position j is simply $|j - i|$. A token T can be characterized in terms of the distance to a token S. The hypothesis we aim to prove in this contribution is that by choosing carefully such characterization it is possible to map texts to a relatively low-dimensional space in which authorship identification is possible with simple classifiers. At the same time, such embedding allows specialists to look into the writing pattern of authors from a different perspective.

The rest of the contribution continues as follows. In Sect. 2 we briefly describe the state-of-the-art of AA algorithms. In Sect. 3 we describe our algorithm to tackle with AA, and some results are presented in Sect. 4. Finally, we offer some discussion and conclusions in Sect. 5.

2 State-of-the-Art

The identification of features that allow the correct attribution of texts is an open-ended task. A seminal work based on shallow networks, word2vec, allowed the construction of a feature space able to capture some aspects that offered an approximation of semantics purely based on syntactic aspects [16]. The idea of embeddings built by weighting the relative frequency of appearance of words was further developed in a series of interesting models and reached a milestone with the appearance of Transformers [13].

Transformers are a family of deep learning architectures able to cope with the local context in which signals, often words, occur. By weighting each word in a context window, the achieved embedding captures deep connections between words. Those connections have impacted several areas of Natural Language Processing, including translation [17], topic classification [18], among others.

Transformers have been applied in the AA in several contexts [19]. In [20], authors develop a method able to generate embeddings of authors based on their texts from which it can be decided if a novel text was written by some of the candidate authors. In [21], authors introduce a method based on Transformers to break the double-blind review process in a path similar to AA.

Deep representations of language models come in several flavours. Large language models (LLM) refers to a representation, mainly in terms of probability distributions, of sequences of words or tokens. Language models are trained over usually large datasets, known as corpora.

Of particular interest to AA is a LLM known as BERT, after Bidirectional Encoder Representations from Transformers (BERT) [22] refers to a family of language models that encode contextual representations. BERT is pre-trained with unlabeled corpora (the entirety of the English Wikipedia, as well as the Brown Corpus). The pre-training serves as a base layer of a model to build from. Once BERT was trained from that corpora, a process known as transfer learning allows its use in several contexts. BERT relies on a self-attention mechanism, which is made possible by the bidirectional Transformers at the core of its architecture [23].

3   A Novel Embedding

Let $\mathbf{T}$ be a text. $\mathbf{T}$ can be seen as a list of tokens $[T_0, T_1, T_2, ...]$. A token $T \in \mathbf{T}$ is any word, number of symbol. Each token is indexed by its position or order of appearance in $\mathbf{T}$. T_0 refers to the first token in $\mathbf{T}$, T_1 to the second, and so on. The number of symbols in $\mathbf{T}$ is denoted by $|\mathbf{T}|$. A given token can appear multiple times within the text. In the tokenization process, capital letters are converted to small letters.

The distance between tokens T_i and T_j in $\mathbf{T}$, denoted by $\sigma(T_i, T_j)$, is the number of tokens that separates them, that is $|i - j|$. A particularly relevant case is the distance between the token at position i, T_i and the previous appearance of that same token. We will refer to that distance as $\delta(T_i)$. If it is the first appearance of token T_i, we will make $\delta(T_i) = 0$. In order to compare texts of different size, $\delta(T_i)$ is escalated to the range $[0, 1]$ by dividing it by $|\mathbf{T}|$. On the other hand, $\sigma(T_i, T_j)$ is not normalized since, in general, the range of values is similar in texts of different size, and rarely exceeds $|\mathbf{T}|^2$.

The algorithm analyzes $\mathbf{T}$ and keeps a record of the position in which each token appears. A novel token η in $\mathbf{T}$ is a token that appears for the first time in $\mathbf{T}$. At the beginning, $\eta = T_0$. If the second token is different from the first, as is usual the case in many texts, $\eta = T_1$. The position of η is omitted for clarity, but is implicitly maintained for comparisons. Table 1 shows as an example the analysis of the phrase "a rose is a rose by any other name".

Table 1. An example showing the last novel token η for each token T_i, the distance to the previous appearance of token T_i ($\delta(T_i)$), and the distance to the last novel token, $\sigma(T_i, \eta)$. The position of η is omitted for clarity, but it is used to compute $\sigma(T_i, \eta)$.

i	Token	η	$\sigma(T_i, \eta)$	$\delta(T_i)$
0	a	a	0	0
1	rose	a	1	0
2	is	rose	1	0
3	a	is	1	3
4	rose	is	2	3
5	by	is	3	0
6	any	by	1	0
7	other	any	1	0
8	name	other	1	0

From $\sigma(T_i, \eta)$ and $\delta(T_i)$, we can create an embedding that, as we will shortly show, offers at least two relevant aspects. We will refer to the embedding of tokens in $\mathbf{T}$ in that space as $E_m(\mathbf{T})$. As an example, Fig. 1-A shows $E_m(\mathbf{T})$ for *Funes el memorioso*. Each point is a token in $\mathbf{T}$. The red points indicate the mapping of token $T =$*funes*. A token T_i can appear multiple times at different positions within **T**. From the multiple appearances of each token T_i, the expected $\sigma(T_i, \eta)$ and $\delta(T_i)$ are computed. The expected embedding is referred to as $\overline{E_m}(\mathbf{T})$. Still in 1-A, the continuous blue line indicates the expected mapping of token *funes*. The proposed algorithm is focused on the expected embedding of all tokens in the vocabulary. Figure 1-B shows the expected mapping of some of the most frequent tokens of *Funes el memorioso*.

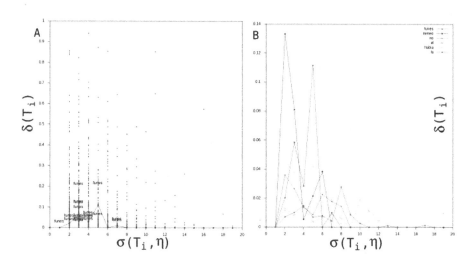

Fig. 1. A. The embedding $E_m(\mathbf{T})$ of *Funes el memorioso*, by Jorge Luis Borges. Each point represents a token T_i in **T**. Each token may represent a word, number or symbol in the text. The text contains 2,690 tokens, with a vocabulary of size 1,120. The x-axis indicates the distance (number of tokens separating) between T_i to the last novel token η, denoted by $\sigma(T_i, \eta)$. The $y-$ axis displays the normalized distance (number of tokens divided by the total number of tokens in **T**) to the previous appearance of T_i, $\delta(T_i)$. The token *funes*, which appears 20 times, is indicated by red circles. In B, it is shown the expected embedding $\overline{E_m}(\mathbf{T})$, of the six most frequent tokens in **T**. In the x-axis, it is shown the expected $\sigma(T_i, \eta)$, whereas in y it is shown the expected $\delta(T_i)$. Note that from this six characterizations, an expected characterization can also be obtained.

The embedding $\overline{E_m}(\mathbf{T})$ offers information about the use of tokens followed by an author. The lines, or trajectories in $\overline{E_m}(\mathbf{T})$, present a wide range of patterns, and, as it will be shown in the next section, those patterns are helpful since they tend to be stable among texts from the same author, and different from those of a distinct writer.

From the expected embedding $\overline{E_m}(\mathbf{T})$ it is possible to extract relevant information to tackle the AA problem. Since in a given texts several tokens rarely appear, it is convenient to focus only on the $k-$ most frequent tokens. The parameter k is the only free parameter in our proposal.

Our proposal to tackle the AA problem based on $\overline{E_m}(\mathbf{T})$ is depicted in Algorithm 1. It requires a list of authors, and a group of texts for each author. Each text a is represented as a vector of k components. Each component is a tuple denoting the expected $\sigma(T_i, \eta)$ and $\delta(T_i)$ of the k most frequent tokens.

Algorithm 1. Authorship Attribution based on the expected embedding of distance-based attributes

---

Require: Let A be the list of authors. Each author $a \in A$ is represented by $|a|$ texts (a_0 is the first text for author a, and so on). Parameter k sets the limit of the number of tokens to consider (the $k-$ most frequent). Let $\mathbf{S}$ be the text to be attributed.

1: **for** each author a in A **do**
2:     **for** each text i from author a **do**
3:         Compute $\overline{E_m}(\mathbf{T}_a^i, k)$
4:     **end for**
5: **end for**
6: Let $\overline{E_m}(\mathbf{T})$ be the descriptions or embeddings of all texts from all authors.
7: Let $\overline{a}$ be the label of each text a, that is, its author.
8: Train a classifier $\mathbf{C}$ with $\overline{E_m}(\mathbf{T}) : \mathbf{C}(\overline{E_m}(\mathbf{T})) = \overline{a}$.
9: Compute $\overline{E_m}(\mathbf{S})$.
10: Apply $\mathbf{C}$ to $\overline{E_m}(\mathbf{S})$ in order to identify the author of $\mathbf{S}$ from the list A: R = $\mathbf{C}(\overline{E_m}(\mathbf{S}))$.
11: Output: R is the attributed author of text $\mathbf{S}$.

The classifier $\mathbf{C}$ in Algorithm 1 can be any algorithm. In particular, we applied random forests (RF) [24]. RF are an ensemble classifier that creates a set of decision trees, each one trained with a subsample of the training set. The class assigned to a test instance is decided by consulting all the decision trees.

Our algorithm, hereafter referred to as AuADBEBEr, after AUthorship Attribution focused on Distance-Based EmBEddings, aims to tackle the AA problem in a way that takes into account how authors make use of words within a text. As covered in this section, AuADBEBEr characterizes each token in two axis. In the first one, a token is described in terms of the distance between the position it appears and the position if its previous appearance. In the second perspective, a token is described by the distance between its position and the position of the most recent novel token. These characterizations or embeddings allow for an AA approach of syntactic nature, as opposed to models based on semantics or those focused on statistical perspectives such as *bag-of-words* or even deep learning algorithms. In the next section we will show some of the results of applying AuADBEBEr to a dataset of Latin American writers, and compare the performance with a deep learning algorithm.

4   Results

We are interested in studying writing styles, or stylistics, of Latin American writers from a structural perspective. That is, we are more interested in the patterns authors follow instead on semantic-oriented semantics. Our requirements imposed two constraints into the use and development of AA algorithms. The first one is that we are interested in answering in an interpretable way why a certain author was attributed the authorship of a text. This is the reason we developed the present algorithm. The second constraint is that of language. Since the texts we studied are either in Portuguese or in Spanish, we have to count with databases in those two languages. In order to conduct a fair comparison between AuADBEBEr and state-of-the-art models, a direct comparison with a model trained by BERT was not possible. For that, we relied on a Spanish [25] and Portuguese [26] equivalents of BERT.

Table 2 shows the list of authors we investigated. It is also shown the number of texts from each author. A total of 350 texts, mainly short stories, from twenty different authors were analyzed. From this database, we conducted two series of experiments.

Table 2. The list of authors whose ouvres were analyzed.

Name	ID	Country	Number of texts
Jorge Luis Borges	JLB	Arg	30
Juan Rulfo	JR	Mex	20
Rubem Fonseca	RF	Bra	20
Carlos Fuentes	CF	Mex	20
Clarise Lispector	CL	Bra	20
Rosario Castellanos	RC	Mex	10
Carlos Drummond de Andrade	CDA	Bra	20
Joaquim Machado de Assis	JMA	Bra	20
Bioy Casares	BC	Arg	12
Alejo Carpentier	AC	Cub	12
Amparo Dávila	AD	Mex	8
Elena Garro	EG	Mex	10
Augusto Roa Bastos	ARB	Par	20
Josefina Pla	JP	Par	20
Horacio Quiroga	HQ	Uru	8
Mercedes Rein	MR	Uru	12
Roberto Bolaño	RB	Chi	20
Victoria Orjikh	VO	Chi	6
Alberto Fuguet	AF	Chi	20
Mario Vargas Llosa	MVL	Per	6
Pilar Dughi	PD	Per	6
Magela Baudoin	MB	Bol	12
Oscar Soria	OS	Bol	6
Augusto Monterroso	AM	Gua	12

The first set of experiment is leave-one-out. For a writer a, one of her/his *ouvres* is kept out of the training set, while all other texts from this and other authors are part of the training set. The selected *ouvre*, r, is the one to be attributed. The trained classifier is then interrogated about the r. This scheme is repeated for each of the texts of each author, and a record of the classification, or, in this case, attribution, is maintained. If the authorship was correctly attributed, the true positive rate was increased. If the authorship was not correctly identified, the false positive rate was incremented. A confusion matrix was maintained in order to verify if the algorithm was prone to confound a certain writer with another with higher frequency.

In the second set of experiments, $\sim 20\%$ of the texts from each author were selected for validation, or, in our case, attribution. Since this a stochastic process, we conducted 10 Monte Carlo experiments. For each Monte Carlo iteration, the training set was generated by selecting 80% of the texts from each author. In particular, for author a, the number of his/her texts selected for training was $\lceil |a| \times 0.8 \rceil$. Once the training was completed, the author of each of the texts in the validation dataset was asked to the classifier. Again, a confusion matrix was maintained, and the true and false positive rates were increased accordingly.

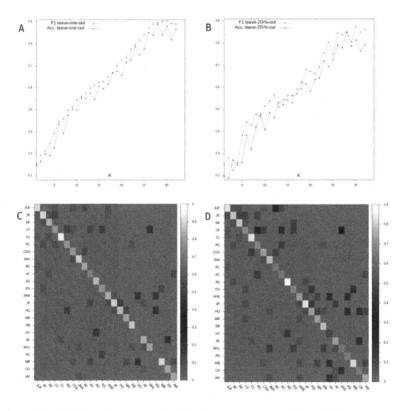

Fig. 2. F1 and accuracy for the leave-one-out and leave-20% out.

Figure 2 shows the results of applying AuADBEBEr to the dataset shown in Table 2. In A and B, it is shown the accuracy and $F1$ scores for the leave-one-out and for the leave-20%-out cases. It is observed that for the conducted experiments the best results were achieved when the $k = 30$ most frequent tokens were used to generate the embedding $\overline{E_m}(\mathbf{T})$. The confusion matrix for the leave-one-out case is shown in C, whereas the corresponding confusion matrix for the second case (leave-20%-out) is shown in D. It can be observed that in the two cases, the confusion is rather low. Both confusion matrices correspond to the $k = 30$ case.

The comparison of results obtained by AuADBEBEr with those obtained by the Spanish and Portuguese implementations of BERT is shown in Fig. 3. It is shown the quotient of the metric obtained by AuADBEBEr and the one achieved by BERT. A quotient greater than 1 indicates that AuADBEBEr outperforms BERT, whereas a quotient less that 1 indicates the opposite. It is observed that for small values of k, BERT achieves a better performance. This trend is reversed for relatively large values of k.

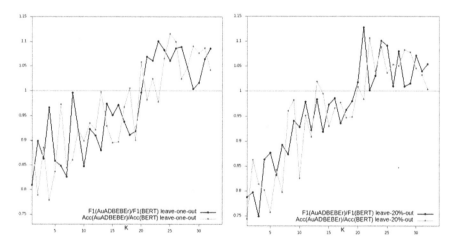

Fig. 3. Comparison of performance between AuADBEBEr and BERT models. It is shown the quotient of the F1 score obtained by AuADBEBEr for the specified k parameter and the BERT model for the leave-one-out case (A). In B, it is shown the corresponding comparison for the leave-20%-out scenario.

5   Conclusions and Discussion

The linguistic study of texts created by professional writers is an open-ended endeavor, involving linguistics, art historians, computer scientists, literary critics, among other professionals. Counting with novel and interpretable descriptions is useful to unveil profiles followed by authors.

In this contribution, we have described a novel algorithm able to create characterizations or embeddings of texts, based on distance-related concepts. In particular, our approach characterizes a token in position or order of appearance i in terms of both, the number of tokens separating it from its previous appearance, and the number of tokens between i and the position of the most recent novel token. A novel token is a token previously unseen within the analyzed text.

In our approach, the position of tokens is taken into account by keeping record of appearance. Since a token may appear several times in a text, that token may be represented by multiple points in the embedding space. From that embedding, the expected position is obtained. By computing the expected description of all tokens in the vocabulary, a text can be fully mapped. In particular, in our experiments we have detected that only the $k \sim 30$ most frequent tokens are needed. Thus, each text can be embedded in a k- dimensional space.

With the proposed embedding, we are able to provide a framework for the authorship attribution problem. Texts from several authors are mapped into the distance-based embedding or space. A classifier is trained in order to approximate a function relating the position of texts in the attribute space with the corresponding label or author. A text to be attributed is then mapped into the embedding space. The trained classifier takes as its input the description of the text, and offers as a response the most likely author of the text. In particular, we applied random forests as classifiers.

Our algorithm, named AuADBEBEr after AUthorship Attribution focused on Distance-Based EmBEddings, was applied in a set of 350 texts from 24 writers. Our algorithm offers at least three advantages. Firstly, the results were in many cases better than those obtained by a Transformer architecture. In particular, we compared our method with a Spanish and Portuguese version of BERT. As a second positive aspect, since the embedding space in which our algorithm is based is clearly defined, our method offers an explicit and interpretable answer to the question of why the text was attributed to a specific author. The third advantage of AuADBEBEr is the computational complexity. The mapping from a text to the attribute space is quadratic, and the classification stage can also be conducted with an algorithm of low complexity. The low complexity contrasts with the training of deep architectures.

We have provided in this contribution evidence to support our hypothesis, which, to remind the reader, can be stated as follows. The number of words separating consecutive appearances of a certain token, together with the number of words separating a token from the last novel word, form the basis to create an embedding from which the authorship of a text can be accurately attributed. Our purely syntactic approach allows a rational and solid framework to look into deeper properties of how writers make use of words.

Although our results are encouraging, our algorithm has to be extensively evaluated in larger datasets. This constitutes part of our ongoing work. Another point to be fully clarified is the parameter k, that refers to the most frequent tokens within a text that are to be selected to create the embedding. So far, we have only provided an approximate answer to this relevant point, but we plan to have a better idea of the correct value in future versions of our work. The software accompanying this manuscript will be fully available upon acceptance.

Acknowledgments. Authors would like to thank DGAPA PAPIIT for financial support under projects TA101323 and TA100721.

Availability. Software is available at https://anomalocarisproject.github.io/

References

1. Burke, M.: Stylistics: from classical Rethoric to cognitive neuroscience, pp. 1–16. In
2. Argamon, S., Burns, K., Dubnov, S.: The structure of style: algorithmic approaches to understanding manner and meaning (2010). https://doi.org/10.5555/1869899
3. Tomatsu, R.A.: Computational analysis of literary style: comparison of Kawabata Yasunari and Mishima Yukio. In: Re-Visioning Boundaries Conference of The School of Languages and Comparative Cultural Studie (2006)
4. Herrmann, B., Jacobs, A., Piper, A.: Computational Stylistics, pp. 460–489. In: Kuiken, D., Jacobs, A. (eds.) Handbook of Empirical Literary Studies. De Gruyer (2022)
5. Manning, C., Schutze, H.: Foundations of statistical natural language processing. MIT Press (2010)
6. Joula, P.: Authorship analysis and attribution. In: Schintler, L.A., McNeely, C.L. (eds.) Encyclopedia of Big Data. Springer, Cham (2022). https://doi.org/10.1007/978-3-319-32010-6_522
7. Gómez-Adorno, H., Sidorov, G., Pinto, D., Vilariño, D., Gelbukh, A.: Automatic authorship detection using textual patterns extracted from integrated syntactic graphs. Sensors **16**, 1374 (2016). https://doi.org/10.3390/s16091374 (2016)
8. Joula, P.: Verifying authorship for forensic purposes: a computational protocol and its validation. Forensic Sci. Int. **325**, 110824 (2021). https://doi.org/10.1016/j.forsciint.2021.110824
9. Abuhamad, M., Rhim, J., AbuHmed, T., Ullah, S., Kang, S., Nyand, D.: Code authorship identification using convolutional neural networks. Future Generation Comput. Syst. **95**, 104–115 (2019).https://doi.org/10.1016/j.future.2018.12.038
10. Garrad, P., Maloney, L., Hodges, J.: The effects of very early Alzheimer's disease on the characteristics of writing by a renowned author. Brain **128**, 250–260 (2004)
11. Cortez, C.: Risky books, rejected authors. Novos Estudos CEBRAP. http://dx.doi.org/10.25091/S01013300201800030007 (2018)
12. Neme, A., Lugo, B., Cervera, A.: Authorship attribution as a case of anomaly detection: a neural network model. Int. J. of Hybrid Intelligent Systems. (2011). https://doi.org/10.3233/HIS-2011-0142
13. Vaswani, A., et al.: Attention is all you need. In: Advances in Neural Information Processing Systems, pp. 5998–6008 (2017)
14. Abbasi, A., Javed, A.R., Iqbal, F. et al.: Authorship identification using ensemble learning. Sci. Rep. **12**, 9537 (2022). https://doi.org/10.1038/s41598-022-13690-4
15. Neme, A., Pulido, J., Muñoz, A., Dey, T., Hernández, S.: Stylistics analysis and authorship attribution algorithms based on self-organizing maps. Neurocomputing (2015). https://doi.org/10.1016/j.neucom.2014.03.064

16. Mikolov, T.: Distributed representations of words and phrases and their compositionality. In: Advances in Neural Information Processing Systems (2013)

17. Yan, J., Meng, F., Zhou, J.: Multi-unit transformers for neural machine translation. In: Proceedings of the 2020 Conference on Empirical Methods in Natural Language Processing (EMNLP), pp. 1047–1059. Association for Computational Linguistics (2020)

18. Zandie, R., Mahoor, M.: Topical language generation using transformers. Nat. Lang. Eng. **29**(2), 337–359 (2023). https://doi.org/10.1017/S1351324922000031

19. Fetoun, M., Al-Yahya, M.A.: Transformer-based approach to authorship attribution in classical Arabic texts. Appl. Sci. **13**, 7255 (2023). https://doi.org/10.3390/app13127255

20. Huertas-Tato, J., Martin, A., Huertas-Garcia, A., Camacho, D.: Generating authorship embeddings with transformers. In: 2022 International Joint Conference on Neural Networks (IJCNN), pp. 1–8. Padua, Italy (2022). https://doi.org/10.1109/IJCNN55064.2022.9892173

21. Bauersfeld, L., Romero, A., Muglikar, M., Scaramuzza, D.: Cracking double-blind review: authorship attribution with deep learning. PLoS ONE **18**(6), e0287611 (2023). https://doi.org/10.1371/journal.pone.0287611

22. Devlin, J., Chang, M., Kenton, L., Toutanova, K.: BERT: pre-training of deep bidirectional transformers for language understanding. arXiv:1810.04805v2 (2018)

23. Radford, A., Narasimhan, K., Salimans, T., Sutskever, I.: Improving language understanding by generative pre-training. https://www.bibsonomy.org/bibtex/273ced32c0d4588eb95b6986dc2c8147c/jonaskaiser (2018)

24. Breiman, L.: Random forests. Mach. Learn. **45**, 5–32 (2001). https://doi.org/10.1023/A:1010933404324

25. Cañete, J., Chaperon, G., Fuentes, R., Ho, J., Kang, H., Pérez, J.: Spanish pre-trained BERT model and evaluation data. PML4DC at ICLR 2020 (2020)

26. Souza, F., Nogueira, R., Lotufo, R.: BERTimbau: pretrained BERT models for Brazilian Portuguese. In: Cerri, R., Prati, R.C. (eds.) BRACIS 2020. LNCS (LNAI), vol. 12319, pp. 403–417. Springer, Cham (2020). https://doi.org/10.1007/978-3-030-61377-8_28

Comparing Transformer-Based Machine Translation Models for Low-Resource Languages of Colombia and Mexico

Jason Angel[1] , Abdul Gafar Manuel Meque[1] ,
Christian Maldonado-Sifuentes[2] , Grigori Sidorov[1(✉)] ,
and Alexander Gelbukh[1]

[1] Instituto Politécnico Nacional (IPN), Centro de Investigación en Computación
(CIC), Mexico City, Mexico
{gafar_meque,sidorov,gelbukh}@cic.ipn.mx
[2] Conahcyt, Mexico City, Mexico
christian.maldonado@conahcyt.mx

Abstract. This paper offers a comparative analysis of two state-of-the-art machine translation models for Spanish to Indigenous languages of Colombia and Mexico, with the aim of investigating their effectiveness and limitations under low-resource conditions. Our methodology involved aligning verse pairs text using the Bible for twelve Indigenous languages and constructing parallel datasets for evaluation using BLEU and ROUGE metrics. The results demonstrate that transformer-based models can deliver competitive performance in translating from Spanish to Indigenous languages with minimal configuration. In particular, we found the Opus-based model obtained the best performance in 11 of the languages in the test set but, the Fairseq model performs competitively in scenarios where training data is more scarce. Additionally, we provide a comprehensive analysis of the findings, including insights into the strengths and limitations of the models. Finally, we suggest potential directions for future research in low-resource language translation, specifically in the context of Latin American indigenous languages.

Keywords: Low-resource languages · Machine translation ·
Indigenous languages

The work was done with partial support from the Mexican Government through grant A1-S-47854 of CONAHCYT, Mexico, grants 20232138, 20232080, and 20231567 of the Secretaría de Investigación y Posgrado of the Instituto Politécnico Nacional, Mexico. The authors thank the CONAHCYT for the computing resources brought to them through the Plataforma de Aprendizaje Profundo para Tecnologías del Lenguaje of the Laboratorio de Supercómputo of the INAOE, Mexico, and acknowledge the support of Microsoft through the Microsoft Latin America PhD Award.

1   Introduction

Indigenous languages, as crucial aspects of cultural heritage, play an important role in preserving the identity and history of indigenous communities. However, many of these languages are facing rapid decline and even extinction due to globalization, migration, and lack of resources for their preservation. In Mexico and Colombia, these languages are an essential part of their rich cultural diversity, with Mexico alone being home to around 68 indigenous languages, and Colombia having around 65 indigenous languages spoken throughout the country. Despite the large number of languages and their cultural significance, there is a lack of resources and tools to support their preservation, documentation, and revitalization.

In recent years, machine translation has made significant progress, providing powerful tools to break language barriers and facilitate communication among speakers of different languages. However, the majority of these advancements have been focused on widely spoken languages, while low-resource languages, including indigenous ones, have received much less attention. The development of machine translation models for these low-resource languages can contribute to their documentation, revitalization, and preservation efforts.

This paper aims to explore the possibilities of using state-of-the-art machine translation models to translate Spanish to several indigenous languages from Mexico and Colombia. By analyzing the performance of different models, we hope to gain a better understanding of the strengths and limitations of current translation models and uncover the factors that contribute to their performance and identify potential avenues for improvement.

Ultimately, our work seeks to serve as a foundation for future research, contributing with models and dataset baselines to compare the performance of coming NLP techniques as part of the ongoing effort of preserving and promoting the linguistic and cultural diversity of indigenous communities.

2   Indigenous Languages in this Research

In this section, we provide a brief linguistic overview of the twelve Indigenous languages included in our research and highlight some of their distinctive phonological, morphological, and syntactic features. At the end of this section, we introduce Table 1, which describes these languages in terms of the linguistic family, word order, population reported in the last census, the country (either Colombia or Mexico), and their respective ISO 639-3 codes. This language information was retrieved from the Ethnologue [2][1]

The Mazahua is a language that exhibits complex morphological structures, including the use of morphemes for encoding direct and indirect objects. Also

---

[1] The Ethnologue is widely recognized as the most authoritative source on the languages of the world.

it has a specific word order and syntactic structures, which may involve head-marking and dependent-marking grammar. Moreover, it displays specific alignment patterns in its ditransitive constructions and it has specific information structures and sentence forms that may involve the use of focus, topic, and other discourse-related elements [14].

The Huichol is a complex language with more than 40 prefixes and around 50 verbal suffixes and various types of suffixes, including thematic, derivational, and those related to argument structure, valency, modes of action, clause relationships, time, aspect, and formal register [9].

The Mixteco and Mazateco share the same consonants, variants of the languages present some variations in the pronunciation of certain phonemes depending on the region. As tonal languages, they use morphological markers rather than intonation to indicate questions [18]. Moreover, the Mixteco phonological inventory is characterized by a large number of contrasting nasal vowels [16] it is known for its complex system of numeral classifiers too [17].

Puebla Nahuatl, exhibits a rich system of morphology, including the use of affixes to convey grammatical information [5]. Guerrero Nahuatl follows a different word order but is polysynthetic, thus, single words can convey complex ideas through the use of affixes [5]. Nahuatl languages have influenced significantly modern Mexican Spanish which exhibits numerous loanwords from Nahuatl [7].

Epena, features a highly agglutinative morphology, with numerous affixes to mark tense, aspect, and mood, as well as evidentiality, which conveys the source of information [3].

Cacua, is on the verge of extinction. It is unique in that it follows an object-subject-verb (OSV) word order, which is rare among the world's languages.

Nasa, have been recently considered as part of the larger Barbacoan language family and has a rich system of morphology, with various inflectional and derivational processes that made it difficult to classify for many years in a specfic language family [8].

Kogi is an agglutinative and tonal language with a complex system of noun classes. Interestingly, Kogi people have a deeply spiritual and ecological connection with their environment, and their language reflects this relationship [23].

Wayuu is part of the larger Maipurean language family. The language is known for its complex system of classifiers and its extensive use of reduplication [4].

Camsá is characterized by its complex system of noun classification and a highly agglutinative morphology [19].

3 Methodology

This section describes the creation of the dataset and the experimentation setting used to conduct the experiments. The dataset creation includes source and preprocessing details, while the experimentation setting explains the models and metrics used for the experiments.

Table 1. Description of Indigenous languages of Colombia and Mexico.

Language	ISO 639-3	Family	Word order	Population	Census	Country
Mazahua	maz	Otomanguean	VSO	154,000	2020	Mexico
Huichol	hch	Uto-Aztecan	SOV	60,300	2020	Mexico
Mazateco	maq	Otomanguean	VSO	237,000	2020	Mexico
Mixteco	mim	Otomanguean	VSO	150,000	2011	Mexico
Nahuatl, Puebla	azz	Uto-Aztecan	VSO	200,000	2007	Mexico
Nahuatl, Guerrero	ngu	Uto-Aztecan	SVO	125,000	2000	Mexico
Epena	sja	Emberá	SOV	7,050	2018	Colombia
Cacua	cbv	Maku	OSV	150	2018	Colombia
Nasa	pbb	Paezan	SOV	243,000	2018	Colombia
Kogi	kog	Chibcha	SOV	15,800	2001	Colombia
Wayuu	guc	Arawak	VSO	380,000	2018	Colombia
Camsá	kbh	Isolate	SOV	7520	2018	Colombia

3.1 The Datasets Creation

The present study has utilized a set of linguistic resources that comprises twelve distinct indigenous languages, specifically six from Colombia and six from Mexico that were aligned with their correspondent translation in Spanish. These languages have been meticulously obtained from a version of the Holy Bible online [1], which is a well-known and widely recognized language source for low-resource language studies. The popularity of the Bible for linguistic studies relies on the number of high-quality translations it has had to a diversity of languages for religious purposes, making it a valuable and easily accessible resource for researchers in the field. Additionally, the Bible is highly advantageous for developing automated translation models, as it is organized into chapters and verses, allowing for a precise and reliable alignment of text across multiple languages. It is important to mention that according to eBible.org [1] their Spanish Bible uses a simplified language (syntax and more conventional vocabulary) that incorporates a more basic vocabulary than most Spanish Bibles, which is particularly convenient for our goal as this choice also simplifies the translation task from Spanish to the low-resources languages. This process concluded in an alignment of approximately 7930 verses for each language, representing parallel texts as a pair of verses (i.e., "Spanish-text, indigenous-language-text").

After the alignment process, the data is prepared for use in the machine translation models. To achieve this, the data undergoes two steps: preprocessing and splitting into training, validation, and testing sets. The preprocessing step involves tokenizing and segmenting the words, as well as generating the vocabulary. Once this is complete, the data is split into training, validation, and testing sets, with 80% of the available data allocated for training, 10% for validation, and the remaining 10% for testing. In total, the training set comprises approximately 6,305 samples, while the validation and testing sets contain 790 samples each. The final outcome is a suitable dataset for the specific machine translation task of each indigenous language. Table 2 presents the statistics of our datasets used for training, validation, and testing splits of our machine translation models. These statistics specify the number of types, the number of tokens in each set, as well as the percentage of unknown words in the validation and test sets. These statistics provide an overview of the language availability in our datasets and are taken into consideration for detailed analysis of our models' performance in the Sect. 4.1.

Table 2. Token statistics of our dataset.

Token stat	maz	hch	maq	mim	azz	ngu	sja	cbv	pbb	kog	guc	kbh
num types	25k	43k	22k	19k	38k	33k	29k	24k	34k	41k	35k	38k
train tokens	235k	100k	225k	298k	219k	149k	155k	220k	123k	158k	175k	161k
valid tokens	30k	12k	28k	37k	27k	19k	20k	28k	15k	20k	22k	20k
test tokens	29k	12k	29k	37k	27k	19k	19k	27k	15k	20k	22k	20k
val unknown	2%	21%	2%	1%	7%	9%	5%	2%	10%	10%	8%	10%
test unknown	2%	22%	2%	1%	7%	8%	5%	2%	10%	10%	7%	11%

3.2   Experimentation Setting

In this study, we employed two state-of-the-art Natural Language Processing (NLP) models to conduct our experiments. These models are Fairseq and Opus-mt-en-es, which we will refer to as M1 and M2 respectively, for convenience. These models were chosen for their strong performance in previous research and their potential to improve translation quality for low-resource languages.

- **Fairseq (M1):** our first model is based on Fairseq [20] an extensible library built on PyTorch that allows the creation of customized encoder-decoder models to address a variety of text generation tasks, including translation, summarization, and paraphrasing, among others. Moreover, models trained using Fairseq have proven to be reliable and efficient for a variety of MT tasks [6,10,25], its versatility and accuracy make it a popular choice for NLP researchers and developers worldwide.
- **Opus-mt-en-es (M2):** Opus models [22] have been trained on a large parallel corpus and are based on Marian [11] a state-of-the-art transformer-based MT model with efficient training and decoding capabilities. For this study, we use the Opus pre-trained model that was designed for translating text from English to Spanish with the purpose of leveraging the knowledge it already has in Spanish.

We employed the same configuration for all of the Natural Language Processing (NLP) models used in this study. The models were trained with a learning rate of 5.00E-05 and a train batch size of 16, while the evaluation batch size was also set to 16. We used the Adam optimizer with betas set to (0.9,0.999) and an epsilon value of 1e-08. A linear learning rate scheduler was applied, and the models were trained for a total of 10 epochs. It is worth noting that the values used in our NLP model configuration are the default values found in the Hugging Face library, which have been extensively tested and found to work well in a wide range of NLP applications and therefore are highly convenient for future comparison with this work.

To assess the effectiveness of our models, we utilized BLEU and ROUGE as the chosen metrics for scoring. Although both evaluate lexical overlap, they offer different perspectives in evaluating our model's performance. Generally, BLEU emphasizes n-gram precision, while ROUGE is recall-oriented [24]. In addition, ROUGE-L may be a better evaluation metric for MT systems in Indigenous languages because it takes into account word order by measuring the longest common subsequence between the generated translation and the reference translation.

4   Results

In this section, we present the results and findings of the experiments conducted to evaluate the performance of our machine translation models. Two tables are presented, providing a detailed report of our experiments using different models and metrics across twelve Indigenous languages. Table 3 compares the performance of our proposed models for the validation set and Table 4 the results for the test set. Please note that for the sake of being efficient in the use of space, the results tables use the abbreviations M1 and M2 to refer to our models Fairseq and opus-mt-en-es respectively, similarly, the names of the Indigenous languages were replaced by their corresponding ISO 639-3 code.

Table 3. Results for the validation split.

	BLEU		Rouge-1		Rouge-2		Rouge-L	
Lang	M1	M2	M1	M2	M1	M2	M1	M2
maz	1.50	4.37	0.45	0.31	0.18	0.31	0.17	0.26
hch	2.34	1.99	0.46	0.19	0.20	0.19	0.19	0.17
maq	2.01	6.66	0.44	0.30	0.19	0.30	0.17	0.24
mim	2.58	5.66	0.54	0.43	0.25	0.43	0.20	0.31
azz	1.81	3.83	0.44	0.26	0.19	0.26	0.18	0.22
ngu	1.75	5.67	0.43	0.29	0.18	0.29	0.16	0.26
sja	1.70	2.80	0.44	0.28	0.18	0.28	0.17	0.22
cbv	1.35	5.86	0.40	0.32	0.16	0.32	0.16	0.25
pbb	1.97	1.30	0.48	0.21	0.20	0.21	0.18	0.17
kog	1.92	1.77	0.47	0.13	0.19	0.13	0.20	0.12
guc	1.16	1.58	0.35	0.29	0.14	0.29	0.15	0.23
kbh	2.53	4.17	0.51	0.29	0.21	0.29	0.20	0.24

Table 4. Results for the test split.

	BLEU		Rouge-1		Rouge-2		Rouge-L	
Lang	M1	M2	M1	M2	M1	M2	M1	M2
maz	1.70	4.12	0.46	0.30	0.19	0.30	0.18	0.25
hch	2.27	2.42	0.47	0.19	0.20	0.19	0.19	0.17
maq	2.05	6.75	0.46	0.30	0.19	0.30	0.18	0.24
mim	2.49	5.63	0.52	0.43	0.25	0.43	0.19	0.31
azz	1.94	4.22	0.44	0.26	0.19	0.26	0.18	0.23
ngu	2.25	5.46	0.44	0.30	0.19	0.30	0.17	0.26
sja	1.67	2.68	0.45	0.27	0.19	0.27	0.17	0.22
cbv	1.47	6.14	0.40	0.31	0.16	0.31	0.16	0.25
pbb	1.66	1.01	0.49	0.21	0.20	0.21	0.19	0.17
kog	2.03	2.29	0.49	0.15	0.20	0.15	0.19	0.13
guc	1.25	2.39	0.34	0.29	0.13	0.29	0.15	0.23
kbh	2.32	4.21	0.52	0.29	0.21	0.00	0.20	0.24

4.1   Analysis of Results

To emphasize the challenges posed by low-resource conditions, we undertook a correlation analysis to examine how dataset characteristics impact model performance. This quantitative exploration revealed compelling insights into the significance of these resources for model efficacy. Our analysis unveiled a negative correlation of -0.531 between model performance and the number of types. Furthermore, we observed a compelling positive correlation of 0.648 between model performance and the number of tokens. These findings align with the unique characteristics of indigenous languages, where the task of modeling becomes increasingly intricate as vocabulary cardinality rises while the frequency of contexts for such types remains limited.

Then, we analyzed the specific performance of each model per language, which provided us with valuable insights into the strengths and limitations of our models. By examining the results of Bleu's metrics, we noticed that the Opus-based model (M2) outperformed the other two models in all languages. It is worth mentioning Fairseq (M1) demonstrated competitive performance despite lacking previous knowledge of the Spanish language that the Opus-based model had. The strengths of the Fairseq-based model become evident in circumstances where there is less resources available and therefore, making accurate predictions becomes harder. To note it, please consider the dataset stats presented in previous Table 2, it shows that Fairseq overcomes the Opus-based model performance for Nasa language (pbb)[2] by a range of 0.6 according to Bleu metric in both validation and test sets. Fairseq (M1) also proved to perform well for the

---

[2] Nasa language (pbb) is the hardest language to translate according to our results out of the twelve languages being presented.

Huichol language (hch) which is the one with the lowest resources in this study because of few number of tokens in the three dataset splits and the high number of unknown words being equal to 21%.

Lastly, we found that our models achieve comparable results across all (twelve) languages in both the validation and test sets. This is a good sign that our models are generalizing well across different languages despite of the lack of training data.

5 Related Works

It is worth noting that because of the few existing works in the wide diversity of low-resource languages such as indigenous languages, the existing works are not directly comparable to ours in terms of languages, datasets, and metrics. Here we provide an overview of recent research in neural machine translation (NMT) for low-resource language that we take into consideration for designing our perspective in this study and believe is relevant to mention for future research.

The paper *Neural Machine Translation of Rare Words with Subword Unit* [21] is a work previous to modern transformer-based models that focused on modeling open-vocabulary translation by encoding rare and unknown words as sequences of subword unit. It demonstrates that neural machine translation (NMT) systems can effectively perform open-vocabulary translation by representing rare and unseen words as sequences of subword units. The aim of this approach is to leverage the relationship between languages that may be encoded as loanwords, cognates, and compounds among others. We are interested in this work to see if we can leverage this approach for modeling unknown words from Indigenous languages, however, no good results arose probably because beyond loanwords there is little overlapping from lexicon in the Indigenous language and Spanish.

In their work *Phrase-Based Neural Unsupervised Machine Translation* [13] the authors highlight the challenges of performing machine translation when there is no language pair availability, i.e., unsupervised translation. Although the work aims to translate German to English the relevance of this kind of proposal are very important for Indigenous languages where language pair corpora are often limited to the Bible and a couple of short documents more like constitutions [15]. A similar approach is presented in [12] however this work actually focuses on low-resource languages by exploiting its similarities with a high-resource language. The core of the proposal is using transliteration models in order to transform the data from the high-resource language into data similar to the low-resource language. The results are impressive considering no true parallel corpora were used and the method is worth be revisited using modern transformer-based models. However, the major constraint for applying this approach to our scenario relies on identifying a high-resource language that is similar enough to each of our target Indigenous languages, which may pose a real challenge for languages with low documentation such as the Camsá language which is an isolated language.

6   Conclusion

The importance of preserving indigenous languages cannot be overstated, as they are essential for maintaining the cultural diversity of our world and preserving the unique knowledge and traditions of indigenous communities. The development of machine translation models specifically designed for low-resource languages can provide new tools to support their preservation and revitalization efforts, contributing to a more inclusive and linguistically diverse future.

Based on our experiments and analysis, we have found that the Opus-based and Fairseq-based models exhibit good performance across all the tested languages, with some variation depending on the specific language and evaluation metric used. Our results also demonstrate the advantage of using a pre-trained model with prior knowledge of the language being translated, as seen in the superior performance of our Opus-based model.

Ultimately, we hope our findings provide valuable insights for researchers and practitioners interested in working with indigenous languages in other parts of the world, and in the spirit of this end, we make our code and dataset freely available.

6.1   Future Work

Overall, our findings suggest that while there is still much room for improvement in low-resource language translation, here we summarize some of the directions we may want to take:

– **Evaluate translations back to Spanish**: while we have evaluated translations from Spanish to indigenous languages it is important to provide a complete picture of the model's effectiveness and perform an error analysis from the generated translations.
– **Leverage the similarities between languages**: We plan to experiment with models that represent similar languages in the same space, specifically languages with similar word order or from the same family that also has been geographically close until the current times, and evaluate their performance against the models developed in this study.
– **Explore a combination of metrics to create more robust translation models**: We believe that combining different evaluation metrics, such as BLEU and ROUGE-L would better assess the performance of machine translation models for indigenous languages and provide more accurate evaluations of their capabilities.
– **Building a comprehensive parallel corpus of Latin American indigenous languages**: We believe that creating such a corpus, drawing on resources such as the Bible is a feasible and important contribution to the field. In addition to facilitating the study of individual languages, this corpus could serve as a resource for developing and refining machine translation models that perform well for low-resource languages more broadly. By providing a more comprehensive view of the linguistic and cultural diversity of the

region, this initiative could also contribute to the broader goals of preserving and celebrating indigenous languages and cultures.

References

1. Ebible.org. https://ebible.org/. Accessed 10 Apr 2023
2. Ethnologue.com. https://www.ethnologue.com/. Accessed 10 Apr 2023
3. The world atlas of language structures. https://wals.info/. Accessed 22 Apr. 2023
4. Aikhenvald, A.Y.: Morphology in Arawak languages. In: Oxford Research Encyclopedia of Linguistics (2020)
5. Amith, J.D., Smith-Stark, T.C.: Transitive nouns and split possessive paradigms in central Guerrero Nahuatl. Int. J. Am. Linguist. **60**(4), 342–368 (1994)
6. Bhardwaj, S., Alfonso Hermelo, D., Langlais, P., Bernier-Colborne, G., Goutte, C., Simard, M.: Human or neural translation? In: Proceedings of the 28th International Conference on Computational Linguistics, pp. 6553–6564. International Committee on Computational Linguistics, Barcelona, Spain (2020). https://doi.org/10.18653/v1/2020.coling-main.576, https://aclanthology.org/2020.coling-main.576
7. Canger, U.: Philology in america: Nahuatl: what loan words and the early descriptions of Nahuatl show about stress, vowel length, and glottal stop in sixteenth century Nahuatl and Spanish. Historical linguistics and philology, pp. 107–118 (1990)
8. Curnow, T.J., Liddicoat, A.J.: The barbacoan languages of Colombia and Ecuador. Anthropol. Linguist. **40**, 384–408 (1998)
9. Gómez, P.: Factores perceptuales y semánticos en la adquisición de la morfología en huichol. Función **17**(18), 175–204 (1998)
10. Guzmán, F., et al.: The FLORES evaluation datasets for low-resource machine translation: Nepali-English and Sinhala-English. In: Proceedings of the 2019 Conference on Empirical Methods in Natural Language Processing and the 9th International Joint Conference on Natural Language Processing (EMNLP-IJCNLP), pp. 6098–6111. Association for Computational Linguistics, Hong Kong, China (2019). https://doi.org/10.18653/v1/D19-1632, https://aclanthology.org/D19-1632
11. Junczys-Dowmunt, M., et al.: Marian: fast neural machine translation in C++. In: Proceedings of ACL 2018, System Demonstrations, pp. 116–121. Association for Computational Linguistics, Melbourne, Australia (2018). https://doi.org/10.18653/v1/P18-4020, https://aclanthology.org/P18-4020
12. Karakanta, A., Dehdari, J., van Genabith, J.: Neural machine translation for low-resource languages without parallel corpora. Mach. Transl. **32**, 167–189 (2018)
13. Lample, G., Ott, M., Conneau, A., Denoyer, L., Ranzato, M.: Phrase-based & neural unsupervised machine translation. In: Proceedings of the 2018 Conference on Empirical Methods in Natural Language Processing, pp. 5039–5049 (2018)
14. López Marín, A., Mora-Bustos, A.: Los adverbios en mazahua de san pedro potla. Forma y Función **28**(2), 183–213 (2015). https://doi.org/10.15446/fyf.v28n2.53549
15. Mager, M., et al.: Findings of the Americasnlp 2021 shared task on open machine translation for indigenous languages of the Americas. In: NAACL-HLT 2021, p. 202 (2021)
16. Marlett, S.A.: Nasalization in mixtec languages. Int. J. Am. Linguist. **58**(4), 425–435 (1992)
17. McKendry, I.: Two studies of mixtec languages, Master thesis (2001)

18. De la Mora, O., et al.: El mazateco de oaxaca. In: V Jornadas Internacionales de Investigación en Filología Hispánica 21, 22 y 23 de marzo de 2012 La Plata, Argentina. Identidades dinámicas. Variación y cambio en el español de América. Universidad Nacional de La Plata. Facultad de Humanidades y Ciencias de la (2012)

19. O'Brien, C.A.: A grammatical description of Kamsá, a language isolate of Colombia, Ph. D. thesis, University of Hawai'i at Manoa (2018)

20. Ott, M., et al.: Fairseq: a fast, extensible toolkit for sequence modeling. In: Proceedings of the 2019 Conference of the North American Chapter of the Association for Computational Linguistics (Demonstrations), pp. 48–53. Association for Computational Linguistics, Minneapolis, Minnesota (2019). https://doi.org/10.18653/v1/N19-4009, https://aclanthology.org/N19-4009

21. Sennrich, R., Haddow, B., Birch, A.: Neural machine translation of rare words with subword units. In: Proceedings of the 54th Annual Meeting of the Association for Computational Linguistics (Volume 1: Long Papers), pp. 1715–1725 (2016)

22. Tiedemann, J., Thottingal, S.: OPUS-MT - building open translation services for the world. In: Proceedings of the 22nd Annual Conference of the European Association for Machine Translation, pp. 479–480. European Association for Machine Translation, Lisboa, Portugal (2020). https://aclanthology.org/2020.eamt-1.61

23. Witte, F.X.P., Xué, F.: Living the law of origin: the cosmological, ontological, epistemological, and ecological framework of kogi environmental politics, Ph. D. thesis, University of Cambridge (2018)

24. Yang, A., Liu, K., Liu, J., Lyu, Y., Li, S.: Adaptations of ROUGE and BLEU to better evaluate machine reading comprehension task. In: Proceedings of the Workshop on Machine Reading for Question Answering, pp. 98–104. Association for Computational Linguistics, Melbourne, Australia (2018). https://doi.org/10.18653/v1/W18-2611, https://aclanthology.org/W18-2611

25. Yin, X., Gromann, D., Rudolph, S.: Neural machine translating from natural language to SPARQL. Futur. Gener. Comput. Syst. **117**, 510–519 (2021)

Disaster Tweets: Analysis from the Metaphor Perspective and Classification Using LLM's

Tania Alcántara[✉], Omar García-Vázquez, Hiram Calvo, and José A. Torres-León

Laboratorio de Ciencias Cognitivas Computacionales, Centro de Investigación en Computación, Instituto Politécnico Nacional, Mexico City, Mexico
{talcantaram2020,hcalvo,jtorresl2019}@cic.ipn.mx

Abstract. Nowadays, social networks, specially Twitter (now X), allow the spread of information about all topics; since this platform is completely open, there is little to none restriction on what a user can post, hence, creating a lack of confidence and trust on the information available. However, the information on Twitter sometimes have hidden meanings, as the users use metaphors to define their ideas. This paper analyzes and classifies a set of texts labeled as disaster and non-disaster, where those labeled as non-disaster include metaphorical context, focusing on the metaphorical tweets and their interaction with large language models such as BERT, RoBERTa and DistilBERT. These experiments showed an improvement compared with the state-of-the-art approaches, demonstrating that these models capture proper metaphorical text representations.

Keywords: LLM · Classification · Natural Language Processing · BERT · RoBERTa · DistilBERT · Metaphors

1 Introduction

The number of words used to communicate an idea can vary, depending on the complexity of the idea. In general, the objective is to provide the message in the clearest and most possible way for the receiver. However, today the communication canons have changed, with the revolution of text messages, people tend to use "texting shorthand" which is the abbreviation of letters and words. In some social networks, the use of shorthand has increased when delimiting words per message, which leads users to use conceptual metaphors.

The platform that defines users the most and where the use of conceptual metaphors increases is Twitter, where the user can write information in real time, through tweets, which are spun from an identifier called a hashtag (an identifier word that is preceded by the numeric symbol #).

This practicality so that any user can publish, means that the information can be shared in real time, which becomes useful when a disaster occurs, since

H. Calvo et al. (Eds.): MICAI 2023, LNAI 14392, pp. 106–117, 2024.
https://doi.org/10.1007/978-3-031-47640-2_9

users can provide detailed information minute by minute and update it. This implies that there is both false and true news flowing constantly.

On some cases, users not only spread false news, but also confuse information with the use of figurative language[1] as metaphors to express their ideas.

Metaphors alone shouldn't affect a message meaning, but on the other hand, if a user uses a metaphor that trivializes a disaster, it could generate more attention in these types of *tweets*. An example of a metaphor, *A #tsunami of problems*, where it is not referring to a real tsunami, but to numerous situations that might feel like a tsunami to the writer.

In this work, the analysis and classification of tweets with natural disaster language was carried out, through deep learning methods. The data set includes two categories, called "disasters" and "non-disasters"; those that are disasters are texts with true information about disasters, and those labeled as non-disasters are mostly texts with metaphors.

2   Context and Motivation

In recent years, there has been great interest in understanding language. From the appearance of attention mechanisms converted into *Transformers* [1] to the most popular ones such as BERT [1] or GPT [2], where the key is that "attention" that is put in the text allows the model to learn relationships between texts and long-term dependencies [1]. In this work, we focused on the understanding and comparison of BERT, RoBERTa and DistilBERT, since Roberta and DistilBERT are variants of BERT, experimentation with this type of language models is of special interest.

On the other hand, a main interest has been placed in understanding how and why language is generated and in some cases, not only to classify but to understand why LLM's are better in this type of text. It is fundamental to understand the concepts of language and why humans are capable of processing certain types of texts, such as metaphors. The understanding of this type of texts will allow us to provide our algorithms with the ability to improve the conceptual relationships of the text.

2.1   Conceptual Metaphor

Human cognition is a topic that continues to be deeply studied, especially the ability we have to make sense of sentences. One of the most interesting phenomena is what we call conceptual metaphor, which, in the area of semantics, represents an idea in another concept [3]. This means that the human being uses his physical experiences, or a conceptual base, to generate another in an abstract way.

---

[1] Figurative: Said in a sense: That it does not correspond to the literal of a word or expression, but is related to it by an association of ideas. https://dictionary.cambridge.org/es/diccionario/ingles-espanol/figurative.

In the beginning, it was believed that the metaphor served only as a poetic resource, but pioneers of cognitive linguistics propose that it should not be seen just like that, instead, it should be conceived as present in daily life, citing the following: "pervasive in everyday life, not just in language but in thought and action" [4,5].

To create a metaphor, a root is required, which is called **source domain**, which is the origin of the conceptual structure, the second is the **target or target domain**, in which it is given that final structure to the sentence [3].

To better understand this, we will use a class metaphor used by [3] and [4] *"TIME IS MONEY"*, in this case we find a formula, where the source domain is time, since It shows us that time is not literally money, but that it takes concepts for the target domain, in a more abstract way, such as in other expressions like *WASTE OF TIME* or *TO WASTE TIME.*

Another important point to highlight is the main criteria for qualifying and classifying metaphors, which are explicitly domains. When a source domain exists, it is said that they tend to belong to other domains where bodily experiences were directly obtained [6]. A clear example of this can be seen in the so-called *"primary metaphors"*, which work 100% as an experiential basis, such as the phrase *THE BODY IS A CONTAINER* [7]. Another type of metaphors are orientations, those referring to a position, to a feeling, such is the example of *HAPPY IS UP* and *SAD IS DOWN* [4], in these specific metaphors can denote that it is not isolated and cognition is shown to be present, since we see an order to systems [6].

Conceptual metaphors should not be confused with metaphorical linguistic expression. Conceptual metaphors are abstract and are represented in multiple ways. Linguistic expressions, can vary from one language to another. Speaking in Spanish, the metaphor **"HIPOTECANDO SU TIEMPO"** is not possible in English, but a metaphor such as **"SAVE TIME"** can be expressed.

We must take into account that metaphors are created for different purposes, in [6] we are shown the most relevant assumptions:

- **One-way:** Metaphors that typically provide structure from source to target domain and not vice versa.
- **Productivity:** They have the ability to adapt to the language over time.
- **Highlighting and Hiding:** Highlights only certain aspects in a limited way.
- **Metaphorical implications:** Projections from the source domain to the target domain allow inferences to be made.
- **Degrees of consciousness and automaticity:** Metaphors are usually concepts that part of the cognitive unconscious understand without realizing it.
- **Corporeal Motivation:** It has been noted that some metaphors in their source domain are more concrete, that is, they have a motivation.
- **Invariance:** The source domain consistent with the inherent structure of the target domain

2.2 Large Language Models

Large Language Models or LLM are Deep Learning based algorithms that use the Transformer [1] architecture. These models are trained on large amounts of text data in a given natural language, with the goal that they can learn to predict the probability of occurrence of a word or sequence of words [8].

Another key to LLM's is word sequence probability learning, so the model tries to predict the next word or phrase based on the previous context. This is achieved thanks to their training procedure, where they learn the semantic, syntactic and pragmatic relationships between words and how they are combined to form coherent words. Quite a few LLM's exist, and they can vary in their complexity, from n-gram based models to more advanced architectures such as neural networks, such as the Transformers used in BERT [1] and GPT [2].

To begin with, we will talk about BERT (Bidirectional Encoder Representations from Transformers) which is a language model developed by Google in 2019, BERT was a watershed in natural language processing (NLP) [1]. The peculiarity of BERT is that "bidirectional" system, which means that it performs a reading from right to left and from left to right, allowing it to better capture the context and coherence of the sentences. The way BERT works is based on the Transformers architecture, which introduces the idea of "attention", which allows the model to learn relationships between text, instead of processing it sequentially. Compared to recurrent architectures (which are the ancestors of attention mechanisms), which had problems handling long-term dependencies, the Transformer uses the attention mechanism to capture connections, that allows for language consistency. The Transformer [1] architecture is based on the key idea of "attention" which allows processing text sequences in parallel, improving the speed and efficiency of the model.

An optimized version of BERT is RoBERTa [9], that according to the authors, it has improved training by increasing in 1000 % the data. Some of the improvements they have introduced are: a larger batch size; removal of next sentence prediction, instead including dynamic masking so that it changes during each training epoch. Speaking of data, this includes texts from CommonCrawl News, websets, and Common Crawl Stories, as well as the training data used to train BERT.

Finally, DistilBERT [10] is a "distilled" version of BERT, which has only 95% of the performance and half of the parameters. DestilBERT eliminates tokens and only uses half of the layers, starting with a smaller neural network. The main idea is that once it has been trained, its outputs can be approximated to a smaller one, this through Kulback and Leiber approximation functions. Specifically, it has no token, pooler embeds, and preserves only half of the layers of Google's BERT. DistilBERT uses a technique called distillation, which approximates Google's BERT, that is, the large neural network for a smaller one. The idea is that once a large neural network has been trained, its full output distributions can be approximated using a smaller network. This is in a sense similar to the posterior approximation. One of the key optimization functions used for posterior approximation in Bayesian statistics is the Kulback Leiber divergence, and naturally it has been used here as well.

3   State of the Art

There have been different works related to disaster events and metaphor identification, some of which we will explore below.

Parrilla-Ferrer et al. [11] use an automatic binary classification through Nayve Bayes and Support Vector Machine apply with a dataset developed in the 2012 flood in Habagat. To train the models, the authors used a characteristics' extractor that functioned through probability and Bayes' theorem. The result got for the accuracy's metric was below 50% and precision's metric was below 80%.

Chanda, A.L et al. [12] explored a different option with the DisasterTweet's dataset. They applied BERT embedding with two combination (softmax and Bi-LSTM) and done comparission with the traditional embeddings methods (GloVe. Skip-gram and FastText). The best results with traditional method was 72.93% in accuracy's metric, and 74.43% F1's metric with logistic regression combination with bag of words and the best result with BERT was 83.51% in accuracy's metric, and 74.43% F1's metric.

Song G. et al. [13] the principal appeal is the creation for learning channel combinate with SentiBERT can be created a contextual embedding through sentiment, also a bidireccional memory with attention and 1D convolutional network. They get good results in the metrics precision, recall and f1 score and the best result was obtained in recall metric with 92.271%. [14], **Saji, B.,** and their colleagues conducted an analysis using the same dataset. They placed particular emphasis on data preprocessing, which included the removal of URLs, "@" signs, and mentions, as well as lemmatization, conversion to lowercase, and the elimination of stop words. They also applied "one-hot" encoding. For the construction of the classification model, they chose to use a Long Short Term Memory (LSTM) neural network, achieving an accuracy of 95% on the training set.

In another study conducted by the author self-identified as **"wisdomml"** referenced as [15], a similar preprocessing approach was employed compared to that used by Saji, B., and their colleagues, with the exception of including the removal of non-alphabetic characters and the application of tokenization. Feature extraction was performed using the TF-IDF (Term Frequency-Inverse Document Frequency) technique, combined with the use of bi-grams and tri-grams. For classification, Naive-Bayes classifiers and a "Passive Aggressive" classifier with cross-validation were used. The most noteworthy results of the study were as follows: 80.03% accuracy using bi-grams and Naive-Bayes, 86.68% precision using tri-grams and Naive-Bayes, and an F1 score of 75.18% using tri-grams and the "Passive Aggressive" classifier.

4   Data Analysis

4.1   Dataset

Disaster Tweets [16] is a data set developed by the Kaggle platform. The principal objective to this task is provided an initial challenge in Natural Language Processing.

The dataset is in a .csv format that includes 5 columns (id, keyword, location, text, and target); Next, a description of the content will be made by column:

- **id:** Identifier of the row.
- **keyword:** Key word with which the natural disaster was tagged, the set has around 223, for example: *ablaze*, burning; *sunk*, sunken; *survive*, surviving; *panic*, panic; *police*, police; among some others. It may be empty.
- **location:** Location of the disaster, it can be a city, country, street or town (for example, beach or forest). It may be empty.
- **text:** It is the text called *tweet*, where the information is written.
- **target:** Indicates whether the text is a disaster or not: **0** indicates that it is not a disaster; **1** indicates that it is a disaster.

In the Table 1 you can see an extract of the data set.

Dataset Distribution: The training data set has 7613 tweets: 4342 **(57%)**, labeled 0, and 3271 **(43%)**, labeled 1.

Word Distribution: On Twitter, it is quite common to be able to string or combine data, even if it is not strictly related. The Fig. 1 shows the cloud of *tweets* labeled as disaster and the Fig. 2 shows the cloud of *tweets* labeled as non-disaster.

Word Length: As we have mentioned, on Twitter there is a maximum length of words that as of today is 280 words. Figure 3 shows the graph of the average of the *tweets*, where we can Note that most *tweets* have an average of 140 words, which corresponded to the maximum character limit in 2017.

Table 1. Extract from the Disaster Tweets training dataset [16]

id	keyword	location	text	target
48	ablaze	Birmingham	@bbcmtd Wholesale Markets ablaze http://t.co/lHYXEOHY6C	1
49	ablaze	Est. September 2012 - Bristol	We always try to bring the heavy. #metal #RT http://t.co/YAo1e0xngw	0
52	ablaze	Philadelphia, PA	Crying out for more! Set me ablaze	0
363	annihilation	United States	Are souls punished annihilation? http://t.co/c1QXJWeQQU http://t.co/Zhp0SOwXRy	0
364	annihilation		@CalFreedomMom @steph93065 not to mention a major contributor to the annihilation of Israel	1
365	annihilation		@willienelson We need help! Horses will die!Please RT &	1
396	apocalypse	ColoRADo	I'm gonna fight Taylor as soon as I get there.	0
397	apocalypse	sindria	ohH NO FUKURODANI DIDN'T SURVIVE THE APOCALYPSE BOKUTO FEELS HORRIBLE my poor boy my ppor child	1

Fig. 1. Most relevant words with positive *hashtag* in *DisasteerTweets*

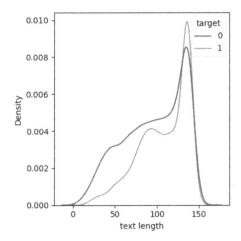

Fig. 2. Most relevant words with negative *hashtag* in *DisasteerTweets*

Fig. 3. Length of words in the set *DisasteerTweets*

4.2   Preprocessing

As we have seen, the set of *dissaster tweets* has peculiarities, that is due to the nature of the platform from which they were extracted. Therefore, some classic replacements and deletions are necessary and add to this a deep analysis of the data to perform the following:

1. **Deletion**
   - (a) Special characters
   - (b) Hashtags
   - (c) Users
   - (d) URL
2. **Replacement**
   - (a) Contractions
   - (b) Informal abbreviations
   - (c) Slang
   - (d) Types
   - (e) Aronyms

Table 2 shows some examples of this analysis for removal and replacement.

In addition to the initial preprocessing, a preprocessing oriented to the architecture of the LLM's must be carried out.

Table 2. Examples of elimination and replace

Special characters	Replace
å£3 million	3 million
fromåÊwounds	from wounds
Contractions	**Replace**
shouldn't	should not
Can\x89t	C|annot
Character entity references	**Replace**
&gt;	>
&lt	<
Typos, slang and informal abbreviations	**Replace**
w/e	whatever
USAgov	USA government
TRAUMATISED	traumatized
lmao	laughing my ass off
Trfc	Traffic

As the first phase of this, BERT's own tokenization is carried out, where the necessary tokens are added for the model to process the tweets; As a second phase, the labels are transformed from their numerical form to a form that the model understands.

Since this work is oriented to large language models, no extra preprocessing was necessary, since what is intended is that the model can infer the context that is being presented.

5   Models

5.1   BERT

It was decided to use BERT-base-cased, since good results have been shown with this model, performing correct finetuning. A learning rate was defined that takes as a minimum value a number widely practiced in the state of the art, but with the difference that this value changes with each epoch, adjusting according to an update schedule. A batch size of 12 elements was defined, the validation batch size will be 6 elements, this according to the definitions found in [1]. The Table 3 shows the modification of the hyperparameters.

5.2   RoBERTa

As part of the hyperparameters, a learning rate was defined that, as the epochs progressed, this rate would change its value to try to mitigate the problem of local minima. A batch size of 12 elements was defined, since according to the literature and the processing capacity of the equipment where the tests were carried out, it is the best option. If this number were a smaller value, there would be a much higher probability that it would not be arrived at a real generalization. Similarly, the same value was defined for the validation batch size. The following table shows the hyperparameters that were modified for this model. The Table 3 shows the modification of the hyperparameters.

5.3   DistilBert

DistilBERT allows to be modified more aggressively as it is a small version that the others LLM's. The hyperparameters was considered limited to this case. The Table 3 shows the modification of the hyperparameters.

Table 3. Modified hyperparameters proposed for BERT, RoBERTa and DistilBERT LLM

Hyperparameters	Values		
	BERT	RoBERTa	DistilBERT
Maximum sentence length	180	180	180
Minimum learning rate	0.00004	0.00005	0.00005
Batch size	12	12	24
Evaluation batch size	6	12	18

6 Results

The results obtained with the Dissater Tweets data set in the BERT, RoBERTa and Distil BERT models can be seen in the table. In Table 4, for the accuracy metric in validation A.

Table 4. BERT, Roberta and DestilBERT results with Dissater Tweets for the Accuracy metric

Model	Metrics		
	Accuracy	F1	Precision
BERT	**98.73%**	**96.98%**	**97.49%**
RoBERTa	**98.29%**	**96.33%**	**97.94%**
DistilBERT	**98.70%**	**96.58%**	**97.21%**

The results obtained in this analysis can be directly compared with the works, [13–15] and since they use the same data set. But, although the set is the same, the authors of each one of the articles do not focus on the analysis of the contextual data, only on their classification, and we can see that the results obtained are superior, showing that our analysis was correct. In the Table 5 you can see this comparison.

Table 5. Comparison with the state of the art.

Comparison	Metrics		
	Accuracy	F1	Presicion
wisdomml [15]	80.03%	75.18%	86.68%
Chanda, A.L. et al., M. [12]	83.51%	83.16%	-
Song G. et al. [12]	- %	89.59%	89.87%
BERT	**98.73%**	**96.98%**	**97.49%**
RoBERTa	**98.29%**	**96.33%**	**97.94%**
DistilBERT	**98.70%**	**96.58%**	**97.21%**

7 Conclusion and Future Work

In this article, the analysis and automatic classification of *tweets* on the *DisasterTweets* dataset was presented, through BERT, RoBERTa and DistilBERT, which are very similar to each other. Despite the fact that there are multiple automatic classification works with this data set and even superior results, this was not the only objective achieved.

As can be seen, conceptual metaphors are a matter of human cognition, since creating them involves a base and a goal, and understanding them requires knowledge to associate them. By introducing these metaphors to these variants of LLM's, good results could be obtained.

By conducting experiments, it is possible to verify that techniques grounded in the "LLM's" approach are more effective in capturing the essential features required for metaphor classification compared to methodologies representing the current state of research in this field.

This work shows us that "attention" was important, since it allows the model to identify the context that determines the polarity of the fragment, in addition to the fact that the other data provided by the dataset was not required, such as the location where the events occurred because the complexity of the problem lies in the context of the tweets.

As a future endeavor, it is essential to persist in our efforts to comprehend metaphors. This will be achieved through an in-depth analysis of data, implementing an analysis involving the classification and dissection of the utilized models. The objective is to accurately identify and pinpoint where the key to understanding this type of text lies.

References

1. Vaswani, A., et al.: Attention is all you need. In: Proceedings of the 31st International Conference on Neural Information Processing System, pp. 6000–6010 (2017)
2. Radford, A., Narasimhan, K., Salimans, T., Sutskever, I.: Improving language understanding by generative pre-training (2018)
3. Soriano, C.: La metáfora conceptual. In: Ibarretxe-Antuñano, I., Valenzuela, J. (eds.) Lingüística Cognitiva, pp. 97–121, Anthropos, Barcelona (2012)
4. Lakoff, G., Johnson, M.: Metaphors We Live By. Chicago University Press, Chicago (1980)
5. Devlin, J., Chang, M.W., Lee, K., Toutanova, K.: BERT: pre-training of deep bidirectional transformers for language understanding. In: Proceedings of the 2019 Conference of the North American Chapter of the Association for Computational Linguistics: Human Language Technologies, Volume 1 (Long and Short Papers), pp. 4171–4186. Association for Computational Linguistics (2019)
6. Morales, B.C.: Teoría de la metáfora conceptual y teoría de la metáfora deliberada: propuestas complementarias. Estudios de Lingüística Aplicada **68**, 165–198 (2018)
7. Grady, J., Taub, S., Morgan, P.: Primitive and compound metaphors. In: Goldberg, A.E. (ed.) Conceptual Structure, Discourse and Language, pp. 177–187. Center for the Study of Language and Information, Stanford (1996)
8. Radford, A., Wu, J., Child, R., Luan, D., Amodei, D., Sutskever, I.: Language models are unsupervised multitask learners. OpenAI Blog **1**(8), 9 (2019)
9. Liu, Y., et al.: Roberta: a robustly optimized BERT pretraining approach. arXiv preprint arXiv:1907.11692 (2019)
10. Sanh, V., Debut, L., Chaumond, J., Wolf, T.: DistilBERT, a distilled version of BERT: smaller, faster, cheaper and lighter. arXiv preprint arXiv:1910.01108 (2019)

11. Parilla-Ferrer, B.E., Fernández, P.L., Ballena, J.T.: Automatic Classification of Disaster-Related Tweets (2015)
12. Chanda, A.K.: Efficacy of BERT embeddings on predicting disaster from Twitter data. arXiv.org (2021). https://arxiv.org/abs/2108.10698
13. Song, G., Huang, D.: A sentiment-aware contextual model for real-time disaster prediction using twitter data. Future Internet **13**(7), 163 (2021). https://doi.org/10.3390/fi13070163
14. Saji, B.: Disaster Tweet Classification Using LSTM - NLP. Analytics Vidhya (2022). https://www.analyticsvidhya.com/blog/2022/05/disaster-tweet-classification-using-lstm-nlp/
15. wisdomml. Disaster Tweets Classification Using Machine Learning & NLP Approach - Wisdom ML. Wisdom ML (2022). https://wisdomml.in/disaster-tweets-classification-using-machine-learning-nlp-approach/
16. Natural Language Processing with Disaster Tweets Stepanenko, Viktor. Disaster Tweets [Dataset] (2021). https://www.kaggle.com/datasets/vstepanenko/disaster-tweets

LLM's for Spanish Song Text Analysis and Classification Using Language Variants

Omar García-Vázquez, Tania Alcántara[(✉)], Hiram Calvo, and Grigori Sidorov

Centro de Investigación en Computación, Instituto Politécnico Nacional, Mexico City, Mexico
{talcantaram2020,hcalvo,sidorov}@cic.ipn.mx

Abstract. Feelings are the affective state of mind, which are produced in the brain and are caused by an emotion. This feelings have been transferred in multiple ways, such as texts, paintings music. Music transmits different emotions, which makes it even more important to know what kind of feelings are found within a song, which can be, among many others, positive, negative or neutral. Through this work, the texts of two different datasets of songs in the Spanish language were analyzed and classified, this through BERT, RoBERTa and DistilBERT. These experiments showed an improvement compared with previous works and improvement with the use of these methods.

Keywords: Classification · BERT · RoBERTa · DistilBERT · Natural Language Processing · LLM's · Songs

1 Introduction

Feelings are a capacity that human beings have, this through a combination of biological, social, cultural and above all neural factors. Neurobiology says that the brain triggers responses according to the interpretation of stimuli and cultural learning, in addition to cognitive processes. As people grow, this ability to feel and transmit feelings to different areas develops, not only in people, but in poems, texts and nowadys in songs.

Music is capable of activating emotional areas and even evoking memories, through rhythmic scores. But the rhythm is not the only conduit of emotions, but the texts and those words that the authors use to express sadness, happiness or emotions. The classification of this type of emotions can be done through PLN [1].

This search for emotions in sentences is not a simple matter, since they are usually subjective sentences, which state facts, because opinions and feelings are inherently subjective. In addition to this subjectivity, we are faced with language variants, since there are differences in the words in the Spanish spoken in Mexico or the one spoken in Chile or Spain.

H. Calvo et al. (Eds.): MICAI 2023, LNAI 14392, pp. 118–127, 2024.
https://doi.org/10.1007/978-3-031-47640-2_10

During this work we carried out an analysis of sentiments in song texts, working with two different datasets in Spanish: One with mixed Spanish and the other with Mexican Spanish, created specifically for this work and performing the behavioral comparison of sentiments and language, this through LLM's methods.

2   Motivation and Theoretical Concepts

Sentiment analysis is a topic that has been on the rise, especially with the rise of GPT [2], but there hasn't really been an emphasis on determining some language differences. Focusing on the Spanish language, on the lexicon between countries that speak this language. However, there are perceptible linguistic differences by hearing and writing, especially between the regions of Spain and Latin America.

The Spanish-American part has the greatest richness in terms of variants of the Spanish language, arising from contact between indigenous populations and existing idioms. Derived from the above, when analyzing the datasets, it was noticed that there are variants in terms of the results of the classification for two datasets.

Different emotions can be extracted, but the most classic are positive, negative or neutral [3]. The way to approach sentiment analysis has several approaches, but during this work we will focus on a classic approach to compare its performance with the two datasets.

Another important point regarding these datasets is the language in which they were written, Spanish, and for which it is interesting to test the large language models that were trained with large amounts of data and include the Spanish language and those multilanguage models that were made for this purpose.

2.1   Large Language Models

Large Language Models (LLM) are natural language processing models based on the [4] transformer architecture. LLM's are trained with large amounts of information, with the goal that they memorize the context and know the type of information due to the sequence of words.

Speaking of specific language models, BERT or Pre-training of Deep Bidirectional Transformers for Language Understanding is a pre-trained model developed by google [5]. BERT was trained with large amounts of data, and its main function is to capture contextual relationships between words in a long text or a simple paragraph. The difference of BERT with other language models is the full context of both directions, since it goes from left to right and from right to left, it adapts to different languages and domains. On the other hand, BERT multilanguage or multilingual, is an extension of the original model, to train various languages [6].

Multilanguage models offer several advantages [6]:

- **Resource Efficiency:** It is designed to work with a wide variety of languages, rather than having a separate model for each language.

- **Language Representations:** Share knowledge between the languages that was trained and take advantage of it to improve the performance in another language.
- **Better performance:** The performance may vary depending on the language being used.
- **Mixed Set:** Mental representations of various languages help learn patterns and linguistic structures unique to each language.

One of the most popular multilanguage models is BERT, which is a pre-trained model in 102 languages [5]. The multilanguage BERT model contains the same principles as BERT, in broad strokes the model concatenates two sentences to learn the language structure, so it has to predict whether the two sentences were following each other or not. In this way, the model learns an internal representation of the English language.

Finally, we find the DistilBERT model, this model is a "distilled" version of the BERT multilingual model. This model is capable of making differences between English and other languages. The model has 6 layers, 768 dimensions and 12 heads, totaling 134 million parameters. On average, DistilmBERT is twice as fast as BERT-base.

3   State of the Art

There are multiple works around the classification of feelings. In [7] a polarity classification is proposed, with a set of Thai songs, based purely on the text of the songs. They propose the use of a lexicon and the use of traditional machine learning techniques. Of the different parts of a song (title, verses, chorus, pre-chorus, chorus and bridge) where it was only decided to use the chorus and the verses as corpus, since it is thought that these two parts are where there is more probability that the theme of the song will be found.

In the case of [8], three genres were used as tags (inspirational, funny and romantic) in order to use association mining on the training data and find out which tag the keywords in the song text belong to. After this task, the Naive Bayes model was used to calculate probability. They find a maximization of the probability of observing the words that were actually found in the example texts, thus improving the usual independence of Naive Bayes.

For [9] an ontology called *SentiWordNet* was used, which includes scores related to the positive or negative aspects of words. The ontology was used for the extraction of characteristics of feelings, all this in the texts of songs, to find the mood to which these songs belong. The experiments were developed in a corpus of 185 songs and three different classification algorithms were used; Naive Bayes, *K-Nearest Neighbor* and Support Vector Machines (SVMs *Support Vector Machine*).

[10] compares the performance of some *Word embedding* models, previously trained on song lyrics analysis and movie review polarity tasks. The results show that *tweets* are the best for song lyrics analysis, while Google *News* and

Common Crawl are the best for movie analysis, since the vocabulary that used in these portals is very similar in both cases. Models trained with GLoVe slightly outperform those trained with Skip-grams.

On the other hand, it was found that there are combinations of models that are not commonly used for classification, such as CNN [11]. This model combines CNN and bidirectional LSTM networks to capture relevant text features at different levels. These experiments performed on different sets demonstrated an *accuracy* of 90.66%

In relation to the dataset in question, the work presented in reference [12] stands out, where conventional approaches to feature extraction were used, which were combined with the use of CNN and RNN to capture relevant aspects. Experiments conducted in this context revealed remarkable results, with an accuracy of 80.1% achieved by using the recurrent neural network (RNN), while the convolutional neural network (CNN) demonstrated a performance of 78.1%.

This study addresses how the fusion of traditional feature extraction techniques with more modern approaches, such as CNN and RNN, can lead to promising results in the classification task. The significant precision obtained using these methodologies highlights the effectiveness of these hybrid combinations for analyzing and categorizing texts. These findings underline the importance of methodological innovation to improve the capacity of analysis and classification in contexts related to artistic expressions and beyond.

4   Datasets

The first dataset, called ***Textos de Canciones en Español*** [13], is a private PLN corpus developed at the Natural Language Processing Laboratory of the Center for Computing Research of the National Polytechnic Institute[1].

The set is made up of 91 songs, all written in the Spanish language without discrimination, that is, it has variants of Spanish from Latin America and Spain, with varied rhythms (bachata, pop, ballad, among others).

Each song was sectioned into small paragraphs manually, following a sense of the sentence, that is, there are no incomplete ideas or sentences that end in stop words, which gives a total of 1,477 data.

For song tagging, a method developed by the authors of the ensemble was used. For the labeling, 3 main emotions were considered: S, neutral; P, positive; N, negatives. The Table 1 represents the distribution of the dataset, it can be noted that it is an unbalanced set.

For this work, the dataset was divided into **80%** for training and **20%** for validation.

The second dataset, called **Song Texts in Mexican Spanish** [14], is a private corpus developed for this work. The set is made up of 200 songs, all written in the Spanish language with the Mexican Spanish variant, with the genres of *banda, pop, regional mexicano, rock* and *cumbia*. Each song was sectioned into

---

[1] **Textos de Canciones en Español**, to consult or ask for access, contact sidovor@cic.ipn.mx.

Table 1. Distribution of the corpus Texts of Songs in Spanish, Dataset 1 [13]

Feeling	No. Sentences	Percentage
S	97	6.67%
P	780	52.80%
N	600	40.53%

small paragraphs manually, following a sense of the sentence, that is, there are no incomplete ideas or sentences that end in stop words, which gives a total of 4,555[2].

For the labeling, 3 main emotions were considered: S, neutral; P, positive; N, negatives. The Table 2 represents the distribution of the dataset.

Table 2. Distribution of the Texts of Songs in Mexican Spanish corpus, Dataset 2 [14].

Feeling	No. Sentences	Percentage
S	1574	34.56%
P	1368	30.03%
N	1613	35.41%

For this work, the dataset was divided into **80%** for training and **20%** for validation.

5   Solution Proposal

5.1   Preprocessing

To obtain the best results, it is necessary to prepare the data of a text with the classic mechanisms of data preprocessing, for example:

– **Removal:**
    1. Spell check.
    2. Stop words.
    3. Slashes and backslashes.
    4. Numbers.
    5. Line breaks.
    6. Parentheses.
    7. Double blank spaces.

---

[2] **Song Texts in Mexican Spanish**, to consult or access it, write to talcantaram2020@cic.ipn.mx.

After the initial preprocessing, a preprocessing oriented to the architecture of the LLM's must be carried out.

As the first phase of this preprocessing, BERT's own tokenization is performed, where the necessary tokens are added for the model to process the song fragments and as a second phase, the labels are transformed from their numerical form to a form that the model understands. Since this work is oriented to large language models, no additional preprocessing was necessary, since what is intended is that the model can infer the context that is being presented.

5.2   Classification

The models used for this task were the following:

1. BERT-base-multilingual-cased
2. RoBERTa-base
3. DistilBERT-base-multilingual -cased

Since 2 datasets collected and constituted in different ways are being analyzed, a different maximum phrase length must be considered for each case. For dataset 1, a sentence length of no more than 300 characters was taken, while dataset 2 must have a length of no more than 150 characters.

5.3   BERT-Base-Cased

As the second model, the base version of multilingual BERT was chosen, taking into account capital letters, since excellent performance of this model has been demonstrated. Some of the hyperparameters described in the previous model are preserved, since they worked correctly. A learning rate was defined that takes as a minimum value a number widely practiced in the state of the art, but with the difference that this value changes with each era, adjusting according to an update itinerary. A batch size of 36 elements was defined, the validation batch size will be 36 elements.

The Table 3 shows the hyperparameters that were modified for this model in the two datasets.

Table 3. Modified hyperparameters proposed for the BERT LLM

Hyperparameters	Value dataset 1	Value dataset 2
Maximum sentence length	300	150
Minimum learning rate	0.00004	0.00005
Batch size	36	36
Evaluation Batch size	36	36

5.4   RoBERTa-Base

Since this model is a modification of BERT where the pre-training phase of the phrase was removed and it was trained with mini batches and different learning rates, it is of great help to the classification of the dataset as it is equally separated by small batches of information.

As part of the hyperparameters, a learning rate was defined that as the epochs progressed, this rate would change its value to try to mitigate the problem of local minima. A batch size of 24 elements was defined since, according to the literature and the processing capacity of the equipment where the tests were carried out, it is the best option, since if a smaller value were chosen, there would be a much higher probability that it would not be arrived at a real generalization.

In the same way, the same value was defined for the validation batch size, since for this type of model will react positively. The Table 4 shows the hyperparameters that were modified for this model based on both datasets.

Table 4. Modified hyperparameters proposed for the RoBERTa LLM

Hyperparameters	Value dataset 1	Value dataset 2
Maximum sentence length	300	150
Minimum learning rate	0.00004	0.00005
Batch size	24	24
Evaluation Batch size	24	24

5.5   DistilBERT-Base-Multilingual-Cased

As the last model, the base version was chosen, taking into account capitalization of the multilingual DistilBERT model, where what is intended is to be a lighter, faster version of BERT, thus obtaining accurate predictions using a limited amount of resources.

The Table 5 shows the hyperparameters that were modified for this model in the two datasets.

Table 5. Modified hyperparameters proposed for the DistilBERT LLM

Hyperparameters	Value Dataset1	Value Dataset2
Maximum sentence length	300	150
Minimum learning rate	0.00004	0.00005
Batch size	48	48
Evaluation Batch size	48	48

6   Results

The results obtained with the datasets in the BERT, RoBERTa and DistilBERT models can be seen in the table. In Table 6, for the accuracy metric in validation A.

Table 6. BERT, RoBERTa and DistilBERT results for the Accuracy, F1 and precision metrics

| Models/Datasets | Metrics | | | | | |
| | Accuracy | | F1 | | Precision | |
	Dataset 1	Dataset 2	Dataset 1	Dataset 2	Dataset 1	Dataset 2
BERT	95.58%	92.35%	94.68%	91.26%	93.03%	90.42%
RoBERTa	95.66%	92.29%	94.99%	91.72%	93.29%	90.60%
DistilBERT	95.83%	92.63%	95.08%	91.53%	93.68%	90.23%

It is important to mention that the comparison cannot be 100% direct, since the state of the art, nor the proposal in this article, use the same dataset, but it is important to highlight the average results in similar tasks, and thus determine a improvement in future work. The Table 7 shows the comparison of the results obtained with the state of the art.

Table 7. Comparative table of the state of the art and results obtained.

Clasificador	Accuracy
RoBERTa Dataset1	**95.66%**
BERT Dataset1	**95.58%**
DistilBERT Dataset1	**95.83%**
RoBERTa Dataset2	**92.29%**
BERT Dataset2	**92.35%**
DistilBERT Dataset2	**92.36%**
CNN-BiLSTM [11]	90.66%
Genre Classification [8]	85%
RNN-SentimentSongs [12]	80.1%
CNN-SentimentSongs [12]	78.4%
SentiWordNet 2 [9]	71%
SentiWordNet 1 [9]	69%
Thai Songs [7]	62%
QWE [10]	61%

7   Conclusions and Future Work

In this article, the analysis and automatic classification of song texts in their Spanish language variants was presented through BERT Multilenguaje, RoBERTa and DistilBERT Multilenguaje, which are very similar to each other.

As can be seen, the models that were trained with datasets with Spanish language, such as RoBERTa, generate good results and quite competitive as those obtained with multilanguage models, such as BERT and DestilBERT. In addition to this, it was possible to observe that the use of LLM's is a great tool, which allows the model to identify the context that determines the polarity of the fragment.

It can be seen that dataset one obtained better results than dataset two, this despite the fact that it was more unbalanced and dataset one provides us with a greater amount of data, this is due to the fact that the sentences were longer and that helped the models better determine the context.

Another important point is the pre-processing of the data, but this can be achieved thanks to the analysis prior to the classification, superior results are obtained than without it, in addition to the generalization of the models.

This work shows us that "attention" is a fundamental issue in this type of work, and, although the old models do not work badly, the models that have been pretrained generalize better.

As future work, it is necessary to continue working on the comprehension of the texts, and to improve the paragraphs of the dataset.

References

1. Poria, S., Cambria, E., Hazarika, D., Majumder, N., Zadeh, A., Morency, L.P.: Context-dependent sentiment analysis in user-generated videos. In: Proceedings of the 55th Annual Meeting of the Association for Computational Linguistics (Volume 1: Long Papers), pp. 873–883. Association for Computational Linguistics (2017). https://doi.org/10.18653/v1/P17-1081
2. Radford, A., Wu, J., Child, R., Luan, D., Amodei, D., Sutskever, I.: Language models are unsupervised multitask learners. OpenAI blog 1(8), 9 (2019)
3. Xue, B., Zhang, M., Browne, W.N., Gao, J.: Sentiment analysis and opinion mining. WIREs Data Min. Knowl. Discovery 10(4), e1370 (2020). https://doi.org/10.1002/widm.1370
4. Vaswani, A., et al.: Attention is all you need. In: Proceedings of the 31st International Conference on Neural Information Processing System, pp. 6000–6010 (2017)
5. Devlin, J., Chang, M.W., Lee, K., Toutanova, K.: BERT: pre-training of deep bidirectional transformers for language understanding. arXiv preprint arXiv:1810.04805 (2018)
6. Pires, T., Schlinger, E., Garrette, D.: How multilingual is multilingual BERT?. arXiv preprint arXiv:1906.01502 (2019)
7. Srinilta, C., Sunhem, W., Tungjitnob, S., Thasanthiah, S.: Lyric-based sentiment polarity classification of Thai songs. In: Proceedings of the International Multi Conference of Engineers and Computer Scientists, vol. 1 (2017)

8. Giras, A., Advirkar, A., Patil, C., Khadpe, D., Pokhare, A.: Lyrics Based Song Genre Classification. Journal of Computing Technologies, 3. Recuperado de (2014). http://jctjournals.com/feb2014/v4.pdf

9. Kumar, V., Minz, S.: Mood classification of lyrics using SentiWordNet. In: 2013 International Conference on Computer Communication and Informatics, pp. 1–5 (2013). https://doi.org/10.1109/ICCCI.2013.6466307

10. Çano, E., Morisio, M.: Quality of Word Embeddings on Sentiment Analysis Tasks. CoRR, abs/2003.03264. Recuperado de https://arxiv.org/abs/2003.03264 (2020)

11. Pham, V.Q., Nguyen, D.T., Nguyen, T.H.: CNN-BiLSTM model for document-level sentiment analysis. J. Inf. Telecommun. 1(3), 832–847 (2020)

12. Omar, G.V.: Análisis automático de sentimientos en textos de canciones, Repositorio Dspace (2022). http://tesis.ipn.mx/handle/123456789/30409

13. Sidorov, G.: Corpus Textos de Canciones en español. Laboratorio de Procesamiento de Lenguaje Natural, Centro de Investigación en Computación (2019)

14. Alcántara, T., Desiderio, A., García-Vázquez, O., Calvo, H.: Corpus Textos de Canciones en español mexicano, Laboratorio de Ciencias Cognitivas Computacionales, Centro de Investigación en Computación. T (2023)

Bioinformatics and Medical Applications

Boosting Kidney Stone Identification in Endoscopic Images Using Two-Step Transfer Learning

Francisco Lopez-Tiro[1,5], Daniel Flores-Araiza[1], Juan Pablo Betancur-Rengifo[4], Ivan Reyes-Amezcua[3], Jacques Hubert[2], Gilberto Ochoa-Ruiz[4(✉)], and Christian Daul[5(✉)]

[1] Tecnologico de Monterrey, School of Engineering and Sciences, Monterrey, Mexico
[2] CHU Nancy, Service d'urologie de Brabois, 54511 Nancy, France
[3] CINVESTAV Unidad Guadalajara, Zapopan, Mexico
[4] Erasmus Mundus Master in Medical Imaging and Applications (MAIA), Université de Bourgogne, Dijon, France
gilberto.ochoa@tec.mx
[5] CRAN (UMR 7039), Université de Lorraine and CNRS, 2 avenue de la Forêt de Haye, 54518 Vandœuvre-lès-Nancy cedex, France
christian.daul@univ-lorraine.fr

Abstract. Knowing the cause of kidney stone formation is crucial to establish treatments that prevent recurrence. There are currently different approaches for determining the kidney stone type. However, the reference ex-vivo identification procedure can take up to several weeks, while an in-vivo visual recognition requires highly trained specialists. Machine learning models have been developed to provide urologists with an automated classification of kidney stones during an ureteroscopy; however, there is a general lack in terms of quality of the training data and methods. In this work, a two-step transfer learning approach is used to train the kidney stone classifier. The proposed approach transfers knowledge learned on a set of images of kidney stones acquired with a CCD camera to a final model that classifies images from endoscopic images. The results show that learning features from different domains with similar information helps to improve the performance of a model that performs classification in real conditions (for instance, uncontrolled lighting conditions and blur). Finally, in comparison to models that are trained from scratch or by initializing ImageNet weights, the obtained results suggest that the two-step approach extracts features improving the identification of kidney stones in endoscopic images.

Keywords: Deep learning · Transfer learning · Endoscopy

1 Introduction

The formation of kidney stones in the urinary tract is a public health issue [1,2]. In industrialized countries, 10% of the population suffers from an episode of kidney stones during their lifetime, and the risk of recurrence increases up to 40% [3,4]. Determining the root cause of kidney stone formation is crucial to avoid relapses through personalized treatments [3,5,6].

© The Author(s), under exclusive license to Springer Nature Switzerland AG 2024
H. Calvo et al. (Eds.): MICAI 2023, LNAI 14392, pp. 131–141, 2024.
https://doi.org/10.1007/978-3-031-47640-2_11

Therefore, different approaches for visually identifying the most common types of kidney stones have been proposed in recent years [7,8]. The Morpho-Constitutional Analysis (MCA) is the reference method for the identification of extracted kidney stones [9]. This ex-vivo procedure consists of two complementary analyses on the extracted kidney stones, which were fragmented with a laser. The fragments are visually inspected under a microscope to observe the colors and textures of their surface and section. Then, an infrared-spectrophotometry analysis enables to identify the molecular composition of the kidney stone [10]. However, the MCA results are only available after some weeks. This delay makes it difficult to establish an immediate and appropriate treatment for the patient. To complicate the matters, in modern ureteroscopic procedures, kidney stones are pulverized with a laser during surgery [11]. As a result, the biochemical composition can be altered by the laser during the pulverization, making the MCA procedure challenging in some cases.

Endoscopic Stone Recognition (ESR) is a promising technique to immediately determine the type of kidney stones during the ureteroscopy (i.e., in-vivo recognition). The advantage of ESR is twice: kidney stones can be pulverized instead fragmented, and an appropriate treatment can be immediately defined. ESR is only based on a visual inspection of in-vivo endoscopic images observed on a screen. For trained urologists, ESR results are strongly correlated with those of MCA [12]. However, only a few highly trained experts are nowadays able to recognize the type of kidney stones using only endoscopic images. Moreover, the visual classification by urologists is operator dependent, subjective, and the required experience is long to acquire [13].

Several studies have been proposed to automate ESR [12,14,15]. Deep Learning (DL) based methods led to promising results. However, one of the challenges of these methods is the lack of a large image dataset for the model training. In addition, the similarity of the data distribution is another important factor to obtain a good model. Consequently, this suggests a trade-off between the amount of available data, and the data distribution to fit the network weights adequately. The majority of the DL-based models report fine-tuning of weights learned from distributions other than kidney stone images (i.e.,ImageNet [16]).

Transfer Learning (TL) is used when features learned from a given domain can bring appropriate knowledge to another domain (for which the available image dataset is too small to train a large model from scratch [18,19]). In the context of ureteroscopy, a large dataset of in-vivo images is currently not available, and collecting such a large dataset of endoscopic images during ureteroscopies is a long term work. However, images of ex-vivo kidney stone (acquired with CCD cameras) are available. Due to their similarity in color, texture and morphological features, TL can be used to distill knowledge from CCD-camera images into the final classifier of the images acquired with endoscopes. Based on this idea, a two-step TL model to classify kidney stones is proposed. The model uses a homogeneous, as well as a heterogeneous TL phase using a ResNet50 architecture pre-trained with the ImageNet dataset.

To validate our proposal, the approach transfers knowledge learned on a small dataset of images acquired with CCD cameras to a final model that classifies endoscopic images. The results obtained in this work improve those reported

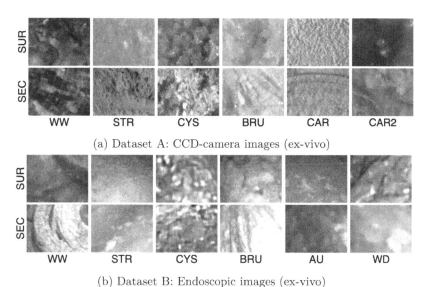

(a) Dataset A: CCD-camera images (ex-vivo)

(b) Dataset B: Endoscopic images (ex-vivo)

Fig. 1. Examples of ex-vivo kidney stone images acquired with (a) a CCD camera [9] and (b) an endoscope [17]. SEC and SUR stand for section and surface views, respectively. The class types (WW, STR, CYS, BRU, AU, and WD) are defined in Table 1.

in the state of the art (up to 10% in surface and section views measured with accuracy) for six classes of kidney stones in endoscopic images.

The rest of this paper is organized as follows. Section 2 provides an overview of the ex-vivo datasets, namely the CCD (digital) camera image and endoscopic image sets. Section 2 also presents the two-step TL approach. Section 3 compares the performances of the two-step TL approach with those of the methods of the literature. Finally, Sect. 4 concludes this contribution and proposes perspectives.

2   Materials and Methods

2.1   Datasets

Two kidney stone datasets were used in our experiments (see Table 1): images were acquired with standard CCD cameras, and endoscopic images with an ureteroscope. The dataset's main characteristics are described below.

Dataset A, [9]. This ex-vivo dataset of 366 CCD camera images (see, Fig. 1a) is split in 209 surface and 157 section images, and contains six different stone types sorted by sub-types denoted by WW (Whewellite, sub-type Ia), CAR (Carbapatite, IVa), CAR2 (Carbapatite, IVa2), STR (Struvite, IVc), BRU (Brushite, IVd), and CYS (Cystine, Va). The fragment images were acquired with a digital camera under controlled lighting conditions and with a uniform background.

Dataset B, [17]. The endoscopic dataset consists of 409 images (Fig. 1b). This dataset includes 246 surface, and 163 section images. Dataset B involves the same classes as dataset A, except that the carbatite stones (sub-types IVa1, and IVa2) are replaced by the weddelite (sub-type IIa) and uric acid (IIIa) classes. The images of dataset B were captured with an endoscope by placing kidney stone fragments in an environment simulating in a realistic way the shape and color or ureters (for more details, see [17]). These images are visually close to in-vivo images since the fragments were acquired with an ureteroscope and by simulating a quite realistic the clinical in-vivo scenes.

Table 1. Description of the two ex-vivo datasets.

Dataset A. *M. Daudon et al.* [9]

Subtype	Main component (Key)	Surface	Section	Total
Ia	Whewellite (WW)	50	74	124
IVa1	Carbapatite (CAR)	18	18	36
IVa2	Carbapatite (CAR2)	36	18	54
IVc	Struvite (STR)	25	19	44
IVd	Brushite (BRU)	43	17	60
Va	Cystine (CYS)	37	11	48
Number of images dataset A		209	157	366

Dataset B. *J. El-Beze et al.* [17]

Subtype	Main component (Key)	Surface	Section	Total
Ia	Whewellite (WW)	62	25	87
IIa	Carbapatite (CAR)	13	12	25
IIIa	Carbapatite (CAR2)	58	50	108
IVc	Struvite (STR)	43	24	67
IVd	Brushite (BRU)	23	4	27
Va	Cystine (CYS)	47	48	95
Number of images dataset B		246	163	409

Due to the small size, and class imbalance of the two datasets, patches were extracted from the images to increase and balance the number of training and testing samples. The two last lines of Figs. 1a and 1b show such patches. As demonstrated in previous works [15,20,21], the use of square patches of appropriate size allows to capture sufficient color and texture information for the classification. In addition, the use of patches instead of full surface and section images allows for augmenting and balancing the datasets. According to [21], a patch size of 256×256 pixels was chosen for the A and B datasets. A patch overlap of at most 20 pixels is set to avoid redundant information inside the image of a same kidney stone fragment. A total of 12,000 patches were extracted, both for dataset A and dataset B (1,000 patches per kidney stone type and view).

The patches of each dataset were "whitened" using the mean m_i and standard deviation σ_i of the color values I_i^w for each RGB channel with $I_i^w = (I_i - m_i)/\sigma_i$,

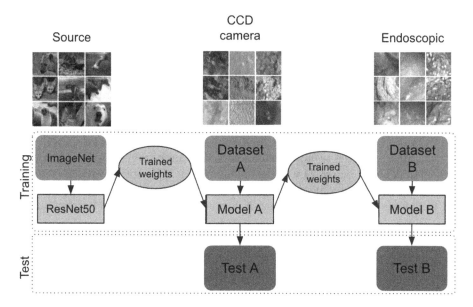

Fig. 2. Two-step TL workflow. Model A was initialized with the weights of a ResNet50 network pre-trained with ImageNet, and fine-tuned with Dataset A. Next, Model B starts with the weights learned from Model A and is finally fine-tuned with Dataset B.

with i = R, G, B. The strategy for partitioning the training and testing set was 80% and 20%, respectively. To avoid data leakage in the datasets, a random, non-repeating dataset partitioning strategy was used (in contrast to previous works that used repeated images in both sets).

2.2   Two-Step Transfer Learning

Depending on the difference between two image domains, TL can be classified into homogeneous and heterogeneous transfer techniques. Homogeneous TL (HoTL) is applicable when specific datasets relating to a particular domain are available, even if the later is only "similar" to the images of the target domain (i.e., the dataset from which the knowledge is transferred does not exactly match the target dataset, but carries similar information). On the other hand, heterogeneous TL (HeTL) is the case where the datasets of the source and target domains differ [18,22]. Furthermore, when a reduced amount of training data is available, it is recommended to initialize the weights of architectures with pre-trained values rather than random values (i.e., TL from the scratch) [18]. Thus, in the first step of the proposed two-step strategy, a large dataset (ImageNet) is used to transfer knowledge into a network (ResNet50) which is fine-tuned by the smaller kidney stone image set acquired under controlled acquisition conditions (dataset A). After this HeTL step, an HoTL is used, this second step exploiting dataset B including endoscopic images close to dataset A, but with more image quality variability as really encountered in ureteroscopy.

First TL Step: HeTL. Figure 2 shows the workflow of the two-step TL process. The first step is the HeTL phase in which the weights are initialized. To do so, a ResNet50 architecture was pre-trained with ImageNet [16], and used to train a model able to classify the six types of kidney stones from dataset A (see Table 1). In this HeTL step, gaussian blur and geometrical transformations are only applied to the training images with the aim of preparing the model for dataset B. A batch size of 24 was used along with a SGD optimizer with a learning rate of 0.001 and momentum of 0.9. Fully connected layers with 768,256,128 and 6 neurons were added with batch-normalization, ReLU, and a dropout of 0.5.

Second TL-Step: HoTL. The HoTL occurs in the second step of the TL-process. It consists in transferring the knowledge (weights) of the trained model from the HeTL into dataset B to differentiate between the six types of kidney stones (see Table 1). The initial weights of model B are those after the fine-tuning of model A with dataset A, model B being finally fine-tuned with dataset B. The purpose of this approach is to improve the generalization performance of model B, and facilitate the extraction of robust features [23]. Geometric transformations were applied to the patches, since the image quality variability in dataset B is naturally high, while this variability is limited in dataset A. Moreover, 30 epochs were also executed with a SGD optimizer, but with a larger learning rate of 0.01 since it was expected that the model had less to learn. However, fully connected layers were not added since the idea was to use the model without further modifications to the architecture.

3   Results and Discussion

Three different experiments were carried out to assess the performance of the two-step TL approach presented in Sect. 2.2 using patch dataset described in Sect. 2.1. The ability of the two-step TL approach (see Fig. 2) to predict kidney stone types on endoscopic and CCD-camera images was evaluated with surface (first experiment), and section patches (second experiment). In the third experiment, based on a "mixed" dataset, the performance of the two-step TL approach was evaluated by simultaneously using surface and section patches. In previous works based on DL [15,20,21] it has been reported that the combination of kidney stone patch types improves the classification process over models trained with only one patch type. Furthermore, mixing patch types closely simulates the way experts perform MCA and ESR [9,10]. The results of our experiments are summarized in Table 2 and discussed below.

Table 2. Mean ± standard deviation determined for each metric quantifying the results for each patch type set (fragment surface patches, section patches, and both patch types mixed) and for various TL strategies after 5 executions. Accuracy, Precision, Recall, and F1-Score were used to measure over six classes the performance of the models for each TL strategy.

Patch type	TL strategy	Accuracy	Precision	Recall	F1-Score	Dataset	Training details
Surface	No TL	0.582 ± 0.033	0.588 ± 0.028	0.582 ± 0.033	0.579 ± 0.028	A	Baseline (no TL) trained on dataset A
	No TL	0.702 ± 0.012	0.718 ± 0.010	0.702 ± 0.012	0.701 ± 0.008	B	Baseline (no TL) trained on dataset B
	HeTL only	0.649 ± 0.050	0.655 ± 0.039	0.649 ± 0.050	0.642 ± 0.046	A	Baseline + TL with ImageNet weights
	HeTL only	0.820 ± 0.033	0.833 ± 0.029	0.820 ± 0.033	0.818 ± 0.032	B	Baseline + TL with ImageNet weights
	HeTL + HoTL	$\mathbf{0.832 \pm 0.012}$	$\mathbf{0.845 \pm 0.012}$	$\mathbf{0.832 \pm 0.012}$	$\mathbf{0.829 \pm 0.012}$	**B**	**Baseline + TL with ImageNet +TL dataset A**
Section	No TL	0.592 ± 0.039	0.627 ± 0.029	0.592 ± 0.039	0.596 ± 0.039	A	Baseline (no TL) trained on dataset A
	No TL	0.738 ± 0.022	0.772 ± 0.015	0.738 ± 0.022	0.722 ± 0.023	B	Baseline (no TL) trained on dataset B
	HeTL only	0.824 ± 0.022	0.834 ± 0.020	0.824 ± 0.022	0.820 ± 0.023	A	Baseline + TL with ImageNet weights
	HeTL only	0.873 ± 0.041	0.897 ± 0.021	0.873 ± 0.041	0.872 ± 0.043	B	Baseline + TL with ImageNet weights
	HeTL + HoTL	$\mathbf{0.904 \pm 0.048}$	$\mathbf{0.915 \pm 0.037}$	$\mathbf{0.904 \pm 0.048}$	$\mathbf{0.903 \pm 0.050}$	**B**	**Baseline + TL with ImageNet +TL dataset A**
Mixed	No TL	0.594 ± 0.021	0.610 ± 0.023	0.594 ± 0.021	0.596 ± 0.020	A	Baseline (no TL) trained on dataset A
	No TL	0.760 ± 0.024	0.773 ± 0.029	0.760 ± 0.024	0.752 ± 0.024	B	Baseline (no TL) trained on dataset B
	HeTL only	0.800 ± 0.013	0.809 ± 0.013	0.800 ± 0.013	0.797 ± 0.013	A	Baseline + TL with ImageNet weights
	HeTL only	0.837 ± 0.032	0.848 ± 0.030	0.837 ± 0.032	0.834 ± 0.035	B	Baseline + TL with ImageNet weights
	HeTL + HoTL	$\mathbf{0.856 \pm 0.001}$	$\mathbf{0.868 \pm 0.002}$	$\mathbf{0.856 \pm 0.001}$	$\mathbf{0.854 \pm 0.001}$	**B**	**Baseline + TL with ImageNet +TL dataset A**

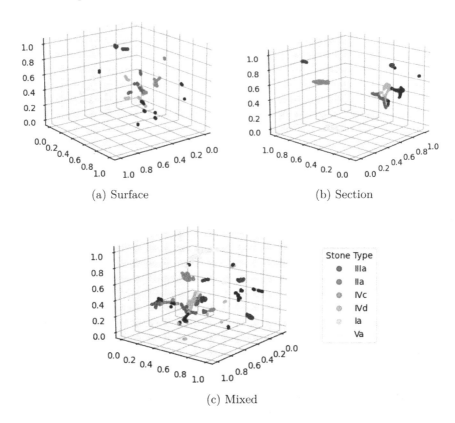

(a) Surface

(b) Section

(c) Mixed

Fig. 3. UMAP-ICN dimensionality feature reduction [24]. (a) Surface, (b) section, and (c) mixed patch sets. The visualizations were generated in the second step of the "HeTL+HoTL" strategy (see Fig. 2).

3.1 Two Step TL-Approach Results

Experiment 1. From the surface patch results, it can be seen that the weights heterogeneously transferred from ResNet50 to model A (the "HeTL only" strategy applied on dataset A, see Table 2) led to an accuracy of 0.649 ± 0.050 that is useful to avoid training the model from scratch (0.582 ± 0.033 for the "No TL" strategy applied on dataset A). Although the performance of "HeTL only" remains low, it is also noticeable that the two-step TL strategy ("HeTL+HoTL") of Fig. 2 improves significantly the identification performance, obtaining an overall accuracy of 0.832 ± 0.012 (18% increase compared the "HeTL only").

Experiment 2. For section patches, the results of "HeTL only" (0.824 ± 0.022) applied on dataset A are promising. This high performance was reached due to the rich textural information in section patches which is not present in surface patches. An accuracy of 0.904 ± 0.048 was obtained for "HeTL+HoTL" applied on dataset B. Although the 8% increase from "HeTL only" to the

Table 3. Comparison of the performance of various kidney stone identification methods. The value of the accuracy over all classes was determined with dataset B for all methods.

Method	Surface	Section	Mixed
Martinez, et al. [20]	0.562 ± 0.233	0.466 ± 0.128	0.527 ± 0.189
Black, et al. [14]	0.735 ± 0.190	0.762 ± 0.185	0.801 ± 0.138
Estrade, et al. [12]	0.737 ± 0.179	0.788 ± 0.106	0.701 ± 0.223
This contribution	$\mathbf{0.832 \pm 0.012}$	$\mathbf{0.904 \pm 0.048}$	$\mathbf{0.856 \pm 0.001}$

"HeTL+HoTL" strategy was smaller for section dataset as for surface patches, this accuracy was the highest one in all three experiments.

Experiment 3. The "HeTL" strategy applied on mixed patches of dataset A, led to an accuracy of 0.8 ± 0.013. This performance in increased by 5% by the "HeTL+HoTL" strategy which has an accuracy of 0.856 ± 0.001. In previous contributions it has been reported that the simultaneous use of surface and section led to the highest performance. This observation is not confirmed here, since the best results were obtained for section patches in experiment 2.

In general, the results obtained for the surface, section and mixed patch sets improve the results obtained from scratch, in the same way as using weights trained with ImageNet. Table 2 shows that, in comparison to a learning from scratch, all TL-strategies improve the values of all four performance criteria, whatever the dataset. The UMAP-ICN visualisation [24] of Fig. 3 represents the features extracted in the last step of the "HeTL+HoTL" strategy. It is visible that for all patch types, the inter-class distance is high and the intra-class distance is weak.

3.2 Comparison with the State-of-the-art

Table 3 details the performance of reference DL-based methods used to identify the type of kidney stones using endoscopic image patches. These methods were [12,14,20] were all implemented and evaluated on dataset B (endoscopic dataset), and compared to the TL-approach described in this contribution. The results demonstrate that the two-step TL model outperforms the solutions described in [12,14,20] in terms of accuracy. Thus, DL-strategies involving a pre-training with a general database, followed by a first tuning with a specific database, and ending with a final tuning with the target database can effectively lead to an improved performance on different data distributions without the need of a large amount of data.

4 Conclusion and Perspective

It was demonstrated that it is possible to classify six different types of kidney stones using a small datasets of endoscopic images, the strategy being first to pre-learn the model with images acquired under controlled acquisition conditions (CCD camera) and then to exploit a fine tuning of the model using images captured in conditions simulating in a realistic way an ureteroscopy. This study confirms that it is easier for a neural network to adjust the weights learned on similar distributions and adapt them to a multiple class task. It is desirable that models of this type should be adapted to identify kidney stones using the complete endoscopic images instead of patches. We believe that the proposed approach will facilitate training on whole-image models when the datasets are reduced in the number of images.

Acknowledgments. The authors wish to acknowledge the Mexican Council for Science and Technology (CONAHCYT) for the support in terms of postgraduate scholarships in this project, and the Data Science Hub at Tecnologico de Monterrey for their support on this project. This work has been supported by Azure Sponsorship credits granted by Microsoft's AI for Good Research Lab through the AI for Health program. The project was also supported by the French-Mexican ANUIES CONAHCYT Ecos Nord grant 322537.

References

1. Hall, P.M.: Nephrolithiasis: treatment, causes, and prevention. Clevel. Clin. J. Med. **76**(10), 583–591 (2009)
2. Kasidas, G.P., Samuell, C.T., Weir, T.B.: Renal stone analysis: why and how? Ann. Clin. Biochem. **41**(2), 91–97 (2004)
3. Kartha, G., Calle, J.C., Marchini, G.S., Monga, M.: Impact of stone disease: chronic kidney disease and quality of life. Urol. Clin. **40**(1), 135–147 (2013)
4. Scales, C.D., Smith, A.C., Hanley, J.M., Saigal, C.S., Urologic Diseases in America Project, et al.: Prevalence of kidney stones in the United States. Eur. Urol. **62**(1), 160–165 (2012)
5. Friedlander, J.I., Antonelli, J.A., Pearle, M.S.: Diet: from food to stone. World J. Urol. **33**(2), 179–185 (2014). https://doi.org/10.1007/s00345-014-1344-z
6. Viljoen, A., Chaudhry, R., Bycroft, J.: Renal stones. Ann. Clin. Biochem. **56**(1), 15–27 (2019)
7. Daudon, M., Jungers, P.: Clinical value of crystalluria and quantitative morpho-constitutional analysis of urinary calculi. Nephron Physiol. **98**(2), 31-p36 (2004)
8. Estrade, V., Daudon, M., Traxer, O., Meria, P.: Why should urologist recognize urinary stone and how? The basis of endoscopic recognition. Prog. Urol. **27**(2), F26–F35 (2017)
9. Corrales, M., Doizi, S., Barghouthy, Y., Traxer, O., Daudon, M.: Classification of stones according to Michel Daudon: a narrative review. Eur. Urol. Focus **7**(1), 13–21 (2021)
10. Daudon, M., et al.: Comprehensive morpho-constitutional analysis of urinary stones improves etiological diagnosis and therapeutic strategy of nephrolithiasis. C. R. Chim. **19**(11–12), 1470–1491 (2016)
11. Keller, E.X., et al.: Fragments and dust after holmium laser lithotripsy with or without "Moses technology": How are they different? (2019)
12. Estrade, V., et al.: Towards automatic recognition of pure and mixed stones using intra-operative endoscopic digital images. BJU Int. **129**(2), 234–242 (2022)

13. Coninck De, V., Keller, E.X., Traxer, O.: Metabolic evaluation: who, when and how often. Curr. Opin. Urol. **29**(1), 52–64 (2019)
14. Black, K.M., Law, H., Aldoukhi, A., Deng, J., Ghani, K.R.: Deep learning computer vision algorithm for detecting kidney stone composition. BJU Int. **125**(6), 920–924 (2020)
15. Lopez, F., et al.: Assessing deep learning methods for the identification of kidney stones in endoscopic images. In: 2021 43rd Annual International Conference of the IEEE Engineering in Medicine & Biology Society (EMBC), pp. 2778–2781. IEEE (2021)
16. Deng, J., Dong, W., Socher, R., Li, L.-J., Li, K., Fei-Fei, L.: ImageNet: a large-scale hierarchical image database. In: 2009 IEEE Conference on Computer Vision and Pattern Recognition, pp. 248–255. IEEE (2009)
17. El Beze, J., et al.: Evaluation and understanding of automated urinary stone recognition methods. BJU Int. **130**(6), 786–798 (2022)
18. Raghu, M., Zhang, C., Kleinberg, J., Bengio, S.: Transfusion: understanding transfer learning for medical imaging. In: Advances in Neural Information Processing Systems, vol. 32 (2019)
19. Wen, Y., et al.: On the effective transfer learning strategy for medical image analysis in deep learning. In: 2020 IEEE International Conference on Bioinformatics and Biomedicine (BIBM), pp. 827–834. IEEE (2020)
20. Martínez, A., et al.: Towards an automated classification method for Ureteroscopic kidney stone images using ensemble learning. In: 2020 42nd Annual International Conference of the IEEE Engineering in Medicine & Biology Society (EMBC), pp. 1936–1939. IEEE (2020)
21. Ochoa-Ruiz, G., et al.: On the in vivo recognition of kidney stones using machine learning. arXiv preprint arXiv:2201.08865 (2022)
22. Zhuang, F., et al.: A comprehensive survey on transfer learning. Proc. IEEE **109**(1), 43–76 (2020)
23. Yosinski, J., Clune, J., Bengio, Y., Lipson, H.: How transferable are features in deep neural networks? In: Advances in Neural Information Processing Systems, vol. 27 (2014)
24. Mendez-Ruiz, M., Garcia, I., Gonzalez-Zapata, J., Ochoa-Ruiz, G., Mendez-Vazquez, A.: Finding significant features for few-shot learning using dimensionality reduction. In: Batyrshin, I., Gelbukh, A., Sidorov, G. (eds.) MICAI 2021. LNCS (LNAI), vol. 13067, pp. 131–142. Springer, Cham (2021). https://doi.org/10.1007/978-3-030-89817-5_10

Automatic Assessment of Canine Trainability Using Heart Rate Responses to Positive and Negative Emotional Stimuli

Cristian A. Ospina-De la Cruz[1], Humberto Pérez-Espinosa[1,2(✉)],
Mariel Urbina-Escalante[3], Verónica Reyes-Meza[3(✉)], and Jorge Ríos-Martínez[4]

[1] CICESE-UT3, Tepic, Nayarit, Mexico
crisalod@cicese.edu.mx
[2] Instituto Nacional, de Astrofísica, Óptica y Electrónica, Tonantzintla, Puebla,
Mexico
humbertop@inaoep.mx
[3] Doctorado En Ciencias Biológicas, Universidad Autónoma de Tlaxcala,
Tlaxcala, Tlaxcala, Mexico
veronica.reyesm@uatx.mx
[4] Universidad Autónoma de Yucatán, Merida, Yucatán, Mexico
jorge.rios@correo.uady.mx

Abstract. Canine trainability is an important characteristic for working and companion dogs, but assessing it accurately is a challenging task. In this study, we propose a novel approach to evaluate canine trainability by measuring their heart rate responses during behavioral trials. We conducted behavioral tests on a group of 10 dogs of the Siberian Husky breed and recorded their heart rates using a wearable sensor Polar OH1. The behavioral trials consisted of eight tests that induced different emotional reactions. We analyzed the heart rate data using statistical and machine learning techniques to identify patterns and correlations with the dogs' performance in the trials. Our results indicate that heart rate responses during behavioral trials are significantly correlated with the dogs' trainability, as measured by the high correlation (0.77 Pearson's correlation index) and the small error (1.54 MAE on a rating scale from 1 to 10) showed by the trained regression model. We conclude that heart rate variability is a useful feature for distinguishing between highly trainable and less trainable dogs. Our approach provides a reliable and non-invasive method for assessing canine trainability, which could be useful for breeders, trainers, and owners in selecting and training dogs.

Keywords: Dog heart rate · dogs trainability · machine learning

1 Introduction

The evaluation of canine trainability is a challenging task, as it often relies on subjective assessments from trainers and handlers and can be influenced by

H. Calvo et al. (Eds.): MICAI 2023, LNAI 14392, pp. 142–156, 2024.
https://doi.org/10.1007/978-3-031-47640-2_12

various environmental and genetic factors [3]. Recent studies have shown that physiological measures, such as heart rate responses, can provide objective and reliable indicators of canine behavior and cognition. Heart rate variability, which reflects the variability of the time between heartbeats, has also been proposed as a useful indicator of cognitive and emotional processes in dogs [1]. The characteristics of heart rate in dogs vary depending on factors such as size, age, and behavior, it can be used as an indicator of a dog's physical condition and cardiovascular health, and can be monitored during exercise and training to ensure the dog's safety and well-being [2].

Heart rate can serve as an indicator of canine trainability, as changes in heart rate can reflect conditioning, fear, anticipation, and pain in dogs [19]. However, the accuracy of heart rate as a measure of canine trainability is not well established. A study aimed at evaluating the accuracy of heart rate measurements using three smartwatch models designed for human use when applied to dogs found that the accuracy of heart rate measurements varied between models [25]. Other factors, such as intelligence, breed, and temperament, can also affect a dog's trainability [15]. There is currently no standardized method for identifying and assessing the trainability of dogs, so researchers have used different approaches and methodologies [13]. Evaluating canine trainability requires a comprehensive approach that considers various factors and uses multiple assessment methods [5]. Emotion induction trials can be used to assess the training ability of dogs. Studies have shown that dogs' emotional states can influence their behavior and performance during training sessions [3].

Some studies have focused on using machine learning techniques to analyze physiological and behavioral data in dogs. For example, a study used machine learning algorithms to identify patterns in the heart rate and movement data of dogs and to predict their responses to different types of stimuli [7]. Another study used a machine learning approach to classify dog barks based on their acoustic features and to identify the emotional states of the dogs [20]. Other studies have also used machine learning to track dog exploratory behavior [21], estimate their posture [4], and recognize dog behavior based on multimodal data [9]. These studies suggest that machine learning techniques can be used to analyze physiological and behavioral data in dogs and to gain insights into their responses to different stimuli. More research is required to evaluate the positive affective states associated with training methods.

In this study, we aimed to investigate the relationship between heart rate responses and trainability in dogs using emotion induction trials. Our main objective was to evaluate the heart rate in dogs subjected to positive and negative tests. We hypothesized that HR would increase by 5 to 30 beats per minute during NP compared to HR taken during PP and that all measurement methods would agree well. Our work encompasses five key components: (1) the development of a robust data collection protocol, (2) the application of the protocol and systematic organization of information, (3) preprocessing and thorough data cleaning, (4) characterization of heart rate, and (5) training of a model to capture the nuanced relationship between heart rate and trainability. In general, our approach provides a promising method for assessing canine trainability using physiological measures and highlights the potential of statistical and machine-learning techniques to improve our understanding of canine behavior and cognition. These data are available for research purposes upon request from the authors.

2   Methodology

We propose a method for assessing the trainability of dogs based on the analysis of their heart rates during negative and positive tests. It is consistent with studies where heart rate is used to assess emotional arousal [22] in many different animal species in diverse contexts, for example, to study social interaction or to quantify the activation of the physiological stress response for animal welfare. Regarding human emotion recognition based on heart rate signals our approach is similar to the proposal of [12] where a small heart rate sensor was placed on the underwear of volunteer pregnant women who reported their feelings via a smartphone application. Machine learning algorithms were employed to predict four different emotions from heart rate variability features. Also in [18] ML algorithms predicted three emotional states (happy, sad, and neutral). Heart rate was collected by using a smart bracelet while the user was watching videos aimed to induce corresponding emotions. By contrast, recent methods in machine learning-based human activity recognition [10] which include heart rate as a feature are not using it alone but combined with inertial sensors. Also, ECG seems to be more precise in estimating heart rate than PPG (like POLAR OH1). The method comprises four main steps (see Fig. 1) dataset generation, pre-processing, feature extraction, and automatic modeling of trainability. For the training process, labels assigned by an expert were used, based on the 4 criteria evaluated in the official certifications: obedience, emotional stability, independence and motivation to play [11]. The data were prepared and transformed into a suitable format during the preprocessing step. The heart rates were recorded and stored in the database for each test, followed by sampling. In the characterization step, the heart rate signal was processed to extract the most relevant characteristics for each specific task. Subsequently, in the modeling step, a model was trained for each regression task, with careful selection of optimal hyperparameters for training.

2.1   Development of the Protocol for Dataset Generation

Although there are some tasks for dog evaluation, most of them are designed to evaluate their behavior in general. For our research, we developed a protocol that included the 4 criteria evaluated in the official certifications in positive and negative contexts, which we named Protocol for Testing Canine Behavior and Trainability (PTCBT), drawing upon expertise in neuroethology, canine training, and veterinary medicine. During our tests, all the dogs were exposed to identical situations, at the same time, and were scored by the same observer.

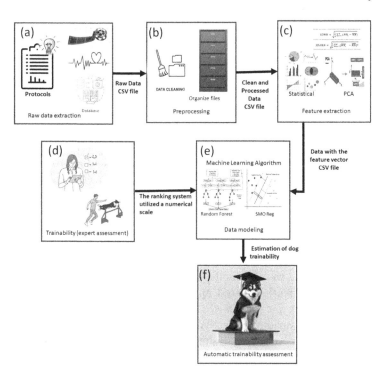

Fig. 1. Flow diagram illustrating the information processing steps in the proposed method

Our PTCBT protocol has adhered to bioethical guidelines to ensure the well-being of the animals involved in scientific research and the ethical aspects in the design and development of artificial intelligence systems, including the privacy of owners.

Materials. In addition to behavioral record formats, we conducted interviews with the owners and caretakers of the dogs. We used 1) Sony HDR-CX405, Sony CX240, and Vixia HF R80 camcorders with their respective tripods. 2) Harmless miniature explosives for children (pop-pop snappers). 3) Novelty Toy (hard plastic rose bone with an included squeaker of 14 cm.) 4) Food rewards (Chicken Tender Prime Nutrition 100 g.) 5) Polar OH1 optical heart rate sensor attached to a belt worn by the dog.

Scenarios. The working area for conducting the positive and negative tests was 5×12 m, excluding the abandonment test that was applied outdoors. At-home activities provided a controlled space to conduct the experiments. Approximately 2.5 m of space was utilized to ensure an adequate distance for carrying out the tasks. The location of the camcorders served as a reference point.

Participant Dogs Selection. We selected a group of 10 adult Siberian Husky dogs, females in anestrus and intact males, ranging from 1 to 6 years of age. The owners of each dog provided their consent for their dogs to participate in the investigation. Siberian Huskies were chosen for their established history in search and rescue operations, as they possess desirable physical traits such as endurance, strength, and the ability to withstand cold temperatures.

2.2   Experimental Procedure

Before data collection, we obtained permission from dog owners to visit their homes. Each test application lasted approximately 5 min. To capture the dog's behavior from multiple perspectives, the tests were recorded using three video cameras positioned at various angles. We placed the Polar OH1 device with a belt attachment mechanism that was designed to be adjustable for dogs of different weights. It was placed on the caudal region of the abdomen, which is an area devoid of hair.

The handler reported that the belt was easy to put on, the device did not change the dog's usual behavior and showed no signs of discomfort.

For each test, a 2-minute recording was initiated prior to the stimulus presentation to capture the dog's habitual behavior. Following this, the stimulus was applied for 1 min and the recording continued for an additional 2 min. This allowed for comprehensive observation of the dog's behavior throughout the test session. The tests were conducted in two stages, with a two-day interval between them. This approach was implemented to minimize the influence of carryover effects or biases that could impact the results. By allowing a sufficient time gap between stages, we aimed to ensure that the dog's responses in each stage were independent and not fully influenced by the previous stage. This design decision contributes to the validity and reliability of the study's findings.

Positive tests

1. Food (AL): The owner put dog food on the floor and actively preventing the dog from eating it. If the dog managed to eat the food despite the owner's efforts, another portion of food was provided. If the dog did not eat the food after one minute, it was given as a reward.
2. Novelty Toy (JN): The owner was provided with a novelty toy to play with their dog for one minute. The owner's goal was to motivate the dog and engage them in the game.
3. Own Toy (JP): The dog was provided with its favorite toy, and the owner was instructed to engage in play for one minute.
4. Caresses (CA): The dog was petted by the owner for 1 minute.

Negative tests

1. Thunder(TR): Six snappers were detonated during a one-minute period, with each spark separated by 10 seconds.
2. Intruder(IN): A designated unfamiliar individual was asked to knock on the door of the house for one minute.
3. Abandonment (AB): The owner tied the dog and left the area, creating a situation where the dog was temporarily placed in a new setting. The test lasted four minutes.
4. Frustration (FR): The owner was instructed to go through the usual behaviors and cues that indicate they are going to take their dog for a walk, but without actually taking the dog outside.

2.3   Ethical Considerations

All experimental procedures were approved by the Institutional Animal Care and Use Committee of the Universidad Autónoma de Tlaxcala they were designed following the guidelines of the Animal Welfare Act.

2.4   Obtained Dataset

After applying our experimental protocol, we gathered both video recordings and a CSV file with recorded heart rate values for each test (see the Fig. 2, we present the raw recorded values of heart rate, showing two example tests: a positive one (Caresses) and a negative one (Abandonment)). In total, we recorded over 160 videos, each with a duration of 4 ± 0.5 min. The heart rate sampling frequency was set at one hertz.

We organized the collected data into 10 directories, one for each dog. Every directory was divided into eight subdirectories: food, novelty toy, own toy, caresses, thunder, intruder, abandonment, and frustration.

Data Preprocessing. During the data cleaning process, we discovered that some heart rate data from the tests were incomplete, as the sensor used failed to capture certain periods. To fill in the gaps we utilized linear interpolation.

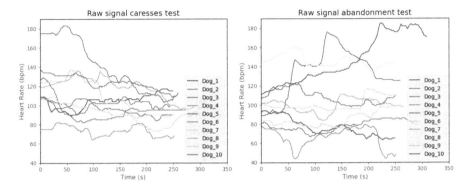

Fig. 2. In this figure, we present the raw recorded values of heart rate, showing two example tests: a positive one (Caresses) and a negative one (Abandonment).

To prevent outliers from affecting the results, we identified and handled them accordingly. The resulting clean dataset was saved in a new directory, while the original data was kept intact. We have named this dataset the Canine Heartbeat Evaluation and Analysis for Reactive Triggers (HEART) corpus. This dataset will be available for research purposes.

Feature Extraction. In order to assess dogs' trainability using heart rate changes during behavioral tests, we must first describe the patterns of heart rate that occur during each test. To capture the relevant information, we designed a set of three time-domain types of attributes.

The first type of attribute involves calculating two statistical indices from the heart rate readings. These indices are the RR intervals (60000/HR), the standard deviation of normal-to-normal intervals (SDNN), and the root mean square of successive differences (RMSSD). These indices have been previously used in works analyzing heart rate variability [23]. The second type of attributes consists of calculating basic elements of statistical analysis, such as mean, median, standard deviation, variance, min, max, and the differences between max and min, as well as the 25%, 50%, and 75% interquartile range. Finally, the third type of attributes involves principal component analysis (PCA) indices [6]. This technique reduces the dimensionality of high-dimensional feature vectors, increasing interpretability while minimizing information loss. In this work, we used PCA as a feature to analyze heart rate rather than using it as the typical dimensionality reduction technique, as is usually done. This decision was based on similar studies [17] in which PCA successfully captured the changes in dimensionality and qualitative echocardiography resulting from an endurance training program with healthy dogs. Before extracting PCA, we applied a Min-max normalization to the completed data. We selected the five components with the highest contribution rates, namely PC1, PC2, PC3, PC4, and PC5.

Our feature set consists of a total of 17 heart rate attributes extracted from each of the behavioral test data. The result is a vector with a length of 8×17 composed of different tests (8) of descriptors (17) of heart rate.

Trainability Score. Trainability was determined by an expert based on the International Search and Rescue Dog Organization criteria [11] (La toya 2017; IRO, 2019) which are: Obedience (ability to follow instructions on the first command), Independence (security and tranquility of the dog when staying away from its owner), Motivation to play (motor activation response to the handler's invitation) and Emotional stability (ability to remain calm despite adverse circumstances). To ensure an accurate assessment of each dog's trainability, a systematic approach was employed. The trainer recorded the latency, frequency, and duration of behaviors such as dog pulling, barking, howling, standing, hopping, running, and wagging, from the videos recorded in every task. Also registered observations encompassing various factors influencing trainability, such as stimuli that hindered the dog's response to correction, as well as the dog's emotional state before, during, and after the correction was applied. These records were intended for later analysis. In order to gather essential information and establish a comprehensive context, the owners underwent interviews prior to the test administration. A considerable duration of approximately 15 d was dedicated to familiarizing the dogs with the testing environment before the beginning of the actual tests. This acclimation period allowed the dogs to become accustomed to the trainer, potentially minimizing confounding factors during the evaluation process. Upon completion of the tests, the 10 dogs were ranked based on their performance. The ranking system followed a numerical scale, with 1 indicating the highest level of trainability and 10 representing the lowest. This ranking system provided a clear indication of the relative trainability among the dogs.

Data Modeling. In order to estimate the trainability score described in Sect. 2.4, we trained a machine learning model using the feature set described in Sect. 2.4. The model takes these features as input and provides an output that estimates the trainability of dogs.

We utilized the software Weka, a collection of machine learning algorithms that supports several tasks including feature selection and regression [24]. To select the most important features for estimating the trainability score, we employed Weka's feature selection functionality. This allowed us to avoid the curse of dimensionality, which refers to the challenges associated with analyzing and organizing data with many attributes but few samples. We found that utilizing seven features provided us with the best results through several trials.

We utilized the training of regression models to find the relationship between the heart rate attributes and the trainability score, which is a numerical variable that ranges from 1 to 10. A value of 1 represents the most trainable dog, while a value of 10 represents the least trainable. In all experiments, we implemented a 10-fold cross-validation scheme due to the limited sample size of the experimental data. This validation scheme is the same as a leave-one-dog-out validation and allows us to avoid biases and overfitting. We utilized the Random Forests and Support Vector Machines algorithms for regression.

Table 1. Dataset statistical information

Test	mean	std	min	Q1	Q2	Q3	max
AB	108.12	21.08	67.00	96.97	107.41	122.04	140.93
AL	106.89	27.52	74.01	79.61	104.82	134.95	140.28
CA	94.82	**12.00**	76.85	84.25	97.41	103.50	**111.71**
FR	108.73	**33.11**	76.82	80.98	96.43	131.28	**162.73**
IN	109.94	30.34	69.03	94.61	102.76	132.08	160.29
JN	98.64	25.60	72.59	77.99	90.76	118.90	138.67
JP	111.70	12.82	96.15	102.79	107.85	116.44	135.31
TR	113.86	25.87	84.32	91.14	109.22	138.46	152.77

Table 2. Most and less correlated tests.

Most correlated tests			Less correlated test		
Test_1	Test_2	r	Test_1	Test_2	r
TR	FR	**0.83**	TR	AL	0.11
AB	IN	**0.77**	AL	IN	0.1
FR	CA	**0.69**	TR	JN	0.09
IN	FR	**0.64**	JP	AB	0.08
TR	CA	0.62	AB	JN	**0.05**
CA	IN	0.56	JN	FR	**0.04**
JN	CA	0.54	JP	JN	**0.03**
AB	TR	0.52	JP	AL	**0.03**

3   Results

We identified the best descriptors by statistical analysis are summarized in Table. 1. We included the mean, standard deviation, min, max, and 25% (Q1), 50% (Q2), and 75% (Q3) interquartile ranges. We can see from the Table. 1 that the means and min values are similar, but there is greater variability in the standard deviation (33.11) and max (162.73) values. In particular, we can see that the FR value makes a difference, as it is highlighted in bold to facilitate its identification. When finding a high standard deviation, it indicates that the data of the heart rate in the FR test have a large variability and dispersion with respect to the mean, suggesting that there is greater excitement and changes in heart rate. We found that in the CA test, its max(111.71) and standard deviation(12.00) are the lowest values in the entire dataset. On the other hand, a low standard deviation indicates that the data is closer to the mean, suggesting that the heart rate remains stable.

We show the Pearson Correlation coefficients (see Table. 2) were used to analyze the relationship between different heart rate variables in dogs for different tests. With all of this, we were able to find and analyze that for each test, the behavior of heart rate is similar in terms of the reaction it generates in dogs. We found that the most correlated pairs of tests seen in Table. 2 are TR-FR (0.83), AB-IN (0.77), FR-CA (0.69), and IN-FR (0.64). Similarly, we identified those with less correlation, which are located in the same aforementioned table, these are: AB-JN (0.05), JN-FR (0.04), JP-JN (0.03), and JP-AL (0.03).

The results of the experiments conducted using the SMO Reg and Random Forest machine learning algorithms are presented in Tables 3 and 4, respectively. As described in Sect. 2.4, the feature vector comprises attributes from the eight tests in which the dog participated. Two approaches were evaluated: training models using all attributes and training models using only the top 7 attributes. The evaluation metrics employed to assess the model quality included Pearson's correlation coefficient (Correlation), mean absolute error (MEA), and root mean squared error (RMSE). Ideally, the best models exhibit a correlation coefficient close to 1, and both error metrics close to zero, given that the dogs are rated on a scale of 1 to 10. Achieving an error of less than one would be considered ideal. Additionally, the analysis was performed considering the information from the eight tests applied to each dog, individual information from each test, and the combined information from the two tests that showed the best results separately.

For both training algorithms, using only the top 7 attributes yielded improved results due to the limited sample size of 10. While good results were obtained by using information from all the tests with both algorithms, the best overall performance was achieved by the SMO Reg algorithm using the best 7 attributes and information solely from two tests, namely Frustration and Play with a novel toy. This configuration produced a correlation coefficient of 0.77, indicating a significant positive correlation between heart rate attributes and dog trainability. The mean absolute error of 1.54 is considered acceptable for assigning a satisfactory trainability rating to a dog. The seven attributes used to obtain the best results were: max Frustration, 75% quartile Frustration, Media Frustration, PCA 5 Novelty toy, PCA 1 Frustration, min Frustration, and 50% quartile Frustration.

4   Discussion

Heart rate is considered a good indicator of emotional response in dogs [16], however, most studies include tasks that induce discomfort, and there are few studies that explore also positive emotions. In this work, we designed an experimental protocol that included both kinds of emotions and we evaluated them

Table 3. Results with SMO Reg

	Using all the attributes			Using the best 7 attributes		
Test	Correlation	MEA	RMSE	CORR	MEA	RMSE
All	−0.28	4.06	4.27	**0.69**	1.86	2.08
AB	−0.74	5.13	6.07	−0.68	4.53	5.38
AL	−0.28	9.54	16.95	0.33	2.75	3.26
CA	0.13	4.08	4.96	0.21	3.04	3.53
FR	**0.75**	1.83	2.18	**0.60**	2.31	2.46
IN	0.26	4.96	6.09	0.09	2.82	3.61
JN	0.51	1.93	2.55	0.40	1.95	2.77
JP	0.39	2.85	3.09	0.43	2.21	2.70
TR	0.36	3.48	4.28	0.46	2.20	2.63
FR + JN	0.62	1.93	2.25	**0.77**	1.54	1.83

Table 4. Results with Random Forest

	Using all the attributes			Using the best 7 attributes		
Test	Correlation	MAE	RMSE	Correlation	MEA	RMSE
All	**0.36**	2.97	3.29	**0.74**	0.79	1.26
AB	−0.92	3.39	3.97	−0.87	3.61	4.04
AL	−0.02	2.84	3.18	0.15	2.74	3.08
CA	−0.07	2.97	3.37	0.17	2.69	3.01
FR	0.16	2.49	3.04	**0.43**	2.15	2.67
IN	−0.20	2.82	3.31	0.15	2.60	3.09
JN	−0.70	3.33	3.86	−0.48	2.93	3.44
JP	−0.36	2.95	3.33	−0.28	4.06	4.27
TR	0.23	2.61	3.09	0.20	3.27	4.03
FR + JP	−0.64	2.87	3.40	**0.47**	2.12	2.56

through repeated recordings. The development and implementation of our proto-col PTCBT (see Sect. 2.1) have been fundamental for the creation of our HEART database, Sect. 2.4. Our dataset contains the record of the cardiac frequencies from eight different tests, providing confidence to this research and opening new possibilities in data collection. The objective of eliciting diverse heart rate responses in positive and negative tests and associating them with trainability was achieved. Even considering that breeding, raising, and training dogs is a long and expensive process that often fails, identifying the most trainable dogs using an objective measure, such as heart rate, will avoid investing resources and reduce the stress caused by training unsuitable dogs [13]

As discussed in Sect. 2.4, the equation $RR = \frac{60000}{HR}$ enabled us to calculate RR intervals, which in turn allowed us to analyze certain characteristics such as SDNN and RMSSD in the time domain. While we successfully obtained these values, their performance did not yield any significant insights for the final results. The POLAR sensor was very helpful because it allowed us to measure and collect heart rate data. However, there were some limitations of the Polar band as it was originally designed for humans it does not have the same accuracy for all sizes of dogs In future studies, we will explore the use of a heart rate monitor band specifically designed for dogs to ensure accurate measurements. It is important to note that certain dogs may find the current Polar band uncomfortable, potentially affecting their heart rate, however, it is worth mentioning that the dogs were given a familiarization period to gradually adapt to the strip band.

The processed data and statistical analysis helped to understand the relation among the tests, we found that the FR, TR, AB, and IN tests provided relevant information. Likewise, we were able to identify tests that had less similarity, such as AB, JN, JP, and AL. With all this information collected and saved, we were able to create a vector with the necessary attributes, including the 8 tests and 17 attributes, as well as adding expert ratings on trainability. All this work has provided a solid methodology for further research.

From the best seven attributes used to obtain the final results, we were able to use five in the statistical analysis. These were: max Frustration, 75% Frustration quartile, Mean Frustration, min Frustration, and 50% Frustration quartile. A great value was placed on the statistical results. The attributes of the calculations were also contributed by PCA 5 "Toy novelty" and PCA 1 "Frustration", which are of great relevance. In the context of data analysis, the results PC1 and PC5 could be the first and fifth principal components respectively, selected to explain the largest amount of variation in the data used in the analysis. This could be explained because the stress associated with frustration has been associated with learning abilities [14]. Furthermore, it has been reported that frustration changes the learning rate during training [8].

It is very important to highlight that the SMO Reg and Random Forest algorithms were the most suitable for this work due to their ability to understand the specific dataset used in the experiments and handle non-linear relationships between input and output variables, which may be present in the attributes. Additionally, it should be noted that there is a risk of overfitting the training data, which could lead to better generalization performance on unseen test data. We obtained a correlation coefficient of 0.77 (from Random Forest), highlighting the importance of two specific tests (FR + JN), indicating a significant positive correlation between heart rate attributes and the dog's training ability. It is also important to note that calculating all samples as well as individual samples provided us with useful control and comparison parameters.

One potential explanation for the strong correlation between heart rate and trainability is that heart rate variability is linked to cognitive flexibility, which is a key component of successful training. Dogs with higher levels of heart rate variability may be better able to adapt to changing situations and learn new tasks, leading to improved performance in training and cognitive tasks. The use of machine learning algorithms allowed us to identify specific heart rate features that were most strongly correlated with trainability, providing more precise and accurate prediction models than traditional statistical methods. The identification of these predictors has important implications for the selection and training of service dogs, as it may be possible to use heart rate measures to identify dogs with high potential for success. However, it is important to note that our study was limited to a small sample size and may not generalize to all dog breeds. Further research is needed to evaluate the effectiveness of heart rate measures in predicting trainability across a broader range of dog populations and to explore the underlying mechanisms of the observed correlations.

Our study provides preliminary evidence that heart rate measures during cooperation induction trials and response time are strong predictors of trainability in dogs, and that machine learning algorithms can be effective in identifying these predictors. This work may inform the development of new training and selection methods for working and service dogs, leading to more successful outcomes in these important roles. We emphasize the importance of interdisciplinary work as the key to success and advancement in the knowledge and solution of theoretical and practical problems.

5   Conclusions

In this study, we evaluated the use of heart rate responses during emotion induction trials to predict trainability in dogs, using statistical and machine learning techniques. Our findings suggest that heart rate variability measured during emotional tests are strong predictors of trainability in dogs, and that machine learning algorithms can be effective in identifying these predictors.

The identification of heart rate features that are most strongly correlated with trainability may inform the development of new training and selection methods for working and service dogs, leading to more successful outcomes in these important roles. However, our study was limited by a small sample size and may not generalize to all dog breeds or populations, highlighting the need for further research in this area.

Overall, this study provides promising preliminary evidence that heart rate responses during emotional trials can be used to estimate trainability in dogs, and that machine learning techniques can provide more accurate prediction models than traditional statistical methods. Further research is needed to explore the underlying mechanisms of these correlations and to evaluate the effectiveness of heart rate variability measures in predicting trainability across a broader range of dog populations.

Acknowledgements. We thank CONAHCYT for funding CF-2019/2275, postdoctoral grant 2815847 and Master's degree grant 1081073. We are deeply grateful to the owners of the dogs who participated in this study, as their willingness to open their homes on multiple occasions made this research possible.

References

1. Abate, S.V.: Animal-assisted therapy for cardiac conditions. In: Animal Assisted Therapy Use Application by Condition, pp. 147–164. Elsevier (2023)
2. Bidoli, E.M., Erhard, M.H., Döring, D.: Heart rate and heart rate variability in school dogs. Appl. Anim. Behav. Sci. **248**, 105574 (2022)
3. Bray, E.E., Otto, C.M., Udell, M.A., Hall, N.J., Johnston, A.M., MacLean, E.L.: Enhancing the selection and performance of working dogs. Front. Vet. Sci. **8**, 430 (2021)
4. Brugarolas, R., Roberts, D., Sherman, B., Bozkurt, A.: Posture estimation for a canine machine interface based training system. In: 2012 Annual International Conference of the IEEE Engineering in Medicine and Biology Society, pp. 4489–4492. IEEE (2012)
5. Vieira de Castro, A.C., Araújo, Â., Fonseca, A., Olsson, I.A.S.: Improving dog training methods: efficacy and efficiency of reward and mixed training methods. Plos one **16**(2), e0247321 (2021)
6. Dandil, E., Polattimur, R.: PCA-based animal classification system. In: 2018 2nd International Symposium on Multidisciplinary Studies and Innovative Technologies (ISMSIT), pp. 1–5. IEEE (2018)
7. Hussain, A., Ali, S., Kim, H.C., et al.: Activity detection for the wellbeing of dogs using wearable sensors based on deep learning. IEEE Access **10**, 53153–53163 (2022)
8. Jakovcevic, A., Elgier, A.M., Mustaca, A.E., Bentosela, M.: Frustration behaviors in domestic dogs. J. Appl. Anim. Welfare Sci. **16**(1), 19–34 (2013)
9. Kim, J., Moon, N.: Dog behavior recognition based on multimodal data from a camera and wearable device. Appl. Sci. **12**(6), 3199 (2022)
10. Kulsoom, F., Narejo, S., Mehmood, Z., Chaudhry, H.N., Butt, A., Bashir, A.K.: A review of machine learning-based human activity recognition for diverse applications. Neural Comput. Appl. **34**(21), 18289–18324 (2022). https://doi.org/10.1007/s00521-022-07665-9
11. La Toya, J.J., Baxter, G.S., Murray, P.J.: Identifying suitable detection dogs. Appl. Anim. Behav. Sci. **195**, 1–7 (2017)
12. Li, X., et al.: Heart rate information-based machine learning prediction of emotions among pregnant women. Front. Psychiatry **12** (2022). https://doi.org/10.3389/fpsyt.2021.799029, https://www.frontiersin.org/articles/10.3389/fpsyt.2021.799029
13. Marcato, M., Kenny, J., O'Riordan, R., O'Mahony, C., O'Flynn, B., Galvin, P.: Assistance dog selection and performance assessment methods using behavioural and physiological tools and devices. Appl. Anim. Behav. Sci. **254**, 105691 (2022)
14. McEwen, B.S., Sapolsky, R.M.: Stress and cognitive function. Curr. Opin. Neurobiol. **5**(2), 205–216 (1995)
15. Moser, A.Y., Brown, W.Y., Bennett, P., Taylor, P.S., Wilson, B., McGreevy, P.: Defining the characteristics of successful biosecurity scent detection dogs. Animals **13**(3), 504 (2023)
16. Palestrini, C., Previde, E.P., Spiezio, C., Verga, M.: Heart rate and behavioural responses of dogs in the Ainsworth's strange situation: a pilot study. Appl. Anim. Behav. Sci. **94**(1–2), 75–88 (2005)
17. Restan, A.Z., et al.: Conditioning program prescribed from the external training load corresponding to the lactate threshold improved cardiac function in healthy dogs. Animals **12**(1), 73 (2021)

18. Shu, L., et al.: Wearable emotion recognition using heart rate data from a smart bracelet. Sensors **20**(3) (2020). https://doi.org/10.3390/s20030718, https://www.mdpi.com/1424-8220/20/3/718

19. Shull, S.A., Rich, S.K., Gillette, R.L., Manfredi, J.M.: Heart rate changes before, during, and after treadmill walking exercise in normal dogs. Front. Vet. Sci. **8**, 202 (2021)

20. Vehkaoja, A.: Description of movement sensor dataset for dog behavior classification. Data Brief **40**, 107822 (2022)

21. Völter, C.J., Starić, D., Huber, L.: Using machine learning to track dogs' exploratory behaviour in the presence and absence of their caregiver. Anim. Behav. **197**, 97–111 (2023)

22. Wascher, C.A.F.: Heart rate as a measure of emotional arousal in evolutionary biology. Philos. Trans. R. Soc. B: Biological Sciences **376**(1831), 20200479 (2021). https://doi.org/10.1098/rstb.2020.0479, https://royalsocietypublishing.org/doi/abs/10.1098/rstb.2020.0479

23. Wess, L., et al.: Effect of cooperative care training on physiological parameters and compliance in dogs undergoing a veterinary examination-a pilot study. Appl. Anim. Behav. Sci. **250**, 105615 (2022)

24. Witten, I.H., Frank, E.: Data mining: practical machine learning tools and techniques with java implementations. ACM SIGMOD Rec. **31**(1), 76–77 (2002)

25. Yanmaz, L.E., Okur, S., Ersoz, U., Senocak, M.G., Turgut, F.: Accuracy of heart rate measurements of three smartwatch models in dogs. Top. Companion Anim. Med. **49**, 100654 (2022)

LSTM-Based Infected Mosquitos Detection Using Wingbeat Sound

Marco Haro[1], Mariko Nakano[1]([✉]), Israel Torres[1], Mario Gonzalez[2], and Jorge Cime[3]

[1] Instituto Politecnico Nacional, 04420 Mexico City, Mexico
mnakano@ipn.mx
[2] Universidad Veracruzana, Poza Rica, Veracruz, Mexico
[3] Instituto Nacional de Salud Publica, Cuernavaca, Morelos, Mexico

Abstract. Dengue fever is one of the most important mosquito-borne disease in the world. To avoid its spread, it is necessary to detect accurately and quickly the infected Aedes mosquitoes and eliminate them. Under the hypothesis of the change of behaviors of the mosquitoes when they are infected by dengue virus, we proposed a discrimination scheme of the infected mosquitoes from the healthy ones using their wingbeat signal. We constructed acoustic chamber in which a condense and omni-directional microphone capture sthe wingbeat signal as clear as possible under the noisy environment. The proposed scheme is based on Long-Short Term Memory (LSTM) neural networks with two LSTM layers and two Fully-Connected (FC) layers. Time-frequency representation of wingbeat signal is used as input data. We identified the Spectogram, among several time-frequency representations, as the best input data for this task. Some hyperparameters of LSTM-based proposed system are adjusted after several trials. The discrimination accuracy obtained by the proposed scheme is approximately 89.35%, which is 5% better than the previously proposed method based on machine learning techniques such as K-Nearest Neighbor (KNN) and Support Vector Machine (SVM).

Keywords: Infected Mosquitos · Dengue fever · Wingbeat Sound · LSTM · STFT · Spectral Analysis · Acoustic Camera

1 Introduction

Dengue fever is one of the mosquito-borne diseases caused by the arbovirus transmitted from, mainly, Aedes aegypti (Ae. aegypti) mosquito to human. According to the report of the Centers for Disease Control and Prevention (CDC), approximately four billion peoples, which is almost half of the whole population of the world, are at risk of contracting dengue fever [1]. It causes approximately 90% of the cases of arbovirus in the last ten years according to the report of the Pan-American Health Organization [2]. A dangerous variant is the dengue hemorrhagic since the ill people may die, in this case the mortality rate is 2–5%

if the patients receive an adequate treatment. If patient of dengue hemorrhagic not receive any treatment, the mortality rate is up to 20%.

Fumigation by spraying pesticides is the current strategy to mitigate the spread of dengue. However, it causes irreversible environmental pollution and creates an economic burden on local governments. If an accurate detection of infected mosquitos by dengue fever virus can be done, meaningful and efficient vector control can be performed, avoiding further transmission of dengue fever.

Some scientists reported the behavior change of the infected mosquitos compared with the behavior of uninfected mosquitos. For example, Xiang et al. observed that the infected female Aedes mosquitos bite more frequently to get the same amount of blood as uninfected mosquitos [3,4]. This behavior change causes further propagation of the dengue fever due to increase number of bites. Also, in [5], authors documented the increase of the locomotor activity of the infected mosquitos. These observations about the changes of the infected mosquito's behavior provides a hypothesis about the change of flight forms. And by analyzing mosquito wingbeat sounds, it may be possible to accurately detect infected mosquitoes.

To date, mosquito's wingbeat sound has been used mainly to classify the mosquito's genera or mosquito's species [6–8] as vector surveillance task. In [6], mosquito's wingbeats of six different species are captured by opt-electronics devices. Two of these six species belong to Aedes mosquitos which are Ae. aegypti and Ae. albopictus. Other two species belong to Anopheles, An. arabiensis and An. gambiae, the rest two species belong to Culex, being C. pipiens and C. quinquefaciatus. The authors of [5] created a database with a large amount of wingbeat data and publicly provides it. Also, they performed classification using several Convolutional Neural Networks (CNNs), such as VGG, ResNet, Inception, among others. Authors of [7] proposed Mosquito's genera classification using lightweight neural networks based on Long-Short Term Memory (LSTM) for portable installation purpose. The work reported in [8] classifies mosquito's species by obtaining wingbeat sounds by smartphones for the purpose of population monitoring of different species of mosquitos.

Under the hypothesis mentioned above, in [9] we proposed infected mosquito's discrimination algorithm using several spectral analysis methods. We extracted 15 spectral features using spectral analysis, such as spectral Rolloff, Spectral Centroid, Spectral Spread, Spectral Contrast, Spectral Flux, Spectral Flatness and Spectral Slop, from spectrogram of wingbeat sounds. Well-known classifiers such as Support Vector Machines (SVM), K Nearest Neighbor (KNN) and Logistic Regression were used for discrimination. The best detection accuracy 84.32% is provided by the KNN classifier with K is equal to 3 [9].

In this paper we propose a scheme to discriminate infected mosquitos from healthy ones. The main contributions of this work are:

- We propose a LSTM-based scheme to discriminate infected mosquitos from healthy ones.
- We report a methodology to construct an acoustic chamber to eliminate several types of noise, such as voice and environmental noise.

– We compared the proposed scheme against other schemes to assess its performance.

The proposed scheme achieves a higher discrimination performance than the best detection accuracy obtained by machine learning techniques reported by [9].

The rest of this paper is organized as follows: In Sect. 2, we provide the design of the acoustic chamber used for recording of mosquito's wingbeat sound together with description of generated database. The proposed LSTM-based discriminator of infected mosquitos is described in Sect. 2.2. We provide experimental results in Sect. 3, and finally we conclude this paper in Sect. 4.

2   Acoustic Chamber Design and Database Construction

In this section, we describe an acoustic chamber used for wingbeat sound recording, which designed ourselves, the conditions of female Ae. aegypti mosquitos used in the experiment, such as age and days after infection as well as environment condition such as temperature, humidity, and environmental noise. Additionally, we provide description of wingbeat sound database.

Acoustic Chamber. We constructed an acoustic chamber using materials that blocks the external noise to capture wingbeat signal of mosquitos as clear as possible. Figure 1 shows the acoustic chamber. It has an omnidirectional microphone, which introduce from small hole of chamber. The chamber has two holes, one is in the top of the chamber, and another is in left side of the chamber. If we use the top hole for microphone, the side hole is used to insert and extract a mosquito. The size of acoustic chamber is as follows: lower width. upper width, height and depth are 24 cm, 19 cm, 17 cm and 16 cm, respectively.

2.1   Recording Condition and Dataset Construction

We recorded the wingbeat sound of 100 female Ae. aegypti mosquitos, where 50 of these mosquitoes were inoculated with dengue virus cerotype II (DENV2) by feeding them with infected blood 2 days before the recording took place, and the rest of 50 mosquitoes were healthy. All mosquitos had 6-days old. The temperature and humidity of the laboratory was approximately 26 °C–28 °C and humidity was approximately 80%. The sampling frequency was set to 48 kHz and the recording duration varies depending on the activities of each mosquito, which ranges from 2 sec to 8 sec. Main noise sources were human voice and engine sound of some machines in the laboratory where the recording was carried out.

We measured the potential of the sound in each recoding to detect and eliminate silence periods. After that we segmented each data into segments of duration of one second with 25% overlapping. In total we get 772 segmented data of infected mosquitoes and 772 segmented data for healthy mosquitos. Figure 2 shows two examples of wingbeat signal recorded under the above condition

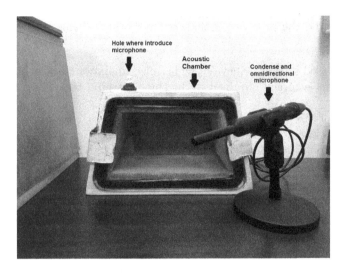

Fig. 1. Acoustic chamber and condense and omnidirectional microphone used for recording.

together with its time-frequency representation obtained using the Short Time Fourier Transform (STFT). All data were divided into training set, validation set and test set, with the proportion of 75%, 15% and 10%, respectively.

2.2 Proposed LSTM-Based Scheme

The proposed LSTM-based scheme is composed by two LSTM layers with 64 neurons and two Fully Connected (FC) layers with dropout mechanism to reduce overfitting. Several hyperparameters including number of LSTM layers, FC layers, dropout rate, optimizer and activation function are adjusted empirically. Figure 3 shows the proposed scheme and Table 1 shows the hyperparameters used in the proposed scheme. Input data of the proposed classifier is a time-frequency representation of one second wingbeat signal without any preprocessing. As the time-frequency representation, we used three methods, which are Spectrogram, Spectrogram with Mel frequency scale (Mel spectrogram) and Mel-frequency cepstral coefficients (MFCC).

3   Experimental Results

To identify the best method for time-frequency representation, firstly we evaluate the discrimination accuracy provided by Spectrogram, Mel Spectrogram and MFCC. Table 2 shows the results. As we can observe from this table, the Spectrogram provides the highest accuracy compared against the other two methods, so we selected Spectrogram as time-frequency representation. We think that a possible reason of this accuracy difference may be due to the frequency scaling used in Mel Spectrogram and MFCC. This frequency scaling is based on

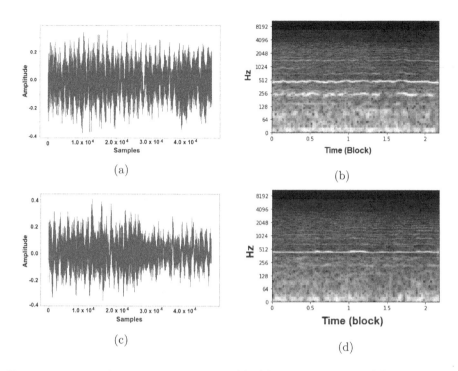

Fig. 2. Two examples of wingbeat signals. (a), (c) wingbeat signals, (b), (d) spectrograms of (a) and (c), respectively.

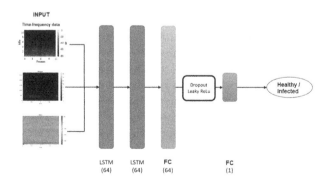

Fig. 3. Proposed LSTM-based scheme to discriminate infected mosquitos.

Table 1. Hyperparameters used in LSTM Neural Network.

Hyperparameters	Values
Initial Learning Rate	0.00001
Optimizer	Adam, $\beta_1 = 0.9$, $\beta_2 = 0.999$
Number of epochs	100
Dropout rate	0.3
Batch size	1
Activation function	Leaky ReLU, Sigmoidal (last layer)
Loss function	Binary Cross-Entropy

human auditory system to distinguish sound; however, difference of wingbeat sounds between healthy and infected mosquitos may be inaudible by human and frequency scaling may be influencing the results.

Table 2. Accuracy comparison among three time-frequency inputs.

Time-frequency data	Accuracy (%)
Spectrogram	89.35
Mel Spectrogram	60.51
MFCC	79.85

Figure 4 shows the confusion matrix obtained in the proposed scheme using Spectrogram as input data. We can observe from this figure, the confusion of wingbeat signals of healthy mosquitoes with those of infected ones is only 3.9%; however, about 20% of infected mosquitoes were confused with the healthy ones. The latter confusion rate must be reduced because the regions, where infected mosquitoes are found, cannot be detected and therefore a timely fumigation cannot be performed. The possible solution is the introduction of uncertainty in the last layer, that is depends on the value calculated by the sigmoidal activation function to compute the uncertainty rate. The uncertainty rate can be used for the human decision making about fumigation.

The performance of proposed scheme is compared with the previous methods proposed by [9] in Table 3. We can observe from the Table 3, the proposed method improves the discrimination accuracy approximately 5% compared with the best performance (KNN k = 3) of [9].

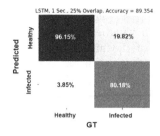

Fig. 4. Confusion Matrix obtained using proposed scheme with Spectrogram as input data.

Table 3. Comparison of detection accuracy of proposed method against the previous methods.

Method	Accuracy (%)
KNN $K = 3$ [9]	84.32
KNN $K = 5$ [9]	80.39
SVM Linear [9]	80.39
SVM Radial [9]	78.84
Proposed	**89.35**

4   Conclusions

In this paper, we proposed a discrimination scheme of infected mosquitos from the healthy ones using wingbeat signal recoded by condenser omnidirectional microphone, in which we used neural networks with two LSTM layers, and two FC layers with dropout mechanism. We identified the Spectrogram as time-frequency representation as input signal because other representations, such as Mel spectrogram and MFCC provide unfavorable results. The discrimination accuracy obtained is 89.35%, which is approximately 5% better than the proposed method based on other machine learning techniques [9].

From the confusion matrix given by Fig. 4, we observe that the false negative error, which is the algorithm decides erroneously the infected mosquitos as healthy ones, is relatively large, being approximately 20%. This situation indicates us two issues: the first one is uncertainty in the decision taken by proposed system, and the second one is uncertainly of real infection in mosquitoes. To attend the first issue, instead of binary decision, "infected" or "healthy", we can add the third decision "uncertainty", considering probabilities of "infected" decision. If probability of "infected" is smaller than one threshold values (for example 0.65) and lager than another threshold value (for example 0.35), the decision can be "uncertainty". In this case, the final decision can be taken by human. The second issue is related to the fact that not all mosquitoes, fed on blood containing dengue virus, acquire the infection. Real infection in a mosquito can be detected by molecular biology.

As far as we know, our proposal and [9] are the unique works aimed to identify infected mosquitos using their wingbeat signals. Almost all works related to the detection or discrimination of the infected mosquitos are based on biological methods. So, we were able to compare our method only against the methods proposed by [9].

Acknowledgements. Marco Haro wishes to thank the National Council for Humanity, Science, and Technology (CONAHCyT) of Mexico for their support during the development of this research.

References

1. CDC Homepage about Dengue. https://cdc.gov/dengue/about/index.html
2. Pan American Health Organization, weekly epidemiological update for dengue, chikungunya and zika in 2022. https://ais.paho.org/PAHOArboBulletin2022.pdf. (in Spanish)
3. Xiang, B., et al.: Dengue virus infection modifies mosquito blood-feeding behavior to increase transmission to the host. Proc. Natl. Acad. Sci. U.S.A. **119**(3) (2021)
4. Mendez-Luzi, P., et al.: Potential impact of a presumed increase in the biting activity of dengue-virus-infected Aedes aegypti females on virus transmission dynamics. Mem. Inst. Oswaldo Cruz **106**(6), 755–758 (2011)
5. Lima-Camara, T., et al.: Dengue infection increase the locomotor activity of Aedes aegypti female. PLOS ONE **6**(3), e17690 (2011)
6. Fanioudakis, E., Geismar, M., Potamitis, I.: Mosquito wingbeat analysis and classification using deep learning. In: Campisi, P. (ed.) Proceedings of 26th European Signal Processing Conference, Rome, Italy, 3–7 September 2018, pp. 2410–2413 (2018)
7. Toledo, E., et al.: LSTM-based mosquito genus classification using their wingbeat sound. In: Fujita, H. (ed.) Proceedings of New Trends in Intelligent Software Methodologies, Tools, and Techniques, Cancun, Mexico, 21–23 September 2021, pp. 293–302 (2021)
8. Mukundarajan, H., Hol, F., Castillo, E., Newby, C., Prakash, M.: Using mobile phones as acoustic sensors for high-throughput mosquito surveillance. eLife **6**, e27854 (2017)
9. Haro, A., Nakano, M., Cime-Castillo, J., Lanz-Mendoza, H., Gonzalez-Lee, M., Perez Meana, H.: Infected mosquito detection system using spectral analysis. Front. Artif. Intell. Appl. **355**, 669–677 (2022)

FAU-Net: An Attention U-Net Extension with Feature Pyramid Attention for Prostate Cancer Segmentation

Pablo Cesar Quihui-Rubio[1], Daniel Flores-Araiza[1], Miguel Gonzalez-Mendoza[1], Christian Mata[2,3], and Gilberto Ochoa-Ruiz[1(✉)]

[1] School of Engineering and Sciences, Tecnologico de Monterrey, Monterrey, Mexico
gilberto.ochoa@tec.mx
[2] Universitat Politècnica de Catalunya, 08019 Barcelona, Catalonia, Spain
[3] Pediatric Computational Imaging Research Group, Hospital Sant Joan de Déu, 08950 Esplugues de Llobregat, Catalonia, Spain

Abstract. This contribution presents a deep learning method for the segmentation of prostate zones in MRI images based on U-Net using additive and feature pyramid attention modules, which can improve the workflow of prostate cancer detection and diagnosis. The proposed model is compared to seven different U-Net-based architectures. The automatic segmentation performance of each model of the central zone (CZ), peripheral zone (PZ), transition zone (TZ) and Tumor were evaluated using Dice Score (DSC), and the Intersection over Union (IoU) metrics. The proposed alternative achieved a mean DSC of 84.15% and IoU of 76.9% in the test set, outperforming most of the studied models in this work except from R2U-Net and attention R2U-Net architectures.

Keywords: Segmentation · U-Net · Attention · Uncertainty Quantification · Prostate Cancer · Deep Learning

1 Introduction

Prostate cancer (PCa) is the most common solid non-cutaneous cancer in men and is among the most common causes of cancer-related deaths in 13 regions of the world [9].

When detected in early stages, the survival rate for regional PCa is almost 100%. In contrast, the survival rate when the cancer is spread to other parts of the body is of only 30% [3]. Magnetic Resonance Imaging (MRI) is the most widely available non-invasive and sensitive tool for detection of PCa, due to its high resolution, excellent spontaneous contrast of soft tissues, and the possibility of multi-planar and multi-parametric scanning [5]. Although MRI is used traditionally for staging PCa, it can be also be used for the PCa detection through the segmentation of Regions of Interest (ROI) from MR images.

The use of image segmentation for PCa detection and characterization can help determine the localization and the volume of the cancerous tissue [7]. This highlights the importance of an accurate and consistent segmentation when detecting PCa.

H. Calvo et al. (Eds.): MICAI 2023, LNAI 14392, pp. 165–176, 2024.
https://doi.org/10.1007/978-3-031-47640-2_14

However, the most common and preferred method for identifying and delimiting prostate gland and prostate regions of interest is by performing a manual inspection by radiologists [1]. This manual process is time-consuming, and is sensitive to specialists' experience, resulting in a significant intra- and inter-specialist variability [14]. Automating this process for the segmentation of prostate gland and regions of interest, in addition to saving time for radiologists, can be used as a learning tool for others and have consistency in contouring [11].

Deep Learning (DL) base methods have recently been developed to perform automatic prostate segmentation [6]. One of the most popular methods is U-Net [16], which has been the inspiration behind many recent works in literature.

In this work, we propose an automatic prostate zone segmentation method that is based on an extension of Attention U-Net that combines two types of attention, pyramidal and additive. We also include the pixel-wise estimation of the uncertainty.

The zones evaluated in this work are the central zone (CZ), the peripheral zone (PZ), transition zone (TZ), and, in the case of a disease, the tumor (TUM), different from other works, which only evaluate CZ and PZ [10].

The rest of this paper is organized as follows: Sect. 2 describes previous works dealing with the prostate segmentation. Section 3 describes the dataset used in this work, the proposed architecture, as well as the experimental setup to evaluate it. In Sect. 4 the results of the experiments are presented and discussed and Sect. 5 concludes the article.

2   State-of-the-Art

In medical imaging, one of the best known DL models in the literature for segmentation is U-Net, which consists of two sub-networks: an encoder with a series of four convolutions and max-pooling operations to reduce the dimension of the input image and to capture its semantic information at different levels. The second sub-network is a decoder that consists of four convolution and up-sampling operations to recover the spatial information of the image [16]. The work from Zhu et al. [18] proposes a U-Net based network to segment the whole prostate gland, obtaining encouraging results. Moreover, this architecture has served as the inspiration for some variants that enhance the performance of the original model. One example is the work from Oktay et al. [13], which proposes the addition of attention gates inside the original U-Net model with the intention of making the model focus on the specific target structures. In this architecture, the attention layers highlight the features from the skip connections between the encoder and the decoder. Many others extension architectures have been proposed since U-Net was released, some of them include Dense blocks [17], residual and recurrent blocks [2], even novel architectures implemented transformers blocks named Swin blocks in order to obtain Swin U-Net [4].

All the mentioned models had demonstrated great results in many biomedical image datasets. However, in this work we focused on PCa segmentation, in particular, the main zones of the prostate, which has not been deeply investigated by some of these models.

3   Materials and Methods

3.1   Dataset

This study was carried out in compliance with the Centre Hospitalier de Dijon. The dataset provided by these institutions consists of three-dimensional T2-weighted fast spin-echo (TR/TE/ETL: 3600 ms/ 143 ms/109, slice thickness:1.25 mm) images acquired with sub-millimetric pixel resolution in an oblique axial plane. The total number of patients from the dataset are 19, with a total of 205 images with their corresponding masks used as a ground truth. The manual segmentation of each with four regions of interest (CZ, PZ, TZ, and TUMOR) was also provided, this process was cautiously validated by multiple professional radiologists and experts using a dedicated software tool [12, 15].

The entire dataset contains four different combination of zones, being: (CZ+PZ), (CZ+PZ+TZ), (CZ+PZ+Tumor), and (CZ+PZ+TZ+Tumor) with 73, 68, 23, and 41 images respectively. For the purpose of this work, the dataset was divided in 85% for training and 15% for testing, keeping a similar distribution in both sets of data, having a total of 174 images for training, and 31 for testing.

In Fig. 1 examples of images from every possible combination of zones in the dataset are presented.

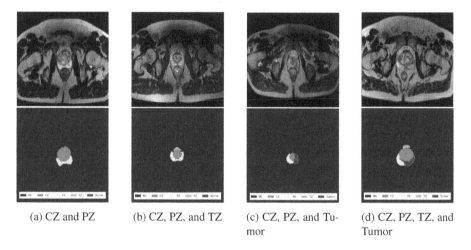

(a) CZ and PZ   (b) CZ, PZ, and TZ   (c) CZ, PZ, and Tumor   (d) CZ, PZ, TZ, and Tumor

Fig. 1. Sample images from every possible combination of zones in the dataset are presented in the upper row. Their respective ground truth masks are shown in the lower row.

3.2   Feature Pyramid Attention

The work of Yonkai et al. [9] introduces the feature pyramid attention (FPA) network to capture information at multiple scales. It contains three convolutional blocks of different sizes (3×3, 5×5 and 7×7) to extract the features from different scales. These are then integrated from smaller to bigger, to incorporate the different scales. In our work, the attention map is multiplied by the features from the skip connection after a 1×1 convolution. A visual representation of this attention block is presented in Fig. 2.

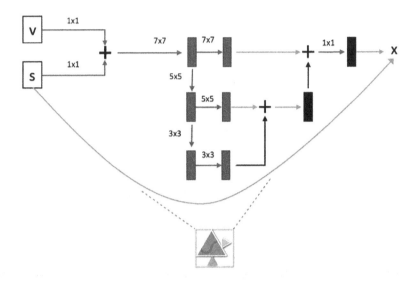

Fig. 2. The feature pyramid attention block. It consists of three convolutional blocks of 3×3, 5×5, and 7×7 which responses are integrated to capture the context of each level.

3.3   Proposed Work

This contribution proposes the Fusion Attention U-Net (FAU-Net), an Attention-U-Net-based extension with pyramidal and additive attention. The proposed model is used to perform the segmentation of five different regions from the PCa dataset described in Sect. 3.1.

Attention U-Net implements attention gates (AG) into the U-Net architecture to highlight salient features that are passed through the skip connections, these gates allow the network to disambiguate irrelevant and noisy responses in skip connections, leaving only the relevant activations to merge [13]. In the architecture proposed, we used AGs in the last three levels of the architecture. Meanwhile, in the first level, the implementation of a FPA was carried out to give further attention in those layers, were more data could be leaked. In Fig. 3 an entire representation of the architecture is shown.

A comparison between U-Net [16], Attention U-Net [13], Dense U-Net [17], Attention Dense U-Net [8], R2U-Net [2], Attention R2U-Net, Swin U-Net [4] and the proposed FAU-Net was done to validate the results obtained.

Most of the works in the literature perform the segmentation task of only two zones, and the number of works that consider a third zone (TZ) is limited, mainly because the

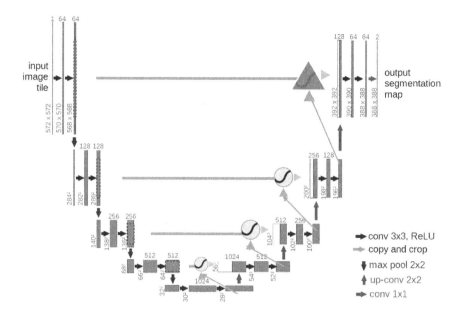

Fig. 3. Proposed Fusion Attention U-Net model. The input image first goes through the contracting path. The boxes represent the feature map at each layer, and the blue boxes represent the cropped feature maps from the contracting path. (Color figure online)

boundaries are more delimited than zones such as TZ or Tumor. In this work we used a private dataset which incorporates the TZ and, in some cases, a tumor. This zone is important because it could lead to a proper diagnosis or treatment if a tumor is present.

Therefore, we proposed an attention-based model to perform segmentation with a dataset of only T2-weighted images with 4 prostate zones, and compare the results against other models proposed in the literature. We analyzed the segmentation of the prostate zones using different metrics to choose the best DL architecture. Finally, we did a qualitative analysis of the predictions of each model.

In Table 1 is shown the number of parameters, which are different for each model, being the one with the lowest number the original U-Net, and the Swin U-Net with the highest number of parameters. FAU-Net has only around 160,000 more parameters than U-Net and Attention U-Net, being the third model with less parameters.

All the models were trained with the same dataset for 145 epochs, using Adam optimizer with a learning rate of 0.0001, batch size of 6, and categorical cross-entropy as loss function. The performance was evaluated using F1-score and Intersection over Union (IoU) as the main metrics. All the training was done using a NVIDIA DGX workstation, using a V100 GPU.

Table 1. Count of trainable parameters for each model analyzed during this work.

Model	Number of parameters
U-Net	1,940,885
Attention U-Net	1,995,409
FAU-Net	**2,158,505**
Dense U-Net	4,238,389
Attention Dense U-Net	4,271,521
R2U-Net	6,003,077
Attention R2U-Net	6,036,081
Swin U-Net	26,598,344

4   Results and Discussion

The results of this work are divided in two subsections for further analysis and comparison between the models: quantitative and qualitative.

4.1   Quantitative Results

Table 2 shows a summary of results for the evaluation of the eight studied architectures in two metrics (DSC and IoU) and loss value. Each evaluation corresponds to the mean value of the metrics for all the prostate zones and images in the test set. The bold values represent the model that achieved the best metric score within all of them.

Table 2. The model performance evaluation was conducted using the Categorical Cross-Entropy (CCE) as the loss function. The metrics were designated with either an upward (↑) or downward (↓) arrow to indicate whether higher or lower values were desirable. Bold values and green highlights denote the best metric score achieved among all models.

Model	IoU ↑	DSC ↑	Loss ↓
U-Net	70.76	80.00	0.0138
Dense U-Net	74.53	83.65	0.0225
Swin U-Net	75.24	83.91	0.0124
Attention U-Net	74.92	84.01	0.0114
Attention Dense U-Net	75.12	84.01	0.0211
FAU-Net	75.49	84.15	**0.0107**
R2U-Net	76.60	85.30	0.0131
Attention R2U-Net	**76.89**	**85.42**	0.0120

As expected, the extended U-Net architectures performed better than the original U-Net architecture. For instance, the Dense U-Net model showed an improvement of approximately 5% in both metrics. However, the Swin U-Net model, based on Swin Transformers and considered one of the best architectures available, did not perform as well on the dataset used in this study. It outperformed U-Net and Dense U-Net models in both metrics by 6%, and Attention U-Net and Attention Dense U-Net in the IoU metric by only 0.4% and 0.1%, respectively. The subpar performance of this model could be attributed to various factors, but the most likely explanation is the small size of the dataset and the high number of training parameters, which may have led to overfitting.

Incorporating attention modules into U-Net and Dense U-Net models resulted in significant improvements compared to models without them. Attention U-Net outperformed U-Net by more than 5% in both metrics. Meanwhile, Attention Dense U-Net achieved the same DSC score as Attention U-Net and a higher IoU score by approximately 1%. These results indicate that attention modules are beneficial for obtaining better prostate segmentation, even with a relatively small dataset.

The proposed FAU-Net architecture in this study incorporated two types of attention: additive attention, as used in previous models, and pyramidal attention, consisting of attention modules in a cascade fashion. The objective of this model was to focus on the most complex features of each prostate image and obtain better information, and the results support this hypothesis. FAU-Net achieved IoU and DSC values of 75.49% and 84.15%, respectively, improving U-Net results by more than 6%. However, this architecture was surpassed by R2U-Net and Attention R2U-Net.

R2U-Net and Attention R2U-Net are architectures that rely on recurrent residual blocks, which aid in extracting more information from deeper image features. In this study, Attention R2U-Net was the top-performing model overall, achieving metric scores greater than 76% for IoU and 85% for DSC, with a loss value of 0.0120.

To gain a comprehensive understanding of the segmentation metrics in biomedical images, particularly related to the prostate, it is important to examine specific tissue zones. After analyzing the segmentation metrics through the full test set from the dataset, Fig. 4 shows the IoU scores obtained from each image in each prostate zone. Each model is represented by a different color, and each test image is represented by a colored dot with the corresponding value. However, it's essential to note that not all images in the set had the same distribution, resulting in fewer dots in the boxplot for prostate zones such as TZ and Tumor. Nonetheless, the performance trends of the models in each particular zone can be analyzed.

Undoubtedly, the central and peripheral zones are the easiest for all models to segment, with only a few images having low IoU values. However, segmenting the peripheral zone appears slightly more challenging, likely due to its smaller size. The proposed FAU-Net was the best model overall for these two zones, with a mean IoU score of 82.63% and 72.55% for CZ and PZ, respectively. In contrast, the worst model was U-Net, with values below 80% for CZ and 67% for PZ.

As for the transition zone and tumors, the variation between the models is more noticeable in Fig. 4. Most models had lower values for outliers in the transition zone, achieving mean IoU scores lower than 60% in all of them except R2U-Net, which managed to reach a mean score of 61% in TZ.

Prostate tumors are a challenging task for segmentation due to the different types of geometry and boundaries between other tissues or zones. However, unlike TZ, most of

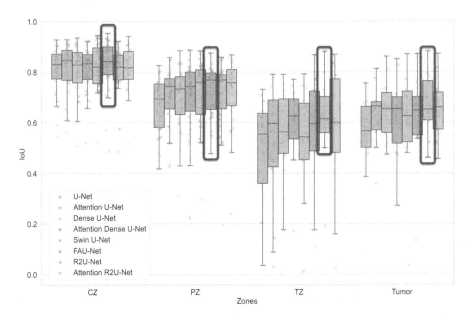

Fig. 4. The IoU scores obtained for each prostate zone from all images in the test set were compared between models. A line represents the median uncertainty value obtained, dots represent the particular score for each image, and the best model for each zone is indicated with a red box. (Color figure online)

the models managed not to have many outliers when segmenting the tumor, and most reached values higher than 60%. The worst model for segmenting the tumor was U-Net, with a mean IoU score of only 57%. On the other hand, the best model, R2U-Net, surpassed this model by 10%, obtaining a mean IoU score of 67%.

4.2 Qualitative Results

A visual inspection was carried out of the segmentation results of the eight models discussed in this study. This analysis of results complements the previous quantitative analysis based on the metrics. In this inspection, the images from the test set were visually compared to their corresponding ground truth, and conclusions were stated.

Figure 5 presents a qualitative comparison between each model's prediction in four different example images from the dataset, with all the possible combinations of zones. The first two rows show the original T2-MRI image of the prostate and below its corresponding ground truth. Then, each row represents prediction of the different models.

Starting from the base model U-Net, it is clear that U-Net had difficulty correctly segmenting all pixels, especially in images with tumors, for example in image C, this model missed many pixels that corresponded to the Tumor; this could be a wrong lead for a radiologist who is relying upon this model. Nevertheless, even though a Tumor is present in example D, U-Net segments most of the pixels better than in the previous example, at least from a visual perspective.

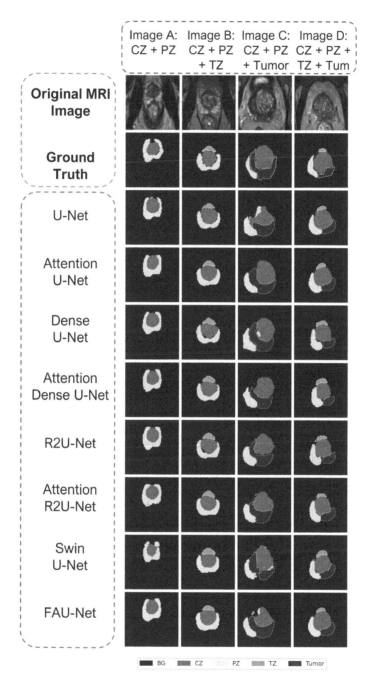

Fig. 5. Image comparison of segmentation results using U-Net-like architectures. All possible combinations of zones available in the dataset are used as examples for conducting predictions on MRI images.

Based on qualitative analysis, some models, such as Attention U-Net, R2U-Net, and FAU-Net, performed better in segmenting all prostate zones, including the Tumor. Compared to the other models, these models produced smoother and more complete segmentation in images with three or more zones. However, it should be noted that FAU-Net misclassified some pixels as TZ in example C, which does not include TZ.

It is clear that images with only two zones (CZ and PZ) are easier to segment for all the models, which are the bigger and more present ones in the dataset. Some models in examples C and D include more pixels in the smaller zones, resulting in a smoother segmentation; although this looks great from visual analysis, compared to the ground truth, that prediction is incorrect; thus, relying solely on visual analysis is not advisable.

As a qualitative conclusion of the predictions based on the examples from Fig. 5, it can be demonstrated that Attention U-Net and R2U-Net are the models with the best segmentation performance overall. However, based on the metrics and a visual analysis from the entire test set, in general the best performance was obtained by FAU-Net, R2U-Net, and Attention R2U-Net.

5   Conclusion

In this work, we proposed a U-Net extension using two attention blocks: additive and pyramidal. From the results shown in Sect. 4, we can conclude that the proposed architecture, FAU-Net, outperforms most of the studied architectures in this work. Moreover, other alternatives like R2U-Net and Attention R2U-Net, are still better suited to perform over this particular dataset than the proposed architecture. Furthermore, FAU-Net presents great metrics score and although it struggles in particular zones like TZ and Tumor, it is the best model to segment the CZ and PZ regarding the segmentation metrics in our dataset.

Considering that the results obtained are promising, further investigation can be done by improving the FAU-Net architecture to achieve even better results. For instance, a future implementation of feature pyramid attention module in the R2U-Net architecture can lead to promising results using the dataset studied in this work for prostate segmentation. Also, trying more combinations of the attention modules and/or adding more levels to the architecture can produce interesting results.

Acknowledgments. The authors wish to acknowledge the Mexican Council for Science and Technology (CONAHCYT) for the support in terms of postgraduate scholarships in this project, and the Data Science Hub at Tecnologico de Monterrey for their support on this project.

This work has been supported by Azure Sponsorship credits granted by Microsoft's AI for Good Research Lab through the AI for Health program. The project was also supported by the French-Mexican ANUIES CONAHCYT Ecos Nord grant 322537.

References

1. Aldoj, N., Biavati, F., Michallek, F., Stober, S., Dewey, M.: Automatic prostate and prostate zones segmentation of magnetic resonance images using DenseNet-like U-net. Sci. Rep. **10** (2020). https://doi.org/10.1038/s41598-020-71080-0

2. Alom, M.Z., Hasan, M., Yakopcic, C., Taha, T.M., Asari, V.K.: Recurrent residual convolutional neural network based on U-net (R2U-net) for medical image segmentation. CoRR abs/1802.06955 (2018)

3. AstraZeneca: A personalized approach in prostate cancer (2020). https://www.astrazeneca.com/our-therapy-areas/oncology/prostate-cancer.html. Accessed 17 Oct 2021

4. Cao, H., et al.: Swin-Unet: Unet-like pure transformer for medical image segmentation. In: Karlinsky, L., Michaeli, T., Nishino, K. (eds.) ECCV 2022. LNCS, pp. 205–218. Springer, Cham (2023). https://doi.org/10.1007/978-3-031-25066-8_9

5. Chen, M., et al.: Prostate cancer detection: comparison of T2-weighted imaging, diffusion-weighted imaging, proton magnetic resonance spectroscopic imaging, and the three techniques combined. Acta Radiologica **49**(5), 602–610 (2008). https://doi.org/10.1080/02841850802004983. https://www.tandfonline.com/doi/abs/10.1080/02841850802004983

6. Elguindi, S., et al.: Deep learning-based auto-segmentation of targets and organs-at-risk for magnetic resonance imaging only planning of prostate radiotherapy. Phys. Imaging Radiation Oncol. **12**, 80–86 (2019). https://doi.org/10.1016/j.phro.2019.11.006. https://www.sciencedirect.com/science/article/pii/S2405631619300569

7. Haralick, R., Shapiro, L.: Image segmentation techniques. Comput. Vis. Graph. Image Process. **29**(1), 100–132 (1985). https://doi.org/10.1016/S0734-189X(85)90153-7. https://www.sciencedirect.com/science/article/pii/S0734189X85901537

8. Li, S., Dong, M., Du, G., Mu, X.: Attention Dense-U-Net for automatic breast mass segmentation in digital mammogram. IEEE Access **7**, 59037–59047 (2019). https://doi.org/10.1109/ACCESS.2019.2914873

9. Liu, Y., et al.: Automatic prostate zonal segmentation using fully convolutional network with feature pyramid attention. IEEE Access **7**, 163626–163632 (2019). https://doi.org/10.1109/ACCESS.2019.2952534

10. Liu, Y., et al.: Exploring uncertainty measures in Bayesian deep attentive neural networks for prostate zonal segmentation. IEEE Access **8**, 151817–151828 (2020). https://doi.org/10.1109/ACCESS.2020.3017168

11. Mahapatra, D., Buhmann, J.M.: Prostate MRI segmentation using learned semantic knowledge and graph cuts. IEEE Trans. Biomed. Eng. **61**(3), 756–764 (2014). https://doi.org/10.1109/TBME.2013.2289306

12. Mata, C., Munuera, J., Lalande, A., Ochoa-Ruiz, G., Benitez, R.: MedicalSeg: a medical GUI application for image segmentation management. Algorithms **15**(06) (2022). https://doi.org/10.3390/a15060200. https://www.mdpi.com/1999-4893/15/6/200

13. Oktay, O., et al.: Attention U-net: learning where to look for the pancreas (2018). https://doi.org/10.48550/ARXIV.1804.03999

14. Rasch, C., et al.: Human-computer interaction in radiotherapy target volume delineation: a prospective, multi-institutional comparison of user input devices. J. Digit. Imaging **24**(5), 794–803 (2011). https://doi.org/10.1007/s10278-010-9341-2

15. Rodríguez, J., Ochoa-Ruiz, G., Mata, C.: A prostate MRI segmentation tool based on active contour models using a gradient vector flow. Appl. Sci. **10**(18) (2020). https://doi.org/10.3390/app10186163. https://www.mdpi.com/2076-3417/10/18/6163

16. Ronneberger, O., Fischer, P., Brox, T.: U-net: convolutional networks for biomedical image segmentation. In: Navab, N., Hornegger, J., Wells, W.M., Frangi, A.F. (eds.) MICCAI 2015. LNCS, vol. 9351, pp. 234–241. Springer, Cham (2015). https://doi.org/10.1007/978-3-319-24574-4_28

17. Wu, Y., Wu, J., Jin, S., Cao, L., Jin, G.: Dense-U-Net: dense encoder-decoder network for holographic imaging of 3D particle fields. Opt. Commun. **493**, 126970 (2021). https://doi.org/10.1016/j.optcom.2021.126970. https://www.sciencedirect.com/science/article/pii/S0030401821002200

18. Zhu, Q., Du, B., Turkbey, B., Choyke, P.L., Yan, P.: Deeply-supervised CNN for prostate segmentation. CoRR abs/1703.07523 (2017). http://arxiv.org/abs/1703.07523

Implementation of a Digital Electromyographic Signal Processor Synthesized on an FPGA Development Board for Biocontrol Systems

J. Brandon Mañón Juárez[(✉)] and Eusebio Ricárdez Vázquez

Centro de Investigación En Computación, Instituto Politécnico Nacional, 07738 Ciudad de México, Mexico
{jmanonj2023,ericardez}@cic.ipn.mx

Abstract. This paper presents the design and synthesis of a digital electromyographic signal processor applying dedicated processing methods and pattern recognition for the classification of upper limb movements of the human body. To accelerate the digital processing of EMG signals and reduce the implementation hardware, the system is integrated with a Field Program Gate Array in which the digital processing techniques are implemented at hardware level, from signal filtering to pattern recognition and classification, also, the analog to digital converter of a microcontroller is used for the acquisition of the EMG signal. The modules necessary for the first steps of digital processing are designed and synthesized in Verilog HDL. After obtaining and characterizing the signal, from registered signal values in MATLAB, the simple perceptron training algorithm is used to obtain the synaptic weights of the perceptron, which are then implemented in the FPGA design for the perceptron module in hardware. After implementing the complete system and performing the tests, the signals obtained are analysed with their classification and the percentage of success, with results of 70% and 80% person A and 60% and 80% for persond B for contraction and extension, respectively; it should be noted that the complete system was only tested on two people.

Keywords: electromyography · digital signal processing · artificial neural network · FPGA

1 Introduction

Within the scope of computer engineering are some systems that process information whose variables are continuous in time and which can be modeled computationally either by software or hardware, making better use of the resources that comprise them. Some systems that are frequently modeled through computation are the biological ones; a particular case is those used for the analysis of muscular ailments or the control of prosthesis through electromyographic signals

(EMG) [5] which are electrical signals that the muscles produce in response to the electrical signal sent by the brain to the motor neurons that make up the muscle and cause the movement.

An electromyographic signal acquisition, conditioning and processing system is defined as the set of elements that interact with each other to capture the electrical signals produced by the muscular movement of some part of the body, then the signal is prepared to have it or obtain information with specific characteristics and at the end calculations or operations are performed to perform some action from the results of the signal. The signal processing system is usually embedded in a single computing device that consists of the necessary elements for each stage. Despite the progress in terms of computing and information processing capabilities, the needs and requirements for the design and implementation of EMG signal processing systems require devices that, despite their high speed, low energy consumption, resource optimization and reduced device size.

Some prototype projects that process EMG signals present areas of opportunity in terms of design, on the one hand in hardware design to reduce size and implementation space, improve energy consumption by reducing the number of devices to a minimum and replacing analog filters with digital ones, just to mention a few, and on the software side it is suggested to accelerate the processing capacity, optimize the implementation algorithms, as well as the implementation of pattern recognition and classification stages. This work is aimed at the integration of digital signal processing techniques to cover part of the areas of opportunity in the prototypes as described by [3,11] as well as the acceleration of EMG signal processing through the implementation of a field programmable gate array (FPGA), in which pattern recognition and classification are also implemented by means of an artificial neural network model. It is emphasized that the application of the system is for general purpose use so it can be implemented in different use cases.

2   Related Work

Digital signal processing systems applied to electromyography are developed according to the needs of the case study or biomedical application and the techniques used vary according to the requirements and design specifications, however, many systems have common characteristics and specifications in both design and implementation. Cases such as [1,6] where an EMG signal acquisition bracelet is used, what varies is the type of device, respectively, while one is commercial and integrates more types of sensors, the other is designed only for acquisition by electrodes, but both acquire the information wirelessly and is processed in MATLAB.

In the designs of [4,7,9] the analog conditioning stage is designed, in the first case a robotic arm is controlled by pattern recognition through connection to a BeagleBone development board, in the second case an avatar of a mobile device game is controlled to perform muscle rehabilitation in a playful and supervised way, for the third case the system is only used to analyze the behavior of the EMG signal, however, in all three cases the conditioning stage covers a large size and space by requiring many electronic components in the analog bandpass filter stage.

In the prototypes that perform digital signal processing using an FPGA there are several techniques, for example, [2] who proposes two architectures of FIR (finite impulse response) type digital filters, the first in series and the second in parallel where it is highlighted that the parallel architecture, despite using more FPGA resources, the processing speed and filtering time are better compared to the serial architecture. In [10] a specific way of performing digital processing of electromyographic signals is defined, although it uses an analog conditioning stage, the digital processing has stages that perform complex calculations such as Fast Fourier Transform, dimensionality reduction, segment variance extraction, as well as its mean value. The prototype obtains a percentage higher than 66% of success in the classification of the three movements, it is highlighted that although some stages are executed in parallel, the process control is by means of a state machine which resembles the sequential execution of the processing.

3   Methods and Materials

Based on the characteristics of a digital signal processing system, a design proposal is defined that takes into account techniques that cover the areas of opportunity of the existing prototypes; the diagram of the proposal is shown in Fig. 1.

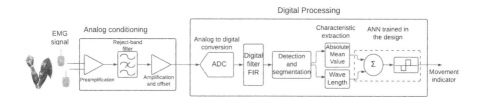

Fig. 1. Digital Signal Processing for EMG signal block diagram

The EMG signal is obtained from the muscle movement of wrist contraction or rotation by two electrodes placed on the user's upper limb, it is taken to the analog conditioning stage in which a gain is obtained in the signal by means of an instrumentation amplifier. Then band-pass filtering is performed for 60 Hz that corresponds to the noise of the power supply installation and the signal is conditioned with a displacement and amplification for processing in a digital device. In the digital stage the analog to digital conversion is performed, each sample is transferred to the FPGA to pass through the digital bandpass filter and start the segmentation of the ranges with considerable information of the EMG signal. From each segment two characteristics are obtained, absolute value and wavelength, which in the simple perceptron stage allow to obtain a movement classification that is performed

3.1 Analog Signal Conditioning

The analog signal conditioning stage is divided into three parts: preamplification, band-reject filter and displacement. Considering [7], the instrumentation amplifier used is the INA128 to which, in order to obtain an EMG signal gain of approximately 2.5, a gain resistor $R_G = 33K\Omega$ is connected. Likewise, the band reject filter is also taken from [7] and the values of its components are defined as shown in Fig. 2, for which, the filter capacitor $C_0 = 68nF$, the quality factor $Q = 5$, the filter resistor $R_0 = 3.9K\Omega$, and the resistor for the quality accuracy $R_Q = 39K\Omega$.

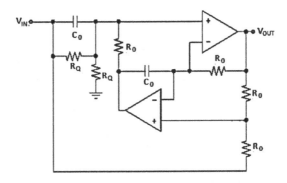

Fig. 2. Band-reject filter

For signal displacement and amplification, an amplifier in differential configuration is used to meet, from Eq. 1, the displacement required for the EMG signal.

$$V_o = 1.5V_{sEMG} + 1.5V. \tag{1}$$

From Eq. 1, value 1.5 is factorized and taken to Eq. 2, which corresponds to the differential amplifier, so now $R_{10}/R_9 = 1.5$, and it is the gain factor.

$$V_o = \frac{R_{10}}{R_9}(V_2 - V_1). \tag{2}$$

Figure 3 shows the analog signal conditioning circuit, in the signal displacement stage, is used the differential amplifier with gain of 1.5, and proposing for $R_{10} = R_8 = 18K\Omega$ in Eq. 2, is obtained $R_{11} = R_9 = 12K\Omega$. From the circuit a module is designed for PCB implementation and connection to the development board for digital processing.

3.2 Analog to Digital Conversion

The EMG signal has a frequency between 50 and 500 Hz, according to [10], it concentrates its highest energy between 50 and 250 Hz, taking into account the

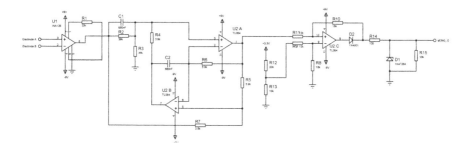

Fig. 3. Signal Conditioning Schematic

Nyquist theorem for signal sampling, it is defined that the sampling frequency is 1100 Hz, i.e. $2.2f_{sEMG}$. The analog to digital converter of the SAMD21 microcontroller is used to acquire the EMG signal, the conversion is configured with a resolution of 10 bits per sample. Also, due to the programming model of the microcontroller and the distribution of its pins, a data transfer format to the FPGA is required, so shift registers are implemented through which the analog to digital conversion bits are received and then the processing result bits are transmitted to the microcontroller. Figure 4 shows the block diagram of the microcontroller elements and the FPGA modules that interact in the processing.

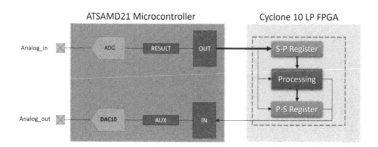

Fig. 4. FPGA and Microcontroller interconnection

3.3   Digital Filter

The digital filter is designed using MATLAB's Filter Designer Toolbox, in which the filter type, cutoff frequencies and, since it is a digital filter operating binary values, the word size and the format of the binary values are defined. After designing the filter, the code is generated in Verilog corresponding to the hardware to be configured in the FPGA. The word format assigned for the values is 22 bits of fixed point type, of which 10 are for the fractional part, 11 for the integer part and one sign bit.

3.4   Signal Segmentation and Characteristic Extraction

A signal segmentation stage is required in which significant and not false movements are identified, so it is convenient to identify at what moment a movement is carried out with the continuous comparison of the ranges of the signal samples. Similarly, when identifying a motion, a significant number of samples should be obtained from which to obtain features, in this case the mean absolute value and wavelength of the segment. Equations 3 and 4 define how to obtain the number of samples required from the signal.

$$N_{min} = \frac{T_{min}}{T_s} \tag{3}$$

$$N_{max} = \frac{T_{max}}{T_s} \tag{4}$$

As a function of the minimum and maximum times of the EMG signal (T_{min} and T_{max}) and the sampling period (T_s).The number of samples in the project is 50, where two signal cycles and a tolerance of six samples are taken into account due to the speed of signal capture.

Figure 5 shows the signal segmentation algorithm for subsequent implementation with Verilog.

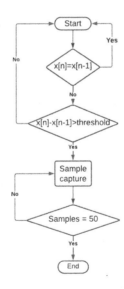

Fig. 5. Sample capture flow diagram

At the start of segmentation each sample is processed in the absolute mean value and wavelength, as suggested [8], extraction modules to obtain a segment characteristic value. Equation 5 corresponds to the absolute mean value (AMV) and Eq. 6 to the segment wavelength (WL).

$$AMV = \frac{1}{N} \sum_{i=1}^{N} |x_i| \tag{5}$$

$$WL = \sum_{i=1}^{N} |x_i - x_{i-1}| \tag{6}$$

From the above equations N represents the number of samples, x_i is the value of a given current sample at the output of the filter, x_{i-1} is the previous sample stored in an accumulator register. Each equation is described in Verilog with which its equivalent abstraction in hardware is obtained, as shown in Figs. 6 and 7

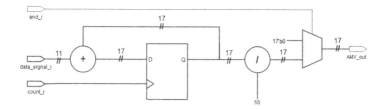

Fig. 6. AMV module RTL schematic

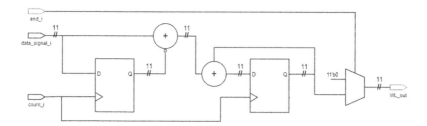

Fig. 7. WL module RTL schematic

3.5 Characteristic Classification

After extracting the features of each segment, the results are routed to the inputs of the simple perceptron for pattern recognition and motion classification to be performed. The simple perceptron is defined according to Eqs. 7 and 8.

$$\tilde{y} = \sum_{i=1}^{N} x_i w_i + \theta \tag{7}$$

$$\widehat{y} = \begin{cases} 1 : \widetilde{y} > 0 \\ 0 : \widetilde{y} \le 0 \end{cases} \tag{8}$$

where $\widetilde{y}$ corresponds to the prediction value as a function of the features x_i and the synaptic weights w_i, θ corresponds to the prediction trend threshold shift. Finally $\widehat{y}$ corresponds to the prediction or decision that is made as a result of the perceptron activation function.

Weights w_i are obtained by training the perceptron, i.e., they are defined as a synaptic learning threshold which is stored after learning or training the perceptron.

$$\widetilde{y} = AMV * w_1 + WL * w_2 + \theta \tag{9}$$

In Eq. 9 the perceptron model is defined considering the characteristics obtained in the segmentation. By defining the equations in Verilog, the weights are obtained by being described in hardware as a ROM memory with stored values for each feature. Finally, by obtaining the hardware equivalent of the perceptron model, the classification is decoded into a two-bit label where 01 represents arm contraction and 10 represents wrist rotation. Figure 8 shows the RTL diagram corresponding to the perceptron module designed with Verilog.

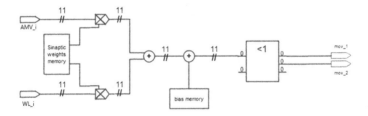

Fig. 8. Perceptron RTL diagram

3.6   Module Integration and Implementation

The implementation process consists of two stages, the first one has to do with the training of the neural network and the second one with its application to pattern recognition. In the training stage, the device is connected to the computer via USB, a MATLAB script is executed in the computer which begins to acquire the values of the filtered and segmented signal from the FPGA. With the acquisition stage and MATLAB scripts the perceptron training and the synaptic weights are obtained. When the synaptic weights are defined, they are formatted in 22-bit fixed-point format in order to load those values into a .hex format file that is in turn defined in the initialization configuration of the ROMs that make up the simple perceptron module in Verilog. After the training procedure and definition of synaptic weights, the Verilog project must be recompiled to reload the design in the FPGA and reconfigure it with the trained perceptron.

In the application to pattern recognition, the device no longer requires connection to a computer because the system becomes independent as it already has the configuration of digital processing and training of the perceptron in the FPGA. The user again has to put on the electrodes, however, it is only to recognize the movements that are made, the device displays two LEDs the result of the classification label that identifies the movements.

4   Results and Analysis

In the digital processing stage, the ideal digital filter shows stability in the behavior depending on the specifications given, however, when performing an adjustment and transition of the values to be processed in fixed-point binary format, the behavior of the filter is altered, as shown in Fig. 9.

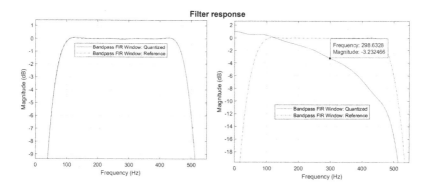

Fig. 9. Digital Filter design response a) Without modifying word b) Modifying word

Despite the behavior of the digital filter, the signal is attenuated in the range of frequencies higher than 500 Hz, as shown in Fig. 10.

In the implementation to obtain the segmented signal, the acquisition of the information is obtained from five people for six seconds for each user sample and for each of the two movements to be recognized; the values are automatically recorded in a text file. The values acquired by the device and stored in the text files are plotted in MATLAB, Fig. 11 shows the data graphs of the movement performed by all the sample users and grouped in one register for wrist contraction and rotation. Likewise, with the segmented signal obtained previously, the classification of both movements can be seen when executing the training algorithm.

The synthesis of the main project for the digital processing stage reports the FPGA resource consumption that, for the Cyclone 10 LP device model 10CL016YU256C8G whose capacity is 15,408 logic elements uses 1,147 logic

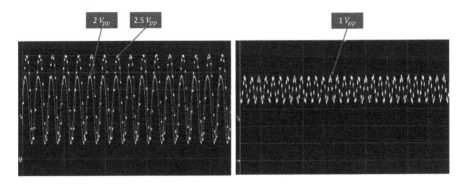

Fig. 10. Signal Filtering

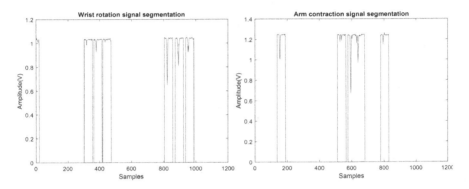

Fig. 11. Movements signal graphics

elements, that is, less than 10% of the FPGA for the implementation of the complete module, so it is defined that it is possible that at least 5 equal modules can be implemented in the FPGA.

Training the perceptron with the segmented values allows finding a hyperplane of separation for the movements. In a MATLAB script the data is sorted to assign classification according to the movements and subsequently the perceptron training algorithm is executed with which the synaptic weights w_1 and w_2 are obtained after a separation hyperplane is found for the registered values. Figure 12 shows the final result of the perceptron training which identifies that it was possible to train and classify with the implemented system. Triangles indicate contraction and asterisks indicate wrist rotation.

Regarding the percentage of prediction successes of the device, when implemented independently and tested in two people, of ten repetitions for contraction of which in person A only seven prediction were asserted and for person B only six. Thus, it is determined that, for the first test, the percentage was 65 percent correct. For the wrist rotation movement, in person A and person B the assertion was eight of ten movements. of the movements in this case the percentage of prediction is 80%. Since the system was tested on only t, it is necessary to use

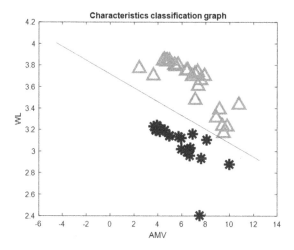

Fig. 12. Training and classification

the system on more people to be more certain of the percentage of performance as well as the factors that influence a change in response and accuracy.

5   Conclusions and Future Work

The application of mathematical models and basic machine learning algorithms like perceptron for artificial neural networks by means of computation at the software or hardware level is possible based on the knowledge of the technologies used. When software interacts with hardware, great computing power is achieved. In the development of the project, digital signal processing algorithms are implemented at software and hardware level, it is identified that both implementations may differ in accuracy, however, the results are similar. It leaves a wide panorama of opportunities in the perspective that computer engineering is not only software development but also hardware development and that both can interact for the optimization of the computation of real world models.

In the case of signal processing and segmentation algorithms, as well as the simple perceptron model, it is observed that for some algorithms that are represented in a flowchart and that are executed sequentially when implemented with structured programming languages, they can also be implemented at the hardware level, which causes their operation to be independent of the previous execution of a program segment and at the same time interact with other stages, which gives greater speed for processing.

The influence of the word format stands out in the accuracy of the results, so improvements can be made by parameterize the data format in general for the entire system, i.e., defining from the analog to digital conversion, the design of digital filters and digital processing, the format that the values should have to avoid loss of information and accuracy.

The development board has a wireless communication module so that, in order to improve the system, it can be implemented to transfer the signal acquisition without requiring USB communication.

From the report of resources used by the module, it is defined that it is possible to implement replicas or at least increase the number of perceptrons to be able to classify more movements. Similarly, it is possible that the firmware necessary for the training of the perceptron is carried out in the microcontroller and not depend on a computer.

References

1. Arias, A.M.: Prototipo de mano roboótica controlado mediante señales electromiográficas con un dispositivo comercial. Computación y Sistemas **25**(2), 307–315. México (2021)
2. Artetxe, Q.I.: Procesado digital de señales mediante circuitos integrados reconfigurables. Filtros de respuesta impulso finita (FIR). Universidad del País Vasco. España (2014)
3. Basáñez, M.M.: Diseño e implementación de un sistema de adquisición, procesamiento y clasificación de señal mioeléctrica para prótesis transhumeral de tres grados de libertad. INAOE, México (2008)
4. Cantillo. M.A.: Procesamiento de señales EMG en un sistema embebido para el control neuronal de un brazo robótico. Revista Colombiana de Tecnología Avanzada **32**(2), 139–147. Colombia (2018)
5. Chowdhury, R.H., Reaz, M.B., Ali, M.A., Bakar, A.A., Chellappan, K., Chang, T.G.: Surface electromyography signal processing and classification techniques. Sensors. **13**, 12431–12466 (2013)
6. Gómez, C.M.: Desarrollo de un sistema inalámbrico asistencial para la monitorización a distancia y clasificación de señales electromiográficas en pacientes con movilidad reducida. Universidad de Antioquia, Colombia (2022)
7. Hernández, M.J.: Sistema de rehabilitación muscular de antebrazo mediante un videojuego para dispositivos Android. Instituto Politécnico Nacional, Mexico (2017)
8. Geethanjali P., Ray K.K.: EMG based man-machine interaction-A pattern recognition research platform. Robot. Auto. Syst. **62**(6), 864–870. India (2014)
9. Proaño, G.D.: Sistema de adquisición de señales EMG de superficie multicanal para prótesis de miembro superior. Universidad Politécnica Salesiana, Ecuador (2019)
10. Reyes L.D.: Implementación en FPGA de un clasificador de movimientos de la mano usando señales EMG. Redes de Ingeniería, **6**(1), 85–94. Colombia (2015)
11. Tenesaca, L.E.: Desarrollo del prototipo de un sistema de control para prótesis de mano asistida mediante señales electromiográficas. Universidad Politécnica Salesiana, Ecuador (2020)

BEC-1D: Biosignal-Based Emotions Classification with 1D ConvNet

Juan Eduardo Luján-García$^{(\boxtimes)}$ (ID), Marco A. Cardoso-Moreno(ID),
Cornelio Yáñez-Márquez(ID), and Hiram Calvo(ID)

Centro de Investigación en Computación, Instituto Politécnico Nacional, 07738
Mexico City, Mexico
{jlujang2020,mcardosom2021,cyanez,hcalvo}@cic.ipn.mx
https://www.cic.ipn.mx

Abstract. Biomedical signals can be used to diagnose several affections of the human body. Nonetheless, they can also be used to describe a more general behavior of specific organs and how they respond according to the feelings and emotions of a person. Therefore, the YAAD dataset, which contains electrocardiogram (ECG) and Galvanic Skin Response (GSR) signals, is used in order to detect and classify seven different emotions from 25 different subjects. Stimulus is provoked to the subjects by exposing them to watch a collection of different videos that evoke emotions, such as anger, happiness, sadness, among others. Two different subsets are used in this research, a single-modal and multi-modal signals. In this work, we propose a series of preprocessing techniques to clean and resample the original signals, then a simple 1-dimensional convolutional neural network is implemented to perform the classification task. Moreover, two different types of validation methods were used to validate our results. We have achieved an accuracy over 95% for both validation methods on the multi-modal subset and an accuracy over 85% for the single-modal subset.

Keywords: emotion classification · biomedical signal · signal preprocessing · convolutional neural network · electrocardiogram · ECG · galvanic skin response · GSR

1 Introduction

Emotion recognition plays a significant role in Human-Computer Interaction systems (HCI) [12]; having good performance in such systems can greatly impact the outcome of several applications, for example, online learning, where having the computer recognize the emotional state of the user can improve feedback, and therefore learning; psychological diagnosis could also benefit from emotion recognition, since the therapist would be able to know exactly how the patient is feeling; additionally, these systems can help interaction, in both ways, of people who cannot explicitly express their feelings, such as newborn, elderly people, among others.

© The Author(s), under exclusive license to Springer Nature Switzerland AG 2024
H. Calvo et al. (Eds.): MICAI 2023, LNAI 14392, pp. 189–200, 2024.
https://doi.org/10.1007/978-3-031-47640-2_16

Emotions have been subject of study from the perspective of several disciplines, giving as a result a plethora of terminology, where different researchers attribute different meanings to the same word [7]. Therefore, it is important to determine what is considered an emotion when trying to classify, or recognize, it from a Machine Learning (ML) perspective; according to Oatley and Jenkins [18], emotions elicit both, physiological and psychological effects, that are reflected in muscular and motor expressions, as well as in neurological functions. This definition allows for the detection of emotion based on physiological signals, under the assumption that such physiological, motor and neurological effects would be present in the readings of different types of sensors.

In this regard, several techniques have been used for this task, such as: Electroencephalography (EEG), Electrocardiography (ECG), Galvanic Skin Response (GSR), Heart Rate Variability (HRV), Respiration Rate Analysis (RR), among others [8].

In this paper we selected the Young Adult's Affective Dataset (YAAD) [6], which holds a collection of both, ECG and GSR signals, as well as self annotated labels from a set of seven different emotions, for up to 25 experimental subjects, divided in two experiments: single-modal and multi-modal classification. Our proposal consists of a small 1D Convolutional Neural Network (CNN) of five layers; for validation, two approaches were tested: a hold-out split of approximately 80% for training (10–11 subjects) and the rest for testing (2 subjects, with no validation split) and, for robustness, a Leave-One-User-Out (LOUO) procedure. In neither case, data from a given subject was present in both training and test sets, i.e., special care was taken so that no subject was used for training and testing, in order to avoid data leakage.

The rest of the paper is structured as follows: Sect. 2 presents an overview of related works in the field; Sect. 3 explains the materials and methods utilized for this work; Sect. 4 is the cornerstone of this paper, since it is here where we introduce our proposal in depth—both for the preprocessing stage, as well as the model's architecture—; in Sect. 5 we present the results obtained from our experiments; lastly, Sect. 6 offers some conclusions based on our observations.

2   Related Works

Emotion recognition has been studied from several angles, mainly from facial gestures, speech, gestures and physiological and biomedical signals. Nevertheless, facial gestures and images have several limitations since these features are dependent on factors such as social masking, culture, gender and age. On the other hand, physiological responses are involuntary, i.e., cannot be masked, thus, making up for a more reliable source from which to recognize emotions [1,12,16,20].

2.1   Facial Gestures

In terms of what has been done with facial gestures and images, Canal and his colleagues [3] carried on an extensive review on the subject. They conclude, by means of a statistical analysis, that traditional classifiers achieved, in general, better precision when compared to Neural Network based models; nevertheless, Neural Networks show greater generalization capabilities.

2.2 EEG Signals

[24] develop a method that allows to classify images with respect to three categories: positive, neutral and negative, depending on what kind of emotion a given image will evoke on people. [19] proposed an approach involving the preprocessing of EEG signals (obtained in a multichannel setup) so that they can be converted to multi-spectral topology images; the presented model is a recurrent CNN that obtained a test accuracy of 90.62% when classifying positive and negative valence for emotions.

2.3 ECG Signals

Goshvarpour and colleagues [11] collected ECG signals from 47 students using the pictorial emotion elicitation paradigm; they presented several images corresponding to four different emotion classes, and after preprocessing the data with Wavelet Transform and using a Least Squares Support Vector Machine (LS-SVM) to classify each emotion against the rest, they found statistically significant differences in each class when compared to its corresponding rest. In [9] a CNN with attention mechanisms is proposed for ECG emotion recognition; the main points of the proposal is that they found larger kernel sizes to achieve better performance with respect to those with conventional, small sizes. Attention mechanisms were implemented spatial and channel-wise, and where the channel attention made more contribution to the model's performance.

2.4 GSR Signals and Multi-modal Emotion Recognition

Patil and colleagues [20] presented a method using facial emotion recognition and GSR, developing a system that is able to run on Raspberry Pi and Arduino architectures, allowing for a real-time system. In [23] vision computer techniques for eye-tracking signals along with EEG signals were used in conjunction with a Deep Gradient Neural Network for emotion classification.

More generally, several datasets have been created with the purpose of emotion recognition by means of multi-modal signals, i.e., combining several types of signal sources to better classify emotion responses. For instance, the DREAMER database [13], which consists of EEG and ECG data of emotion elicitation from audiovisual stimuli. Based on this dataset, there is the work of Song [21], where a Dynamical Graph CNN is proposed, where the multichannel EEG features, and relationship over channels are modeled by means of a graph. Also, in [5] a Regional-Asymmetric CNN is proposed, consisting of temporal, regional and asymmetric feature extraction stages.

Another dataset widely studied is the AMIGOS dataset [17], formed by EEG, ECG, and GSR signals generated while 40 participants were watching emotional videos. Gahlan et al. [10] proposed an Empirical Mode Decomposition (EMD)-based methodology in order to extract significant features, followed by a Feed-Forward Neural Network; the proposed methodology was tested on both, the DREAMER and AMIGOS datasets, getting an increase between 5 to 6% in accuracy. In similar fashion, Bota and her colleagues [2] proposed an interpersonal Weighted Group Synchrony approach, trying to leverage group phenomena which improves classification performance; the AMIGOS dataset was tested by covering different group sizes, the experimental results show that taking into account group information does, in fact, improve classification.

Lastly, and of more importance to our research, there is the YAAD dataset [6]; formed by ECG and GSR signal data mapped, by subjects' self-annotation, to seven emotions. As of today, the only work by that has reported to work with this dataset is that of Alam et al. [1]; they performed a feature extraction—of statistical features relevant in signal analysis—procedure before the classification phase, which was carried on with the use of traditional ML classifiers, such as: Random Forest, SVM, k-Nearest Neighbors (kNN) and Decision Trees. The validation procedure was 5-fold cross validation over all samples, without any distinction between subjects.

3   Materials and Methods

This section aims to describe the materials and methods employed to this research. In the first place, the used dataset is mentioned. Secondly, 1-D CNNs are introduced. Finally, the performance metric used to evaluate the results is explained.

3.1   Young Adult's Affective Data Dataset

For this work, we have used the Young Adult's Affective Data (YAAD) dataset, presented by Dar et al. [6], which contains different biosignals of subjects exposed to stimulus of seven different emotions through video visualization. The YAAD dataset is composed by two subsets: a single-modal subset which contains ECG signals from 13 subjects up to three rounds for some of them, resulting in 154 single-channel samples; a multi-modal subset which contains 3 rounds of both ECG and GSR signals from another 12 different subject, resulting in 252 two-channel samples. ECG signals were acquired at a sampling frequency of 128 Hz and have a duration of 39 s. On the contrary, GSR samples have a sampling frequency of 256 Hz and the same duration.

3.2   1-D Convolutional Neural Networks

CNNs are a subset of Deep Learning (DL) algorithms. Specifically, 1D CNNs have proven to be useful in tasks involving signal analysis procedures [4]. Therefore, biomedical and physiological signals are suitable to be analyzed by 1D CNNS.

As with most DL-based algorithms, 1D CNNs are trained using forward and backpropagation; the forward pass allows for a loss value calculation based on how different the output of the model is with respect to the ground truth, while the backward pass adjusts the parameters of the network by computing the gradients of the loss value obtained. The training process is, in fact, an optimization one, which is commonly carried out by a variant of the Gradient Descent algorithm [15]. One dimensional convolutions allow to automatically extract and learn meaningful representations from the input data (signals) with aims to use them to solve a problem [14].

3.3   Performance Metrics

The YAAD dataset is balanced, since it contains the same number of samples per subject for the multi-modal subset and two or three samples per subject for the single-modal subset. As a result, the metric that is the best suitable to evaluate the classification of this proposal is the accuracy. In a binary classification task, accuracy takes into account the correct classified instances among the total of instances, this is the sum of the true positives (tp) and true negatives (tn) divided by the sum of false positives (fp) and false negatives (fn) and correct classified tp and tn. These values can be obtained from a confusion matrix (Fig. 1) that shows the status of each classified sample by the model.

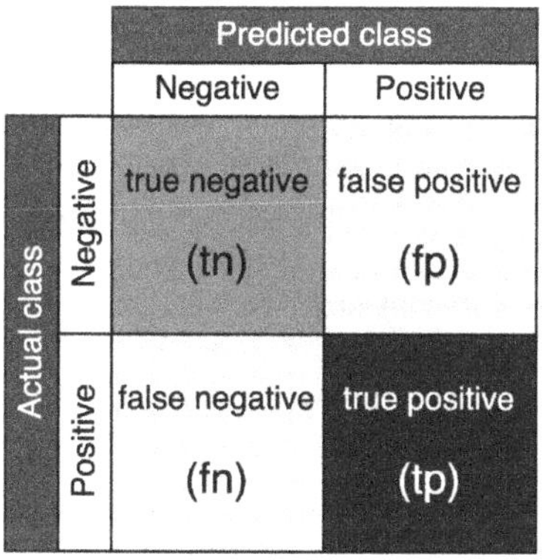

Fig. 1. Confusion matrix diagram.

The following Eq. (1), shows the definition of accuracy.

$$accuracy = \frac{tp + fn}{tp + tn + fp + fn} \qquad (1)$$

In this work, the definition of the accuracy is extended to the multi-class classification problem.

4   Proposal

In this section, our proposal and framework is fully described. A full process to aim to classify the biosignals is presented.

4.1   Signal Preprocessing

Start Dropping and Scaling. Firstly, the original work by Dar et al. [6] mentioned that in the first five seconds the stimulus has not yet begun. Therefore, we compute the mean of the first 5 s of each signal on the training set and drop those non-stimulus seconds from each one, then, we subtract the computed mean from each signal on both the training and test sets to scale them using a "base noise". At this time, we keep signals with a duration of 34 s. Figure 2(a) and Fig. 2(b), shows the before and after of the signals.

Filtering. After scaling the signals, filtering over the cut signals was performed by using a second-order passband Butterworth filter with a range of [0.5–15] Hz. The differences between different class examples become more evident after filtering the signals. Figure 2(c) shows an example after filtering the signals of Fig. 2(b).

Decimation and Normalization. After filtering the signals, we observed that the form of the signals was clearer compared to the beginning. So, we decided to apply decimation in order to reduce the length of the signals but conserving the shape of them. We applied decimation with a factor of 2, that is equivalent to applying a Max Pooling with a windows size of 2.

After reducing the number of points, we normalize all the signals using Min Max normalization to put them into the [0, 1] range. Moreover, depending on its modality, we compute different statistics according to the channel (for multi-modal only). Statistics were computed over the train set and applied to both the training and test set. Lastly, following Fig. 2(d) shows the final preprocessed signals used to train the model.

Model. Finally, we have implemented a 1D-CNN as our model to classify the preprocessed signals. Our model consists only of four convolutional layers followed by a MaxPooling layer. Then, flattening of the features maps is used to obtain a 1-dimensional vector and at the end, the final layer is composed by seven units with softmax activation in order to obtain the final predictions (Fig. 3).

5   Results

Our experimental framework was as follows. We use Google Colab to perform our experiments. We did not use the GPU instances, due to the simplicity of the model. We implemented our experiments with Python 3.10 as a programming

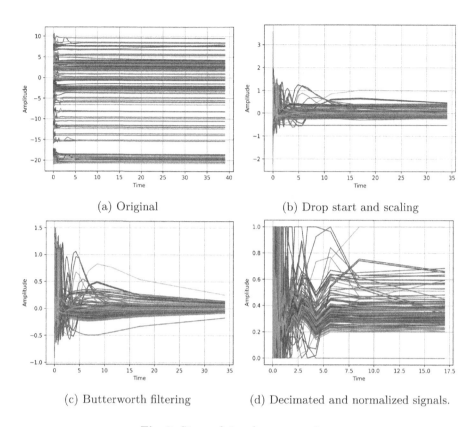

(a) Original

(b) Drop start and scaling

(c) Butterworth filtering

(d) Decimated and normalized signals.

Fig. 2. Steps of signal preprocessing.

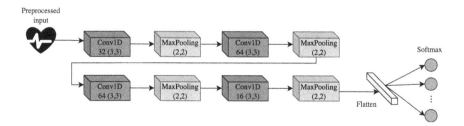

Fig. 3. Diagram of proposed 1D-CNN model.

language and TensorFlow 2.12 as DL framework. Also, we implemented the filtering of the biosignals with SciPy library [22]. For training, a validation set was not used due to the limited data of the dataset, we trained the model up to 25 epochs for each subset, but we observed that after 15 epochs it began to overfit. We found the best results by selecting the number of epochs by trial and error between 10 and 15. We used Adam as optimization algorithm with a learning rate of 0.0005 and a weight decay of 0.05. Finally, we use both tanh and ReLU activation functions in the hidden layers, selecting the model with the best results.

5.1   Validation Methods and Evaluation

We performed two different validation procedures over the experiments. A hold-out fixed partition, leaving the last two subjects out from the training set of each configuration—single-modal and multi-modal—, and use them as part of the test set (Fig. 4(a)); secondly, we performed LOUO which, essentially, is based on the leave-one-out cross validation method, that leaves only one pattern (or data sample) out of the training set so that it is used for testing purposes. This process is repeated with each sample on the dataset. In the particular case of LOUO, instead of leaving one sample out from the whole dataset, all samples of a given subject are left out of the training partition and are used as the testing set instead. A visual explanation of how LOUO works is shown in Fig. 4(b). As a result, by using LOUO we obtain deterministic results due the nature of the method itself. Moreover, by using this cross-validation method, we avoid data leakage, preventing that samples of any individual are present in both the training and testing sets at any time.

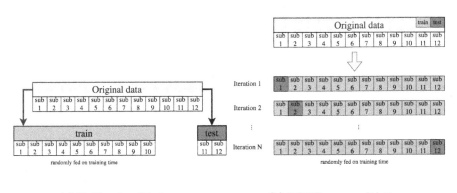

(a) Hold-out validation.   (b) LOUO cross-validation.

Fig. 4. Validation methods applied to YAAD dataset.

5.2 Classification Results

Hold-Out Modality. For the single-modal subset, we found the best result following training the model during 14 epochs and using ReLU on each hidden layer of the model. The confusion matrix can be found in the following Fig. 5(a).

On the other hand, for the multi-modal subset, we obtained the best results by training the model during 12 epochs and using tanh activation function for each hidden layer. The results are showed in the following Fig. 5(b).

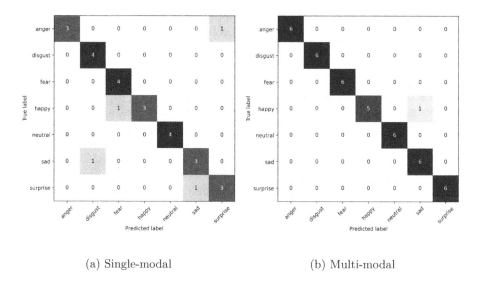

(a) Single-modal   (b) Multi-modal

Fig. 5. Confusion matrices of hold-out validation modality.

As seen in Fig. 5, when using only ECG signals we have some mistaken predictions of anger, happy, sad and surprise emotions. On the other hand, when using both ECG and GSR signals, we only get one misclassification of happy as sad.

LOUO Modality. By using LOUO cross-validation, we evaluate each subset by the number of subject within each one. Therefore, we compute the accuracy of each trial and then, average them to obtain the final result. The following Table 1, shows the computed accuracies for both hold-out and LOUO modalities.

Finally, as seen in Table 1, the results for the single-modal are not favorable when using LOUO validation. On the contrary, performance of the model over the multi-modal signals is very similar in both validation methods.

Table 1. Classification accuracies on both modalities.

Modal	Accuracy hold-out	Accuracy LOUO
Single-modal	0.8571	0.5952
Multi-modal	0.9762	0.9523

6 Conclusions

We have introduced a comprehensive approach comprising a preprocessing framework and a straightforward 1D convolutional model to classify two distinct categories of biomedical signals, namely ECG and GSR, across seven distinct emotional states: anger, disgust, fear, happiness, sadness, surprise, and neutrality. Our approach encompasses the incorporation of two distinct validation strategies to assess its efficacy: hold-out validation, which ensures that subjects are exclusively assigned to either the training or testing group but not both, and leave-one-user-out cross-validation.

With hold-out validation, our model has demonstrated commendable accuracy, achieving 0.8571 for single-modal signals and an impressive 0.9762 for multi-modal signals. Nevertheless, when subjected to leave-one-user-out cross-validation for single-modal signals, the accuracy drops to 0.5952. In stark contrast, the model's performance remains consistent for multi-modal signals, attaining an accuracy of 0.95. It is noteworthy that results obtained through leave-one-user-out cross-validation underscore the model's reliability, as it promotes a more robust generalization representation, particularly crucial for datasets containing intricate and noisy biosignal data.

Furthermore, our findings highlight a noteworthy observation: while ECG signals alone do not provide as comprehensive descriptions as GSR signals when individuals undergo emotional experiences induced by audiovisual stimuli, our model's multi-modal approach capitalizes on this distinction to deliver enhanced predictive performance.

The strengths of our proposal are worth emphasizing. Firstly, the neural network architecture chosen for our model possesses inherent variance, enabling it to extract generalizable features from non-stationary biosignals, which often exhibit distinct patterns among different subjects. Secondly, the meticulous selection of validation methods ensures that our model is never tested on data from subjects used for training. This not only bolsters its generalizability but also yields competitive accuracy, affirming its robustness in making predictions suitable for real-world applications.

Lastly, the simplicity of our CNN model, comprised of just four convolutional layers and a softmax classifier, makes it highly accessible for training, eliminating the need for specialized hardware like GPUs or accelerators. A standard CPU is sufficient, further enhancing the practicality of our proposal for deployment in real-life scenarios beyond laboratory settings.

Acknowledgements. The authors gratefully acknowledge the Instituto Politécnico Nacional (Secretaría Académica, Comisión de Operación y Fomento de Actividades Académicas, Secretaría de Investigación y Posgrado, Centro de Investigación en Computación) and the Consejo Nacional de Humanidades Ciencias y Tecnologías (CONAH-CYT) for their economic support to develop this work.

References

1. Alam, A., Urooj, S., Ansari, A.Q.: Human emotion recognition models using machine learning techniques. In: 2023 International Conference on Recent Advances in Electrical, Electronics & Digital Healthcare Technologies (REED-CON), pp. 329–334. IEEE (2023)
2. Bota, P., Zhang, T., El Ali, A., Fred, A., da Silva, H.P., Cesar, P.: Group synchrony for emotion recognition using physiological signals. IEEE Trans. Affect. Comput., 1–12 (2023)
3. Canal, F.Z., et al.: A survey on facial emotion recognition techniques: a state-of-the-art literature review. Inf. Sci. **582**, 593–617 (2022)
4. Chollet, F.: Deep Learning with Python, 2nd edn. Manning Publications, Shelter Island (2021)
5. Cui, H., Liu, A., Zhang, X., Chen, X., Wang, K., Chen, X.: EEG-based emotion recognition using an end-to-end regional-asymmetric convolutional neural network. Knowl. Based Syst. **205**, 106243 (2020)
6. Dar, M.N., Rahim, A., Akram, M.U., Gul Khawaja, S., Rahim, A.: YAAD: young adult's affective data using wearable ECG and GSR sensors. In: 2022 2nd International Conference on Digital Futures and Transformative Technologies (ICoDT2), pp. 1–7 (2022). https://doi.org/10.1109/ICoDT255437.2022.9787465
7. Davou, B.: Interaction of emotion and cognition in the processing of textual material. Meta **52**(1), 37–47 (2007)
8. Dzedzickis, A., Kaklauskas, A., Bucinskas, V.: Human emotion recognition: review of sensors and methods. Sensors **20**(3) (2020). https://doi.org/10.3390/s20030592. https://www.mdpi.com/1424-8220/20/3/592
9. Fan, T., et al.: A new deep convolutional neural network incorporating attentional mechanisms for ECG emotion recognition. Comput. Biol. Med. **159**, 106938 (2023)
10. Gahlan, N., Sethia, D.: Three dimensional emotion state classification based on EEG via empirical mode decomposition. In: 2023 International Conference on Artificial Intelligence and Applications (ICAIA) Alliance Technology Conference (ATCON-1), pp. 1–6. IEEE (2023)
11. Goshvarpour, A., Abbasi, A.: An emotion recognition approach based on wavelet transform and second-order difference plot of ECG. J. AI Data Mining **5**(2), 211–221 (2017)
12. Jerritta, S., Murugappan, M., Nagarajan, R., Wan, K.: Physiological signals based human emotion recognition: a review. In: 2011 IEEE 7th International Colloquium on Signal Processing and its Applications, pp. 410–415 (2011). https://doi.org/10.1109/CSPA.2011.5759912
13. Katsigiannis, S., Ramzan, N.: Dreamer: a database for emotion recognition through EEG and ECG signals from wireless low-cost off-the-shelf devices. IEEE J. Biomed. Health Inform. **22**(1), 98–107 (2017)
14. LeCun, Y., Bengio, Y., Hinton, G.: Deep learning. Nature **521**(7553), 436–444 (2015). https://doi.org/10.1038/nature14539

15. Lecun, Y., Bottou, L., Bengio, Y., Haffner, P.: Gradient-based learning applied to document recognition. Proceed. IEEE **86**, 2278–2324 (1998)
16. Lin, W., Li, C.: Review of studies on emotion recognition and judgment based on physiological signals. Appl. Sci. **13**(4), 2573 (2023)
17. Miranda-Correa, J.A., Abadi, M.K., Sebe, N., Patras, I.: AMIGOS: a dataset for affect, personality and mood research on individuals and groups. IEEE Trans. Affect. Comput. **12**(2), 479–493 (2018)
18. Oatley, K., Keltner, D., Jenkins, J.M.: Understanding Emotions. Blackwell Publishing (2006)
19. Ozdemir, M.A., Degirmenci, M., Izci, E., Akan, A.: EEG-based emotion recognition with deep convolutional neural networks. Biomed. Eng./Biomedizinische Technik **66**(1), 43–57 (2021)
20. Patil, V.K., Pawar, V.R., Randive, S., Bankar, R.R., Yende, D., Patil, A.K.: From face detection to emotion recognition on the framework of Raspberry pi and galvanic skin response sensor for visual and physiological biosignals. J. Electr. Syst. Inf. Technol. **10**(1), 1–27 (2023)
21. Song, T., Zheng, W., Song, P., Cui, Z.: EEG emotion recognition using dynamical graph convolutional neural networks. IEEE Trans. Affect. Comput. **11**(3), 532–541 (2018)
22. Virtanen, P., et al.: SciPy 1.0: fundamental algorithms for scientific computing in Python. Nat. Meth. **17**, 261–272 (2020). https://doi.org/10.1038/s41592-019-0686-2
23. Wu, Q., Dey, N., Shi, F., Crespo, R.G., Sherratt, R.S.: Emotion classification on eye-tracking and electroencephalograph fused signals employing deep gradient neural networks. Appl. Soft Comput. **110**, 107752 (2021)
24. Yang, M., Lin, L., Milekic, S.: Affective image classification based on user eye movement and EEG experience information. Interact. Comput. **30**(5), 417–432 (2018)

Feature Selection and Classification for Searching Light at Night Exposure and Students' Weight Relationship

Christian Sánchez-Sánchez[1](✉)(iD), Alfredo Piero Mateos-Papis[1],
Natalí N. Guerrero-Vargas[2], Alberto Manuel Ángeles-Castellanos[2],
and Carolina Escobar[2]

[1] Universidad Autónoma Metropolitana, Unidad Cuajimalpa, 05348 Ciudad de
México, México
{csanchez,amateos}@cua.uam.mx
[2] Universidad Nacional Autónoma de México, Departamento de Anatomía, Facultad
de Medicina, 04510 Ciudad de México, México
natalinadi@facmed.unam.mx, mangeles_castellanos@unam.mx,
cescobar@comunidad.unam.mx

Abstract. Circadian rhythm is essential for living beings. This rhythm
regulates sleeping and waking patterns, hormone production, eating
habits, digestion, and body temperature in humans and other animals.
Prolonged use of Light at Night (LatN) has become a factor that can confuse biological clocks. In our research, we utilized ANOVA to perform feature selection and classification algorithms to explore the potential correlation between night-time light exposure and medical surgeon students'
weight. Our findings revealed that incorporating LatN exposure data
resulted in enhanced classification outcomes. With this additional information, and not including BMI and height as features, the classifier was
better equipped to distinguish between those who are overweight/obese
compared to when only the students' weight was considered.

Keywords: ANOVA Feature Selection · Classification Algorithms ·
Light at Night exposure

1 Introduction

Circadian rhythm is essential for living beings. In some animals, like humans,
this rhythm controls when they should sleep and wake up, hormones released,
eating habits and digestion, and body temperature [1].

Some scientists have researched circadian rhythm by watching humans or
organisms with similar biological clock genes. To understand the adverse effects
but also the possible treatments for some diseases.

Although artificial light has brought great benefits to society, its prolonged
use has become a factor that can confuse biological clocks. That is why it has

H. Calvo et al. (Eds.): MICAI 2023, LNAI 14392, pp. 201–210, 2024.
https://doi.org/10.1007/978-3-031-47640-2_17

raised the interest in knowing the effect of overexposure to artificial lighting, emitted by light bulbs or electronic devices, on the weight of humans.

This research surveyed medical surgeon students at a Mexico City university. The questions were about their general information (age, weight, gender) and circadian disruption markers like wake up and bedtime on weekdays and weekends, breakfast, meal, and dinner times. Other questions were about the Light at Night (LatN) intensity and exposure students have through light bulbs, cellphones, or other electronic devices. From the survey results, a question emerged: Can we find relationships between LatN exposure and people's weight? That is to say, LatN attributes can help to predict if people are overweight/obese or not.

Through the use of Analysis of Variance (ANOVA), this research was able to determine the attributes that are most effective in classifying whether a person is overweight/obese or not. Once a set of characteristics were chosen, it was noticed that some of them provided information about LatN exposure, so those attributes were used to train a classifier with 13 different algorithms. The obtained results were compared against a baseline (explained better in the experiments section), in order to determine if taking into account LatN exposure information improved Classification results.

This paper is structured as follows: in the next section, related work is described. In Sect. 3 the data description is given, and in Sect. 4 it is shown information about the experiments' design and configuration details. The results of the experiments can be found in Sect. 5. Finally, conclusions and future work are in Sect. 6.

2   Related Work

Regarding the influence of LatN on animal's weight, some scientists have discovered that some animals under LatN overexposure have put on weight even though they didn't have changes in their caloric intake. For example, Arble et al. [2] observed a more significant weight gain in mice fed only during the light phase (resting) compared to mice fed only during the dark phase (active period) in a similar research Fonken et al. [3] noticed that mice were kept in constant light; they gained more weight than mice under a light/dark cycle. Similarly, rats fed during the light phase increased weight gain compared with rats fed only during the dark phase [4].

Brainard et al. [5] reports that melatonin secretion is potently inhibited by exposure to sufficient levels and durations of nighttime lighting in both rodents and humans. Short-duration sleep is associated with an elevated risk for obesity at all ages in humans [6].

McFadden E. and Colleagues [7] surveyed 113,000 women aged 16 or older living in the United Kingdom. Using multinomial logistic regression, they examined the association between exposure to light at night and obesity. They found a significant association, which was not explained by potential confounders they could measure.

Yong Seo Koo et al. [8] showed an approach where using univariate logistic regression analysis, they revealed a significant association between high outdoor lighting at night and obesity, but also, with multivariate logistic regression analyses, they showed that high outdoor LatN was significantly associated with obesity after adjusting for age and sex and other confounding factors including age, sex, educational level, type of residential building, monthly household income, alcohol consumption, smoking, consumption of caffeine or alcohol before sleep.

On the other hand, other studies have, as reported in [9, 10], said that morning light exposure helps to reduce body fat. And according to Karlsson et al. [11], shift work was associated with increased obesity, blood pressure, cholesterol, and hypertriglyceridemia in men and increased risk for obesity, hypertension, and hypertriglyceridemia in women.

It is essential to say that it isn't easy to find studies about LatN exposure in Mexican people.

3 Data Description

First, it is important to mention that all surveyed participants consented to using their data in this research.

To know the factors that affect circadian rhythm and can influence overweight/obesity, a group of researchers from the Faculty of Medicine apply a survey to the medical surgeon students. Through the questions, they collected general information like age, weight, height, and patterns in daily habits like 1) Sleep and wakefulness; 2) meal times; 3) LatN exposure, and 4) electronic device usage at night.

The answers include information on weekday and weekend patterns. The data was compiled in a tabular format where each row represents the information of each interviewed, and each column represents each answer of the 67 questions. At the end, a matrix with 67 columns was obtained, and for this research, an expert manually selected 31 of them. A new column, called "OBESITY, was added to the matrix" which indicates whether the student is overweight or obese. This information was gathered by calculating the Body Mass Index (BMI) of each individual. If the BMI is 25 or higher, the value in the column is "yes," and "no" otherwise. This last column was selected as the class or category for classification purposes.

The other 31 features (answers to the questions) are the next:

- General information: 2 attributes (weight and gender),
- Sleep times during week and weekend: 2 attributes
- Available sleeping information: 4 attributes
- Meals among week: 3 attributes
- Meals among weekend: 3 attributes
- Food consumption, in general: 8 attributes
- Light at night: 3 attributes
- Use of electronic devices before bed: 6 attributes

After wrong data was excluded, in total 2485 registries were collected.

The main objective of this research is to find if there is a relationship between LatN exposure and people's weight.

For example, during the Exploratory Data Analysis of two LatN features, it was noted that the percentage of overweight/obese individuals (the red color in graphics) was higher among those who reported greater exposure to LatN. This trend can be observed in Fig. 1.

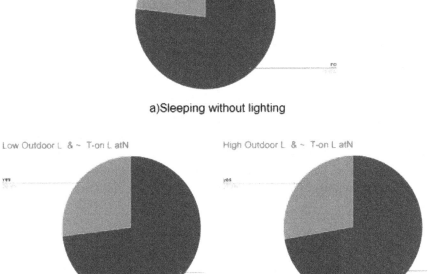

a)Sleeping without lighting

b) Low Outdoor LatN exposure and
Turning on the bedroom light
when waking up at Night

c)High Outdoor LatN exposure and
Turning on the bedroom light
when waking up at Night

Fig. 1. Excerpt of the trend of students based on their exposure to LatN. (Color figure online)

Unfortunately, the sample of people who reported high outdoor light intensity exposure and turning on their bedroom light if they wake up at night is just 6.4%. People who reported sleeping with low outdoor light intensity exposure and turning on their bedroom light were 15.7%. Meanwhile, 25% of people said sleeping without lighting. The remaining percentage was distributed among various configurations of sleeping with high and low outdoor light intensity exposure and turning their bedroom light on or not at night. Although analyzing this data couldn't come to any conclusion, it provided some valuable insights. Therefore, it was determined to carry out the ensuing experiments.

4 Experiments

4.1 Experiments Design

To answer the research question stated in the Introduction two experiments were designed.

1. The BMI helps to determine if a person is overweight/obese (BMI ≥ 25) or not (BMI < 25). But for calculating BMI, it is necessary to have the person's weight and height. And because the student's height wasn't considered a feature in the data for this research, just the attribute "WEIGHT" was used in the first experiment or baseline to train several classification algorithms. The Accuracy metric (Number of correct predictions/Total number of predictions) helped us to determine how well the classification was done.
2. To verify if LatN exposure was an important factor in determining if a person is overweight/obese or not, the following steps were done: a) Feature selection (from one attribute to 31 attributes) using Analysis of Variance (ANOVA) and train a classifier, evaluate Accuracy for each classifier and chose the set of attributes with the higher score. b) It was checked that in the selected set of attributes, there were features related to LatN exposure and then, c) Train twelve classification algorithms using the selected set of features and evaluate, applying the Accuracy metric, to resolve how well the classifier decide if a person is overweight/obese or not.

Subsequently, the best results obtained from experiments 1 and 2 were compared because if the results of the second experiment were better than the first one, it would mean that LatN attributes help to decide if a person is overweight/obese. So There could be a relationship between peoples' weight and LatN.

4.2 Configuration Details of Experiments

The twelve classification algorithms used for each experiment were the following: KNN with three neighbors, Support Vector Machines SVM (lineal y kernel RBF-gamma 2 y C 1-), Decision Tree (max_depth $= 7$), Random forest (max_depth $= 7$, n_estimators $= 10$, max_features $= 4$), Multilayer Perceptron (alpha $= 1$), AdaBoost, Naïve Bayes, Quadratic Discriminant Analysis QDA, Gaussian Process Classifier (1.0 * RBF (1.0)) and Logistic Regression. The rest of the parameters, those not mentioned previously, had the default value.

When generating random values for training-test splitting and inside of specific classification algorithms such as Support Vector Classification (SVC), Random Forest, and Decision Tree and others with cross-fold validation, a seed was established to ensure the reproducibility of all experiment results. The whole data was split into training, validation, and test subsets, and also all values were scaled using Standard Scaler function.

The experiments were performed using Python, especially the Sklearn library, for the classification algorithms. To do feature selection (ANOVA), the function SelectKBest was used with the parameter score_func = f_classif. The function SelectKBest was used to select from one to thirty-two attributes, and for each selection, an SVC algorithm was trained. The thirty-two classifiers were evaluated using the Accuracy metric, and the set of attributes with the higher score was selected to train the rest of the classification algorithms to assess their scores against the results obtained in the first experiment.

5   Experiments Results

5.1   Results of Experiment 1

Using just the 'Weight' attribute, the twelve classification algorithms were trained, and the following Accuracy results were obtained (see Table 1):

Table 1. Classifiers Accuracy using just "Weight" attribute.

Algorithm	Accuracy	Time (Training/Score)
KNN (3)	0.826	0.002 s/0.029 s
RBF SVM	0.875	0.079 s/0.028 s
Decision Tree	0.85	0.002 s/0.002 s
Random Forest	0.857	0.017 s/0.003 s
MLP	0.878	0.430 s/0.001 s
AdaBoost	0.88	0.120 s/0.010 s
Naive Bayes	0.875	0.001 s/0.001 s
QDA	0.875	0.007 s/0.003 s
Linear SVC	0.875	0.006 s/0.001 s
Linear SVM	0.875	0.035 s/0.009 s
Gaussian PC	0.875	16.043 s/0.019 s
Logistic R	0.875	0.004 s/0.001 s

It's important to mention that the results reported in the previous table are the score obtained by trying the classifier with the validation set. The accuracy of choosing the Linear SVC classifier and trying it with the test set was 0.892. Similar results were obtained using the rest of the classifiers.

5.2   Results of Experiment 2

According to the subsection "a", defined in 2nd experiment design, each attribute selection (from one to 31) was used to train a Classifier, employing the Support

Vector Machines (with a Linear Kernel). Then the results from each selection were compared, and the configuration of attributes with the highest score were chosen. With the purpose to find the score of each set of attributes, the classifier was evaluated through cross-validation, using ten folds.

The configuration of selected attributes, because it's highest score, was obtained with 18 characteristics (with an average score, obtained from the cross-validation results, of 0.889 Accuracy).

The selected attributes were the next: Weight (WEIGHT), Genre (GENRE), Sleeping Time on Weekdays (S TIME W), Sleeping Time on Weekends (S TIME WE), Wake up Timing (WAKEUP T), Midpoint of sleep (S MIDPOINT), Weekdays and Weekend Bedtime differences (DIFFERENCE ST), Feeding window on Weekdays (FEED WINDOW W), Dinner and Midpoint of sleep difference on Weekdays (D&BT T W), Feeding windows on Weekdays and Weekend difference (F WINDOWS DIF), Feeding windows Average (FW AVE), Main Meal JetLag (MAIN MEAL JL), Outdoor Light Intensity while sleeping (OUTDOOR LIGHT), The Intensity of lighting while sleeping (L INTENSITY), Turn lights on when waking up at night (TO L), Electronic Devices usage at night on Weekdays (ED U AN W), Electronic Devices usage at night on Weekend (ED U AN WE), Cell Phone usage on Weekends (CELLPHONE U WE).

The Table 2 displays the ANOVA scores, as well as the score (for distance between classes/compactness of classes), along with the names of the attributes. The names of the selected attributes are highlighted in bold.

From the selected attributes, the last six provide information on LatN exposure. This fulfills the condition in subsection "b," allowing the application of subsection "c." As a result, the classifier was trained using 18 attributes, and the obtained outcomes are shown in Table 3.

As in the previous experiment, the results reported in Table 3 are the score obtained by trying the classifier with the validation set. The accuracy of choosing the Linear SVC classifier and trying it with the test set was 0.904.

Comparing the results of the baseline (first experiment) and the second experiment, it seems to be helpful to use LatN exposure information in order to improve the classification.

As a final step, a statistical significance test (T-test) was applied to the results (from the first and second experiments). The null hypothesis "H0: There is no difference in the accuracies obtained from a classification using LatN" was rejected with a p-value of 0.001661, so it was concluded that the results of the second experiment were higher than the first.

Table 2. Scores of Features

SCORE	ATTR NAME
1313.236916	**WEIGHT**
4.215098	**GENRE**
2.348877	**S TIME W**
11.476662	**S TIME WE**
1.058688	**WAKEUP T**
0.403851	BEDTIME
0.870622	**S MIDPOINT**
1.256468	**DIFFERENCE ST**
1.193321	**FEED WINDOW W**
0.497424	D&MP T W
2.844227	**D&BT T W**
0.00178	FEED WINDOW WE
0.657725	D&MP T WE
0.703926	D&BT T WE
1.343658	**F WINDOWS DIF**
0.86784	**FW AVE**
2.258247	**MAIN MEAL JL**
0.142906	BREAKFAST JL
0.579498	DINNER JL
0.077947	METABOLIC JL AVE
0.051372	F MP MET JL
0.2671	EATING AT NIGHT
0.858443	**OUTDOOR LIGHT**
1.254109	**L INTENSITY**
3.143894	**TO L**
0.887489	**ED U AN W**
0.734635	**ED U AN WE**
0.038686	ED U DIFF
0.600086	CELLPHONE U W
0.734635	**CELLPHONE U WE**
0.731561	CELLPHONE U DIFF

Table 3. Classifiers Accuracy using 18 selected features.

Algorithm	Accuracy	Time (Training/Score)
KNN (3)	0.816	0.002 s/0.151 s
RBF SVM	0.789	0.186 s/0.101 s
Decision Tree	0.869	0.006 s/0.001 s
Random Forest	0.878	0.023 s/0.003 s
MLP	0.896	1.113 s/0.001 s
AdaBoost	0.88	0.155 s/0.011 s
Naive Bayes	0.866	0.001 s/0.001 s
QDA	0.785	0.005 s/0.001 s
Linear SVC	0.902	0.042 s/0.001 s
Linear SVM	0.9	0.068 s/0.009 s
Gaussian PC	0.893	34.967 s/0.036 s
Logistic R	0.9	0.008 s/0.001 s

6 Conclusions and Future Work

In this research, it was analyzed survey information that was applied to medical surgeon students with the purpose of finding a relationship between LatN and students' weight. First, a feature selection was performed using an Analysis of Variance (from one to 31 attributes). With the selected features, classifiers were trained to decide whether a student is overweight/obese or not. The results of the classifiers were evaluated through the Accuracy metric. The best classification results were obtained using 18 attributes, among which six are related to LatN information.

Different classification algorithms were trained using the same 18 selected features, and similar results were obtained. Those results were compared to the results of the classifier trained only with the "weight" attribute. It was proved that the classifiers trained using LatN information got better scores.

It can be concluded that a relationship between LatN and the students' weight was found; nevertheless, using only the information from the survey, it is difficult to find the kind of relationship. This gave us some ideas about how to follow future research and what information is necessary, for example, more data from the same people in time windows and extending the survey to other students. It would also be interesting to include questions related to types of diets and pre-existing diseases to find if the found relationship prevails.

References

1. U.S. Department of Health and Human Services: Circadian rhythms. National Institute of General Medical Sciences. https://nigms.nih.gov/education/fact-sheets/Pages/circadian-rhythms.aspx. Accessed 4 Sep 2023

2. Arble, D.M., Bass, J., Laposky, A.D., Vitaterna, M.H., Turek, F.W.: Circadian timing of food intake contributes to weight gain. Obesity (Silver Spring) **17**, 2100–2102 (2009)
3. Fonken, L.K., Workman, J.L., Walton, J.C., Weil, Z.M., Morris, J.S., et al.: Light at night increases body mass by shifting the time of food intake. Proc. Natl. Acad. Sci. U.S.A. **107**, 18664–18669 (2010)
4. Salgado-Delgado, R.C., Saderi, N., Basualdo Mdel, C., Guerrero-Vargas, N.N., Escobar, C., Buijs, R.M.: Shift work or food intake during the rest phase promotes metabolic disruption and desynchrony of liver genes in male rats. PLOS ONE **8**(4), e60052 (2013)
5. Brainard, G.C., Rollag, M.D., Hanifin, J.P.: Photic regulation of melatonin in humans: ocular and neural signal transduction. J. Biol. Rhythms **12**(6), 537–546 (1997)
6. Markwald, R.R., et al.: Impact of insufficient sleep on total daily energy expenditure, food intake, and weight gain. Proc. Natl. Acad. Sci. **110**(14), 5695–5700 (2013)
7. McFadden, E., Jones, M.E., Schoemaker, M.J., Ashworth, A., Swerdlow, A.J.: The relationship between obesity and exposure to light at night: cross-sectional analyses of over 100,000 women in the Breakthrough Generations Study. Am. J. Epidemiol. **180**(3), 245–250 (2014)
8. Koo, Y.S., et al.: Outdoor artificial light at night, obesity, and sleep health: cross-sectional analysis in the KoGES study. Chronobiol. Int. **33**(3), 301–314 (2016). https://doi.org/10.3109/07420528.2016.1143480
9. Danilenko, K.V., Mustafina, S.V., Pechenkina, E.A.: Bright light for weight loss: results of a controlled crossover trial. Obes. Facts **6**, 28–38 (2013)
10. Reid, K.J., Santostasi, G., Baron, K.G., Wilson, J., Kang, J., Zee, P.C.: Timing and intensity of light correlate with body weight in adults. PLoS ONE **9**(4), e92251 (2014)
11. Karlsson, B., Knutsson, A., Lindahl, B.: Is there an association between shift work and having a metabolic syndrome? Results from a population based study of 27 485 people. Occup. Environ. Med. **58**(11), 747–752 (2001)

PumaMedNet-CXR: An Explainable Generative Artificial Intelligence for the Analysis and Classification of Chest X-Ray Images

Carlos Minutti-Martinez[1(✉)] , Boris Escalante-Ramírez[1,2] ,
and Jimena Olveres-Montiel[1,2]

[1] Centro de Estudios en Computación Avanzada,
Universidad Nacional Autónoma de México (CECAv-UNAM), Mexico City, Mexico
{carlos_minutti,boris,jolveres}@cecav.unam.mx
[2] Laboratorio Avanzado de Procesamiento de Imágenes,
Universidad Nacional Autónoma de México (LaPI-UNAM), Mexico City, Mexico

Abstract. In this paper, we introduce PumaMedNet-CXR, a generative AI designed for medical image classification, with a specific emphasis on Chest X-ray (CXR) images. The model effectively corrects common defects in CXR images, offers improved explainability, enabling a deeper understanding of its decision-making process. By analyzing its latent space, we can identify and mitigate biases, ensuring a more reliable and transparent model. Notably, PumaMedNet-CXR achieves comparable performance to larger pre-trained models through transfer learning, making it a promising tool for medical image analysis. The model's highly efficient autoencoder-based architecture, along with its explainability and bias mitigation capabilities, contribute to its significant potential in advancing medical image understanding and analysis.

Keywords: Medical Image Analysis · Autoencoder · Explainable Artificial Intelligence · Chest X-Ray

1 Introduction

Medical image understanding is predominantly carried out by skilled medical professionals. However, the limited availability of human experts and the drawbacks of fatigue and imprecise estimation associated with manual analysis limit the effectiveness of medical image interpretation. Convolutional Neural Networks (CNNs) have emerged as powerful tools for image understanding and have demonstrated superior performance to human experts in various image-related task [24].

Deep Learning, specifically CNNs, has shown significant advancements in object recognition, image analysis, and classification tasks. In the medical field, CNNs have found successful applications. However, training CNNs requires a

H. Calvo et al. (Eds.): MICAI 2023, LNAI 14392, pp. 211–224, 2024.
https://doi.org/10.1007/978-3-031-47640-2_18

substantial amount of data and computational resources, and gathering medical image data presents significant challenges, both in terms of cost and time. Transfer Learning (TL) addresses this challenge by fine-tuning pre-trained CNNs from large datasets like ImageNet, reducing the need for extensive medical data. Nevertheless, TL has its limitations due to differences between objects in datasets like ImageNet and medical images, such as varying shapes and image characteristics. Furthermore, pre-trained CNNs from ImageNet come with millions of parameters, posing computational challenges, whereas a medical imaging dataset could potentially be classified more efficiently with a model pre-trained on data similar to medical images.

Additionally, large CNN models lack explainability, a crucial feature for reliable medical image analysis to ensure unbiased results. Moreover, these large models may not be practical in resource-limited areas, where financial, technological, or human resources are scarce but could benefit from this technology. For instance, ranking patients who require urgent attention could be made more accessible with smaller, more explainable models.

Recent surveys underscore the significance of CNNs in medical imaging. Suganyadevi *et al.* [28] review 120 medical imaging research papers with the ResNet architecture standing out for its high performance. It is also mentioned how challenges remain, such as the scarcity of properly annotated data, limited medical imaging datasets compared to general computer vision datasets, and the considerable expenses associated with teaching deep learning models, often requiring high-end GPUs. The use of black-box models is also a major obstacle due to legal ramifications, leading to healthcare professionals' reluctance to rely on them.

Sarvamangala and Raghavendra [24] survey CNNs applications in medical image understanding of some diseases of the brain, breast, lung, colon, skin, eyes, heart and other organs, being classification and segmentation the main tasks performed. The authors mention how CNNs are highly efficient methods of feature extraction, but black-boxes with the need of research in terms of analyzing and understanding output at every layer.

In the context of addressing the lack of large, high-quality labeled datasets, Semi-Supervised (SSL) or Unsupervised Learning (USL) methods have been explored. Solatidehkordi and Zualkernan [27] present a survey of the latest SSL methods proposed for medical image classification tasks, where Virtual Adversarial Training (VAT) is one of the must successful methods, but it keeps having the explainability problem.

Autoencoders, a type of neural network architecture, play a crucial role in USL, serving for dimensionality reduction, feature extraction, and data compression. Comprising an encoder and decoder, autoencoders map input data into a compressed representation (latent space) and then reconstruct the original or variant data from the compressed representation. This architecture finds applications in image denoising, compression, anomaly detection (*e.g.* [7]), and can be a base for more complex models like Variational Autoencoders (VAEs) to generate new data samples with specific characteristics. The latent space can also be used for classification tasks, leading to supervised or semi-supervised models.

There are multiple autoencoders architectures and applications (see [6]). Some of these architectures have proven their effectiveness in various medical imaging tasks. For example, Huang *et al.* [14] proposed an active learning framework called variational deep embedding-based active learning (VaDEAL) that uses a VAE with sampling strategies to improve the accuracy of diagnosing pneumonia and utilizes the latent space for classification. Another study by Raghavendra *et al.* [14] employed a VAE for data imputation on Chest X-Ray (CXR) images, treating high opacity regions as missing data for lung area segmentation using a U-net (see [22]) type segmentation.

Although CXR images are commonly available in medical datasets, their analysis has gained significant attention with the onset of COVID-19 (*e.g.* [3,17,18,21,29]). Many CNN-based works for classifying the disease rely heavily on large CNN models and TL. Some of these approaches address the explainability problem by using Grad-CAM (see [25]) to detect relevant areas in the model's decision-making process and lung segmentation to mitigate biases. However, Grad-CAM may not provide a comprehensive understanding of the model's internal workings. The visualization is limited to highlighting areas but does not provide a explanation of how the model arrived at a particular decision, and lung segmentation may not be sufficient on its own to completely avoid biases, as critical features for decision-making could exist outside or even within the segmented lung areas, such as medical devices like pacemakers, catheters, or tubes (see [19]). Moreover, pre-trained Large-CNN models still face computational burdens for training and prediction.

In this paper, we present the advancements of the PumaMedNet project, which aims to design a CNN architecture for medical image classification with low computational costs for transfer learning, achieving comparable accuracy to current standards while maintaining high explainability and bias detection and mitigation. Our initial release focuses on CXR images, utilizing a denoising β-VAE as the model's backbone. The model is trained and validated on the ChestX-ray14 medical imaging dataset, comprising 112,120 frontal-view X-ray images of 30,805 unique patients with fourteen common disease labels, obtained through NLP techniques from radiological reports. Further validation involves transfer learning on a composite dataset of 19,362 CXR images, including COVID-19 cases not present in the ChestX-ray14 dataset.

Our results demonstrate comparable performance with pre-trained Large-CNN models like ResNet- 18 while enhancing bias mitigation and explainability by exploring the effects of variables in the latent space.

2   Methodology

The methodology of the project was divided into several stages to develop the CNN architecture based on an Autoencoder for medical image classification. The following are the key stages:

2.1 Model Architecture

Base Architecture Selection. An Autoencoder was chosen as the base structure to describe the visual characteristics of the images. The Autoencoder allows generating a vector of latent variables (latent space) that capture essential image information, enabling explainability through the analysis of the latent space, without requiring supervised learning.

Evaluation of Autoencoder Architectures. Several Autoencoder architectures were explored and compared (see [23]). The VAE architecture has a continuous latent space approximation to a normal distribution. A β-VAE [8] is an extension of the standard VAE that incorporates a hyperparameter called β. The β aims to disentangle and control the learned representations in the latent space by a penalization of the KL-divergence between the latent space and a independent normal distribution, resulting in the following characteristics.

- Disentangled Representations: β-VAEs encourage individual latent variables to capture specific features, facilitating precise control and manipulation of the generated data.
- Explainability: The disentangled representations foster more interpretable latent spaces, simplifying the comprehension and analysis of learned features.
- Bias Mitigation: Through explicit disentanglement of variation factors, β-VAEs offer potential for mitigating biases in generated data and the decision-making process of models by adjusting or deactivating factors contributing to bias.

However, the β hyperparameter introduces a trade-off between reconstruction accuracy and disentanglement, necessitating careful selection of this value.

The β-VAE model was expanded by incorporating a classification layer that employs the latent space for classification tasks. Additionally, a denoising/corrective component was integrated by training the β-VAE with defective images as input, and measuring the error between the output and the image without added defects. Figure 1 presents the schematic diagram of the β-VAE model, where an input image which is rotated and flipped horizontally is provided as input, and a corrected image is produced in the output.

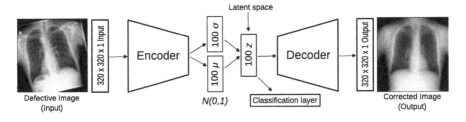

Fig. 1. Schematic diagram of the PumaMedNet-CXR model.

Hyperparameter Optimization. We conducted a series of trial-and-error experiments to optimize the model's hyperparameters, encompassing factors like latent space size, layer count, units per layer, and activation functions. The following details highlight the final architectural characteristics:

- Latent Space Size: The latent space comprises one hundred variables. Although the experiments indicated a feasible size of fifty variables, it was considered beneficial to opt for a larger latent space, useful for when transfer learning is performed across numerous classes.
- Layers: Our architecture employs six layers for the encoding algorithm and another six for decoding, utilizing ConvTranspose2d for deconvolution. Extending the number of layers for the encoder and decoder did not demonstrate enhancements in classification or reconstruction tasks. Excessively deep layers were intentionally avoided to preserve efficiency.
- Activation Functions: A range of activation functions, including ReLU, GeLU, ELU, LeakyReLU, SiLU, and the novel Smish [31], were evaluated. LeakyReLU(0.15) emerged as the most effective choice.
- Batch Normalization: Incorporating batch normalization into each encoder and decoder layer did not yield improvements due to the architecture's limited layer count. Hence, the final model omits batch normalization.
- Dropout: The dropout function introduces redundancy in the latent variables, which is an undesirable feature in the proposed model, potentially compromising explainability, so it was excluded.
- Skip-Connections: While skip-connections were explored to enhance image reconstruction, their introduction consistently affected latent space sensitivity. This reduction in explainability contradicted the model's objectives, leading to their exclusion.
- Classification Layer: This layer comprises two fully connected layers from the latent space to the classes, utilizing ReLU activation. Increasing the layer count resulted in higher classification errors.

This architecture results in a total of 1,405,753 trainable parameters, which is less than lightweight, state-of-the-art architectures tailored for mobile devices, such as MobileNetV3 Small [13], with 2,542,856 parameters.

Loss Function Investigation. Structural Similarity Index [32] (SSIM) is an image quality assessment metric that measures the similarity between two images. It quantifies the structural information, luminance, and contrast similarities, making it a useful alternative to Mean Squared Error (MSE) as a loss function in the autoencoder architecture, which only measures pixel-wise differences.

SSIM is designed to mimic human perception of image similarity, making it more aligned with the human visual system's sensitivity to changes in structure and textures. And its use in Medical Image Analysis as also been studied (see [20]). In addition, Bergmann *et al.* [7] found that it is more useful for Unsupervised Defect Segmentation, where an autoencoder is trained to reconstruct images, and defected on images can be found by differences between reconstruction and the input image. These characteristic can be useful for the model, for a zero-shot training, where classification is possible, even for classes which are not part of the training dataset.

In addition, MSE loss can suffer from gradient saturation, especially when the autoencoder produces images that are far from the ground truth. SSIM mitigates this problem by providing a more informative loss signal during training.

Emphasis on Regions of Interest During Training. To enhance sensitivity towards crucial regions in CXR images, like the lungs, we incorporated a weighted mask during the autoencoder training (Fig. 2). This strategy enabled the model to concentrate on clinically significant areas, thereby refining its performance.

Pre-training. Building upon the methodology proposed by Singh *et al.* [26], who utilized weakly supervised pre-training to enhance image recognition performance, we adopted a similar approach. In our case, the model was pre-trained on three distinct datasets. These include the *Describable Textures Dataset* [9] comprising 5,640 images across 47 classes, the *Textures Classification dataset* [1] containing 8,674 images categorized into 64 classes, and the *Medical MNIST* dataset [4] comprising a substantial collection of 58,954 medical images grouped into 6 classes. For a visual representation of this pre-training process, refer to Fig. 2, which showcases example images and their corresponding reconstructions.

Evaluation and Result Comparison. The ChestX-ray14 dataset comprises 112,120 CXR images, an expansion of the ChestX-ray8 dataset [30], encompassing fourteen common thoracic pathologies: Atelectasis, Consolidation, Infiltration, Pneumothorax, Edema, Emphysema, Fibrosis, Effusion, Pneumonia, Pleural thickening, Cardiomegaly, Nodule, Mass and Hernia. An additional category labeled "No finding" is also included. This dataset serves as the foundation for training and validating the model.

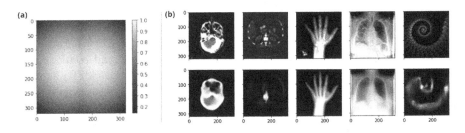

Fig. 2. (a) Weighted mask used for the loss function. Higher weights are assigned to the area of the lungs to prioritize its reconstruction. (b) Samples of original input and reconstruction for the pre-training dataset.

Furthermore, to provide additional validation, TL is conducted on a composite dataset of three categories: Pneumonia, COVID-19, and Normal. These categories were sourced from various publicly accessible datasets [2,10,15,16]. Duplicate images were identified using the Geeqie software [11], detecting images with a visual similarity exceeding 97% and treating them as identical. This validation dataset comprises a total of 19,362 CXR images, with 1,831 images designated for testing. Half of these images correspond to the lung segmentation of the dataset, to introduce visual variability similar to that of the original ChestX-ray14 dataset.

Comparative results were obtained against a fine-tuned pre-trained ResNet-18 model, with 11,689,512 parameters, making it 8.3 times larger than our model.

3   Results

A sample of defective inputs and the corresponding autoencoder outputs, correcting rotation and flipped images, is presented in Fig. 3. Additionally, denoising characteristics were included in the model through Gaussian Blur, Random Equalize, and Random Autocontrast applied to the input images, to be corrected at the output.

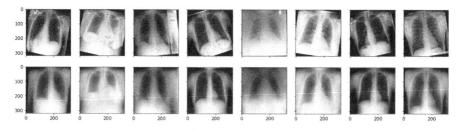

Fig. 3. Sample of input (first row) and reconstructed-corrected images (second row) for the ChestX-ray14 dataset.

Table 1 displays a comparative analysis of various studies involving classification using the ChestX-ray14 dataset. Wang *et al.* [30] examined different CNN architectures (AlexNet, GoogLeNet, VGGNet-16, ResNet-50), with ResNet-50 achieving the best results. Yao *el al.* [33] employed a custom architecture, while Gundel *et al.* [12] utilized an approach based on DenseNet121. Baltruschat *et al.* [5] experimented with different ResNet architectures and achieved results similar to each other.

From the results, it is evident that the smallest architecture with similar performance to PumaMedNet is Baltruschat's ResNet-38 *et al.*, which has at least 16 times as many parameters as PumaMedNet, resulting in PumaMedNet achieving better performance when considering the computational burden.

Table 1. AUC values for different studies on the ChestX-ray14 dataset

| Pathology | Wang et al. | Yao et al. | Guendel et al. | Baltruschat et al. | | | PumaMedNet |
				ResNet-38	ResNet-50	ResNet-101	
Atelectasis	0.700	0.733	0.767	0.763	0.755	0.747	**0.770**
Cardiomegaly	0.810	0.856	**0.883**	0.875	0.877	0.865	0.863
Consolidation	0.703	0.711	0.745	0.749	0.742	0.734	**0.787**
Edema	0.805	0.806	0.835	0.846	0.842	0.828	**0.874**
Effusion	0.759	0.806	0.828	0.822	0.818	0.818	**0.862**
Emphysema	0.833	0.842	**0.895**	**0.895**	0.875	0.868	0.856
Fibrosis	0.786	0.743	**0.818**	0.816	0.800	0.778	0.771
Hernia	0.872	0.775	0.896	**0.937**	0.916	0.855	0.834
Infiltration	0.661	0.673	0.709	0.694	0.694	0.686	**0.710**
Mass	0.693	0.777	**0.821**	0.820	0.810	0.796	0.770
Nodule	0.669	0.718	**0.758**	0.747	0.736	0.738	0.674
Pleural Thicken	0.684	0.724	0.761	0.763	0.742	0.739	**0.783**
Pneumonia	0.658	0.684	**0.731**	0.714	0.703	0.694	0.702
Pneumothorax	0.799	0.805	0.846	0.840	0.819	0.839	**0.861**
Average	0.745	0.761	**0.807**	0.806	0.795	0.785	0.794
No Findings	—	—	—	0.727	0.725	0.720	**0.754**

Figure 4 shows the ROC curves and AUC values for the 15 classes (14 diseases and a "No finding" category) of the ChestX-ray14 dataset. Additionally, ROC-AUC is displayed for CXR type (AP, PA), SEX (M, F), and AGE (above or below the median), which are metadata included in the dataset. The results demonstrate that the model effectively separates CXR type and sex classes and accurately predicts age.

3.1   Latent Space Interpolation

The latent space generated by the model can be used to simulate and explore how the model "understands" specific characteristics. For example, By studying the average values of the latent space for the "No finding" class versus other health conditions, it is possible to modify any image to increase or decrease its health value. The modification is achieved through latent space manipulation, by doing $z_i^* = z_i + \alpha(z_1 - z_0)$, where z_i^* is the modified latent space of the image z_i, z_1 is the average value for the latent space for the class "No finding", and z_1 the average value for any other class. Larger positive α values increase health, whereas larger negative values decrease health.

Figure 5 presents examples of health, age, and sex modifications for some images. Younger versions of the image display a more rounded thorax and better contrast compared to the versions of older patients. Health modification mainly affects lung opacity, being higher for versions of a sicker patient. Changing from female to male results in increased thorax and heart size, as well as shoulders, while the basic structure of the lungs remains the same.

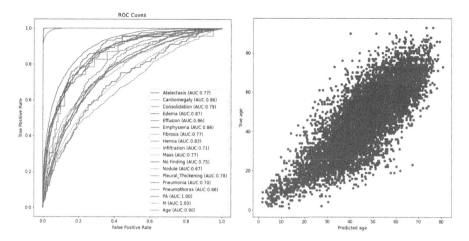

Fig. 4. ROC curves for the 15 classes of the ChestX-ray14 dataset and CXR type (AP or PA), Sex (M or F), Age (above or below the median), and predicted vs True age, reported for the patients in the test dataset.

3.2   Transfer Learning

Fine-tuning the PumaMedNet-CXR model and a ResNet-18 model (which has 8.3 times more parameters), yielded very similar performance metrics, as shown in Table 2.

3.3   Explainability

Although ResNet-18 performed similar in the classification task than PumaMedNet-CXR, our model allows for a better understanding of the decision-making process done by the model. Although ResNet-18 performed similarly to PumaMedNet-CXR in the classification task, our model provides better explainability of the decision-making process. Figure 6 illustrates the effect of varying a latent variable that has been found to be crucial for classification. By varying its values, it changes the size of the heart, likely related to detecting whether the CXR image is AP or PA, as the AP view results in a heart magnification on the X-ray film, because in the AP view the beam enters from front to back.

Latent variable related to any bias can be ignored in the classification task, or randomly changed. Resulting in a model which does not have this bias. Understanding these latent variables allows the avoidance of biases in the classification task without the need for complete model retraining or dataset modification.

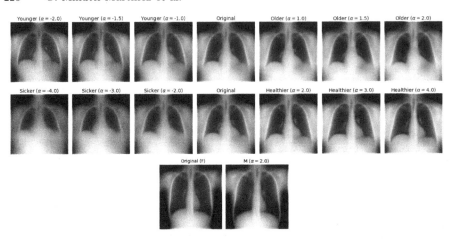

Fig. 5. Decoded images for the modification of the latent space to change the age, health, and sex of the original image. From younger to older (first row), from sicker to healthier (second row), and from female to male (third row).

Table 2. Classification results using PumaMedNet-CXR and ResNet-18

PumaMedNet-CXR

	precision	recall	f1-score	support
COVID19	0.993	0.994	0.994	1224
NORMAL	0.919	0.951	0.935	634
PNEUMONIA	0.981	0.969	0.975	1804

ResNet-18

	precision	recall	f1-score	support
COVID19	0.999	0.998	0.999	1224
NORMAL	0.911	0.951	0.931	634
PNEUMONIA	0.983	0.968	0.976	1804

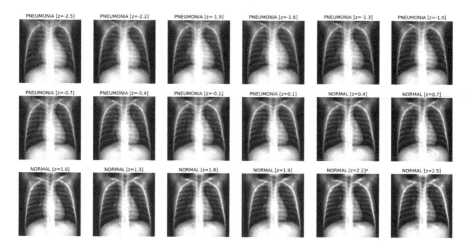

Fig. 6. Model explainability: By varying one of the latent variables most relevant for classification, it can be seen how it changes the size of the heart, resulting in different classifications.

4   Summary and Conclusions

In this study, we presented the PumaMedNet-CXR, an autoencoder-based CNN architecture designed for medical image classification, particularly focusing on Chest X-ray (CXR) images.

We demonstrated the effectiveness of the PumaMedNet-CXR in correcting common defects found in CXR images, such as rotation, flipping, and denoising. The model achieved comparable performance with a ResNet-18 model, despite having significantly fewer parameters, highlighting its efficiency. Furthermore, the explainability offered by the PumaMedNet-CXR allowed us to gain insights into the decision-making process of the model and detect important latent variables relevant for classification.

Through the manipulation of the latent space, we showed how the model can simulate and explore specific characteristics, such as age, health status, and sex.

Additionally, we explored the use of transfer learning to fine-tune the model on a smaller dataset, demonstrating that the PumaMedNet-CXR can achieve similar performance to larger pre-trained models like ResNet-18 while retaining better explainability.

The explainability offered by the model is of great importance in medical image analysis, as it provides transparency in the decision-making process, helps detect potential biases, and enhances the trustworthiness of the model's predictions. Avoiding biases is crucial in ensuring equitable healthcare outcomes for all patients.

Future work will focus on extending this approach to other medical imaging modalities and exploring the model's performance on a broader range of medical conditions, while continuing to prioritize explainability and bias mitigation.

Acknowledgements. This work was supported by the DGAPA's postdoctoral fellowship program (programa de becas posdoctorales) at UNAM and the PAPIIT-DGAPA-UNAM grant IV100420.

Data Availability Statement. The PumaMedNet-CXR model and weights are openly available at https://github.com/cminuttim/PumaMedNet-CXR.

References

1. abin24: Textures classification dataset (2023). https://github.com/abin24/Textures-Dataset
2. agchung: Covid-19 image dataset (2023). https://github.com/agchung
3. Alshmrani, G.M.M., Ni, Q., Jiang, R., Pervaiz, H., Elshennawy, N.M.: A deep learning architecture for multi-class lung diseases classification using chest x-ray (CXR) images. Alex. Eng. J. **64**, 923–935 (2023). https://doi.org/10.1016/j.aej.2022.10.053
4. apolanco3225: Medical mnist classification (2017). https://github.com/apolanco3225/Medical-MNIST-Classification
5. Baltruschat, I.M., Nickisch, H., Grass, M., Knopp, T., Saalbach, A.: Comparison of deep learning approaches for multi-label chest x-ray classification. Sci. Rep. **9**(1), 6381 (2019). https://doi.org/10.1038/s41598-019-42294-8
6. Bank, D., Koenigstein, N., Giryes, R.: Autoencoders (2021)
7. Bergmann, P., Löwe, S., Fauser, M., Sattlegger, D., Steger, C.: Improving unsupervised defect segmentation by applying structural similarity to autoencoders. In: 14th International Conference on Computer Vision Theory and Applications, pp. 372–380 (01 2019). https://doi.org/10.5220/0007364503720380
8. Burgess, C.P., et al.: Understanding disentangling in β-vae (2018)
9. Cimpoi, M., Maji, S., Kokkinos, I., Mohamed, S., Vedaldi, A.: Describing textures in the wild. In: Proceedings of the IEEE Confeerence on Computer Vision and Pattern Recognition (CVPR) (2014)
10. Cohen, J.P., Morrison, P., Dao, L.: Covid-19 image data collection. arXiv 2003.11597 (2020). https://github.com/ieee8023/covid-chestxray-dataset
11. Geeqie: A free open software image viewer and organiser program for UNIX-like operating systems (2023). https://www.geeqie.org/
12. Gündel, S., Grbic, S., Georgescu, B., Liu, S., Maier, A., Comaniciu, D.: Learning to recognize abnormalities in chest x-rays with location-aware dense networks. In: Vera-Rodriguez, R., Fierrez, J., Morales, A. (eds.) CIARP 2018. LNCS, vol. 11401, pp. 757–765. Springer, Cham (2019). https://doi.org/10.1007/978-3-030-13469-3_88
13. Howard, A., et al.: Searching for mobilenetv3 (2019)
14. Huang, J., et al.: Variational deep embedding-based active learning for the diagnosis of pneumonia. Front. Neurorobot. **16**, 1059739 (2022). https://doi.org/10.3389/fnbot.2022.1059739
15. de la Iglesia Vayá, M.,et al.: BiMCV COVID-19+: a large annotated dataset of RX and CT images from COVID-19 patients (2021). https://doi.org/10.21227/w3aw-rv39
16. Kermany, D.: Labeled optical coherence tomography (OCT) and chest X-Ray images for classification (2018)

17. Kumar, S., Mallik, A.: COVID-19 detection from chest x-rays using trained output based transfer learning approach. Neural Process. Lett. **55**(3), 2405–2428 (2023). https://doi.org/10.1007/s11063-022-11060-9
18. Kwon, H.J., Lee, S.H.: A two-step learning model for the diagnosis of coronavirus disease-19 based on chest x-ray images with 3d rotational augmentation. Appl. Sci. 12(17) (2022). https://doi.org/10.3390/app12178668
19. Mathew, R.P., Alexander, T., Patel, V., Low, G.: Chest radiographs of cardiac devices (part 1): lines, tubes, non-cardiac medical devices and materials. S. Afr. J. Radiol. **23**(1), 1729 (2019). https://doi.org/10.4102/sajr.v23i1.1729
20. Mudeng, V., Kim, M., Choe, S.W.: Prospects of structural similarity index for medical image analysis. Appl. Sci. **12**(8) (2022). https://doi.org/10.3390/app12083754
21. Nillmani, Sharma, N., Saba, L., Khanna, N.N., Kalra, M.K., Fouda, M.M., Suri, J.S.: Segmentation-based classification deep learning model embedded with explainable AI for COVID-19 detection in chest x-ray scans. Diagnostics (Basel) **12**(9), 2132 (2022). https://doi.org/10.3390/diagnostics12092132
22. Ronneberger, O., Fischer, P., Brox, T.: U-net: convolutional networks for biomedical image segmentation. In: Navab, N., Hornegger, J., Wells, W.M., Frangi, A.F. (eds.) MICCAI 2015. LNCS, vol. 9351, pp. 234–241. Springer, Cham (2015). https://doi.org/10.1007/978-3-319-24574-4_28
23. Roth, K., Ibrahim, M., Akata, Z., Vincent, P., Bouchacourt, D.: Disentanglement of correlated factors via hausdorff factorized support. In: International Conference on Learning Representations (ICLR) (2023). https://openreview.net/forum?id=OKcJhpQiGiX
24. Sarvamangala, D.R., Kulkarni, R.V.: Convolutional neural networks in medical image understanding: a survey. Evol. Intel. **15**(1), 1–22 (2021). https://doi.org/10.1007/s12065-020-00540-3
25. Selvaraju, R.R., Cogswell, M., Das, A., Vedantam, R., Parikh, D., Batra, D.: Grad-CAM: visual explanations from deep networks via gradient-based localization. In: 2017 IEEE International Conference on Computer Vision (ICCV), pp. 618–626 (2017). https://doi.org/10.1109/ICCV.2017.74
26. Singh, M., et al.: Revisiting weakly supervised pre-training of visual perception models (2022)
27. Solatidehkordi, Z., Zualkernan, I.: Survey on recent trends in medical image classification using semi-supervised learning. Appl. Sci. **12**(23) (2022). https://doi.org/10.3390/app122312094
28. Suganyadevi, S., Seethalakshmi, V., Balasamy, K.: A review on deep learning in medical image analysis. Int. J. Multimedia Inf. Retrieval **11**(1), 19–38 (2022). https://doi.org/10.1007/s13735-021-00218-1
29. Sultana, A., et al.: A real time method for distinguishing COVID-19 utilizing 2D-CNN and transfer learning. Sensors **23**(9) (2023). https://doi.org/10.3390/s23094458
30. Wang, X., Peng, Y., Lu, L., Lu, Z., Bagheri, M., Summers, R.M.: ChestX-ray8: hospital-scale chest x-ray database and benchmarks on weakly-supervised classification and localization of common thorax diseases. In: 2017 IEEE Conference on Computer Vision and Pattern Recognition (CVPR). IEEE, July 2017. https://doi.org/10.1109/cvpr.2017.369
31. Wang, X., Ren, H., Wang, A.: Smish: a novel activation function for deep learning methods. Electronics **11**(4) (2022). https://doi.org/10.3390/electronics11040540

32. Wang, Z., Bovik, A., Sheikh, H., Simoncelli, E.: Image quality assessment: from error visibility to structural similarity. IEEE Trans. Image Process. **13**(4), 600–612 (2004). https://doi.org/10.1109/TIP.2003.819861
33. Yao, L., Prosky, J., Poblenz, E., Covington, B., Lyman, K.: Weakly supervised medical diagnosis and localization from multiple resolutions (2018)

Robotics and Applications

Visual Navigation Algorithms for Mobile Manipulators in Service Shops

J. A. Cisneros Morales[1], E. R. Altamirano Ávila[2], R. Mendivil-Castro[3], and L. A. Muñoz[4(✉)]

[1] Microsoft, Redmond, USA
josci@microsoft.com
[2] ZF Eurofren Investment, Germany & México, Friedrichshafen, Germany
edisonricardo.altamirano@zf.com
[3] University of Essex, Colchester, UK
roberto.mendivilcastro@essex.ac.uk
[4] Tecnologico de Monterrey, Monterrey, Mexico
amunoz@tec.mx

Abstract. In this paper, we present a computer vision-based robotic grasp detection approach which was recognized as the most consistent solution at the AirLab 2021 Challenge. The main objective was to accurately navigate, locate and grasp multiple cans in order to place them on a shelf.

Keywords: Task and Motion Planning · Service Robotics · Vision-Based Navigation · TIAGo[5] robot · Pal Robotics · Visual Grasping · Bin-Packing Problem · robotics retail · ROS · MoveIt

1 Introduction

The dynamics of service robotics adoption varies significantly between developed and developing countries. In certain instances, the rate of adoption in developing countries surpasses expectations, despite the challenges of relatively low wages and a significant technical diaspora. A considerable number of non-automated jobs remain unaddressed, highlighting the untapped potential in these regions. Economists argue that the key driver of national growth is the human factor— the talent of the workforce and the conditions of their work environments. Innovation is a deeply interactive process, necessitating a conducive and challenging environment. Our method enables the detection of optimal grasp points and object classification in a single step by performing classification and grasp detection simultaneously. Instead of utilizing region proposal techniques, we compute graspable bounding boxes in two stages. This model can be extended to dual-arm grasps per object by employing a locally constrained prediction mechanism. Locally constrained models exhibit superior performance, particularly when grasping a diverse array of objects. As a consequence of the international challenge, we pinpoint a technological trend that constitutes a significant integration milestone. Through

H. Calvo et al. (Eds.): MICAI 2023, LNAI 14392, pp. 227–238, 2024.
https://doi.org/10.1007/978-3-031-47640-2_19

the Robot Operating System (ROS), we provide[1] and validate useful components. During the pandemic, a joint venture between Ahold Delhaize and the Delft University of Technology led to the launch of an international competition (see Fig. 1) aimed at developing an open innovation service robotics application. This application is intended to deploy robots in supermarkets[10], convenience stores, and online stores, serving over 54 million customers weekly across the US, Europe, and Indonesia.

Fig. 1. TIAGo Robot at AirLab challenge

2   Industrial Challenge

In several economies, the primary cause of inflation is the scarcity of talent and labor, predominantly in the service sector. This challenge, undeniably attractive and demanding, arises mainly from the technical prerequisites. It entails navigating a mobile robot equipped with elementary grasping capabilities and intricate object manipulation skills to position objects on a shelf. The robot was tasked to identify a table with a collection of objects and subsequently place them on a cabinet-style shelf using its proximity and image capture sensors. It is relatively uncommon for enterprises to regard technology investment as a means to reduce expenses, let alone to enhance productivity. A novel dimension emerges when a firm continuously integrates evolving technologies that challenge new educational paradigms in an open and competitive manner. In these trials and experiences, the spirit of camaraderie, even on virtual platforms, fosters the solidification of learning and, most importantly, the cultivation of a global perspective. Despite the necessity to overcome linguistic obstacles, occasionally, more formidable cultural barriers exist. This article delineates a comprehensive methodology to address these challenges from a computational robotics stand-point. We scrutinize navigation, obstacle circumvention, grasp planning, object manipulation, and task accomplishment. The

---

[1] Available upon request

code for each development within the ROS platform is publicly accessible in a repository. The research delineated herein elucidates contemporary applications of service robotics and highlights potential opportunities.

3   The Problem Formulation

The problem to be solved involves the process of stocking, collecting, and organizing products on supermarket shelves, particularly in the last mile. Employing point cloud segmentation, the automaton initiates by aligning the cans before the shelving unit through the utilization of Algorithm 6. Upon arriving at the table and shelving area, it pivots its gaze towards the table and engages a sophisticated algorithm for detecting tables and cans, harnessing the power of point cloud segmentation. This enables the system to introduce these objects into Moveit's Planning Scene, thereby orchestrating the appropriate arm movement sequences. To enhance the precision of can localization, we have devised a 2D vision approach, which accurately pinpoints the center of each cylinder. Once the objects are identified, a meticulous assessment identifies the can closest to its left arm, whereupon it is expertly grasped. This iterative process is replicated as many times as necessary, each iteration culminating in a distinctive arm trajectory for the automaton. Notably, even in the face of movement perturbations (as elucidated in Fig. 11), the robotic arms exhibit remarkable resilience, equipped with a recovery mechanism. This ensures that, in the event of a failure, the system can make subsequent attempts to execute the task. Thanks to the presence of the robot's reference map, this strategic approach effectively mitigates extraneous movements that might otherwise result in collisions, rendering the entire operation safer and more dependable

4   Development

4.1   Navigation

SLAM (simultaneous localization and mapping) allows the robot to accomplish this task by understanding the environment (mapping) and its position (location). (localization). As a result, autonomous robots can explore their environment securely without clashing with humans or crashing into items.

Path Planning. A path planner uses the laser scan from the TIAGo robot to estimate the robot's position. As part of our autonomous navigation system, we used the PAL Robotics local planner (see Fig. 2) which produces velocity instructions for transmission to a mobile base based on a plan and a cost-map. TIAGo Robot's local planner package has outperformed Timed Elastic Band (TEB) and Dynamic Window Approach (DWA) in our tests.

Mapping. For this work, we used a virtual environment that consisted of a table on which several identical cans remained static, and a shelf next to it on which cans could be stacked. For the TIAGo robot to effectively solve the stacking challenge, it had to travel to two separate locations, scan the entire shelf, pick the items, and arrange them. By using its sensors, the robot discovered its surroundings and determined where the

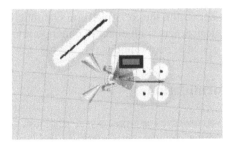

Fig. 2. TIAGo Robot with PAL Robotics' local planner

Fig. 3. Point clouds retrieved from LIDAR and interpretation of the system

table and shelf were located, so it could travel there. To do this, we processed the point cloud data from the robot's laser and discovered all of the clusters. Each of the table's legs as well as the shelf were then identified based on these clusters. It is important for us to locate the left- front leg because it was found by comparing the dimensions of the cluster and using the coordinates of the cluster relative to the shelf to distinguish between the table's legs: the left-front leg is closest to the shelf. A red cross indicates the robot's next position after finding the optimal position. Figure 3 depicts all of the clusters for the simulation, as well as the left-front leg circled in green and the robot's next position.

4.2   Vision

3D Collision Map. A primary goal of our vision system was to detect collisions and constraints. We developed a 3D occupancy grid mapping approach using the MoveIt Planning Scene interface/cite Coleman2014, in proceedings moveit, which offers data structures and mapping algorithms in C++ with Python APIs. We used two different methods to introduce items: first, we enabled the point cloud to automatically create an OctoMap, as shown in Fig. 4, and second, we provided accurate descriptions of the objects. As a result, the robot was aware of all the items it had to consider when traveling from point A to point B, as well as those with which it could interact. OctoMap's design would mean a significant trade-off in time to detect small collision features. As a mitigation, those were added using existing descriptions.

Methods to Detect & Add Collision Objects to the Map - 3D. We believe our system's ability to segment 3D point clouds into numerous homogeneous areas is one of its

Fig. 4. Octomap generated from point clouds

most important features. The points of a certain object can be retrieved using a variety of algorithms, but we most commonly use two. First, the RANSAC Algorithm was implemented for Plane and Cylinder segmentation, as shown in Algorithms 1 and 2. An iterative approach to estimating parameters of a mathematical model in the presence of outliers without letting the outliers affect the estimates. As a second step, our system uses *Euclidean Cluster Extraction* to identify the table, shelf, and cylinders, along with a post-processor to filter the point clouds. A Euclidean Cluster Extraction involves partitioning data according to the minimum distance that must exist between points for them to be considered part of the same group. This implementation allowed TIAGo robot to separate point cloud data into various objects. Figs. 5, 6, 7 demonstrate the result of PCL viewer after utilizing RANSAC Algorithm, Clustering detection, and pass through filters from raw PCL data.

Methods to Detect & Add Collision Objects to the Map - 2D. Despite demonstrating that a 3D projection can be used to resolve an issue like this, it also performed worse than our 2D Vision solution and required more computational power [3]. The cans were located on a planar surface using a 2D approach using circle/ellipse detection [5] as shown in Fig. 6. As the depth picture and intrinsic elements from a calibrated stereo camera were used to project pixels into 3D points, the approaches were implemented using Fig. 8 and Algorithm 3.

Algorithm 1 Detect Table

1: Get latest point cloud
2: Clean points outside of expected z-range
3: **while** table is not found and cloud still has points **do**
4:      Use RANSAC algorithm to obtain candidate plane
5: **if** plane is a table **then**
6:      Calculate plane details
7:      Add plane to the planning scene
8:      break
9:   Remove plane from cloud

Algorithm 2 Detect Shelf and Place Positions

1: Get latest point cloud
2: Clean points outside of expected z-range
3: **while** shelf is not found and cloud still has points **do**
4:      Use RANSAC algorithm to obtain candidate plane
5:      **if** plane is a shelf **then**
6:          Obtain plane details from cloud
7:          Calculate place positions in plane
8:          Publish place positions
9:          break
10:     Remove plane from cloud

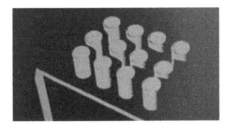

Fig. 5. Point clouds Segmentation of cans

Fig. 6. Point clouds Segmentation of table

Figure 8 also shows how to use this method to add 3D objects to Moveit's Planning Scene.

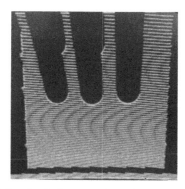

Fig. 7. Point clouds Segmentation of empty space in shelf

Algorithm 3 Detect Cylinders 2D

1: Get latest RGB and depth images
2: Compute circle centers (top of the cans) in RGB image
3: *canPoses* ← []
4: **for** each circle center detected **do**
5:     Deproject circle center in 2D image to a 3D point
6:     Create can pose and append to *canPoses*
7: Remove previous cans from planning scene
8: **for** each *pose* in *canPoses* **do**
9:     **if** *pose* is on the table **then**
10:         Add cylinder to planning scene

4.3 Object Manipulation

Through the use of vision algorithms, the TIAGo robot understood the location of the cans, where to place them, and what obstacles were in the path.

Pick Technique. An algorithm was developed to retrieve the nearest can to the left arm. The TIAGo selection is depicted in Fig. 9 as a pose stamped coordinate of the first can that the robot will pick; TIAGo's selection is depicted with a big red vector originating from the object and a set of smaller arrows surrounding it to show how it might be grasped, which are rotations around the z-axis. The pseudocode is presented in Algorithm 4.

Place Technique. A robot analyzes the shelf to determine where the cans should be placed. The vision algorithms described in the preceding section are used to acquire measurements and the location of the center of the empty area. An algorithm is used to place the six cans in this area after the data is collected. By using a fixed margin to the edge of the empty space and its x center value, the position of the central front can is determined (Yellow Cross, Fig. 10) and the others (Red Cross, Fig. 10) are placed with fixed margins. The pseudocode is presented in Algorithm 5 (Fig. 12).

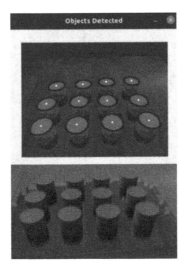

Fig. 8. Can's location with 2D approach and its result in Moveit's Planning Scene

---

Algorithm 4 Pick can loop function

---

function Pick-can-loop(*canList*)
    static: $i := 0$
    while $i <$ lEn(*canList*) **do**
        selectedCan $\leftarrow$ *canList*[*i*]
        for *attempt* $\leftarrow$ 1 to 3 **do**
            pick_can(*selectedCan*)
            if Success **then return** *selectedCan*
            else if Planning Failed **then** break
            else if Invalid Motion Plan **then** break
    return None

Fig. 9. Result of Planning Scene, Position of a can and its possible Grasps.

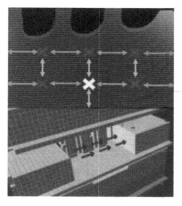

Fig. 10. Point clouds segmentation in the shelf and calculation of the new can's location.

Fig. 11. TIAGo robot placing a can with place server and gazebo link attacher

---

Algorithm 5 Place can loop function

---

    function Place-can-loop(*pickedCan, placesList*)
        while Available place in *placesList* **do**
            place← next-available-place(*placesList*)
            for *attempt* ← 1 to 3 **do**
                place-can(*place, pickedCan*)
                if Success **then return** *place*
                else if Planning Failed **then** break
                else if Invalid Motion Plan **then** break
            Mark *place* as failed place
        return None

Algorithm 6 Strategy

1: Initialization
2: Go to shelf and scan for available places
3: Go to table and scan for cans
4: **while** *True* **do**
5:    Pick-can-loop(*canList*)
6:    **if** picking cans failed **then** break
7:    place-can-loop(*pickedCan,*   *placeMatrix*)
8:    **if** placing can failed **then** break

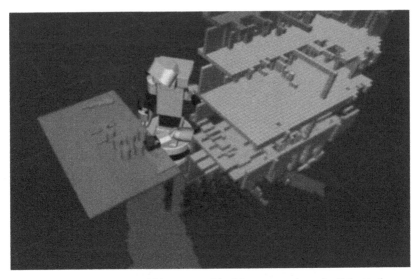

Fig. 12. TIAGo robot grabbing a can with pick server and gazebo link attacher

5 Results

MoveIt [7, 8] is used to manipulate TIAGo's arms. This library offers the required trajectories for a robot's arm to position the end effector in a certain location. A pick and place server was developed for both arms, so the robot can grab and place cans. Moreover, the gazebo_link_attacher library was added in order to attach and detach objects with the gripper, resulting in better performance in the gazebo simulation [4]. We used *OMPL* [6], which contains several cutting- edge sampling-based motion planning techniques; our system uses RRTConnect. In this planning technique, a solution is returned as soon as it is found. *OMPL* does not provide any collision detection or visualization code. To prevent *OMPL* from being tied to a specific collision checker or visualization front end, this was done. This library is designed so that it can be easily incorporated into systems that provide the extra components. It shows a low performance in generating possible robot trajectories using this motion planner. To enhance the system, a pos-processor, such as the one we used, called Covariant Hamiltonian optimization for motion planning (*CHOMP*), is necessary. Gradient-based trajectory optimization simplifies and trains many common motion planning problems. To construct a high-accuracy can grasping and relocation model, a hybrid approach through simulation experiments and dynamic emulation was developed. In the algorithms, we describe three representative approaches (described in the algorithms) for integrating active learning loops and data augmentation to enrich the multidimensional dataset and cultivate the model's accuracy of execution. We investigated several generalized algorithmic design principles and validated them as a final demonstration using data analysis.

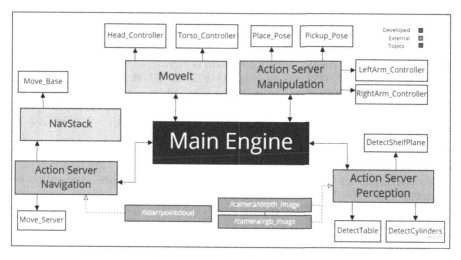

Fig. 13. Main functions diagram

6 Conclusion

Using ellipse detection, we present an accurate computer vision-based approach to robotic grasp detection of several cans. We have developed an approach that recognizes the object and finds a good grasp point in a single step. As opposed to most high-dimensional motion planners, which divide trajectory generation into separate planning and optimization phases, this technique combines covariant gradient and functional gradient approaches to trajectory optimization to create a motion planning algorithm that is solely focused on trajectory optimization. *CHOMP* responds to its surroundings to swiftly move the trajectory out of collision while optimizing dynamical parameters like joint velocities and accelerations. The graspable bounding boxes are computed in two stages, unlike region proposal techniques. By using a locally constrained prediction mechanism, this model can be extended to dual-arm grasps per object. Especially on objects that can be grasped in a variety of ways, the locally constrained model performs significantly better. A useful set of components is presented in Fig. 13 and explained in the proposed algorithms 1–6, from which the community can build upon. The new methods and extensions will incorporate the possibility of handling non-regular objects as well as more complete methods for optimizing the placement and ordering of objects [9]. We continue to work on the extension of these results to be able to incorporate teleoperation capabilities, as well as to incorporate more robust dexterous effector organs such as articulated hands [1] suitable for picking up objects of various shapes whose process requires not only pick and place but even visual servoing for dexterous manipulation [2].

References

1. Munoz, L.A., Bard, C., Najera, J.: Dexterous manipulation: a geometrical reasoning point of view. In: Proceedings of 1995 IEEE International Conference on Robotics and Automation, vol. 1, pp. 458–463 (1995). https://doi.org/10.1109/ROBOT.1995.525326
2. Munoz, L.A.: Robust dexterous manipulation: a methodology using visual servoing. In: Proceedings. 1998 IEEE/RSJ International Conference on Intelligent Robots and Systems. Innovations in Theory, Practice and Applications (Cat. No.98CH36190), vol. 1, pp. 292–297 (1998). Doi: 10. 1109/IROS.1998.724634
3. Fitzgibbon, A., Pilu, M., Fisher, R.B.: Direct least square fitting of ellipses. In: IEEE Trans. Pattern Anal. Mach. Intell. **21**(5), 476–480 (1999). https://doi.org/10.1109/34.765658
4. Koenig, N., Howard, A.: Design and use paradigms for Gazebo, an open- source multi-robot simulator. In: 2004 IEEE/RSJ International Conference on Intelligent Robots and Systems (IROS) (IEEE Cat. No. 04CH37566), vol. 3, pp. 2149–2154 (2004). https://doi.org/10.1109/IROS.2004.1389727
5. Jiang, N., Jiang, Z.: Distance measurement from single image based on circles. In: 2007 IEEE International Conference on Acoustics, Speech and Signal Processing - ICASSP '07, vol. 1, pp. I-809-I- 812 (2007). https://doi.org/10.1109/ICASSP.2007.366031
6. Sucan, I.A., Moll, M., Kavraki, L.E.: The open motion planning library. IEEE Robot. Autom. Mag. **19**(4), 72–82 (2012). https://doi.org/10.1109/MRA.2012.2205651
7. Coleman, D., et al.: Reducing the barrier to entry of complex robotic software: a moveit! case study. J. Softw. Eng. Robot. **5**(1), 3–16 (2014)
8. Görner, M., et al.: MoveIt! Task Constructor for Task-Level Motion Planning. In: May 2019, pp. 190–196. https://doi.org/10.1109/ICRA.2019.8793898
9. Caccavale, R., et al.: A flexible robotic depalletizing system for supermarket logistics. IEEE Robot. Autom. Lett. **5**(3), 4471–4476 (2020). https://doi.org/10.1109/LRA.2020.3000427
10. Costanzo, M., et al.: Can Robots Refill a Supermarket Shelf?: Motion Planning and Grasp Control. IEEE Robot. Autom. Mag. **28**(2), 61–73 (2021). https://doi.org/10.1109/MRA.2021.3064754

NATLOC: Natural Language Object Localization

Erik Ricardo Palacios Garza and Luis Torres-Treviño[✉]

Universidad Autónoma de Nuevo León, San Nicolás de los Garza, Mexico
`luis.torrestrv@uanl.edu.mx`

Abstract. This paper presents a novel approach for interacting with a robot in a virtual environment based on one-shot object localization using an image generator model, an image matching model, and a differentially trained robot. The user provides a textual description of an object, which is used by the image generator model to generate a corresponding image. This generated image is then compared with the visual input from a camera mounted on the differential robot, enabling precise object localization when the object is within the camera's field of view. The robot is trained using Reinforcement Learning techniques to align itself with the requested object. In this way, the robot locates a wide variety of objects solely based on natural language input.

Keywords: One-shot object localization · Image generator model · Reinforcement Learning

1 Introduction

By implementing a computer vision system in a robot, it becomes possible to develop more complex behaviors compared to systems with perception limited solely to sensors. Furthermore, if a communication system is integrated between humans and the robot, tasks or behaviors can be developed that even individuals without robotics expertise could generate in a robot.

There are some works that have attempted to solve task generation for robots using natural language instructions as inputs, such as [1–3]. These models generate tasks based on natural language instructions and an image from the robot's environment as inputs. However, these models have the limitation of only working with pretrained objects. In this work, we will address a method to complete tasks given natural language inputs while having the advantage of working with a much larger variety of objects in the robot's environment.

When it is necessary to locate objects using robotic systems, there are various methods that can be used for both the perception system and the motor system. One can opt to use sensors that measure various characteristics of the environment where the robot is located to determine the location of an object. Image processing algorithms can also be used to enable a robot to perform a specific task with its vision [4]. However, the use of image processing limits the

© The Author(s), under exclusive license to Springer Nature Switzerland AG 2024
H. Calvo et al. (Eds.): MICAI 2023, LNAI 14392, pp. 239–250, 2024.
https://doi.org/10.1007/978-3-031-47640-2_20

robot's capabilities to very specific tasks and objects for each problem. Finally, when a more generalized vision capability is required, deep learning models are used so that the robot in question can recognize and/or locate various objects [5–7]. The disadvantage of employing classification and object detection models is that the robot is restricted to working exclusively with the objects for which the deep learning model has been trained. As a result, a challenge emerges when a more profound generalization of objects that a robotic system should be able to detect becomes necessary.

Taking into account these disadvantages, a model has been proposed in this work where it is intended to have the location of objects with more complex characteristics than those that could be detected with the previously mentioned methods. For this, the coupling of three models from different areas of deep learning is proposed: Image generation from text descriptions, image matching models, and Reinforcement Learning models.

The proposed model takes as input the name or a description of the object that needs to be found. This description is processed by the image generation model, obtaining a representation of the object in RGB format. This image is compared with the image captured by a camera mounted on a differential robot. This comparison is made with the image matching model. When a match has been found between the robot's vision and the reference image, the robot is oriented towards said object using a policy generated by a Reinforcement Learning model. Regarding image generators, there are numerous online models available to accomplish this task. However, when one desires to implement a customized model using these generators, the easiest approach is to implement the DALL-E model from OpenAI using the Hugging Face library corresponding to this model. This model, is a variant of GPT-3 [8], has the ability to generate images from text descriptions, providing a new approach to object recognition and generation. For image matching models, there are different methodologies such as the Speeded-Up Robust Features (SURF) Model [9], Oriented FAST and Rotated BRIEF (ORB) [10], and Scale-Invariant Feature Transform (SIFT) [11]. However, these techniques have limitations in handling significant variations in scale, orientation, and occlusion of objects when the camera is moving, some experiments were made to proof this limitations, in Figs. 1 and 2 it can be observed some of this experiments. Therefore, the DEep Local Features (DELF) algorithm was chosen. It has been recognized for its ability to identify and match local features in images, even in the face of large scale variations and occlusion [12].

Finally, for the generation of behaviors in robots, control theory could be used to perform various tasks [13]. However, keeping the generalization of concepts that are to be addressed in this work, it was decided to use Reinforcement Learning.

Reinforcement Learning has taken on a crucial role in training robots, allowing them to learn from their interaction with the environment to improve their decisions over time. Various Reinforcement Learning methods have been proposed for the navigation and orientation of robots as is mentioned in [14], achieving notable performance in these systems [15]. As can be seen in the literature, one of the quintessential Reinforcement Learning models for robotic systems is Deep Deterministic Policy Gradient (DDPG) [16]. This model is characterized by its rapid convergence towards a desirable policy for most of the tasks that are to be performed with reinforcement agents. This work is based on the aforementioned advances, combining the generation of images from text descriptions, the localization and recognition of objects through deep learning, and the control of robots through Reinforcement Learning. This synergy of techniques presents a promising solution to the problem of object localization in robotics.

2 Theory and Research

2.1 Image Generation

Within the generation of images from text, as its name suggests, the aim is to obtain an image from a description expressed in natural language. Currently, there are different image generation models [17, 18]. In this work, we will focus on the DALL-E model [19] due to its ease of use and the low computational cost offered by its "mini" version.

The architecture of DALL-E consists of an encoder and a decoder. The encoder processes the text input and transforms it into a latent representation, which contains relevant information about the image that will be generated. The decoder takes this representation and generates the corresponding image. It has an architecture similar to that present in the GPT-3 model [8]. However, the generation of the training data was done by compressing and tokenizing this encoded representation of the images and then joining it with the text tokens that describe these images using a transformer [20].

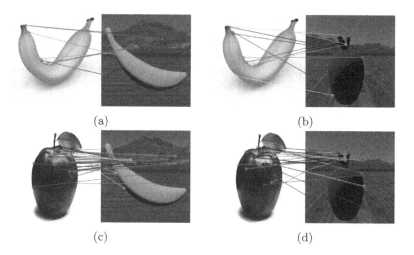

(a)   (b)

(c)   (d)

Fig. 1. Results from the model Brute-Force Matcher

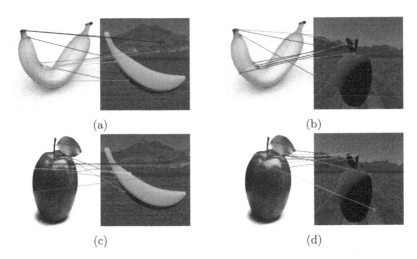

(a)   (b)

(c)   (d)

Fig. 2. Results from the model ORB

2.2   Image Matching Model

Image matching models are used to compare two or more images by analyzing specific features of each one. When there is a relationship between several features of two images, it can be inferred that they belong to the same class.

The extraction of the features of the two images can be performed using different methods. For example, when we talk about the SIFT model, it mostly uses image processing procedures to achieve correct feature extraction. The procedure that SIFT follows for feature extraction is based on the principle of extracting key points using representations at different scales of the images being analyzed, as well as a difference of Gaussians space to find points of interest such as edges and corners in the images. Then, descriptors are constructed based on features extracted from the scales and the difference of Gaussians.

On the other hand, the DELF model, being trained using Deep Learning, can have a better generalization of the features that are extracted from the images. The DELF model uses a convolutional neural network to generate several descriptors in the images. Similarly, an attention layer is trained to select the most relevant descriptors of the image. This allows for a compact and efficient representation of the image in question. Finally, different methodologies can be used to compare descriptors generated between two images and see if they could belong to a common class. Two examples of these methodologies for searching for similar descriptors are KD-tree and RANSAC.

2.3   Reinforcement Learning

The generation of behaviors in robots spans different disciplines, from control theory, swarm robotics, evolutionary algorithms, among others. However, when it comes to generating behaviors that require decision-making in a wide variety of situations, Reinforcement Learning has shown great results in the literature [21,22]. That's why this type of model has been chosen for the control of the robot in this work.

There are different Reinforcement Learning models. For this work, we will use models based on policy gradient, specifically the Deep Deterministic Policy Gradient (DDPG) model, which has been shown in the literature to have a high success rate in developing suitable policies for robot behaviors [23,24].

DDPG is a Reinforcement Learning algorithm that combines policy learning methods and Q learning methods. The goal is to learn a deterministic policy $\mu(s|\theta^\mu)$ that maps states s to actions a, and an action-value function $Q(s, a|\theta^Q)$ that approximates the expected value of the long-term return.

The policy is trained by updating the weights θ^μ of the neural network that implements it. The update is done through the gradient of the loss function:

$$\nabla_{\theta^\mu} J \approx E_{s_t \sim \rho^\beta}[\nabla_a Q(s, a|\theta^Q)|s = s_t, a = \mu(s_t) \nabla_{\theta^\mu} \mu(s|\theta^\mu)|_{s_t}] \tag{1}$$

where J is the objective function to be optimized, ρ^β is a probability distribution over states s, and $E_{s_t \sim \rho^\beta}$ is the expected value of the distribution. The update is done through a stochastic gradient descent process.

The action-value function is trained by updating the weights θ^Q of the neural network that implements it. The update is done through the gradient of the loss function:

$$L(\theta^Q) = E_{(s,a,r,s') \sim D}[(Q(s, a|\theta^Q) - y)^2] \tag{2}$$

where D is a set of experience samples (s, a, r, s'), and y is the learning target, given by:

$$y = r + \gamma Q'(s', \mu'(s'|\theta^{\mu'})_{\theta^{\mu'}}, \theta^{Q'}) \tag{3}$$

where r is the reward received by the agent, γ is the discount factor, and $\theta^{\mu'}$ and $\theta^{Q'}$ are smoothed versions of the parameters of the main networks.

2.4 Differential Robot

The mobile robot configuration used was the differential one, with its mathematical model based on A. Bara [25] as follows:

– Kinematic Model.

$$\begin{bmatrix} \dot{x}_c \\ \dot{y}_c \\ \dot{\theta} \end{bmatrix} = \begin{bmatrix} \frac{r}{2}cos(\theta) - \frac{rd}{2R}sin(\theta) & \frac{r}{2}cos(\theta) + \frac{rd}{2R}sin(\theta) \\ \frac{r}{2}sin(\theta) + \frac{rd}{2R}cos(\theta) & \frac{r}{2}sin(\theta) - \frac{rd}{2R}cos(\theta) \\ \frac{r}{2R} & -\frac{r}{2R} \end{bmatrix} \tag{4}$$

Here, $\dot{x}_c$ and $\dot{y}_c$ are the positions of the robot's center of gravity, r is the radius of the wheels, $2R$ is the separation distance of the wheels, and d is the distance from the central point of the wheels to the robot's center of gravity.

– Dynamic Model.

$$\mathbf{M} \cdot \dot{v} + H(v) = \mathbf{B} \cdot \tau \tag{5}$$

where:

$$\begin{bmatrix} m & 0 \\ 0 & I_p + m \cdot d^2 \end{bmatrix} \begin{bmatrix} \dot{v} \\ \dot{w} \end{bmatrix} + \begin{bmatrix} -m \cdot d \cdot \dot{\theta}^2 \\ m \cdot d \cdot v \cdot \dot{\theta} \end{bmatrix} = \begin{bmatrix} \frac{1}{r} & \frac{1}{r} \\ \frac{R}{r} & -\frac{R}{r} \end{bmatrix} \begin{bmatrix} \tau_d r \\ \tau_d l \end{bmatrix} \tag{6}$$

3   Methodology

As mentioned earlier, a differential configuration robot was used for this work, which was simulated using the Webots (Cyberbotics Ltd.) robotics simulation software. The robot has dimensions of $0.5\,\mathrm{m} \times 0.19\,\mathrm{m} \times 0.3\,\mathrm{m}$, consisting of 4 infrared sensors, an ultrasonic sensor, and a camera. The robot can be seen in Fig. 4.

The robot operates on a square platform of $5\,\mathrm{m} \times 5\,\mathrm{m}$, delimited by a wall of $0.2\,\mathrm{m}$ in height. The robot starts its process at the point (0,0), which is located in the center of the platform with a random orientation from $0°$ to $360°$. Around the robot, different objects are positioned in random order with the same angle of separation on a circular path centered at (0,0) with a radius of 2m. The objects are oriented towards the center of the platform. A representation of the initial conditions of the process can be seen in Fig. 3.

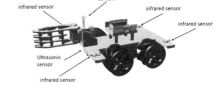

Fig. 4. Robot architecture.

Fig. 3. Example of initial conditions of the process.

The algorithm of this work can be seen in Fig. 6, where it starts with a text input placing the name of the object or describing it. This input is processed by the DALL-E model, generating an image according to the input provided (anchor image). Once this image is obtained, the robot's process to find the object begins.

Once this image is obtained, the process of comparing the images using the DELF model begins. This process tries to find the orientation that has the highest number of shared features between the robot's vision and the anchor image. While no match is found between these two, the robot will execute a search policy to find a match.

This search policy was generated using Reinforcement Learning, specifically the DDPG model, with the following characteristics for the training of the mentioned policy:

- **State:** The state used consists of the robot's position (x,y), its orientation (θ), its linear speed, and its angular speed.
- **Goal:** The goal is the orientation in which the image with the highest number of matches with the anchor image is located, as long as it has already been seen

by the robot. Otherwise, the goal will be a random orientation, promoting a search method.

- **Actions (a):** The robot's actions consist of a single output, which indicates the angular speed of the wheels as well as their direction of rotation, where $a \in [-10, 10]$.

- **Actor and target actor networks:** The architecture of the actor and target actor neural networks consists of an input layer of 6 neurons, which form the concatenated state and goal of the robot, two hidden layers of 512 neurons each with a ReLu activation function, and a single neuron output, which represents the action taken, having tanh as the activation function. The Actor network has a learning rate of 0.0001.

- **Critic and target critic networks:** The architecture of the critic and target critic neural networks consists of an input layer of 7 neurons, which form the state, the goal, and the action taken by the robot, two hidden layers of 512 neurons each with a ReLu activation function, and a single neuron output, which represents the evaluation of the action taken in the state where the robot was. This last layer does not contain an activation function. The critic network has a learning rate of 0.0002.

- **Reward function:** The reward function used is the error between the goal and the robot's orientation, this error being a penalty. In addition to the orientation error penalty, an angular speed penalty was added to achieve damping when the robot reaches its goal. This reward function can be seen in Eq. 7.

The agent's training consisted of two stages. The first stage set a random orientation as the main goal. From an acceptable convergence, the agent's goal changes. Now, while the agent does not locate the main goal, it should be reaching random sub-goals. Once the main goal is visualized, it should orient itself towards it and remain in that orientation.

To specify the goal once found, the centroid of the locations of the matches in the robot's image was used. This can be seen in Fig. 5.

$$Reward = -(e/\pi)^2 - 0.2(\dot{\theta}/\dot{\theta}_{max})^2 \qquad (7)$$

Fig. 5. Example of centroid visualization.

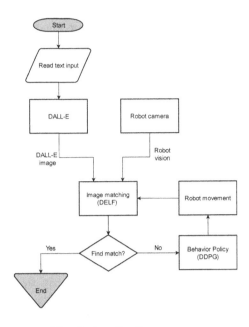

Fig. 6. Localization process.

4 Results

4.1 Agent Training Results

The training of the robot's search policy took approximately 9936 s. This training was carried out on a computer with an i7 processor using an NVIDIA GeForce RTX 2060 GPU. The training can be seen in Fig. 7.

In total, the training was carried out with a total of 15 different objects, obtaining the images shown in Fig. 8 of the objects as the first results.

The average performance of the robot's positioning system can be seen in Figs. 10 and 9, obtaining a precision of the positioning system of 91.33% and a precision of the vision system of 61.3%.

The best case of success was the object "skull", giving a presumption of the positioning system of 96% and a precision of the vision system of 97.6%, while among the worst case is "eraser" with a precision of the positioning system of 94% and a precision of the vision system of 14.2%.

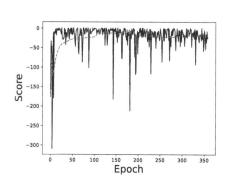

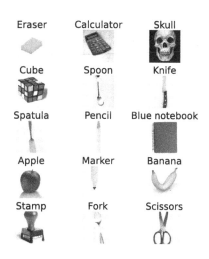

Fig. 8. Objects and prompts

Fig. 7. Training of the search policy

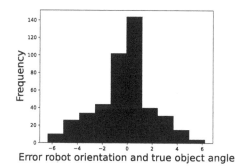

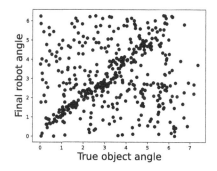

Fig. 9. Histogram of errors between the target orientation and the robot

Fig. 10. Scatter plot between the target orientation and the robot's orientation

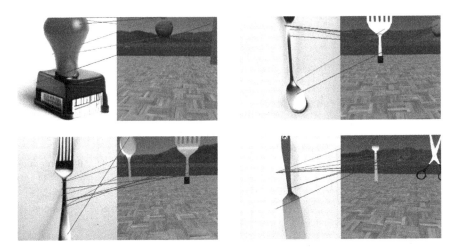

Fig. 11. Examples of false positives.

5 Discussion

The results obtained from the vision system and the positioning system demonstrate an a satisfactory performance of the localization model, despite the low percentage of precision calculated for the vision system. A pattern was observed in the characteristics that differentiate a good case from a bad one. For example, the skull, which has very different characteristics from the rest of the objects, was easily identified by the DELF model. This suggests that the DELF model can be particularly effective in identifying objects with unique and distinctive characteristics. However, the model had difficulties in differentiating between objects with similar characteristics, such as the stamp and the apple or kitchen utensils where in most cases it could correctly differentiate characteristics such as material and shape between objects that were not utensils and those that were, this can be seen in Fig. 11.

This may be considered a limitation of our study and suggests that improvements are needed in the model to increase its ability to differentiate between objects with similar characteristics. In future research, we could explore more advanced deep learning techniques to enhance the model's ability to differentiate between objects with similar characteristics.

As for the positioning system, an adequate approximation towards the object to be found is observed. As is evident, the robot's precision largely depends on the calculation of the centroid, that is, it depends on the number and positioning of the characteristics found with the DELF model.

In comparison with related works such as [1], where a model for zero-shot task generation is presented using a wide variety of scenarios and objects, employing natural language instructions or human videos demonstrating a task and images from the robot as input, and [2], where a 7-degree-of-freedom robot is trained to generate novel tasks that were not seen during training, using natural language instructions and images from the robot as input, another significant work in this area is [3], where another task generation model is presented. However, in this case, it operates on two different image areas using as input one with segmentation of the objects in the picture and a depth map. All these works locate and identify different objects in their environments. However, all these objects are conditioned to be seen during the model's training. In our work, we demonstrate that it is possible to identify a wide variety of objects without pretraining the model on them. Additionally, the model experiences fewer training challenges because it only needs to focus on finding sufficient matches in the images without concerning itself with the diverse characteristics of different objects.

6 Conclusion

This work presents the initial results of a new localization model based on text inputs. The results show acceptable performance, despite limitations in the prompts used and the degrees of freedom of the robot. In particular, the model demonstrated the ability to locate objects with distinctive features, but had difficulties differentiating between objects with similar characteristics. This suggests that the model may be particularly useful for localization tasks involving objects with unique features. However, improvements are needed to increase the model's differentiation capacity. On the other hand, using a natural language-based input facilitates reprogramming the robot's objective, which could significantly enhance the efficiency and flexibility of vision and positioning systems. Taking this into account, the results are promising and suggest that this approach could be a valuable addition to the task of object localization. Future research could explore the use of more advanced deep learning techniques to improve the model's differentiation capacity, as well as incorporate more complex tasks such as interaction with these objects.

References

1. Jang, E., et al.: Bc-z: zero-shot task generalization with robotic imitation learning (2022)
2. Brohan, A., et al.: Rt-1: robotics transformer for real-world control at scale (2023)
3. Shah, P., Fiser, M., Faust, A., Kew, J.C., Hakkani-Tur, D.: Follownet: robot navigation by following natural language directions with deep reinforcement learning (2018)
4. Pan, Y., Yao, Y., Cao, Y., Chen, C., Xiaobo, L.: Coarse2fine: local consistency aware re-prediction for weakly supervised object localization. In: Proceedings of the AAAI Conference on Artificial Intelligence, vol. 37, pp. 2002–2010 (2023)
5. Liu, W., et al.: SSD: single shot multibox detector. In: Leibe, B., Matas, J., Sebe, N., Welling, M. (eds.) ECCV 2016. LNCS, vol. 9905, pp. 21–37. Springer, Cham (2016). https://doi.org/10.1007/978-3-319-46448-0_2
6. Chen, C., et al.: OL-SLAM: a robust and versatile system of object localization and slam. Sensors **23**(2), 801 (2023)

7. Redmon, J., Divvala, S., Girshick, R., Farhadi, A.: You only look once: unified, real-time object detection (2016)
8. Brown, T.B., et al.: Language models are few-shot learners (2020)
9. Bay, H., Ess, A., Tuytelaars, T., Van Gool, L.: Speeded-up robust features (SURF). Comput. Vis. Image Underst. **110**(3), 346–359 (2008)
10. Rublee, E., Rabaud, V., Konolige, K., Bradski, G.: ORB: an efficient alternative to sift or surf. In: 2011 International Conference on Computer Vision, pp. 2564–2571. IEEE (2011)
11. Lindeberg, T.: Scale invariant feature transform (2012)
12. Noh, H., Araujo, A., Sim, J., Weyand, T., Han, B.: Large-scale image retrieval with attentive deep local features. In: Proceedings of the IEEE International Conference on Computer Vision, pp. 3456–3465 (2017)
13. Rojsiraphisal, T., Mobayen, S., Asad, J.H., Vu, M.T., Chang, A., Puangmalai, J.: Fast terminal sliding control of underactuated robotic systems based on disturbance observer with experimental validation. Mathematics **9**(16), 1935 (2021)
14. Quinones-Ramirez, M., Rios-Martinez, J., Uc-Cetina, V.: Robot path planning using deep reinforcement learning (2023)
15. Long, X., He, Z., Wang, Z.: Online optimal control of robotic systems with single critic NN-based reinforcement learning. Complexity **1–7**, 2021 (2021)
16. Lillicrap, T.P., et al.: Continuous control with deep reinforcement learning (2019)
17. Oppenlaender, J.: The creativity of text-to-image generation. In: Proceedings of the 25th International Academic Mindtrek Conference, pp. 192–202 (2022)
18. Ramesh, A., Dhariwal, P., Nichol, A., Chu, C., Chen, M.: Hierarchical text-conditional image generation with clip latents. arXiv preprint arXiv:2204.06125 (2022)
19. Ramesh, A., et al.: Zero-shot text-to-image generation (2021)
20. Vaswani, A., et al.: Attention is all you need. In: Advances in Neural Information Processing Systems, vol. 30 (2017)
21. Haarnoja, T., et al.: Learning agile soccer skills for a bipedal robot with deep reinforcement learning (2023)
22. Akkaya, I., et al.: Solving Rubik's cube with a robot hand. OpenAI (2019)
23. Tsai, C.-H., Lin, J.-J., Hsieh, T.-F., Yen, J.-Y.: Trajectory control of an articulated robot based on direct reinforcement learning. Robotics **11**(5), 116 (2022)
24. He, X., Kuang, Y., Song, N., Liu, F., et al.: Intelligent navigation of indoor robot based on improved DDPG algorithm. Math. Probl. Eng. **2023** (2023)
25. Bara, A., Dale, S.: Dynamic modeling and stabilization of wheeled mobile robot. In: WSEAS International Conference. Proceedings. Mathematics and Computers in Science and Engineering, vol. 11. WSEAS (2009)

Backup Solutions for the Refueling Problem in Foreign Transportation: A Case Study in Mexico

Oliver Cuate$^{(\boxtimes)}$ ⓘ, Ruben Belmont, Lourdes Uribe ⓘ, Gabriela P. Villamar, Ivan G.P., and Cecilio Shamar Sanchez Nava

Instituto Politecnico Nacional, Escuela Superior de Física y Matemáticas, Mexico City, Mexico
{luriber,ocuateg,csanchezna}@ipn.mx,
{rbelmontz1600,fgamboap0800}@alumno.ipn.mx

Abstract. In this paper, we addressed an optimization problem in the bus transportation industry from two points of view. Firstly, we used an integer linear optimization model to describe the problem, and we solved it via a mathematical solver and a genetic algorithm.

The problem to be solved is to minimize the recharged fuel cost necessary to complete a trip on a passenger bus from a Mexican company. Among the assumptions of the problem, we have that the bus can only restore fuel at the stops of the trip, the price of gasoline varies at each stop, and the amount of fuel in the tank always has to be greater or equal to a certain reserve amount and less or equal to the tank's total capacity. It is shown that, under certain conditions, the problem always has a solution since we can choose the strategy of recharging in each city until the tank is full, and in this way, we can reach the next city and complete the trip; however, this approach is far from giving an optimal solution. The integer linear optimization problem arises as a minimization problem with $3n + 1$ constraints, where n represents the number of designated stations that form the trip to be made. In the genetic algorithm approach, the amount of gasoline in the tank was represented as individuals, and suitable mutation and crossover operators were proposed for the problem until a solution yielded good results for the cost function. In the approach with integer linear programming, it was possible to obtain optimal solutions for large instances of the problem in a very short time. Regarding the genetic algorithm, it was possible to get suitable approximations of the optimal points and generate backup solutions for the problem.

Keywords: Genetic algorithm · evolutionary optimization · linear discrete optimization

IPN-SIP 20221947, IPN-SIP 20231045, IPN-SIP 20232208.

1 Introduction

Efficient transportation systems are essential for meeting industry and commerce's growing demands while balancing economic costs. Many transportation problems can be formulated as variations of the shortest path problem [25]. To solve routing problems, the infrastructure in a transportation system is often represented as a graph [15]. Nodes in the graph correspond to significant locations in the design, such as junctions, stations, and starting and ending points. In a simple graph model, a directed arc between two nodes implies a direct link between the corresponding places in the system following the indicated direction. The graph's series of connected arcs (a path) corresponds to a route.

When optimizing transportation systems, some factors can be considered:

- Travel time: The amount of time it takes to travel from one location to another is a significant factor in determining the efficiency of a transportation system [19].
- Energy consumption: The amount of energy used to travel from one location to another is another essential factor to consider [2].
- Environmental impact: The environmental impact of transportation, such as greenhouse gas emissions, is a growing concern [24].
- Cost: The cost of transportation, including both capital and operating costs, is an important factor for businesses and governments [18].

By considering all of these factors, transportation planners can develop efficient and sustainable transportation systems that meet the needs of people and businesses. However, in this paper we focus on the refueling problem which is also widely studied [9,22]. In [21], the authors proposed a new approach to deal with fuel-optimal path planning of multiple vehicles using mixed-integer programming. While in [16] a multi-objective approach is used to find the optimal route by optimizing the fuel consumption.

1.1 Importance of Fuel

Within passenger transport, fuel represents one of the most significant costs for companies; according to [11], in 2014, the expense incurred by motor transportation companies for urban and suburban passenger groups represented 58% of its operational structure, while for foreign transportation, it represented 39.59%, see Fig. 1. The second most significant cost for the companies is related to spare parts, which meant 20.85% for suburban transportation, while foreign transportation reached 13.88% in this area. The third most representative cost for foreign transit is related to toll services and use of infrastructure, which represented 8.21%.

In addition, the fuel price has had a reasonably considerable increase in the last thirteen years, going from 8.24 pesos in January 2010 to 23.87 pesos in September 2023, which implies a price increase of 189.68% [3,12]. According to INEGI [10], inflation of 66.53% is calculated from January 2010 to August 2023.

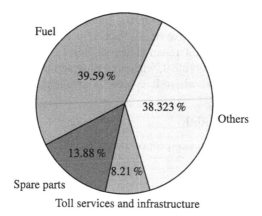

Fig. 1. Passenger transport is the most important cost for companies.

Thus, we obtained a present value of 12.27 pesos, indicating that the fuel price has increased 48.91% compared to January 2010.

It is also worth noting the fuel price by region. Within the different states of the Mexican Republic, one can find prices ranging from 20.09 pesos to 23.87 pesos per liter of diesel [20]. This difference of up to $2.99 per liter of fuel becomes very significant if daily consumption is considered since at least 20,000 liters of fuel are used. This fact becomes essential when considering the itinerary of the coverage routes of the mobility services.

2 Transportation Model

This section will address the costs of foreign transportation, considering that the main objective is to meet customer satisfaction. For this, the following considerations will be taken into account: (a) Every trip must be fulfilled, that is, passengers cannot be left in the middle of their destination; (b) we only considered buses of the Platinum and Gold brands, since they have similar engines and tank attributes, (c) each route contains established fixed stops, buses can only stop and refuel there.

2.1 Problem Statement

As mentioned in Sect. 1.1, one of the most critical costs in foreign transportation occurs in the field of fuel, representing almost 40% of the total cost. In addition, because it is an input that is not recovered (for example, there is the possibility that the tires are reconditioned to extend their helpful life, and with this, the impact of this cost can be reduced), it is vital to optimize the distribution of fuel loads; so that buses always have enough diesel to reach their destination, but simultaneously aiming for a reduction in the costs that involve it.

Currently, at the end of each trip, the tank is filled, which means that the most expensive places are always considered. Taking into account that some trips do not consume all the fuel available in the bus tank, it is intended to adjust the number of liters of fuel to be loaded on each trip to achieve a reduction in the total cost of fuel; this does not mean that less diesel is loaded, but that diesel is loaded where it is most economical, without losing sight of the service attributes. Thus, it will be determined where it is more convenient for us to load fuel.

2.2   Mathematical Model

In this section, we described the proposed model. We defined the following decision variables:

$$
\begin{aligned}
T_c &\leftarrow \text{Bus tank capacity} \\
S_r &\leftarrow \text{Safety reserve} \\
N &\leftarrow \text{Number of fixed stops/fuel loads} \\
T_i &\leftarrow \text{Bus tank at the current stop} \\
S_0 &\leftarrow \text{Travel origin} \\
S_N &\leftarrow \text{Travel destination} \\
U_i &\leftarrow \text{Liters to reach the next stop} \\
C_i &\leftarrow \text{Cost of loading at each stop} \\
L_i &\leftarrow \text{Liters loaded at each stop}
\end{aligned}
$$

Our goal is to minimize the total cost of the trip:

$$
C_T = \sum_{i=1}^{N} C_i L_i,
\tag{1}
$$

subject to the following constraints:

1. All loads must be integers greater or equal to zero. Removing fuel from the tank is impossible, and avoiding loading at some stops is possible.

$$
L_i \geq 0 \ \forall i \in \{1, \ldots, N\}.
\tag{2}
$$

2. The amount of each load must be less than the number of liters needed to fill the bus fuel tank, that is, the capacity of the tank minus the number of liters in the tank after your last trip.

$$
T_i + L_i \leq T_c, \ \forall i \in \{1, \ldots, N\}.
\tag{3}
$$

3. The number of liters at the beginning of each trip must be enough to reach its destination without using the tank safety reserve. In case the trip is too long and the fuel consumption is greater than the tank capacity, an intermediate fixed point must be found at which it is viable to refuel; thus, the trip is divided into two or more stops.

$$
T_i + L_i - U_i \geq S_r \ \forall i \in \{1, \ldots, N\}.
\tag{4}
$$

4. It is important to note that the company already defines all trips and can not be modified. Moreover, due to company policies, all trips start with a full tank, and it means that the last load must be used to achieve it, that is,

$$T_0 = T_c \tag{5}$$
$$N + L_N = T_c. \tag{6}$$

The previously described model is summarized in the following integer optimization problem:

$$\min_{x \in \mathbb{Z}^{2N}} C_T(x) = \sum_{i=1}^{N} C_i x_i, \tag{7}$$

subject to

$$x_i + x_{i+N} \leq Tc, \qquad \forall i \in \{1, \ldots, N\} \tag{8}$$
$$-x_i \leq -S_r, \qquad \forall i \in \{N+1, \ldots, 2N\} \tag{9}$$
$$x_{N+1} = T_c - U_1, \tag{10}$$
$$-x_{i-1} - x_{N+i-1} + x_{N+i} = -U_i, \qquad \forall i \in \{2, \ldots, N\} \tag{11}$$
$$x_N + x_{2N} = T_c, \tag{12}$$
$$x_i \geq 0, \qquad \forall i \in \{1, \ldots, 2N\}, \tag{13}$$

where $x_i = (L_1, L_2, \ldots, L_N, T_1, T_2, \ldots, T_N)^T \in \mathbb{Z}^{2N}$. We will raise the model for a small instance below to facilitate their comprehension and clarity.

2.3   Example

Let's consider the following scenario. We have a trip that departs from City A to City C, with a stopover in City B, and then it returns to City A with the corresponding stopover in City B; that is, a round trip. Table 1 shows the fuel cost at each stop and the liters needed to reach each city in Table 1; we will also assume that $T_c = 595$ and $S_r = 90$.

Table 1. Cost of fuel and liters required to reach each city for the hypothetical example.

Departure City	Fuel Cost	Destination City		
		A	B	C
A	20.99	–	98	–
B	21.86	98	–	250
C	18.11	–	250	–

*Fuel cost given in pesos per liter.

The integer linear programming problem from this data is stated as follows. First, the objective function:

$$C_T(x) = 21.86x_1 + 18.11x_2 + 21.86x_3 + 20.99x_4. \tag{14}$$

The set of Equations (8) –that are related to the maximum capacity of the tank– in matrix form for this example are:

$$\begin{pmatrix} 1\,0\,0\,0\,1\,0\,0\,0 \\ 0\,1\,0\,0\,0\,1\,0\,0 \\ 0\,0\,1\,0\,0\,0\,1\,0 \\ 0\,0\,0\,1\,0\,0\,0\,1 \end{pmatrix} x \le \begin{pmatrix} 595 \\ 595 \\ 595 \\ 595 \end{pmatrix}. \tag{15}$$

While, for the set of equations related to the safely reserve (9), we have:

$$\begin{pmatrix} 0\,0\,0\,0\,-1\,0\,\,\,0\,\,\,\,0 \\ 0\,0\,0\,0\,\,\,0\,-1\,\,\,0\,\,\,\,0 \\ 0\,0\,0\,0\,\,\,0\,\,\,0\,-1\,\,\,0 \\ 0\,0\,0\,0\,\,\,0\,\,\,0\,\,\,0\,-1 \end{pmatrix} x \le \begin{pmatrix} -90 \\ -90 \\ -90 \\ -90 \end{pmatrix}. \tag{16}$$

Regarding the constraints related to the amount of fuel in the tank when the bus arrives at each stop –i.e., (10), (11) (12)– we have:

$$\begin{pmatrix} \,\,\,0\,\,\,\,\,0\,\,\,\,\,\,0\,0\,\,\,1\,\,\,0\,\,\,0\,0 \\ -1\,\,\,0\,\,\,\,\,\,0\,0\,-1\,\,\,1\,\,\,0\,0 \\ \,\,\,0\,-1\,\,\,\,0\,0\,\,\,0\,-1\,\,\,1\,0 \\ \,\,\,0\,\,\,\,0\,-1\,0\,\,\,0\,\,\,0\,-1\,1 \\ \,\,\,0\,\,\,\,0\,\,\,\,\,0\,1\,\,\,0\,\,\,0\,\,\,0\,1 \end{pmatrix} x = \begin{pmatrix} 497 \\ -250 \\ -250 \\ -98 \\ 595 \end{pmatrix}. \tag{17}$$

Finally, we have to add the non-negativity conditions. After solving the problem, we obtain the following:

$$x^* = (0, 348, 0, 348, 497, 247, 345, 247)^T$$

We notice that the fuel price is lower in city C; therefore, getting a full load at that stop seems logical. Based on our example data, this is possible, and a reduction in total cost is achieved compared to the current scheme of filling the tank at each stop.

In Fig. 2, we show the amount of fuel with which a bus reaches each city, followed by the liters it loads in each of them and the liters it leaves with, both for the current approach and the cost reduction approach in the bottom and top of each node, respectively. Although it is a round trip, for clarity, each stop is shown as a different node, starting from city A (in green) and returning to it (in red). Based on the values indicated in Fig. 2, the cost of the travel for the full tank approach is:

$$C_T^F = 98 \cdot 21.86 + 250 \cdot 18.11 + 250 \cdot 21.86 + 98 \cdot 20.99 = 14191.80,$$

while the minimum cost is:

$$C_T^* = 0 \cdot 21.86 + 348 \cdot 18.11 + 0 \cdot 21.86 + 348.0 \cdot 20.99 = 13606.80,$$

which is a saving of 9% per each travel.

Although the optimum of this example can be easily found by solving Problem (7) with a classical mathematical programming method (e.g., [5, 6, 14]), it is important to have options that allow obtaining both backup solutions and alternative solutions [1]. For this reason, we proposed a Genetic Algorithm (GA) with the characteristics described below.

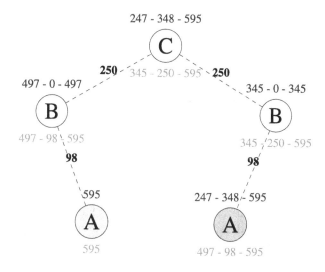

Fig. 2. Representation of the example.

3   Genetic Algorithm

Typically, the cost and distance vectors of a real company trip look like this:

$$C = (21.99, 20.70, 21.59, 20.70, 22.98, 20.70, 21.99, 20.70, 22.59, 20.70, 20.61, 20.7, 23.39)^T$$
$$U = (83, 80, 266, 266, 130, 130, 80, 80, 40, 40, 505, 505, 477)^T.$$

Even though, for confidentiality reasons, the data has been slightly altered, we can observe that on a real route, you can pass through the same city several times; this is for connectivity reasons, and usually, it happens for the most important cities.

We always get the same optimal solution if we solve the problem stated before via a mathematical programming method (we omit the values of T for clarity):

$$L^* = (0, 163, 27, 505, 0, 260, 0, 0, 0, 240, 505, 505, 477)^T.$$

However, the minimum cost of \$59523.03 is also attainable at a different point:

$$\tilde{L}^* = (0, 163, 27, 357, 0, 282, 0, 277, 0, 89, 505, 505, 477)^T$$

Having as many alternatives as possible is of the greatest importance in foreign transportation. Both solutions, L^* and $\tilde{L}^*$, have similar values, but the differences are noticeable in some inputs. For instance, $L_4^* = 505$ and $\tilde{L}_4^* = 357$; in this case, if there is not enough fuel to supply the truck at the fourth stop according to L^*, we recharge 357 liters at the fourth stop, and we update the itinerary according to $\hat{L}^*$.

Due to their random and population-based nature, evolutionary algorithms are an option that will allow a more significant number of choices than classical methods. Evolutionary algorithms are part of evolutionary computing, and they comprise a family of algorithms that search for solutions to problems that are generally complex and difficult to describe mathematically. In particular, Genetic Algorithms (GA) are bio-inspired by the principles of evolution in nature [4,8], and they can produce outstanding solutions, sometimes even optimal ones, of a vast range of search and optimization problems. In addition, they can overcome some problems that some other traditional search and optimization algorithms get stuck in, such as early convergence to local minima or maxima [13,23].

In summary, a GA begins with a random population of potential solutions. Each solution, known as an individual, is evaluated using a fitness function that quantifies its quality. Individuals with higher fitness are more likely to be selected for crossover, which combines their genetic information to create offspring. The mutation is then applied, introducing small random changes in the offspring. This process generates new candidate solutions with potentially improved characteristics that replace the previous generation, ensuring the algorithm evolves as long as we select the right hyper-parameters, such as the probabilities of crossover and mutation, type of mutation, type of crossover, number of generations, and population size.

The main advantages of GAs are the ability to avoid local optima and converge to global optima and attack problems with an excessively complex mathematical representation or without an available mathematical model, as well as the possibility of programming in parallel and the adaptability to change problems over time. On the other hand, there is no guarantee that they found a solution or that such a solution is optimal, and they can become computationally more demanding than traditional algorithms.

3.1 Proposal

In this work, we use the traditional GA with an additional mutation process that allows increasing the exploration of the search and, thus, obtaining assorted individuals.

We represent individuals as an array of integers of the same size as the number of cities, which contains the amount of fuel recharged in each city. Based on this, we can also compute the amount of fuel they have at each town when they are leaving and the amount of fuel they have when they arrive at each city. It is important to point out that we explicitly deal with the constraints in the code via penalty functions; a solution is penalized when one of the following scenarios happens:

- If the individual does not end up with a full tank at the end of the trip.
- If, at any point of the trip, the individual charges more gasoline than the capacity of the tank allows.
- If the individual charges less gasoline at any point of the trip than the established reserve amount.
- If in any city, the individual recharges a negative amount of gasoline.

The penalties are linearly proportional to how many liters an individual violates each constraint. For the crossover, we use a convex linear combination of the parents' arrangements with a random parameter in $[0, 1]$ to produce the offspring; we round the obtained structure. Finally, we adopt a Gaussian mutation of one random element of the individual, and we add a sample of a normal distribution $\mathcal{N}(0, 20)$; we also round the resulting individual before computing its fitness.

3.2   Additional Mutation

Although standard mutations often produce high-quality results, the characteristics of some problems demand specialized mutation approaches [17]. In the transport problem addressed, after analyzing the results of several tests, we observed that there are frequently three consecutive cities where a lot of fuel must be refilled in the first and third cities. In contrast, there is a lower fuel in the second city because the price of gasoline in the first and third cities is lower than in the second city.

For this reason, we include a particular mutation procedure, which detects adjacent trios of stops in which L_i is small but L_{i-1} and L_{i+1} are bigger. Then, we randomly chose one of these trios to slightly vary the amount of gasoline refilled in the first and third cities. We activate this second mutation in the last sixth of the generations when the algorithm can identify these trios.

4   Numerical Results

First, we consider the thirteen-city case described in Sect. 3. For this example, based on real data, we made 15 independent runs with a population size of 100 individuals per 300 generations; the crossover probability was 0.8, while the mutation probability was 0.5 and 0.5 for the additional mutation. We show the best individual of the last generation of each execution in Table 2, where we can appreciate that, in all cases, individuals are different.

We emphasize that all the solutions in Table 2 are optimal; i.e., they are feasible, and their evaluation is the minimum possible cost. In this way, we provide an outstanding example that shows the advantages of the genetic algorithm; we obtained similar results in many other company instances that we cannot include here for confidentiality reasons.

In order to complement this study, we compare random instances ranging from 5 to 60 cities. For the creation of these instances, we used a normal distribution $N(20, 5)$ for the fuel price and a uniform distribution $U(95, 505)$ for the number of liters required to reach each city; in this way, we guarantee that the problem it has a solution. To find the exact solutions of all the instances considered in this article, we utilized the `intlinprog` function of the Matlab software.

The parameters employed for each instance can be found in Table 3. It is worth mentioning that the presented parameters were established by studying

Table 2. Comparative table of the best individual obtained in fifteen different executions of the GA. These solutions have the same cost value of $59523.03 and are feasible points.

| Execution | Liters loaded at each stop | | | | | | | | | | | | |
	L_1	L_2	L_3	L_4	L_5	L_6	L_7	L_8	L_9	L_{10}	L_{11}	L_{12}	L_{13}
1	0	163	27	260	0	293	0	152	0	300	505	505	477
2	0	163	27	266	0	246	0	215	0	278	505	505	477
3	0	163	27	384	0	216	0	102	0	303	505	505	477
4	0	163	27	306	0	225	0	229	0	245	505	505	477
5	0	163	27	362	0	212	0	187	0	244	505	505	477
6	0	163	27	288	0	155	0	150	0	412	505	505	477
7	0	163	27	355	0	212	0	57	0	381	505	505	477
8	0	163	27	262	0	201	0	213	0	329	505	505	477
9	0	163	27	341	0	260	0	99	0	305	505	505	477
10	0	163	27	308	0	197	0	287	0	213	505	505	477
11	0	163	27	361	0	131	0	187	0	326	505	505	477
12	0	163	27	307	0	244	0	166	0	288	505	505	477
13	0	163	27	429	0	20	0	60	0	496	505	505	477
14	0	163	27	435	0	85	0	195	0	290	505	505	477
15	0	163	27	272	0	327	0	119	0	287	505	505	477

Table 3. Parameters for each instance, we include population size (P), number of generations (G), crossover probability (p_c), probability mutation (p_{m1}), probability of additional mutation (p_{m2}).

n	P	G	p_c	p_{m1}	p_{m2}
5,15,20,25	50	300	0.9	0.5	0.5
25,30	100	500	0.9	0.5	0.5
35,40	150	500	0.9	0.5	0.5
45,50,55	200	300	0.8	0.5	0.8
60	250	600	0.8	0.5	0.8

the particular problem. When more nodes were considered, a bigger population was needed. Also, a direct relation between the mutations and the instance size was found. We show the obtained results for 30 independent runs of the GA for each instance in Table 4, where we also include the cost of the full tank approach.

From Table 4, we can conclude that the proposed algorithm provides a lot of variety in individuals due to the additional mutation and that this directly affects large instances since the proposal cannot reach the optimal value. Also, this is due to the particular configuration held in real-world instances and not preserved in random cases. However, the results can serve as backup solutions to the only alternative the mathematical programming method provides. In this way, even though the solutions are not optimal, they offer an acceptable value we can use when implementing the optimal solution is impossible.

Table 4. Numerical results for different random instances.

n	Full Tank	Linear Model	Genetic Algorithm		
			min	mean (std)	max
5	44158.23	43439.11	43439.11	43439.11 (0.0000)	43439.11
10	69473.63	68343.85	68410.49	68531.51 (54.3142)	68573.52
15	66971.17	60636.83	60758.67	61454.56 (347.7122)	62137.83
20	104661.19	92522.93	93601.30	94235.47 (422.5957)	95042.28
25	120925.54	108165.66	109186.49	110358.21 (670.0416)	111392.18
30	152768.19	136464.13	137368.35	137558.67 (192.4864)	138096.08
35	157303.54	136573.19	139175.17	140830.37 (795.7781)	141815.18
40	201954.16	181356.16	190497.55	191886.36 (712.6078)	193402.11
45	225833.61	203626.70	210382.06	212855.63 (1717.5651)	215654.95
50	256620.69	227326.67	233028.59	234661.75 (838.9547)	235887.56
55	314419.75	291680.58	302375.12	304397.32 (1415.8444)	306779.39
60	279417.33	246874.03	259121.66	260579.62 (823.1934)	261630.83

5   Conclusion and Future Work

This work proposed an integer linear optimization problem to solve the refueling problem for a bus company in Mexico. The proposed model adequately solves the desired problem through integer linear programming. However, when observing that the routes provided by the company are multi-modal, it was decided to solve the problem in an additional way using a genetic algorithm that allows obtaining alternative optimal solutions or backup solutions (almost optimal). The algorithm's effectiveness is demonstrated with a problem based on real data and through different random instances. Even though the results shown were analyzed from a statistical point of view, a single execution of the algorithm provides various alternatives to the same instance, which is crucial since gasoline prices change daily.

This problem is vital since a natural extension could use multi-objective optimization that considers functions such as the optimal supply of gasoline stations in each city and the waiting time for recharging, among others. On the other hand, the proposed genetic algorithm seeks to prioritize diversity without losing optimality, which has been studied to a greater extent for multi-objective optimization problems [7]. Finally, being a first approach to the problem, you can work on a fix and improve the method to get better results on routes in general that do not have the local structure.

Acknowledgment. Oliver Cuate and Ruben Belmont acknowledge support from projects SIP 20221947 and SIP 20231045. Lourdes Uribe acknowledges support from project SIP 20232208.

References

1. Beyer, H.G., Sendhoff, B.: Robust optimization-a comprehensive survey. Comput. Methods Appl. Mech. Eng. **196**(33–34), 3190–3218 (2007)
2. Fernández, R.Á., Caraballo, S.C., Cilleruelo, F.B., Lozano, J.A.: Fuel optimization strategy for hydrogen fuel cell range extender vehicles applying genetic algorithms. Renew. Sustain. Energy Rev. **81**, 655–668 (2018)
3. GlobalPetrol: Precios promedio. https://es.globalpetrolprices.com/Mexico/diesel_prices/. Accessed 06 Sept 2023
4. Goldberg, D.E.: Optimization, and machine learning. Genetic algorithms in Search (1989)
5. Gomory, R.E., Baumol, W.J.: Integer programming and pricing. Econometrica: J. Econometric Soc., 521–550 (1960)
6. Gupta, O.K., Ravindran, A.: Branch and bound experiments in convex nonlinear integer programming. Manage. Sci. **31**(12), 1533–1546 (1985)
7. Hernández Castellanos, C.I., Schütze, O., Sun, J.Q., Ober-Blöbaum, S.: Non-epsilon dominated evolutionary algorithm for the set of approximate solutions. Math. Comput. Appl. **25**(1), 3 (2020)
8. Holland, J.: Adaptation in natural and artificial systems, univ. of mich. press. Ann Arbor **7**, 390–401 (1975)
9. Horng, M.-F., Dao, T.-K., Shieh, C.-S., Nguyen, T.-T.: A multi-objective optimal vehicle fuel consumption based on whale optimization algorithm. In: Advances in Intelligent Information Hiding and Multimedia Signal Processing. SIST, vol. 64, pp. 371–380. Springer, Cham (2017). https://doi.org/10.1007/978-3-319-50212-0_44
10. INEGI: Calculadora de inflación. https://www.inegi.org.mx/app/indicesdeprecios/calculadorainflacion.aspx. Accessed 01 June 2023
11. INEGI: Encuesta anual de transportes 2012–2014. https://www.inegi.org.mx/rnm/index.php/catalog/157/variable/V214. Accessed 01 June 2023
12. INEGI: Precios promedio. https://www.inegi.org.mx/app/preciospromedio/?bs=18. Accessed 01 June 2023
13. Joshi, P.: Artificial intelligence with python. Packt Publishing Ltd. (2017)
14. Jünger, M., et al.: 50 Years of integer programming 1958–2008: From the early years to the state-of-the-art. Springer Science & Business Media (2009)
15. Kurant, M., Thiran, P.: Extraction and analysis of traffic and topologies of transportation networks. Phys. Rev. E **74**(3), 036114 (2006)
16. Marie, S., Courteille, E., et al.: Multi-objective optimization of motor vessel route. Marine Navigation Saf. Sea Transp. **9**, 411–418 (2009)
17. Michalewicz, Z., Janikow, C.Z.: Handling constraints in genetic algorithms. In: Icga, pp. 151–157 (1991)
18. Pattnaik, S., Mohan, S., Tom, V.: Urban bus transit route network design using genetic algorithm. J. Transp. Eng. **124**(4), 368–375 (1998)

19. Pellazar, M.B.: Vehicle route planning with constraints using genetic algorithms. In: Proceedings of National Aerospace and Electronics Conference (NAECON'94), pp. 111–118. IEEE (1994)
20. PROFECO: Precios de gasolinas y diésel. https://www.cre.gob.mx/ConsultaPrecios/GasolinasyDiesel/GasolinasyDiesel.html. Accessed 01 June 2023
21. Schouwenaars, T., De Moor, B., Feron, E., How, J.: Mixed integer programming for multi-vehicle path planning. In: 2001 European control conference (ECC), pp. 2603–2608. IEEE (2001)
22. Schulz, A., Suzuki, Y.: An efficient heuristic for the fixed-route vehicle-refueling problem. Transp. Res. Part E Logist. Transp. Rev. **169**, 102963 (2023). https://doi.org/10.1016/j.tre.2022.102963
23. Sheppard, C.: Genetic Algorithms with Python. Packt Publishing Ltd. (2019)
24. Wang, H., Lang, X., Mao, W.: Voyage optimization combining genetic algorithm and dynamic programming for fuel/emissions reduction. Transp. Res. Part D: Transp. Environ. **90**, 102670 (2021)
25. Zajac, S., Huber, S.: Objectives and methods in multi-objective routing problems: a survey and classification scheme. Europ. J. Oper. Res. (2020)

Self-location Algorithm for the Strategic Movement of Humanoid Robots

Moises Omar Leon-Pineda[1] , Ivan Giovanni Valdespin-Garcia[1] ,
and Yesenia Eleonor Gonzalez-Navarro[2]([⊠])

[1] Centro de Investigación y de Estudios Avanzados del Instituto Politécnico
Nacional, Ciudad de México, Mexico
{moises.leon,ivan.valdespin}@cinvestav.mx
[2] Instituto Politécnico Nacional-UPIITA, Ciudad de México, Mexico
ygonzalezn@ipn.mx

Abstract. This work presents an algorithm that enables one or more humanoid robots to position themselves within a specific area by identifying the goal and determining the distance between the robot and the objective. The main objective is to facilitate the operation of the system in soccer-playing robots. To achieve this, two premises are established. Firstly, in the hypothetical scenario where two robots from the same team compete for the ball, the algorithm determines which robot is closer and makes the decision of who will go for the objective, thereby avoiding collisions among the robots. Subsequently, the robot will move towards the target area, i.e., the goal. Secondly, the hypothetical case is considered in which each robot belongs to a different team, and both will attempt to reach the ball before the other.

In both situations, the robot performs the identification of the ball and the other robot, whether friend or foe, in order to determine the distances between the robots and the ball by applying Deep Learning algorithms. For object identification, YOLOv3, a classic model for object identification that uses convolutional neural networks, was retrained. The computer vision is implemented by a RealSense camera which uses stereoscopic vision to calculate the depth of the objects. The robots utilize a self-localization and strategy algorithm, which is executed by each robot's command system. There is no direct communication between the robots in either scenario. However, a wireless communication system between the robot and the computer is required, with Wi-Fi as the initial choice.

The algorithm's performance will be evaluated using measures such as accuracy, precision, and sensitivity, employing tools like the confusion matrix and the Receiver Operating Characteristic (ROC) curve.

Keywords: Humanoid robot · Stereoscopic vision · Computer vision · YOLO · Strategy · Deep learning

---

The authors thanks to Consejo Nacional de Ciencia y Tecnología de México for Master Scholarships CVU No. M. O. Leon-Pineda—1144833 and I. G. Valdespin-Garcia—1147565; and to Y. E. Gonzalez-Navarro—Secretaría de Investigación y Posgrado del Instituto Politécnico Nacional for the support provided for the preparation of this work through the projects SIP 20201539 and SIP 20231572.

H. Calvo et al. (Eds.): MICAI 2023, LNAI 14392, pp. 264–280, 2024.
https://doi.org/10.1007/978-3-031-47640-2_22

1 Introduction

A humanoid robot is a type of robot that resembles a human in appearance and has the ability to autonomously imitate certain aspects of human behavior [1].

Over time, the interest in creating walking machines has persisted. A notable example is the "steam man", designed by George Moore in 1893 [2]. Although it was never built, it laid the groundwork for the development of much more sophisticated humanoid robots, such as the Darwin-OP robot [3]. Darwin-OP is a small humanoid robot (45 cm tall) equipped with senses like vision and hearing.

Currently, fields like artificial intelligence have driven the advancement of these robots through the design and implementation of increasingly complex algorithms. Convolutional networks, for example, have had a significant impact on computer vision, enabling object detection algorithms like YOLO (You Only Look Once) [4], path generation, mapping, and other techniques that enhance the robot's autonomy. As a result, their inclusion in various sectors of everyday life, such as restaurants, homes, healthcare, rescue operations, among others, is increasingly being considered [5].

Due to these advancements, competitions have been organized arround the world to test the capabilities of these robots. One of the most recognized competitions is RoboCup, which initially focused on soccer, with the goal of enabling robots to acquire the necessary skills to compete against and defeat human world champions by the year 2050 [6]. Over time, RoboCup has expanded its scope to include additional categories such as rescue, household tasks, and industry.

The proposed project involves the development and application of a Wi-Fi communication-based algorithm on two Darwin-OP robots. This algorithm aims to identify objects of interest using stereoscopic vision and, by locating the robots, generate a strategy that allows the robot to gain possession of the ball in the proposed scenarios.

2 Antecedents

In the state of the art of orientation detection for humanoid soccer robots, A. Mühlenbrock and T. Laue present a system based on the alignment of the sides of the adversaries' robot feet. This system allows determining the orientation of the opponent robot at distances greater than 2 m, which is crucial due to the robot's movement speed. Three experiments were conducted to verify the system's efficiency, and satisfactory results were obtained by applying a first derivative filter called Sobel, normalized by contrast. The system is capable of recognizing the orientation of a humanoid robot both when it is standing still and when it is walking, and it works in combination with edge detection and color image classification [4]. In contrast to this project, an orientation based on the location of the goal is proposed, and the robots will remain in constant motion.

In the project of training Bioloid robots for playing soccer, J. Hernández Ramírez focuses on developing essential aspects for the efficient navigation of a humanoid robot on a soccer field. The basic movements necessary for a good game were identified, such as walking forward, backward, turning, and lateral movements. These movements are generated through online movement strategies or periodic activities. As for vision, a Havimo module is used to detect the distance between the robot and various objects such as the ball and the goal. Constraints to be considered when designing the robot's poses are also proposed [7].

The guide by E. Sanchez Alvarado and O. M. Rivas Borbon focuses on soccer tactics and strategy. Although it is designed for 11-player matches, each position in the game is addressed, and systems and formations are discussed. In the context of RoboCupSoccer, where only 4 players per team participate, tactics such as zonal marking or man-to-man marking, adapted to robots, are suggested. Attack assembly, its objectives, characteristics, requirements, advantages, disadvantages, as well as well-explained training exercises are also studied [8].

In M. N. Ibarra Bonilla's work on autonomous navigation of robots using localization and routing techniques, a system based on computer vision and fuzzy control implemented in a Lego NXT mobile robot is presented. Obstacles in the environment are detected using an ultrasonic sensor and a camera, and a lighting-tolerant algorithm is obtained. The segmentation of the captured image allows for satisfactory and systematic obstacle detection [9]. In contrast, this project plans to use Python for the algorithm implementation and Darwin-OP robots as a testing platform.

In the coordination and collaboration algorithm for robots in soccer proposed by Awang Hendrianto Pratomo and others, distances between objectives and robots are obtained through artificial vision. The goal is to achieve collaborative robotics that allows for strategic movements planning among robots of the same team, avoiding collisions by deciding who will go after the ball based on proximity [10].

3   Methods and Materials

3.1   Instruments

In order to conduct this research, a series of necessary elements were employed to ensure its proper functioning. The following is a list of the instruments utilized:

- **Test Environment**: A test scenario has been created that simulates a portion of a soccer field, based on competitions such as RoboCup [11] and TalendLand [12]. In RoboCup, there are separate fields for medium-sized and large robots, but in this case, we will focus on the medium-sized field. The dimensions of the fields are as follows: the RoboCup SPL and RoboCup Soccer Humanoid League Kid Size fields have an area of 9 m × 6 m, whereas Talend Land varies in width from 2.5 to 3.5 m and has a length of 1.8 m [6].

- **Darwin-OP Platform**: Darwin-OP (Dynamic Anthropomorphic Robot with Intelligence - Open Platform) is a free platform developed by ROBO-TIS that features an advanced computational system, sophisticated sensors, a good mechanical movement capability, and a monocular vision system [13]. A comparison of the Darwin-OP models can be seen in Table 10 in the appendix. It should be noted that Darwin-OP has been discontinued and replaced by Darwin-OP3. However, for the development of this project, only Darwin-OP robots are available. Therefore, we will be working with this version, making some modifications as presented later on.

- **Vision System**: The Intel RealSense D415 camera is a 3D imaging and depth sensing device that utilizes advanced technology to provide more accurate visual perception. It consists of two lenses and an infrared sensor that enable capturing color and depth images simultaneously. The camera is capable of capturing high-resolution video and generating detailed depth maps, making it suitable for applications such as virtual reality, robotics, object detection, and autonomous navigation. Additionally, the RealSense D415 camera is compatible with a variety of development platforms and frameworks, facilitating its integration into custom projects and applications [14], a comparison of some RealSense cameras can be seen in the Table 11 in the appendix.

- **Processing Board**

  As mentioned before, the algorithm is planned to be implemented on a humanoid robot. Therefore, processing card to be used must be taken into account, as implementing structures like convolutional networks for object identification increases computational cost. A comparison of these cards can be seen in the Table 12 in the appendix.

  However, during the conducted tests, it was observed that the execution was very slow, even with the implementation of the Intel Neural Compute Stick 2 [15]. Upon reviewing the specifications in Table 2, it was noticed that the Darwin-OP3 robot comes with an Intel NUC. Therefore, for this project, the decision was made to use the Intel NUC8i7BEK. The specifications of the Intel NUC8i7BEK are shown in the Table 1, comparing with the NUC of the Darwin-OP3.

- **Split of Training and Validation Set** splitting a dataset into training and validation sets is a critical part of training image recognition models like YOLO (You Only Look Once). This split is done to evaluate the model's performance during training and ensure that it generalizes well to unseen data [16,17]. Here are some general recommendations for splitting the dataset:

  - Split Ratio: A common practice is to use an 80-20 split for training and validation. Adjust the split depending on your dataset size, with options like 90-10 or 95-5 for larger datasets and 70-30 for smaller ones.
  - Randomness: Ensure randomness when splitting data to avoid bias. Shuffle your data before creating training and validation sets to maintain representation.

Table 1. Comparison between Intel NUC8i7BEK and NUC used in Darwin-OP3

Feature	NUC used in Darwin-OP3	Intel NUC8i7BEK
Processor	Intel Core i7	Intel Core i3
RAM	16 GB DDR4	8 GB DDR4
Storage	500 GB SSD	128 GB SSD
GPU	Intel UHD Graphics	Intel HD Graphics
Connectivity	Wi-Fi, Bluetooth, Ethernet	Wi-Fi, Bluetooth, Ethernet
USB Ports	4 × USB 3.0, 2 × USB 2.0	4 × USB 3.0, 2 × USB 2.0
Video Output	HDMI, DisplayPort	HDMI, DisplayPort

- Consider Class Imbalance: Address class imbalance issues by maintaining balance during the split, especially when some classes have significantly more samples. Techniques like stratified sampling can help.
- Consistent Preprocessing: Apply preprocessing consistently in both training and validation sets, such as resizing images or normalizing pixel values. This ensures fair evaluation.
- Cross-Validation: Instead of a single split, consider k-fold cross-validation, where data is divided into k partitions for multiple rounds of training and validation. Each partition serves as the validation set once, providing a more robust performance evaluation.
- Separate Test Set: In addition to training and validation sets, maintain a separate test set untouched during training and validation. This set is used to assess the final model performance.

3.2 Process

Once the necessary instruments were obtained, the following processes were developed:

1. Construction of the test environment: An appropriate test environment was created to carry out the required experiments.

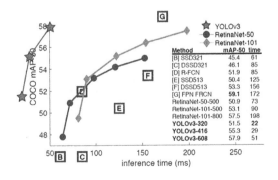

Fig. 1. Advantage from YOLO vs other vision algoritms

2. Vision algorithm:
   – Detection algorithm testing: Various detection algorithms were tested, but in summary, YOLOv3 stands out due to its balance between speed and accuracy in object detection. Its ability to detect multiple objects in real time, versatility across different object classes, and customization through training make it a preferred choice over other image identification algorithms.

   The Fig. 1, provided by the creators of YOLO, compare the advantages of their algorithm relative to others focuses on two key metrics: "inference time (ms)" (inference time in milliseconds) and "COCO mAP" (mean of the average of COCO precision).

3. Database creation:
   – Image acquisition: Images were captured for use in the database. We got a set of 8000 images an were divided in 90% for training and 10% for validation, this because the recomendations of split of training and validation set explained in the section before.
   – Image classification: The acquired images were classified into categories relevant to the study (ball, goal and robot)

4. YOLO installation and training:
   – The YOLOV3 model was installed, and retraining was conducted using the created database. The full process for retraining is in: https://github.com/MLeon8/Rentrenamiento-Yolo
   – The full version of yolov3 and the tiny version are used, which is lighter but also less efficient.

5. Model evaluation: The performance of the trained YOLO model was evaluated through testing and analysis of the obtained results.

6. Depth calculation algorithm:
   – Methods: The methods developed to calculate the depth of detected objects in the images are: BallDistance, GoalDistance, DistanceRobot, DistanceBetweenObjects.
   – Evaluation: The accuracy and effectiveness of the depth calculation methods were assessed.

7. Decision-making algorithm:
   – Scenario Proposal: Various scenarios and decision-making criteria were proposed based on the detection and depth calculation results. These scenarios include "Go for the Ball" and "Don't Go for the Ball". The decision to advance towards the ball is determined by the following conditions:
     • If only the ball is detected, the agent goes for it.
     • When both the enemy and the ball are detected, the agent competes for the ball.
     • In the presence of both the ball and a friendly object, the agent advances towards the ball only if it is closer to the ball than its friend.
     • When the ball, a friend, and an enemy are all detected, the agent calculates the distances between these objects and itself. It decides to advance towards the ball if it is closer to the ball than its friend.

In all other scenarios, the agent does not advance towards the ball.
 – Evaluation: The effectiveness of the decision-making algorithm in selecting actions based on the obtained results was assessed.
8. Integration of algorithms: The different algorithms (vision, depth calculation,
   and decision-making) were combined to create a complete and functional
   system. 8 different scenarios were proposed (see Table 2)

Table 2. Proposed scenarios

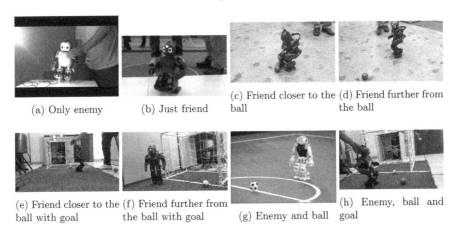

(a) Only enemy   (b) Just friend   (c) Friend closer to the (d) Friend further from
                                      ball   the ball

(e) Friend closer to the (f) Friend further from   (h) Enemy, ball and
ball with goal   the ball with goal   (g) Enemy and ball   goal

The terms "friend" and "enemy" require clarification. In this context, we
define "friend" as robots that are Darwin-OP models with a completely black
appearance, such as those depicted in figures b,c,d,e and f in the Table 2. Additionally, robots are considered "enemies" if they meet any of the following conditions:

1. They are not Darwin-OP robots, as seen in figure g) if Table 2.
2. They are not black Darwin-OP robots, as shown in figure a) in Table 2.
3. They are black Darwin-OP robots but have distinguishing marks identifying
   them as enemies, as illustrated in figure h) in Table 2.

4   Results

4.1   Execution Times

Tests were conducted on the three proposed implementations of the embedded system using 10% of the images used to validate the object identification
algorithm. The goal was to measure the performance of each implementation.
Specifically, we recorded the average response times and the number of recognized objects of interest in each image.

A total of 143 objects of interest were identified in the 80 test images, and it's important to note that these objects were consistently identified across all three devices. This uniformity in detection indicates the algorithm's correctness and underscores the adequacy of the training data.

The response times exhibited variations across the 80 test images for each device. The average response times for each device and algorithm are presented in Table 3:

Table 3. Average Response Times per Image

Device	YoloV3 (seconds)	Yolo-Tiny (seconds)
Raspberry Pi 3B+	More than 120	18
Raspberry Pi 3B+ with Intel Movidius	38	2
Intel NUC	14	0.6

It is important to note that during some of the tests, the Raspberry Pi became overwhelmed, leading to the program's interruption. To ensure accuracy, these instances were excluded when calculating the average response times.

We can confidently assert that this consistency across all devices serves as a strong indicator of the algorithm's reliability and affirms the adequacy of the training dataset. However, to provide a more comprehensive and transparent evaluation of the algorithm's performance, we will present specific data in the subsequent sections. This will include an in-depth analysis using tools such as the Confusion Matrix, ROC curves, and other performance measures. These metrics will further illuminate the algorithm's accuracy and effectiveness in object detection.

4.2   Confusion Matrix and ROC Curves

The results in the YOLO detection algorithm depended on the number of images and the accuracy of the training, in the first training only 2500 images were used for the database, of which only 100 were taken for evaluation; the precision of the training does not fall below 1.2 in the Tiny version and 2 in the full version of YoloV3 and in the literature it indicates that the recommended value is less than 1.

For the second training, a more robust database with 8000 images was used, 800 were taken for evaluation and the training improved, obtaining a precision of 0.53 for the full version of YoloV3 and 0.85 for the Tiny version.

YOLO

For the first training, after evaluating the validation images, the results were shown in Table 4:

These results summarize the detection performance for each class evaluated in the first training.

Table 4. Detection Results_Training 1

Class	Images with Class	Correct Detections	False Negatives	True Negatives
Goalpost	80	53	27	20
Ball	63	38	25	37
Robot	24	10	14	76

Table 5. Confusion Matrix - YOLO Tiny

Class	Positive Prediction		Negative Prediction	
	True Positives	False Negatives	False Positives	True Negatives
Robot	489	91	567	46
Ball	331	64	489	91
Goalpost	9	485	14	565

Table 6. Confusion Matrix - YOLO Full

Class	Positive Prediction		Negative Prediction	
	True Positives	False Negatives	False Positives	True Negatives
Robot	524	28	590	57
Ball	378	35	524	28
Goalpost	5	521	9	584

For the second training, the evaluation was conducted on 10% of the images from the second database. The results showed a total of 1588 objects of interest, with 580 belonging to the "Robot" class, 613 to the "ball" class, and 395 to the "goalpost" class. Each model produced different results, as shown in the confusion matrices in the Tables 5 and 6

The Table 7 summarizes the detection performance of each model during the second training. The table presents the values for TP (true positives), FP (false positives), FN (false negatives), and TN (true negatives), which are essential metrics for evaluating the models' performance in object detection.

Table 7. Summary of Results

Model	TP	FP	FN	TN
YOLO Tiny	1387	30	210	1378
YOLOV3	1492	18	120	1480

These results are crucial for assessing the models' performance in object detection. Below, we will discuss the findings and implications of these results:

- **Model Comparison:** The table demonstrates a comparison between two models, YOLO Tiny and YOLOV3, regarding their object detection performance during the second round of training. YOLOV3 achieved a higher number of true positives (TP) with 1492, while YOLO Tiny had 1387 TP. This indicates that YOLOV3 has a greater capacity to identify objects in this particular training scenario.
- **False positives (FP) and false negatives (FN):** are crucial metrics in assessing the accuracy of object detection models. YOLO Tiny had 30 FP and 210 FN, whereas YOLOV3 had 18 FP and 120 FN. It is noteworthy that

YOLOV3 exhibited better performance in terms of reducing false negatives. This is a significant advantage in applications where accurate object detection is critical.

- **True Negatives:** (TN) represent the correct identification of the absence of objects. Both models displayed a similar number of TN, with YOLO Tiny having 1378 and YOLOV3 having 1480 TN. This suggests that both models effectively identified areas where no objects were present.
- **Implications of Results:** The results provided in the table are instrumental in making informed decisions regarding the selection of an object detection model for specific applications. If minimizing false negatives is a top priority, YOLOV3 appears to be the preferred choice. Conversely, if minimizing false positives is essential, YOLO Tiny may be more suitable.
- **Further Analysis:** These results serve as a foundational assessment of the models' performance. For a comprehensive evaluation, additional metrics such as accuracy and recall should be considered. Moreover, hyperparameter tuning techniques can be explored to enhance the models' performance further

In conclusion, the Table 7 provides important insights into the object detection performance of the two models in the second round of training. The TP, FP, FN, and TN values play a pivotal role in assessing the models' capabilities and are indispensable for making informed decisions in practical applications.

4.3   Performance Evaluation

The performance measures for our models, YOLOV3 Full and YOLOV3 Tiny, are presented in Table 8.

Table 8. Performance Metrics for YOLOV3 Full and YOLOV3 Tiny

Model	Metric					
	Accuracy	Specificity	Sensitivity	Precision	NPV	F1 Score
YOLOV3 Full	0.9395	0.9879	0.92	0.9880	0.925	0.9557
YOLOV3 Tiny	0.8734	0.9786	0.8685	0.9788	0.8677	0.9203

Derived from the overall confusion matrices and performance metrics, ROC curves were plotted to evaluate the model performance. Refer to Fig. 2 for the ROC curve comparison.

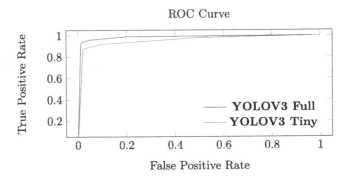

Fig. 2. ROC Curve Comparison

The table presents various performance metrics for two different models, YOLOV3 Full and YOLOV3 Tiny. These metrics provide a comprehensive assessment of each model's performance in terms of accuracy, specificity, sensitivity, precision, NPV, and F1 Score.

- **Accuracy:** Measures overall correctness. YOLOV3 Full achieves an accuracy of 0.9395, while YOLOV3 Tiny scores 0.8734.
- **Specificity:** Reflects the model's ability to identify true negatives. YOLOV3 Full demonstrates higher specificity (0.9879) compared to YOLOV3 Tiny (0.9786).
- **Sensitivity:** Measures the capacity to identify true positives. YOLOV3 Full scores 0.92 in sensitivity, while YOLOV3 Tiny achieves 0.8685.
- **Precision:** Quantifies the accuracy of positive predictions. YOLOV3 Full exhibits higher precision (0.9880) compared to YOLOV3 Tiny (0.9788).
- **Negative Predictive Value (NPV):** Assesses the ability to identify true negatives among negative predictions. YOLOV3 Full scores 0.925 in NPV, while YOLOV3 Tiny achieves 0.8677.
- **F1 Score:** A harmonic mean of precision and sensitivity, providing a balanced measure. YOLOV3 Full achieves an F1 Score of 0.9557, while YOLOV3 Tiny scores 0.9203.

Furthermore, ROC curves were used to visualize and compare the models' performance. The ROC curves plot TPR against FPR at various decision thresholds, with a higher curve indicating better performance.

- **YOLOV3 Full:** The ROC curve (blue) demonstrates excellent performance, with a high TPR even at low FPR values. The AUC quantifies the overall performance.
- **YOLOV3 Tiny:** The ROC curve (red) also shows commendable performance, though with slightly lower TPR compared to YOLOV3 Full at similar FPR values.

Table 9. Performance Measures and ROC Curve

Case	Accuracy	F1 Score	Precision	NPV	Specificity	Sensitivity
1	0.9483	0.9734	1	0.9483	1	0.948
2	0.965	0.9821	0.9931	0.9714	0.9931	0.9714
3	0.955	0.9330	0.9532	0.9168	0.955	0.9136
4	0.9925	0.9879	0.9916	0.9841	0.9916	0.9843
5	0.9194	0.9712	0.9724	0.9701	0.9723	0.9701
6	0.9494	0.9881	0.9824	0.9938	0.9823	0.9938
7	0.91	0.9782	1	0.9547	1	0.9574
8	0.9038	0.9507	0.9987	0.9012	0.9987	0.9071

The YOLO results can be seen in Figs. 3 and 4. In 3, two executions are shown: the upper one with YOLO and the lower one with Tiny YOLO, while in Fig. 4, an image is presented in which the ball, the goal and Robot have been identified. In both runs, classification is carried out on the same image, and the results obtained are surprisingly similar.

Final Algorithm In order to obtain the performance measures and the ROC curve of the final algorithm, 8 different scenarios were proposed, from which 600 samples were taken and based on the results, the values in Table 9 could be obtained:

The algorithm in use can be seen in Figs. 6

The ROC curves presented in Fig. 5 illustrate the performance evaluation of the eight different scenarios. These curves provide valuable insights into the discrimination capabilities of each model by plotting the True Positive Rate (TPR) against the False Positive Rate (FPR) at various thresholds. Generalizing the findings:

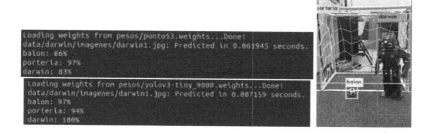

Fig. 3. Results from prediction of Yolo   **Fig. 4.** Prediction from YoloV3

- Exceptional Performance: Cases 1,2,3,4, and 6 exhibit exceptional performance, characterized by ROC curves that rapidly ascend from the origin. The model achieve consistently high TPR while maintaining a low FPR, making them suitable for applications where accurate detection and minimal false positives are crucial.
- Solid Performance: Cases 5, 7 and 8 display solid performance with ROC curves that strike a balance between TPR and FPR. In these cases, the model provide reliable discrimination capabilities and can be well-suited for various practical scenarios.

The choice of a specific model should depend on the specific requirements and priorities of the application. In this case, the ROC curves are valuable tools for assessing and comparing the performance of the classification model in different scenarios, helping to make informed decisions based on their specific objectives, whether that involves optimizing for sensitivity, minimizing false positives, or achieving a balance between the two.

The Fig. 6 present a composition of two subfigures that are used to visualize and compare two aspects related to the algorithm process

(a) This image represents the process that involves calculating distances and identifying objects.
(b) In contrast, this image shows a more complete view of the running process, including various stages and components of the algorithm working together. It is a more comprehensive view of how the process is performed as a whole.

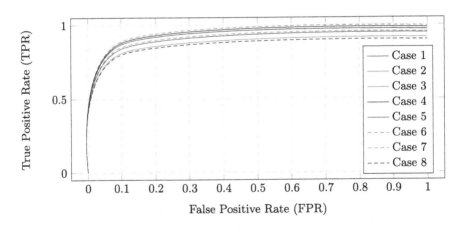

Fig. 5. ROC Curves - Case 1–8

(a) Distance and object identification   (b) Full algorithm running

Fig. 6. Distance calculation results and decision making

5 Conclusions

At the end of this terminal work, the following conclusions were reached.

- Regarding the application of object detection methods:
    - YOLO is a suitable algorithm for real-time detection but requires significant computational resources. Without lighter versions like YOLO-Tiny, implementing it on embedded systems without a powerful processing unit may not be feasible.
    - Some processing units, such as Raspberry Pi 3B+ combined with the Neural Compute Stick 2, can be a viable option for object detection. However, using YOLO may still pose challenges in terms of processing time.
    - The frames per second (FPS) rate depends on various factors, including video quality, which YOLO version is used, the division and subdivision configurations, and any additional post-detection processing steps.
- The training conducted for object detection has proven to be robust, enabling accurate detection of different types of humanoid robots without confusion with humans.
- The appropriate quantity of images in the dataset is crucial for achieving a robust detection system. Dataset with few images can lead to ineffective detection due to limited variety and generalization. Conversely, an excessive amount of images are able to conclude in overfitting, restricting the detection to a single type of robot.
- Although YOLO works as the core algorithm for object detection, the addition of extra processing steps for distance estimation and decision-making has resulted in a custom algorithm. It is important to note that the proper functioning of these components relies heavily on a strong object recognition system.
- The provided metrics and ROC curves offer a comprehensive evaluation of YOLOV3 Full and YOLOV3 Tiny in object detection or classification tasks. These assessments help in selecting the model that best aligns with specific requirements, whether they prioritize accuracy, sensitivity, or a balanced performance.
- Detecting the goalpost may pose challenges in accurately labeling the objects of interest and affect precise distance calculations between objects due to their proximity and the space they occupy in the image.

6 Discussion

- The Self-location algorithm discussed in this study offers promise for enhancing soccer-playing robots' performance but comes with notable limitations. It relies on RealSense camera vision, making it vulnerable to adverse lighting, occlusions, and weather conditions. Wireless connectivity introduces potential latency and instability. YOLOv3's accuracy depends on training data quality. Complex decision-making beyond proximity isn't covered, and the absence of inter-robot communication limits real-time coordination. While promising, the algorithm must address these challenges for effective deployment in dynamic environments like robot soccer matches.
- Implementing the Self-location algorithm in humanoid robots presents ethical, safety, and risk challenges. Ensuring collision avoidance mechanisms is vital to prevent harm. In robot soccer, ethical considerations demand that the algorithm's decisions adhere to game rules for fairness. Privacy concerns arise when robots use computer vision in public spaces, potentially infringing on individuals' privacy. Secure wireless communication is crucial to protect data from unauthorized access. Addressing potential biases in decision-making due to biased or limited training data is imperative for fair robot interactions. These considerations highlight the need for responsible deployment and regulation in the use of such algorithms to ensure safety, ethics, and data privacy.
- Future research in robotic soccer and broader robotics domains should focus on advanced decision-making algorithms, human-robot interaction improvements, multi-robot coordination, robust environmental adaptability, and ethical guidelines and regulations. These directions will pave the way for more capable and responsible robot deployments, addressing challenges in dynamic environments and ensuring safe and ethical use in various applications.

Appendix

A Additional Tables

Table 10. Characteristics of Darwin-OP models

Characteristics	Darwin-OP	Darwin-OP2	Darwin-OP3
Built-in PC	Intel Atom Z530, 1.6GHz 4GB	Intel Atom N2600 Dual-core 1.6GHz	Intel NUC i3 Dual-core
RAM	1GB	DDR3 2GB at 1066MHz	DDR4 8GB at 2133MHz
Actuators	DYNAMIXEL MX-28	DYNAMIXEL MX-28	DYNAMIXEL XM430
Storage	4GB flash SSD	32GB mSATA module	128GB SSD.2 module
Camera	Logitech C905	Logitech C905	Logitech C920
Compatible OS	Linux and 32-bit Windows	Any version of Linux and 32-bit Windows	Any version of Linux and 32/64-bit Windows
Sub Controller	CM-730	CM-740	OpenCR

Table 11. Comparison of Intel RealSense Depth Cameras

Model	Intel SR305	Intel RealSense D415	Intel RealSense D435	Intel RealSense L515
Depth Resolution	640 × 480 px	**1280 × 720 px**	1280 × 720 px	1024 × 768 px
Color Resolution	N/A	**1920 × 1080 px**	1920 × 1080 px	1920 × 1080 px
Horizontal Field of View	65°C	**63.4°C**	85.2°C	70.2°C
Vertical Field of View	50°C	**40.4°C**	58.5°C	55.2°C
Maximum Range	1.6 m	**10 m**	10 m	9 m
Frame Rate	Up to 90 fps	**Up to 90 fps**	Up to 90 fps	Up to 30 fps
Connection	USB 2.0	**USB 3.0**	USB 3.0	USB 3.1 Gen 1
Dimensions	90 × 25 x 25 mm	**99 × 20 x 23 mm**	99 × 20 x 23 mm	61 × 26 x 23 mm
Weight	90 g	**82 g**	83 g	100 g
Key Applications	Hand tracking	**Augmented reality**	Virtual reality	High-resolution 3D scanning

Table 12. Comparison of Processing Boards: Raspberry Pi 4, Jetson Nano, Rock Pi N10

Features	Raspberry Pi 4 [18]	Jetson Nano [19]	Rock Pi N10 [20]
CPU	Broadcom BCM2711, Quad-core	NVIDIA Carmel ARM Cortex-A57	Rockchip RK3399
GPU	VideoCore VI	NVIDIA Maxwell	Mali-T860 MP4
RAM	Up to 8 GB LPDDR4	4 GB LPDDR4	Up to 4 GB LPDDR4
Storage	SD card slot	microSD card slot	SD card slot
Connectivity	Wi-Fi, Bluetooth, Ethernet	Wi-Fi, Bluetooth, Ethernet	Wi-Fi, Bluetooth, Ethernet
USB Ports	2 x USB 3.0, 2 x USB 2.0	4 x USB 3.0, 2 x USB 2.0	2 x USB 3.0, 2 x USB 2.0
HDMI	2 x Micro HDMI	1 x HDMI	1 x HDMI
GPIO	40 GPIO pins	40 GPIO pins	40 GPIO pins
Power Consumption	2.5W - 7.5W	5W - 10W	5W - 10W
Approximate Price	From $ 35	From $ 99	From $ 89

References

1. Siciliano, B., Khatib, O.: Springer Handbook of Robotics. Springer (2016). https://play.google.com/store/books/details/Springer_Handbook_of_Robotics?id=HphMDAAAQBAJ, https://doi.org/10.1007/978-3-540-30301-5
2. Buckley, D.: History Makers - 1893 George Moore's Steam Man. Publisher, 1896. Designed by the Canadian inventor George Moore in 1893, this life-size (6-foot tall) steam-powered android was able to walk at a rate of up to 5 mph. The Walking Steam Man was constructed of tin. The body contained a steam boiler powered by means of a gasoline engine
3. Darwin-op (dynamic anthropomorphic robot with intelligence-Open platform). https://casualrobots.com/robot_Darwin.html. Accessed 07 2023
4. YOLO V3. https://viso.ai/deep-learning/yolov3-overview/. Accessed 07 2023
5. Escobar Hernández, J.C.: La inteligencia artificial y la enseñanza de lenguas: una aproximación al tema. Decires **21**(25), 29–44 (2021). https://doi.org/10.22201/cepe.14059134e.2021.21.25.3
6. RoboCup Humanoid League. https://humanoid.robocup.org, Último acceso: 13 enero 2021
7. Hernández Ramírez, J., et al.: Training bioloid robots for playing football. In: Lecture Notes in Computer Science, vol. 8112 (2013)

8. Sanchez Alvarado, E., Rivas Borbon, O.M.: Táctica y estrategia en futbol. Heredoa (2012)

9. Ibarra Bonilla, M.N.: Navegación autónoma de un robot con técnicas de localización y ruteo. PhD thesis, Tonantzintla, Puebla (2009)

10. Pratomo, A.H., Kwon, D.K., Kim, H.R.: Cooperative strategy for an interactive robot soccer system by reinforcement, pp. 236–242. Control, Automation and Systems (2003)

11. RoboCup - Official Website. https://www.robocup.org/. Accessed Sept 2023

12. TalentLand - Official Website. https://www.talent-land.mx/. Accessed Sept 2023

13. ROBOTIS: Robotis minimal mistakes (2020). https://emanual.robotis.com/docs/en/platform/op3/introduction/

14. Intel. Intel RealSense. Intel Corporation. https://www.intelrealsense.com/depth-camera-d415/

15. Intel. Intel neural compute stick 2, En línea. https://ark.intel.com/content/www/us/en/ark/products/140109/intel-neural-compute-stick-2.html

16. Goodfellow, I., Bengio, Y., Courville, A.: Deep Learning. MIT Press (2016)

17. Szeliski, R.: Computer Vision: Algorithms and Applications. Springer (2010). https://doi.org/10.1007/978-1-84882-935-0

18. Raspberry Pi, En línea. https://www.raspberrypi.org/products/raspberry-pi-4-model-b/

19. NVIDIA. Nvidia desarrollador, En línea. https://developer.nvidia.com/embedded/jetson-nano-developer-kit

20. Radxa (2018). https://wiki.radxa.com/RockpiN10

Learning Neural Radiance Fields of Forest Structure for Scalable and Fine Monitoring

Juan Castorena$^{(\boxtimes)}$

Los Alamos National Laboratory, Los Alamos, NM 48124, USA
jcastorena@lanl.gov

Abstract. This work leverages neural radiance fields and remote sensing for forestry applications. Here, we show neural radiance fields offer a wide range of possibilities to improve upon existing remote sensing methods in forest monitoring. We present experiments that demonstrate their potential to: (1) express fine features of forest 3D structure, (2) fuse available remote sensing modalities and (3), improve upon 3D structure derived forest metrics. Altogether, these properties make neural fields an attractive computational tool with great potential to further advance the scalability and accuracy of forest monitoring programs.

Keywords: Neural radiance fields · Remote Sensing · LiDAR · ALS · TLS · Photogrammetry · Forestry

1 Introduction

With approximately four billion hectares covering around 31% of the Earth's land area [7], forests play a vital role in our ecosystem. The increasing demand for tools that help maintain a balanced and healthy forest ecosystem is challenging due to the complex nature of various factors, including resilience against disease and fire, as well as overall forest health and biodiversity [25]. Active research focuses on the development of monitoring methods that synergistically collect comprehensive information about forest ecosystems and utilize it to analyze and generate predictive models of the characterizing factors. These methods should ideally be capable of effectively and efficiently cope with the dynamic changes over time and heterogeneity. The goal is to provide the tools with such properties for improved planning, management, analysis, and more effective decision-making processes [1]. Traditional tools for forest monitoring, such as national forest inventory (NFI) plots, utilize spatial sampling and estimation techniques to quantify forest cover, growing stock volume, biomass, carbon balance, and various tree metrics (e.g., diameter at breast height, crown width, height) [23]. However, these surveying methods consist of manual field sampling, which tends to introduce bias and poses challenges in terms of reproducibility. Moreover, this approach is economically costly and time-consuming, especially when dealing with large spatial extents.

Recent advancements, driven by the integration of remote sensing, geographic information and modern computational methods, have contributed to the development of more efficient, cost/time effective, and reproducible ecosystem characterizations. These

© The Author(s), under exclusive license to Springer Nature Switzerland AG 2024
H. Calvo et al. (Eds.): MICAI 2023, LNAI 14392, pp. 281–296, 2024.
https://doi.org/10.1007/978-3-031-47640-2_23

advancements have unveiled the potential of highly refined and detailed models of 3D forest structure. Traditionally, the metrics collected through standard forest inventory plot surveys have been utilized as critical inputs in applications in forest health [15], wood harvesting [13], habitat monitoring [24], and fire modeling [16]. The efficacy of these metrics relies in their ability to quantitatively represent the full forest's 3D structure including its vertical resolution: from the ground, sub-canopy to the canopy structure. Among the most popular remote sensing techniques, airborne LiDAR scanning (ALS) has gained widespread interest due to its ability to rapidly collect precise 3D structural information over large regional extents [6]. Airborne LiDAR, equipped with accurate position sensors like RTK (Real-Time Kinematic), enables large-scale mapping from high altitudes at spatial resolutions ranging from 5–20 points per square meter. It has proven effective in retrieving important factors in forest inventory plots [11]. However, it faces challenges in dense areas where the tree canopy obstructs the LiDAR signal, even with its advanced full-waveform-based technology. *In-situ* terrestrial laser scanning (TLS) on the other hand provides detailed vertical 3D resolution from the ground, sub-canopy and canopy structure informing about individual trees, shrubs, ground surface, and near-ground vegetation at even higher spatial resolutions [10]. Recent work by [20] has demonstrated the efficiency and efficacy of ecosystem monitoring using single scan in-situ TLS. The technological advances of such models include new capabilities for rapidly extracting highly detailed quantifiable predictions of vegetation attributes and treatment effects in near surface, sub-canopy and canopy composition. However, these models have only been deployed across spatial domains of a few tens of meters in radius due to the existing inherited limitations of TLS spatial coverage [20]. On the other side of the spectrum, image based photogrammetry for 3D structure extraction offers the potential of being both scalable and the most cost efficient. Existing computational methods for the extraction of 3D structure in forest ecosystems, however, have not been as efficient. Aerial photogrammetry methods result in 3D structure that contains very limited structural information along the vertical dimension and have encountered output spatial resolutions that can be at most only on par with those from ALS [25].

Our contribution seeks to fuse the experimental findings across remote sensing domains in forestry; from broad-scale to in-situ sensing sources. The goal is the ability to achieve the performance quality of *in-situ* sources (e.g., TLS) in the extraction of 3D forest structure at the scalability of broad sources (e.g., ALS, aerial-imagery). We propose the use of neural radiance field (NERF) representations [17] which account for the origin and direction of radiance to determine highly detailed 3D structure via view-consistency. We observe that such representations enable both the fine description of forest 3D structure and also the fusion of multi-view multi-modal sensing sources. Demonstrated experiments on real multi-view RGB imagery, ALS and TLS validate the fine resolution capabilities of such representations as applied to forests. In addition, the performance found in our experiments of 3D structure derived forest factor metrics demonstrate the potential of neural fields to improve upon the existing forest monitoring programs. To the best of our knowledge, the demonstrations conducted in this research, namely, the application of neural fields for 3D sensing in forestry, is novel and has not been shown previously. In the following, Sect. 2 provides a brief overview of neural fields. Sect. 3 includes experiments illustrating the feasibility of neural fields to represent fine 3D structure of forestry while Sect. 4 demonstrates the effectiveness of fusing NERF with LiDAR data by enforcing LiDAR point cloud priors. Finally, Sect. 5 presents results that show the efficacy of NERF extracted 3D structure for deriving forest factor metrics, which are of prime significance to forest managers for monitoring.

2 Background

2.1 Neural Radiance Fields

The idea of neural radiance fields (NERF) is based on classical ray tracing of volume densities [12]. Under this framework, each pixel comprising an image is represented by a ray of light casted onto the scene. The ray of light is described by $r(t) = \mathbf{o} + t\mathbf{d}$ with origin $\mathbf{o} \in \mathbb{R}^3$, unit ℓ_2-norm length direction $\mathbf{d} \in \mathbb{R}^3$ (i.e., $\|\mathbf{d}\|_2 = 1$) and independent variable $t \in \mathbb{R}$ representing a relative distance. The parameters of each ray can be computed through the camera intrinsic matrix $\mathbf{K}$ with inverse $\mathbf{K}^{-1}$, the 6D pose transformation matrix $\mathbf{T}_{m\rightarrow 0}$ of image m as in Eq. (1)

$$(\mathbf{o}, \mathbf{d}) = \left(T^{(4)}_{m\rightarrow 0}, \frac{\mathbf{d}'}{\|\mathbf{d}'\|_{\ell_2}} \right) \quad \text{with}$$

$$\mathbf{d}' = \mathbf{T}^{-1}_{m\rightarrow 0}\mathbf{K}^{-1} \begin{bmatrix} u' \\ v' \\ 1 \end{bmatrix} - T^{(4)}_{m\rightarrow 0} \tag{1}$$

where u', v' are vertical and horizontal the pixel locations within the image and the subscript $^{(i)}$ denotes the i-th column of a matrix. Casting rays $\mathbf{r} \in \mathcal{R}$ into the scene from all pixels across all multi-view images provides information of intersecting rays that can be exploited to infer 3D scene structure. Such information consists on sampling along a ray at distance samples $\{t_i\}^M_{i=1}$ and determine at each sample if the color $\mathbf{c}_i \in [0, .., 255]^3$ of the ray coincides with those from overlapping rays. If it does not coincide then it is likely that the medium found at that specific distance sample is transparent whereas the opposite means an opaque medium is present. With such information, compositing color can be expressed as a function of ray $\mathbf{r}$ as in Eq. (2) by:

$$\hat{C}(\mathbf{r}) = \sum_{i=1}^{N} \left[\underbrace{\left(\prod_{j=1}^{i-1} \exp(-\sigma_j\delta_j) \right)}_{\text{transparency so far}} \underbrace{(1 - \exp(-\sigma_i\delta_i))}_{\text{opacity}} \mathbf{c}_i \right] \tag{2}$$

where $\sigma_i \in \mathbb{R}$ and $\delta_i = t_{i+1} - t_i$ are the volume densities and differential time steps at sample indexed by i, respectively. In Eq. (2) the first term in the summation represents the transparent samples so far while the second term is an opaque medium of color $\mathbf{c}_i$ present at sample i. Reconstructing a scene in 3D can then be posed as the problem of finding the sample locations t_i where each ray intersects an opaque medium (i.e., where each ray stops) for all rays casted into the scene. Those intersections are likely to occur at the sample locations where the volume densities are maximized; in other words, where $t_i = \arg\max_i\{\sigma\}$. Accumulating, all rays casted into the scene and estimating the locations t_i's where volume density is maximized overall rays, renders the 3D geometry of the scene. The number of rays required per scene is an open question; the interested reader can go to [3] where a similar problem but for LiDAR sensing determines the number of pulses required for 3D reconstruction depending on a quantifiable measure of scene complexity.

The problem in Eq. (2) is solved by learning the volume densities that best explains image pixel color in a 3D consistent way. Learning can be done through a multilayer perceptron (MLP) by rewriting Eq. (2) as in Eq. (3) as:

$$\hat{C}(\mathbf{r}) = \sum_{i=1}^{N} \mathbf{w}_i \mathbf{c}_i \tag{3}$$

where the weights $\mathbf{w} \in \mathbb{R}^N$ encode transparency or opacity of the N samples along a ray and $\mathbf{c}_i$ is its associated pixel color. Learning weights is performed in an unsupervised fashion through the optimization of a loss function using a training set of M pairs of multi-view RGB images and its corresponding 6D poses $\{(\mathbf{y}_m, \mathbf{T}_m)\}_{m=1}^{M}$, respectively. This loss function $f : \mathbb{R}^L \to \mathbb{R}$ is the average ℓ_2-norm error between ground truth color and estimation by compositing described as in Eq. (4):

$$\mathcal{L}_C(\mathbf{\Theta}) = \sum_{\mathbf{r} \in \mathcal{R}} \left[\|C(\mathbf{r}) - \hat{C}(\mathbf{r}, \mathbf{\Theta})\|_{\ell_2}^2 \right] \tag{4}$$

Optimization by back-propagation yields the weights that gradually improves upon the estimation of the volume densities. Other important parameters of NERF are distance $\hat{z}(\mathbf{r})$ which can be defined using the same weights from Eq.(2) but here expressed in terms of distance as:

$$\hat{z}(\mathbf{r}) = \sum_{i=1}^{N} \omega_i t_i, \qquad \hat{s}(\mathbf{r})^2 = \sum_{i=1}^{N} \omega_i (t_i - \hat{z}(\mathbf{r}))^2 \tag{5}$$

and $\hat{s}(\mathbf{r})$ defined as the standard deviation of distance. One key issue affecting 3D reconstruction resolution is on the way samples $\{t_i\}_{i=1}^{N}$ for each ray $\mathbf{r} \in \mathcal{R}$ are drawn. A small number of samples N results in low resolution and erroneous ray intersection estimations while sampling vastly results in much higher computational complexities. To balance this trade-off, the work in [17] uses two networks one at low-resolution to coarsely sample the 3D scene and another fine-resolution one used subsequently to more finely sample only at locations likely containing the scene.

3   Are Neural Fields Capable of Extracting 3D Structure in Forestry?

The high capacity of deep learning (DL) models to express data distributions with high fidelity and diversity offers a promising avenue to model heterogenous 3D forest structures in fine detail. The specific configuration of the selected DL model aims to provide a representation that naturally allows the combination of data from multiple sensing modalities and view-points. Neural fields [17] under the DL rubric have proven to be a highly effective computational approach for addressing such problems. However, their application has been only demonstrated for indoor and urban environments.

3.1   Terrestrial Imagery

Expanding on the findings of neural fields in man-made environments, we conducted additional experiments to demonstrate its effectiveness in representing fine 3D structure details in forest ecosystems. Figures 1 and 2 shows the extracted 3D structure of a Ponderosa pine tree in New Mexico, captured using standard 12-megapixel camera phone images collected along an elliptical trajectory around the tree. Figure 1a shows a few of the input example terrestrial multi-view RGB images collected. Figures 1b and 1c presents the image snapshot trajectory represented as red rectangles, along with two 3D structure views derived from a traditional structure from motion (SFM) method [22] applied to the multi-view input images. Note that the level of spatial variability detail provided by this SFM method is significantly low considering the resolution provided by the set of input images.

(a) Terrestrial RGB multi-view imagery of Ponderosa Pine Tree.

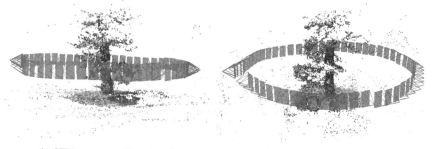

(b) SFM reconstruction view-1   (c) SFM reconstruction view-2

Fig. 1. Even though SFM reconstruction is capable of extracting the 3D structure of tree, its recontruction suffers from sparsity. Such sparsity limits the spatial variability of structure that can be captured thorugh such models.

Can the representational power of modern AI models do better than classical 3D structure extraction methods in Forestry? We extract 3D structure by neural fields using the same input images and obtain the result shown in Fig. 2. Note that much finer spatial variability details can be resolved across the 3D structure including the ground, trunk, branches, leaves. Even fine woody debris as shown in Figs2c-.2d and, bark can be resolved as shown in Figs. 2e-2f in contrast to the result of traditional SFM in Fig. 1. Note that even points coming from images degraded by sun-glare as shown in Fig. 1a landed in the tree within reasonable distances as shown in Fig. 2a, this is significant specially considering the severity of the glare effects present in the 2D RGB images. In general, terrestrial multi-view imagery based NERF can be used to extract fine 3D spatial resolution along the vertical dimension of a tree stand with a level of detail similar to TLS and with the additional advantage of providing color for every 3D point estimate.

(a) Side views illustrating high 3D spatial detail along the vertical tree stem

(b) Tree 3D structure view-5   (c) Fine 3D resolution of forest floor structure

(d) Forest floor 3D structure   (e) Tree trunk view-1   (f) Tree trunk view-2

Fig. 2. Neural field models are capable of extracting fine 3D structure from terrestrial multi-view images in forestry. Reconstructions demonstrate their potential to represent fine scale variability in heterogeneous forest ecosystems.

4   Neural Radiance Fields: A Framework for Remote Sensing Fusion in Forestry

Neural fields, have also demonstrated their ability to provide representations suitable for combining data from multiple sensing modalities in as long as these are co-registered or aligned. The neural fields framework, which extracts 3D structure from multi-view images, enables direct fusion of information with 3D point cloud sources through point cloud prior constraints [21]. Here, we consider the case of fusing multi-view images from an RGB camera and point clouds from LiDAR. The difficulty in fusing camera and LiDAR information is that camera measures color radiance while LiDAR measures distance [5]. Fortunately, the framework of neural radiance fields can be used to extract 3D structure from images thus enabling direct fusion of information from LiDAR. This can be done though a learning function that extracts a 3D structure promoting consistency between the multi-view images as leveraged by standard NERF [17] subject to LiDAR point cloud priors [21] as:

$$\mathcal{L}(\Theta) = \underbrace{\sum_{r \in \mathcal{R}} \left[\|C(\mathbf{r}) - \hat{C}(\mathbf{r}, \Theta)\|_{\ell_2}^2 \right]}_{\mathcal{L}_C(\Theta)} + \lambda \underbrace{\sum_{r \in \mathcal{R}} \left[\|z(\mathbf{r}) - \hat{z}(\mathbf{r}, \Theta)\|_{\ell_2}^2 \right]}_{\mathcal{L}_D(\Theta)} \qquad (6)$$

where the first term $\mathcal{L}_C(\Theta)$ is the standard NERF learning function promoting a 3D structure with consistency between image views while the second term $\mathcal{L}_D(\Theta)$ enforces the LiDAR point cloud priors with $\hat{z}(\mathbf{r}, \Theta)$ given as in Eq.(5). The benefit of imposing point cloud priors into neural fields is two-fold: (1) it enables expressing relative distances obtained from standard 3D reconstruction of multi-view 2D images in terms of real metrics (e.g., meters), and (2) neural fields tend to face challenges in accurately estimating 3D structures at high distances (typically in the order of several tens of meters), where the LiDAR point cloud priors can serve as a supervisory signal to guide accurate estimation, especially at greater distances. This can be beneficial, as distances in aerial imagery are generally distributed around large distances, which may pose challenges for 3D structure extraction methods.

4.1   Filing in the Missing Below-Canopy Structure in ALS Data with TLS

In-situ terrestrial laser scanning (TLS) has been demonstrated as a powerful tool for rapid assessment of forest structure in ecosystem monitoring and characterization. It is capable of very fine resolution including the vertical direction: surface, sub-canopy and canopy structure. However, its utility and application is restricted by limited spatial coverage. Aerial laser scanning (ALS) on the other hand, has the ability to rapidly survey broad scale areas at the landscape level, but is limited as it sparsely samples the scene providing only coarse spatial variability details and it also cannot penetrate the tree canopy. Figure 3a shows a point cloud example collected using a full-waveform ALS system which collects ≈ 10 points per meter square. In Fig. 3a note that the sub-canopy structure is not spatially resolved. In contrast, TLS is finely resolved below the canopy as observed in Fig. 3b.

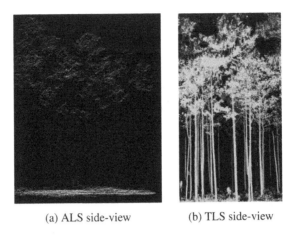

(a) ALS side-view   (b) TLS side-view

Fig. 3. Forest structure from TLS and ALS: ALS provides sparse spatial information and is not capable of resolving sub-canopy detail. TLS on the other hand, provides fine spatial variability and resolution along full 3D vertical stands.

Fortunately, the drawbacks of TLS and ALS scans can be resolved by co-registration which transforms the data to enable direct fusion. Here, we use the automatic and targetless based approach of [4]. This was demonstrated to outperform standard methods [2,8,19] in natural ecosystems and to be robust to resolution scales, view-points, scan area overlap, vegetation heterogeneity, topography and to ecosystem changes induced by pre/post low-intensity fire effects. It is also fully automatic, capable of self-correcting in cases of noisy GPS measurements and does not require any manually placed targets [9] while performing at the same levels of accuracy. All TLS scans where co-registered into the coordinate system of ALS. Once scans have been co-registered they can be projected into a common coordinate system. Illustrative example results for two forest plots where included in Fig. 4 where the two sources: ALS and TLS have been color coded differently, with the sparser point cloud being that of the ALS. Throughout all cases the co-registration produced finely aligned point clouds. In general, the error produced by this co-registration method is <6 cm for the translation and <0.1° for the rotation parameters. The translation error in mainly due to the resolution of ALS at 10 points/meter square.

4.2   Aerial Imagery

Experiments performed on broader forest areas were also conducted. Aerial RGB imagery was collected with a DJI Mavic2 Pro drone at 30 Hz and a 3840 × 2160 pixel resolution. Figures 5a-5f show examples of multi-view aerial image inputs used by the SFM and neural fields models. The forest 3D structure resulting from running conventional SFM [22] on these images is in Figs. 5i-5k illustrating different perspective views. Again, the sequence of rectangles in red illustrate the drone flight path and the snapshot image locations. Note that SFM was capable of resolving 3D structure for the entire scene.

(a) Co-registration Example 1   (b) Co-registration Example 2

Fig. 4. TLS to ALS co-registration: Forest features are well aligned qualitatively between both ALS and TLS sensing.

Applying NERF directly into the RGB imagery dataset, did not result in comparable performance as in the case of the Ponderosa pine tree shown in Sect. 3.1. Without point cloud constraints, the 3D structure extracted by the neural fields in Fig. 5h shows the presence of artifacts at large distances. The main reason for these artifacts is that NERF had difficulties in recovering 3D structures from images with objects distributed at far distances (e.g., ground surface in aerial scanning). Imposing LiDAR point cloud priors we hypothesize can help to alleviate this issue. Here, we follow the methodology of [21] and conduct experiments for fusing camera and LiDAR information through the learning function in Eq.(6). The LiDAR point cloud uses both co-registered TLS and ALS data which provides information to constrain both distances in the mid-story below the canopy and those between the ground surface and the tree canopy. The co-registration approach used to align ALS and TLS point clouds is the one described in Sect. 4.1. Note that TLS information is not available throughout the entire tested forest area; rather, only one TLS scan was collected. We found the information provided by just one single scan was enough to constraint the relative distances in sub-canopy areas throughout the entire scene. Imposing additional constraints through consistency with the input point cloud shown in Fig. 5g, results in the extracted 3D structure shown in Figs. 5l-5n. In this case, the point cloud prior imposes constraints that resolve the associated difficulties at large distances. Note that this reconstruction is significantly less sparser than those shown in Figs. 5i-5j obtained from conventional SFM. NERF+LIDAR results in improved resolution which in turn enables the detection of a much finer spatial variability, specially important for current existing demands in forest monitoring at broad scale. This illustrates the capacity of neural fields models not only to represent highly detailed 3D forest structure from aerial multi-view data but also the possibility of combining multi-source remotely sensed data (i.e., imagery and LiDAR).

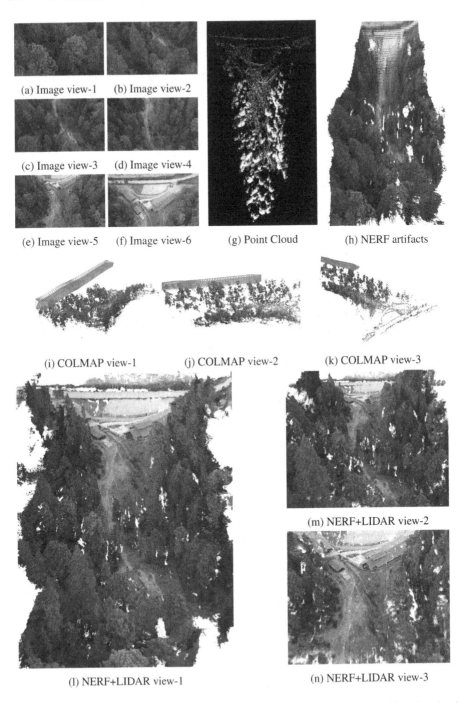

(a) Image view-1   (b) Image view-2

(c) Image view-3   (d) Image view-4

(e) Image view-5   (f) Image view-6   (g) Point Cloud   (h) NERF artifacts

(i) COLMAP view-1   (j) COLMAP view-2   (k) COLMAP view-3

(m) NERF+LIDAR view-2

(l) NERF+LIDAR view-1   (n) NERF+LIDAR view-3

Fig. 5. AI-based extraction of 3D structures from aerial multi-view 2D images + 3D point cloud data inputs. Imposing point cloud priors into 3D structure extraction improves distance ambiguities in structure and resolves artifact issues likely at far ranges.

5   Prediction of Forest Factor Metrics

Demonstration of the described capabilities of neural fields on forest monitoring programs consists here in performance evaluations of 3D forest structure derived metrics. These can include for example number of trees, species composition, tree height, diameter at breast height (DBH), age on a given geo-referenced area. However, since our focus is to demonstrate the usefulness of neural radiance fields for representing 3D forest structure, we only illustrate its potential in prediction of the number of trees and DBH along geo-referenced areas. The data used includes overlapping TLS+ALS+GPS+aerial imagery multi-view multi-modal data collected over forest plot units. Each of these plots represents a location area of a varying size: some of size 20×50 m and others at 15 m radius. The sites in which data was collected is within the boundaries of both Los Alamos National Laboratory and the Bandelier National Monument in New Mexico, USA (the NM dataset). The vegetation heterogeneity and topography variability of the landscape is significantly diverse. The NM site contains high elevation ponderosa pine and mixed-conifer forest: white fir, limber pine, aspen, Douglas fir and Gambel oak and topography is at high elevation and of high-variation (between 5,000–10,200 ft). The TLS data was collected using Leica's BLK360 sensor mounted on a static tripod placed at the center of each plot. The ALS data was collected by a Galaxy T2000 LiDAR sensor mounted on a fixed-wing aircraft. The number of LiDAR point returns per volume depend on the sensor and scanning protocol settings (e.g., TLS or ALS, range distribution, number of scans) and these vary across plots depending on the heterogeneity of the site.

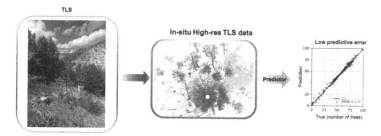

(a) In-situ plot-scale TLS has demonstrated to be an effective tool in estimating plot-level vegetation characteristics

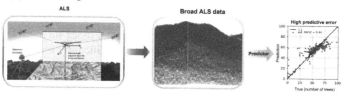

(b) Broad-landscape scale ALS derived prediction, does not have vertical dimension resolution resulting in underestimate predictions

Fig. 6. LiDAR derived vegetation attribute estimation for single TLS and ALS.

Ground truth number of trees per plot was obtained through standard forest plot field surveying techniques involving actual physical measurements of live/dead vegetation composition. Data from a total of 250 plots where collected in the NM dataset. In every forest plot overlapping ALS, GPS, TLS and multi-view aerial imagery data was collected along with the corresponding field measured ground truth. Prediction of the number of trees y_1 per plot given point cloud $\mathbf{X}$, was performed following the approach of the GRNet [26,27]. In general, the methodology consists in computing 2D bounding boxes each corresponding to a tree detection from a birds eye view (BEV). A refinement segmentation approach then follows which projects each 2D bounding box into 3D space. The resulting points inside each 3D bounding box are then segmented by foliage, upper stem and lower stem and empty space and this information is used to improve estimates over the number of trees. This methodology is used independently on several case scenarios comparing the performance of a combination of remote sensing approaches: (1) neural fields (NF) from aerial RGB Images, (2) ALS as in Fig. 6b, (3) TLS as in Fig. 6a, (4) ALS+TLS, (5) NF-RGB images + ALS, (6) NF-RGB images + TLS, (7) NF-RGB Images + TLS + ALS. Note that the TLS, ALS and TLS+ALS prediction results does not make any use of neural fields. Rather, their performance was included only for comparison purposes. Table 1 summarizes the root mean squared error (RMSE) results for each of the tested cases.

Table 1. RMSE Prediction performance of number of trees per plot in NM dataset.

Method	NF-RGB	ALS	TLS	ALS+TLS	NF-RGB+ALS	NF-RGB+TLS	NF-RGB+ALS+TLS
RMSE	10.61	8.44	1.77	1.67	1.41	1.39	1.32

The results in Table 1 corroborate some of the trade-offs between the sensing modalities and in addition some of the advantages gained through the use of neural fields in forestry. First, the superiority of TLS over ALS data on the number of trees metric is mainly due to the presence of information in sub-canopy which is characteristic of in-situ TLS. This in alignment with current demonstrations in the literature which have motivated the widespread usage of in-situ TLS in forestry applications even though it is not as spatially scalable as ALS is [20]. We would have seen the opposite relationships between TLS and ALS, however, in cases when the plot size is significantly higher than the range of a single in-situ TLS scan. A problem which can be resolved by adding multiple view co-registered TLS scans per plot. This limitation is caused as the sensor remains static at collection time which makes it more susceptible to occlusions, specially in dense forest areas where trees can significantly reduce the view of TLS at higher ranges. TLS+ALS overcomes, on the other hand, the limitations of the individual LiDAR platforms by filling in the missing information characteristic of each platform. Structure from neural fields using only multi-view RGB images performed slightly worst than both ALS and TLS. This may be due to the limited number of multi-view images collected per plot, the performance for deriving structure from NERF or to the joint performance of NERF in conjunction with the GRNet. Fortunately, fusing neural fields from multi-view imagery with LiDAR shows a significant improvement overall fused cases (i.e., NF+ALS, NF+TLS and NF+ALS+TLS). We see that the prior supervisory signal imposed by the LiDAR point cloud helps on guiding the resulting 3D structure from NERF to alleviate the artifacts arising at far distances when using multi-view imagery only. We would like to finalize this discussion by highlighting the performance of the NF-RGB+ALS method which is marginally similar to the best performing method (i.e., NF-RGB+ALS+TLS). The benefit of using NF-RGB+ALS is that being both airborne makes the data collection of these two modalities time and cost efficient, in contrast, to in-situ remote sensing methods such as TLS. This has significant implications towards achieving both scalable and highly performing forest monitoring programs. In general, one has to resort to a balance between scalability and performance depending on needs. Our work instead, offers a method which can potentially achieve similar performance as in-situ methods with the benefits of scalability over the landscape scales through computational methods.

Additional experiments were conducted to explore the ability of neural fields from terrestrial based multi-view imagery to achieve a performance near that of TLS in metrics that depend on sub-canopy information. In this case, we evaluated performance on the DBH metric for a total of 200 trees. Ground truth DBH was manually measured in the field for each tree's stem diameter at a height of 1.3m. A total of 5 co-registered TLS scans where used per tree, each collected from a different location and viewing each tree from a different perspective to reduce the effects of occlusion and to remove the degrading effects of lower point LiDAR return densities at farther ranges. Multi-view TLS co-registration was obtained using the method of [4]. Terrestrial multi-view RGB imagery data for NERF was collected around an oblique trajectory around each tree as exemplified in Fig. 1 with $10 - 15$ snapshot images per tree. Algorithmic performance for estimating DBH was compared against TLS, ALS, TLS+ALS and NF-RGB. The estimation approach of [26] relying on stem geometric circular shape fitting at a height of 1.3m over the ground was used following their implementation. Performance is measured as the average error as a percentage of the actual field measured DBH ground truth, following the work of [26]. Comparison results are reported in Table 2.

Table 2. Comparison of sensing modalities on average error DBH estimation.

Method	NF-RGB	ALS	TLS	ALS+TLS
Avg. error %	1.7 %	32.7%	1.3%	3.3%

In Table 2 ALS performs the worst DBH estimation due to its inherited limited sub-canopy resolution. Multi-view TLS on the other hand, performs the best at 1.3% error consistent with TLS superiority findings in [26] for metrics relying on sub-canopy information. However, our neural fields approach from terrestrial imagery performs marginally on par with multi-view TLS, with the additional advantage that RGB camera sensors are simpler to access commercially and significantly cheaper than LiDAR.

In terms of computational specifications, neural radiance fields were trained using a set of overlapping 10–50 multi-view images per scene. The fast implementation of [18] was used with training on the terrestrial and aerial multi-view imagery taking from

30–60 secs per 3D structure extraction (e.g., per plot in the aerial imagery case, per tree in the terrestrial imagery case). Adding the LiDAR constraints was done following the implementation from [21]. The neural radiance architecture is a multilayer perceptron (MLP) with two hidden layers and a ReLU layer per hidden layer and a linear output layer as in [18]. Training was performed using the ADAM optimizer [14] with parameters $\beta_1 = 0.9$, $\beta_2 = 0.99$, $\epsilon = 10^{-15}$ using NVIDIA Tesla V100.

The main limitation of neural fields from aerial multi-view imagery is the presence of occlusion of sub-canopy structure, specially in densely forested areas. In our case, fusion with TLS data can resolve this problem as terrestrial data provides highly detailed sub-canopy information. Additionally, when TLS is unavailable, terrestrial imagery can be used instead. Our 3D structure experiments from terrestrial multi-view information in Sect. 3.1 and the DBH estimation performance results demonstrate that highly detailed structure along the entire vertical stand direction can be extracted by neural fields when image information is available. In the absence of multi-view image data, however, neural fields are not capable of generating synthetic information behind occluded areas and performance on metrics affected by occlusion are expected to yield large errors. This problem can be alleviated through multi-view images capturing the desired areas of interest in the ecosystem.

6   Conclusion

In this work, we proposed neural radiance fields as representations that can finely express the 3D structure of forests both in the *in-situ* and at the broad landscape scale. In addition, the properties of neural radiance fields; in particular, the fact that they account for both the origin and direction of radiance to define 3D structure enables the fusion of data coming from multiple locations and modalities; more specifically those from multi-view LiDAR's and cameras. Finally, we evaluated the performance of 3D structure derived metrics typically used in forest monitoring programs and demonstrated the potential of neural fields to improve performance of scalable methods at near the level of *in-situ* methods. This not only represents a benefit on sampling time efficiency but also has powerful implications on reducing monitoring costs.

Acknowledgements. Research presented in this article was supported by the Laboratory Directed Research and Development program of Los Alamos National Laboratory under project number GRR0CSRN.

References

1. Atchley, A., et al.: Effects of fuel spatial distribution on wildland fire behaviour. Int. J. Wildland Fire **30**(3), 179–189 (2021)
2. Besl, P.J., McKay, N.D.: A method for registration of 3-D shapes. IEEE Trans. Pattern Anal. Mach. Intell. **14**(2), 239–256 (1992). https://doi.org/10.1109/34.121791
3. Castorena, J., Creusere, C.D., Voelz, D.: Modeling lidar scene sparsity using compressive sensing. In: 2010 IEEE International Geoscience and Remote Sensing Symposium, pp. 2186–2189. IEEE (2010)

4. Castorena, J., Dickman, L.T., Killebrew, A.J., Gattiker, J.R., Linn, R., Loudermilk, E.L.: Automated structural-level alignment of multi-view TLS and ALS point clouds in forestry (2023)

5. Castorena, J., Puskorius, G.V., Pandey, G.: Motion guided lidar-camera self-calibration and accelerated depth upsampling for autonomous vehicles. J. Intell. Robot. Syst. **100**(3), 1129–1138 (2020)

6. Dubayah, R.O., Drake, J.B.: Lidar remote sensing for forestry. J. Forest. **98**(6), 44–46 (2000)

7. FAO, U.: The state of the world's forests 2020. In: Forests, biodiversity and people, p. 214. Rome, Italy (2020). https://doi.org/10.4060/ca8642en

8. Gao, W., Tedrake, R.: Filterreg: Robust and efficient probabilistic point-set registration using gaussian filter and twist parameterization. In: Proceedings of the IEEE/CVF Conference on Computer Vision and Pattern Recognition, pp. 11095–11104 (2019)

9. Ge, X., Zhu, Q.: Target-based automated matching of multiple terrestrial laser scans for complex forest scenes. ISPRS J. Photogramm. Remote. Sens. **179**, 1–13 (2021)

10. Hilker, T., et al.: Comparing canopy metrics derived from terrestrial and airborne laser scanning in a Douglas-fir dominated forest stand. Trees **24**(5), 819–832 (2010)

11. Hyyppä, J.: Advances in forest inventory using airborne laser scanning. Remote Sens. **4**(5), 1190–1207 (2012)

12. Kajiya, J.T., Von Herzen, B.P.: Ray tracing volume densities. ACM SIGGRAPH Comput. Graph. **18**(3), 165–174 (1984)

13. Kankare, V., et al.: Estimation of the timber quality of scots pine with terrestrial laser scanning. Forests **5**(8), 1879–1895 (2014)

14. Kingma, D.P., Ba, J.: Adam: a method for stochastic optimization. arXiv preprint arXiv:1412.6980 (2014)

15. Lausch, A., Erasmi, S., King, D.J., Magdon, P., Heurich, M.: Understanding forest health with remote sensing-part ii-a review of approaches and data models. Remote Sens. **9**(2), 129 (2017)

16. Linn, R., Reisner, J., Colman, J.J., Winterkamp, J.: Studying wildfire behavior using FIRETEC. Int. J. Wildland Fire **11**(4), 233–246 (2002)

17. Mildenhall, B., Srinivasan, P.P., Tancik, M., Barron, J.T., Ramamoorthi, R., Ng, R.: NeRF: representing scenes as neural radiance fields for view synthesis. arXiv preprint arXiv:2003.08934 (2020)

18. Müller, T., Evans, A., Schied, C., Keller, A.: Instant neural graphics primitives with a multiresolution hash encoding. ACM Trans. Graph. **41**(4), 102:1-102:15 (2022). https://doi.org/10.1145/3528223.3530127

19. Myronenko, A., Song, X.: Point set registration: coherent point drift. IEEE Trans. Pattern Anal. Mach. Intell. **32**(12), 2262–2275 (2010)

20. Pokswinski, S., et al.: A simplified and affordable approach to forest monitoring using single terrestrial laser scans and transect sampling. MethodsX **8**, 101484 (2021)

21. Roessle, B., Barron, J.T., Mildenhall, B., Srinivasan, P.P., Niebner, M.: Dense depth priors for neural radiance fields from sparse input views. In: Proceedings of the IEEE conference on computer vision and pattern recognition, pp. 12892–12901 (2022)

22. Schonberger, J.L., Frahm, J.M.: Structure-from-motion revisited. In: Proceedings of the IEEE Conference on Computer Vision and Pattern Recognition, pp. 4104–4113 (2016)

23. Tomppo, E., et al.: National forest inventories. Pathways for Common Reporting. European Science Foundation 1, 541–553 (2010)

24. Vierling, K.T., Vierling, L.A., Gould, W.A., Martinuzzi, S., Clawges, R.M.: Lidar: shedding new light on habitat characterization and modeling. Front. Ecol. Environ. **6**(2), 90–98 (2008)

25. White, J.C., Coops, N.C., Wulder, M.A., Vastaranta, M., Hilker, T., Tompalski, P.: Remote sensing technologies for enhancing forest inventories: a review. Can. J. Remote. Sens. **42**(5), 619–641 (2016)

26. Windrim, L., Bryson, M.: Detection, segmentation, and model fitting of individual tree stems from airborne laser scanning of forests using deep learning. Remote Sens. **12**(9), 1469 (2020)

27. Xie, H., Yao, H., Zhou, S., Mao, J., Zhang, S., Sun, W.: GRNet: gridding residual network for dense point cloud completion. In: Vedaldi, A., Bischof, H., Brox, T., Frahm, J.-M. (eds.) ECCV 2020. LNCS, vol. 12354, pp. 365–381. Springer, Cham (2020). https://doi.org/10.1007/978-3-030-58545-7_21

Edge AI-Based Vein Detector for Efficient Venipuncture in the Antecubital Fossa

Edwin Salcedo[✉][ID] and Patricia Peñaloza[ID]

Department of Mechatronics Engineering, Universidad Católica Boliviana "San Pablo", La Paz, Bolivia
{esalcedo,patricia.penaloza}@ucb.edu.bo

Abstract. Assessing the condition and visibility of veins is a crucial step before obtaining intravenous access in the antecubital fossa, which is a common procedure to draw blood or administer intravenous therapies (IV therapies). Even though medical practitioners are highly skilled at intravenous cannulation, they usually struggle to perform the procedure in patients with low visible veins due to fluid retention, age, overweight, dark skin tone, or diabetes. Recently, several investigations proposed combining Near Infrared (NIR) imaging and deep learning (DL) techniques for forearm vein segmentation. Although they have demonstrated compelling results, their use has been rather limited owing to the portability and precision needs to perform venipuncture. In this paper, we aim to contribute in bridging this gap using three strategies. First, we introduce a new NIR-based forearm vein segmentation dnataset of 2016 labelled images collected from 1008 subjects with low visible veins. Second, we propose a modified U-Net architecture that locates veins specifically in the antecubital fossa region of the examined patient. Finally, a compressed version of the proposed architecture was deployed inside an bespoke, portable vein finder device after testing four common embedded microcomputers and four common quantization modalities. Experimental results showed that the model compressed with Dynamic Range Quantization and deployed on a Raspberry Pi 4B card produced the best execution time and precision balance, with 5.14 FPS and 0.957 of latency and Intersection over Union (IoU), respectively. These results show promising performance inside a resource-restricted low-cost device. The full implementation and data are available at: https://github.com/EdwinTSalcedo/CUBITAL

Keywords: Vein detection · Deep learning · NIR Imaging · Edge AI

1 Introduction

Venipuncture is a necessary procedure applied by medical staff, either to draw a blood sample, start an intravenous infusion, or instil a medication. While this procedure can be applied to several regions of the anatomy, doctors prefer the antecubital fossa due to the higher visibility and stability of veins there. Initially,

© The Author(s), under exclusive license to Springer Nature Switzerland AG 2024
H. Calvo et al. (Eds.): MICAI 2023, LNAI 14392, pp. 297–314, 2024.
https://doi.org/10.1007/978-3-031-47640-2_24

physicians identify and ascertain suitability of the median cubital (MC), cephalic (C) and basilic (B) veins in the antecutibal fossa, as depicted in Fig. 1. It is worth mentioning that the median cubital vein is usually refereed as the best site to perform catheterization [6,14]. However, people who do not have good vein visibility might require longer pre-inspection times, which can cause an early start of a trial-and-error venipuncture process to localize a suitable vein. This is the case for children, elderly people, dark-skinned people, and people with overweight or diabetes. Palpation, warm water, tourniquets, NIR vein finders are among some well-known good practices to improve vein visibility. Yet, if veins are still not noticeable, the need for health professionals to assist the next patients might cause bruises, pain, and bleeding to the current one.

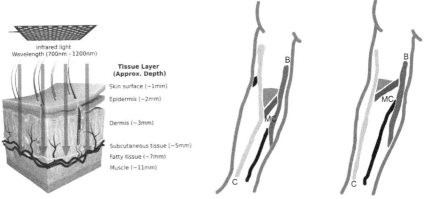

(a) NIR light penetration through skin layers until reaching the subcutaneous tissue where veins and arteries locate.

(b) Samples of vein distributions in the arm region with the antecubital fossa marked in green (adapted from [6]).

Fig. 1. Anatomy of forearm veins in the antecubital region.

Since the beginning of the 2010s, several companies started commercializing hand-held vein finders based on ultrasound, transillumination, or infrared light to facilitate venipuncture. Nowadays, these devices' features range from basic vein visualization enhancement to simultaneous detection and mapping of veins in any part of the body (e.g. AccuVein AV400 and AV500). However, the widespread adoption of these devices has been rather limited owing to their high cost and closed software. Recently, in response to these limitations, several proposal systems based on Computer Vision, Deep Learning, and Near Infrared imaging (NIR) have emerged as promising approaches for vein visualization enhancement [4,7,17,19]. Nevertheless, they are usually designed to improve vein visualization in the entire forearm region, so healthcare professionals must still choose the most suitable region or vein with which they should work. Also, most recent algorithms are oriented to run in a central server, instead of being deployed to portable devices. So, there is still room for research to develop better

AI-based devices that recommend which vein or region to select for venipuncture in real-time and on-site.

Deep learning at the edge can be applied not only for more precise NIR imaging-based vein segmentation, but also to identify which region to choose for venipuncture. Therefore, our proposal aims to extend this body of work with the following contributions:

- A new dataset containing 2016 NIR images with low visible veins in arms is introduced, in tandem with their respective ground truth vein segmentation masks. The dataset also comprise bounding box, centroid and angle annotations for antecubital fossa localization inside the images.
- We test five DL-based semantic segmentation models and perform a thorough comparison, from which we select and modify the best one to also act as a regression model for antecubital fossa localization and arm direction prediction.
- We test the resulting model on four common microcomputers (Raspberry Pi 4B, Raspberry Pi 3B+, Khadas VIM3, and NVIDIA Jetson Nano) and using four common quantization modalities (dynamic range quantization, full-integer quantization, integer quantization with float fallback, and float16 quantization). The best combination is finally implemented in a bespoke, portable device that shows suitable veins in the antecubital fossa.

The remainder of the paper is structured as follows. Section 2 presents the state of the art on vein image acquisition approaches, as well as new DL and Edge AI-related tendencies for vein localization. Section 3 describes the prototyping process of the end device as well as the implemented DL models and metrics. Then, in Sect. 4, we present the experimental results in terms of prediction accuracy and inference time. Finally, Sect. 5 offers conclusions and discusses potential future research threads.

2 Literature Review

Many image acquisition, processing, and visualization techniques have been proposed and released to the market to enhance subcutaneous vein localization. By way of illustration, AccuVein vein finders feature simultaneous localization and mapping using light projections towards the skin. Nevertheless, their prices range from 1800 USD to 7000 USD per unit [5], which keeps them inaccessible for many medical centers in developing countries. In the current section, we present a review on the main technologies and research trends on open-source vein detectors development.

2.1 Image Acquisition Approaches

Two image acquisition approaches can be clearly distinguished for forearm vein localization: transillumination-based and reflectance-based methods. The first ones are more extended in the literature because of its portability and low-cost. They mainly transmit light through the skin and tissue of a body sector, which is then followed and captured by a light sensitive camera at a given wavelength. While regular RGB cameras capture light in the human visible spectrum (400–700 nm), transillumination-based techniques such as multi-spectral imaging or hyper-spectral imaging aim to capture illumination in different ranges of the electromagnetic spectrum, e.g. the ultraviolet range or the infrared range. This approach was widely explored by investigators. For instance, Shahzad et al. [18] propose an illumination wavelength selection algorithm for vein detection using a multi-spectral camera, such that the system can recommend what wavelength to use for a patient based on his skin-tone.

Table 1. Summary of recent forearm vein distribution detector proposals from 2018 to present.

Year & Ref.	Imaging method & Camera	Detection method	End device	Key metrics
2022 [12]	NIR & US	U-Net	PC	0.83 IoU
2022 [11]	NIR, Pi NoIR 2	Image Processing	PCB & VideoCore-IV	74.93 % SSIM
2022 [10]	NIR, OV5647 Omnivision	U-Net	Raspberry Pi 4B	0.68 DSC
2022 [17]	NIR, JAI & DALSA X64-CL	Pix2Pix		0.96 DSC
2021 [19]	NIR & RGB, JAI & DSLR	FCNN	Nvidia Jetson TX2	0.78 Accuracy
2021 [4]	NIR & US, Pi NoIR 2 & US Probe	semi-ResNext-U-Net	Raspberry Pi 4B	0.81 DSC
2018 [1]	NIR & Pi NoIR	Image Processing	Raspberry Pi 2	0.84 Accuracy

Particularly, Near-Infrared light (NIR) has been broadly explored over the past years as a vein visualization enhancing technique. As shown in Fig. 1a, this requires NIR illumination and a special camera able to capture NIR transillumination, which in turn generates digital images. NIR light can go through human skin reaching between 700 nm and 1200 nm depth depending on the person's complexion. Since this range can provide information on a body's temperature and structure, it makes it suitable to capture vein presence in the subcutaneous tissue. Furthermore, oxygenated and deoxygenated hemoglobin, two components of blood, absorb and transmit NIR light better through them. About NIR capture devices, some common cameras available in the market are described in Table 1 (under the "Imaging method & Camera" column) from where we can conclude Raspberry Pi NoIR 1 and 2 are the most frequented NIR cameras for research. For instance, academics in [2] proposed a detection device that combine two NIR cameras to obtain depth information about the subcutaneous layer of an arm and overlapped 3D visualizations of veins to enhance their illustration.

Ultrasound imaging (US) and photoacoustic imaging are amongst the most-used methods in reflectance-based commercial devices for forearm vascular localization. While US provides a high-resolution frame-of-reference for identifying density, flow and perfusion of veins, Photoacoustic Imaging (PI) permits registering important factors such as oxygen saturation, total hemoglobin and the microdistribution of biomarkers. Both solve the problem of finding vessels by reflecting a high frequency sound (US) or non-ionizing light (PI) over a focused part of a body. Then, the return time travel of the reflected waves is registered with an imaging probe as electrical signals [8]. These waves, also known as ultrasonic waves, are detected by ultrasonic transducers to reconstruct physiological organs in living beings. In the case of human vessels, hemoglobine concentration and oxygen saturation are physiological properties that let forming 2D or 3D images with distinguishable contrast between skin tissue and vessels due to their distance with respect to the light source. Combining both US and NIR modalities have recently brought new opportunities for robotic catheterization. For instance, researchers in [4] employed both NIR and US imaging inside a robot to perform venipuncture autonomously. A similar combination of US and NIR imaging was brought to a hanheld robotic device by Leipheimer et al. in [12], where the authors propose the use of machine learning models to safely and efficiently introduce a catheter sheath into a peripheral blood vessel.

2.2   Computer-Based Vein Distribution Localization

Successful venipuncture of intravenous procedures depend on the timely localization of veins. Although a great majority are applied in the antecubital fossa, some procedures require finding veins in lower arm sections. Thus, semantic segmentation of veins over the forearm region is a crucial task that should be performed as precisely and timely as possible. Specifically, semantic segmentation aims to classify each pixel inside a collected image with a label. Most investigations interpret veins anatomically as hollow tube structure that join each other along an image, and they assume two categories for each pixel: vein pixel and background pixel. There are two notorious computer vision-based approaches that are regularly applied for forearm vein segmentation: traditional image processing methods and deep learning architectures.

Image Processing-Based Methods. Segmentation approaches based on traditional image processing methods for NIR, US, multi-spectral, and hyperspectral images usually comprehend steps for contrast and illumination enhancement, morphological operations, vein structure discover, and edge detection. For instance, several investigations apply Histogram Equalisation or Contrast-Limit Adaptive Histogram Equalisation to enhance the contrast of the input images [3,20]. Then, vessel segmentation approaches aim to discriminate regions with veins from the background. Here, vein segmentation techniques can be also classified as vein structure-based, region-based, gradient-based, and pixel-based. For example, Li et al. [13] proposed a convex-regional-based gradient preserving method that use edge information to enhance the low contrast and reduce the noise in NIR images for better vein segmentation. By applying a convex function, they find global minimums as optimal locations to detect veins. Recently, researchers in [11] proposed an image preprocessing system for existing vein detection devices to remove hair digitally from NIR images. They achieved an improvement of 5.04% of Structural Similarity Index (SSIM) with respect to their original vein segmentation algorithm, which shows the relevance of image processing methods for newer approaches.

Deep Learning-Based Methods. Recently, deep learning has demonstrated huge success in detection tasks from visual information due to its generalization power. Recent investigations leverage deep learning-based algorithms to classify pixels as vein or background inside the collected images. In contrast to image processing, deep learning models do not require strict controlled environments, which makes them more suitable to perspective, distance or illumination variations. U-Net based architectures are amongst the most used approaches for vein semantic segmentation [4,10]. Moreover, Shah et al. [17] proposed a forearm vein segmentation model based on the Pix2Pix architecture to translate NIR images of arms into their segmented vascular versions. Their architecture consist of a student, which is a U-Net model that learns to generate new vascular masks from NIR images, and a teacher, which is a PatchGAN-based model that discriminate each generated image into fake or original images. Combined into a common architecture, the approach obtained 0.97 of accuracy. This model outperformed previous methods for forearm vein segmentation.

2.3 Edge AI Methods

During the last years, the advent of better microprocessors has increased the opportunities to bring deep learning models into standalone end devices. Edge AI and Edge Computing are two paradigms that have attracted much of the attention recently. While Edge Computing aims to bring information processing closer to the users, Edge AI is the implementation of artificial intelligence in an edge computing environment. Edge AI-based environments are usually implemented in embedded systems beside Computer Processing Units, Graphics Processing Units (GPUs), Tensor Processing Units (TPUs), Vision Processing Units (VPUs), Field Programmable Gate Arrays (FPGAs), Application-Specific Integrated Circuits (ASICs), or Systems-on-Chip (SoC) [19]. Specifically, development cards such as Nvidia Jetson, Khadas, Neural Computer Stick, or Google Coral can be of huge help to speed up new Edge-AI based applications.

Hardware implementation and Edge AI are important for the present project since venipuncture is applied to patients in situ. So far, several investigations have proposed forearm segmentation algorithms deployed in portable scanners or fixed stations, and the host devices range from Raspberry Pi cards [1,4,10,10,20] to NVIDIA Jetson cards [19]. An updated publication list on vein distribution finders is described in Table 1. To the best knowledge of the authors, the great majority of investigations focuses on general forearm vein segmentation and does not detect specific sites for optimal venipuncture. For instance, Chaoying et al. [19] proposed one of the first investigations to deploy deep learning-based forearm vein detectors on an embedded device with meaningful results: 0.78 of accuracy and 0.31 s per processed frame.

The availability increase of low-cost NIR cameras, such as Pi NoIR, Jai, OV5647, Omnivision, among others, make them suitable for new on-device forearm vein finding applications. For example, Ng. et al. [15] proposed a vein detection and visual guidance system to show the location of veins through a mixed-reality-based interface. They used a HoloLens 2 device and its infrared emitter to obtain new images, which in turn let them segment and visualize veins in real time. Their vein segmentation approach was based on the U-Net architecture with a RegNet-based encoder and achieved 0.89 of precision. In the case of robotized venipuncture, Chen et al. [4] proposed a robotic system solution named Venibot to determine a optimal area on a forearm and perform puncturing autonomously. Their proposal combines US and NIR imaging to control the movements of the venipuncture robot.

3   Material and Methods

To localize the hidden veins of a patient, we developed a Deep Learning-based model that processes NIR images of their forearm and segments the present veins. This model also localizes the antecubital fossa to hide all veins except the ones located in that zone, such that a healthcare practitioner can only see the suitable veins for venipuncture. Later, the algorithm was implemented on an embedded system by applying compression techniques. In the present section, we describe the complete software and hardware implementation process in detail.

3.1   Forearm Vein Segmentation

Dataset Collection and Preprocessing. As stated before, dehydration, young and old age, overweight, dark skin tone, and diabetes are among some factors that can affect patients' veins visibility. Specifically, in the case of young subjects, this series of injections can cause medical trauma, which in turn might cause future self-medication and conflicting feelings when requiring healthcare assistance [14]. Therefore, the present research focused on enhancing the visibility of veins in young patients. 2016 NIR images were collected from both arms of 1008 young subjects during the year 2022. The volunteers, whose age frequency is shown in Fig. 2, were students in elementary and secondary schools in the cities of Sacaba and Santa Cruz, Bolivia. About the setup, each patient located an arm at a time on a flat surface covered with a white fabric for the sake of better contrast. Meanwhile, the initial version of the vein finder depicted in Fig. 5 was located 30 cm above using a lamp arm printed in 3D.

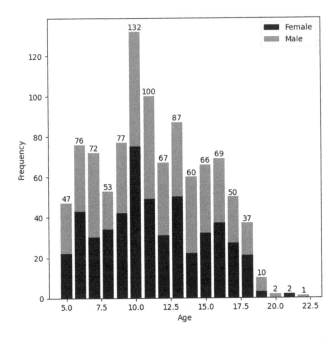

Fig. 2. Age distribution of 1008 subjects who volunteered in the data collection stage.

Given that collecting information from children also requires parental consent, volunteers' parents were asked to sign a consent agreement to use the captured images for research purposes. This resulted in an approximate time of 5 min per subject, making a total of 83.8 h. Data was saved and administered in a laptop's internal memory as CSV files and PNG images using a bespoke Tkinter application. This had the purpose of registering and managing NIR images along the full name, complexion, age, medical condition, gender, and signed consent agreement of volunteers. To form the final version of the base dataset, NIR images were converted to grayscale and enhanced using Contrast-Limit Adaptive Histogram Equalisation (CLAHE). Then, ground-truth was manually annotated with background, arm, and vein segments using Roboflow. Finally, the images were normalized to 512 × 512 pixels to obtain pairs of images and masks suitable for semantic segmentation DL architectures.

To avoid the risk of overfitting, we generated an augmented version of the base dataset applying sequential randomly-selected augmentation techniques. We implemented the following techniques from the ImgAug library: flipping images horizontally, perspective, rotating images in the range of 180° and −180°, blurring images with gaussian and average filters, contrasting with gamma functions, among others. In the end, the augmented version of the dataset contained 8000 images with their corresponding segmentation masks.

Model Selection and Training. The recent progress made on vein subcutaneous segmentation based on NIR imaging in [4,17,19] let us understand the great generalization capabilities of Deep Learning-based (DL) methods with respect to previous approaches. Thus, we focused on implementing various recently proposed generic architectures for semantic segmentation: U-Net, Segnet, PSPNet, DeepLabV3+, and Pix2Pix. The models were implemented using TensorFlow 2.12.0 and Colab Pro+ with NVIDIA A100 GPUs. Besides modelling with both tools, they let us code a unified data loading and munging pipeline for the dataset and experiment parallelly with multiple instances per model, so that optimizing the base code and hyperparameters was completed efficiently. Both versions of the dataset, the base one and augmented one, were split into three subsets: 70% for training, 20% for validation, and 10% for testing.

The available resources provided by Colab limited us to use a batch size of 8 instances per step when training each model. Although all models might have trained longer or shorter times, we made sure to use 10 epochs for a fair comparison. This was also supported by the fact that some models (DeepLabV3+ and Pix2Pix) started overfitting when training longer. We used Binary Cross Entropy (BCE) as the unique loss function for all models to measure the dissimilarity between the ground truth and predicted masks. A mathematical representation of BCE is shown in Eq. 1, where y_i and $\hat{y}_i$ represents a ground truth binary classification vector and a predicted binary classification vector, respectively. Also, in the same equation, T stands for the number of pixels per instance, and f for the sigmoid activation function, as defined in Eq. 2.

$$BCE = -\frac{1}{T}\sum_{i=0}^{T} y_i \cdot log(f(\hat{y}_i)) + (1 - y_i) \cdot log(1 - f(\hat{y}_i)) \tag{1}$$

$$f(s_i) = \frac{1}{1 + e^{-s_i}} \tag{2}$$

Our Pix2Pix implementation was inspired on the work proposed by Zaineb et al. [17], however, we followed the original Pix2Pix architecture proposed by Isola et al. [9]. This base version contained a generator based on the PatchGAN model and discriminator module based on the U-Net architecture. Therefore, we reused our base U-Net architecture and implemented PatchGAN. About the loss functions, we also applied BCE (as defined in Eq. 1) to differentiate the ground truth and generated masks. Yet the generator required to use Mean Squared Error (MSE), commonly defined as in Eq. 3, where M is the number of image pairs (ground truth and predicted masks) and N is the number of pixels per image pair.

$$MSE = \frac{\sum_{i=1}^{N}(x_i - y_i)^2}{M * N} \tag{3}$$

To measure the models precision, metrics such as Pixel Accuracy, Intersection over Union (IoU), Dice Score, Pixel F1Score, and Peak signal-to-noise ratio (PSNR), were calculated according to Eqs. 4, 5, 6, 7, and 8, respectively. These metrics required to process ground truth G and predicted P masks first, with which we quantified the well and wrong classified pixels as True Positive (TP), True Negative (TN), False Positive (FP), or False Negative (FN), as defined in [16].

$$\text{Accuracy} = \frac{TP + TN}{TP+FP+TN+FN} \tag{4}$$

$$\text{IoU} = \frac{|G \cap P|}{|G \cup P|} \tag{5} \qquad \text{DiceScore} = \frac{2 * |P \cap G|}{|P| + |G|} \tag{6}$$

$$\text{F1Score} = \frac{2 * TP}{2 * TP + FP + FN} \tag{7} \qquad \text{PSNR} = 10 * \log_{10}\left(\frac{255^2}{\text{MSE}}\right) \tag{8}$$

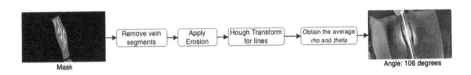

Fig. 3. Angle extraction algorithm.

3.2   Cubital Fossa Localization

Once we found U-Net was the best semantic segmentation architecture for the task, we continued the investigation by experimenting with methods to localize the Antecubital Fossa. This required another labelling iteration to enclose the cubital fossa region with a bounding box in all 2016 NIR images on Roboflow. Moreover, we made sure the bounding boxes' centroids were exactly located in the fossa, which means the center of the bounding boxes' coordinates were located in the median cubital (MC) areas in Fig. 1b. It is worth nothing that the fossa location prediction also required the angle of the examined arm to hide veins out of the antecubital fossa region. So, we labelled the orientation of each arm synthetically by following the process shown in Fig. 3.

As depicted, we worked with the ground truth mask, removed veins, and converted the arm segment into a shape similar to a line by applying a series of morphological erosion operations. Then, we used the OpenCV's function Hough Transform for Lines (HTL) to obtain polar coordinates of lines from an accumulator matrix. According to this matrix, the more concur points in an image, the more probable they depict a line, therefore, HTL obtains a set of θ and ρ where points frequently concur. Given that we started with a single line representing the entire arm, we averaged the θ and ρ values and convert them to a degree value between 0°C and 180°C, starting from the very right in counterclockwise direction.

Obtaining the final version of the dataset let us model the problem as a combination of semantic segmentation and regression tasks. Thus, we integrated a neuronal network to the U-Net architecture. The layers, resolution, and channels of the final architecture are illustrated in Fig. 4. Consequently, we created a multi task loss function to combine BCE and MSE as defined in Eq. 9. We also included the metric Mean Absolute Error (MAE) in the performance analysis stage when training and validating the architecture, as defined in Eq. 10.

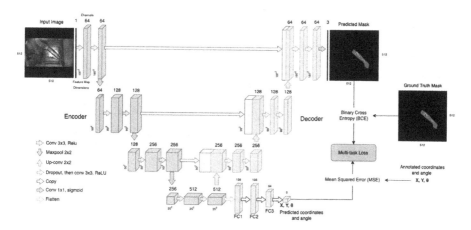

Fig. 4. Final U-Net architecture implemented with TensorFlow for simultaneous forearm vein segmentation, forearm localization and arm angle detection.

$$MutiTaskLoss = BCE + MSE \tag{9}$$

$$MAE = \frac{\sum_{i=1}^{N} |x_i - y_i|}{M * N} \tag{10}$$

Finally, once the model was implemented and tested, we used the compression methods available in TensorFlow Lite to reduce the size of the model and embed it inside the final end device. The implemented approaches were Dynamic Range Quantization, Integer Quantization with Float Fallback, Full Integer Quantization and Float 16 Quantization.

3.3   Hardware Development

Device Design with its Components. The availability of 3D printing technology and standalone microcomputers has opened new possibilities for innovative product design and manufacturing. To prototype the vein finder, we integrated electronic circuitry design, components assembly and 3D printing techniques. Most importantly, the device required initially the implementation and parameter optimization of the NIR imaging system in order to improve the quality of acquired NIR images. The initial version of this system is shown in Fig. 5.

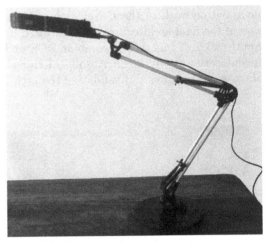

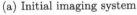
(a) Initial imaging system

(b) 3D printed lamp-shape structure

Fig. 5. Initial prototype used to collect 2006 NIR images

Moving on the development of final vein finder device, we aimed to develop an embedded system to contain a DL architecture for simultaneous vein segmentation and antecubital fossa localization. Then, the testing and compression stages of the final architecture carried out on different cards let us define that Raspberry Pi 4B card was the best choice for the prototype due to its good balance with respect to cost, precision, and inference time. Consequently, it was chosen for on-device image processing and DL model deployment. To enhance portability and autonomy, a Xiaomi portable battery of 10000 mah was connected to the Raspberry Pi 4B card through a Micro-USB cable. For image capture, we included a Raspberry NoIR V2 camera to the Raspberry Pi 4B through a 2 Lane MIPI CSI camera port. A touch screen was also installed to provide a Graphic User Interface (GUI) to the end user. The electronics schematics is presented in Fig. 6.

The illumination matrix of 12 infrared LEDs developed in the initial prototype, as shown in Fig. 5, was included on a perforated breadboard, which was used to assemble the necessary circuits, mainly 100Ω $1/2$ W resistors. The LED matrix was powered by a 9 V battery considering an appropriate resistor for each group of 3 LEDs. In addition, a 5 V relay module was implemented to control the energization of the LED matrix, and an On/Off switch was designed for the device activation. Moreover, a mechanism was implemented to synchronize the Raspberry Pi 4B and the relay module's power, ensuring simultaneous activation and deactivation.

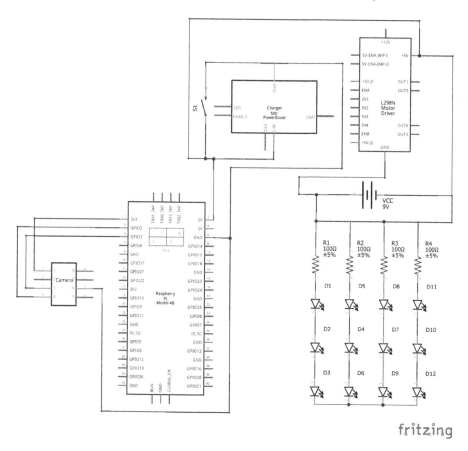

Fig. 6. Electronics schematics

Manufacturing and Assembly. As presented in Fig. 7, the design and implementation of the external case aimed to embed the LED matrix, microcomputer card, battery, powerbank, and camera using 3D printing technology and Polylactic Acid filament (PLA). The top and bottom parts of the casing were printed separately, with careful control of printing parameters to achieve optimal layer adhesion and surface finish. In addition, the battery slot and camera cover were also printed as separate components to facilitate easy assembly and maintenance. The 3D-printed ergonomic case was designed with the software SolidWorks, which let us achieve a lightweight structure and sufficient rigidity, as well as durability and protection for the electronic components. Most importantly, the camera was mounted at the center of the illumination matrix, allowing for higher accuracy in vein detection under a frontal annular lighting setup. The final dimensions of the device are 23 cm × 9.5 cm × 3.5 cm.

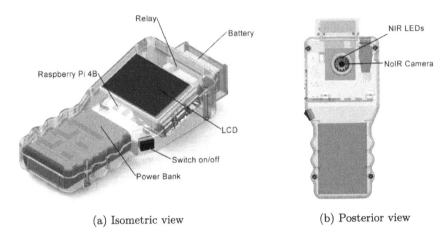

(a) Isometric view   (b) Posterior view

Fig. 7. Vein finder design using the 3D CAD software SolidWorks.

4   Experimental Results

The present section reports the results of the two main detection tasks in the proposal: forearm vein segmentation, and antecubital fossa detection including forearm vein segmentation. It is worth noting the importance of validating the device with the support of medical staff, which is a task to be completed for the present research in the coming months.

4.1   Forearm Vein Segmentation

A summary of the quantitative results of the models (Pix2Pix, U-Net, Segnet, PSPNEt, DeepLabV3+), calculating the metrics defined in Eqs. 4, 5, 6, 7, and 8, is shown in Table 2. The numbers in bold define the lowest or highest performance for each metric. While we aimed to obtain high values for almost all columns, we identified some models weight (shown in the last column) were higher than others. This was an important factor to choose one model over the others. For instance, we noted U-Net as one of the most precise models requiring fewer kilobytes than Segnet or Pix2Pix.

For the augmented dataset, several metrics were affected heavily due to the modifications applied to augmented instances. This was an important aspect in the present research since any portable vein finder should also work in more challenging environments than the one where the base dataset was collected. Therefore, we decided to work with the U-Net architecture.

4.2   Antecubital Fossa Localization

The final model performance was measured considering the metrics MSE and MAE, as defined in Eqs. 3 and 10, respectively. These results are shown in

Table 2. Results comparison for forearm vein segmentation

	Model	IoU	Dice Score	PSNR	Pixel Accuracy	F1-Score	FPS (Frames)	Weight (MBs)
Base dataset	U-Net	0.986	0.050	**70.050**	0.992	**0.992**	**5.940**	1.600
	Segnet	**0.987**	0.055	70.010	**0.993**	**0.992**	4.290	2.100
	PSPNet	0.948	**0.516**	63.590	0.969	0.967	5.630	**1.100**
	DeepLab v3	0.981	0.120	68.620	0.988	0.989	5.770	4.000
	Pix2Pix	0.940	**0.700**	63.610	0.970	0.960	3.880	7.000
Aug. dataset	U-Net	0.959	0.120	68.130	0.967	0.950	**6.020**	1.500
	Segnet	0.935	0.076	**69.780**	**0.975**	**0.992**	4.110	2.000
	PSPNet	0.911	0.522	60.910	0.928	0.967	5.620	**1.200**
	DeepLab v3	**0.956**	0.100	64.670	0.943	0.989	5.380	4.300
	Pix2Pix	0.891	0.531	59.600	0.921	0.960	4.230	6.900

Table 3. Results comparison for forearm vein & antecubital region localization & angle prediction

Model	Multitask loss	MSE	MAE
Modified U-Net & Dynamic Range Quantization	**0.4 ± 0.2**	**42.0 ± 6.0**	**57.7 ± 7.3**
Base Modified U-Net	0.4 ± 0.2	44.6 ± 6.6	59.5 ± 4.7
Modified U-Net & Integer Quantization with Float Fallback	0.41 ± 0.2	58.9 ± 8.6	73.0 ± 9.4
Modified U-Net & Full Integer Quantization	0.45 ± 0.2	60.1 ± 8.3	72.0 ± 9.7
Modified U-Net & Float 16 Quantization	0.55 ± 0.67	76.3 ± 7.2	82.9 ± 1.6

Table 3, from where we could identify that the compression method Dynamic Range Quantization was the best for the model in terms of precision. Consequently, this was the selected model to be deployed in the end device. The final version of the Graphical User Interface developed with PyQT with the final compressed model inside is shown in Fig. 8a. Finally, the final printed device is shown in Fig. 8b.

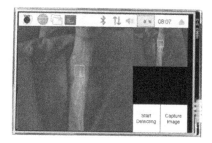

(a) Graphical User Interface developed with PyQT

(b) Final printed vein finder

Fig. 8. Final prototype printed in 3D

5   Conclusions and Future Work

In this study, we addressed the challenges associated to venipuncture by proposing a comprehensive solution that combines Near Infrared (NIR) imaging and deep learning (DL) techniques for precise vein localization in the antecubital fossa. The significance of accurate vein assessment prior to intravenous catheterization cannot be understated, especially for patients with low visible veins due to various factors such as fluid retention, age, obesity, dark skin tone, or diabetes. Our proposal comprehend three principal contributions. We introduced a novel dataset comprising 2016 NIR images of arm veins with limited visibility, accompanied by meticulous annotations that include ground truth images, bounding boxes, centroids, and angle information for precise antecubital fossa identification.

Furthermore, we devised and compared five different deep learning-based semantic segmentation models, ultimately selecting the most suitable one for antecubital fossa localization and direction prediction. Thirdly, the integration of this model into a compact vein finder device, through rigorous testing of various microcomputers and quantization methods, underlined its feasibility and efficiency in real-world applications. The experimental results demonstrated that the compressed model utilising Dynamic Range Quantization, deployed on a Raspberry Pi 4B, achieved optimal performance in terms of execution time and precision balance. This achievement, with an execution time of 5.14 frames per second and an Intersection over Union (IoU) of 0.957, showcased the potential of our approach in a resource-constrained and cost-effective portable device.

For future work and a better identification of veins for venipuncture, other imaging modalities could be combined. We noted the importance and challenges of locating the median cubital vein. Its automatic detection opens avenues for future exploration in computer vision applications. In addition, suitable vein recommendation according to a given intravenous procedure should be also considered in future research to enhance venipuncture procedures and patient care.

References

1. Adi Surya Gunawan, I.P., Sigit, R., Gunawan, A.I.: Vein visualization system using camera and projector based on distance sensor. In: 2018 International Electronics Symposium on Engineering Technology and Applications (IES-ETA), pp. 150–156. arXiv, Berlin, October 2018. https://doi.org/10.1109/ELECSYM.2018.8615501

2. Ai, D., et al.: Augmented reality based real-time subcutaneous vein imaging system. Biomed. Opt. Express. **7**(7), 2565–2585 (2016). https://doi.org/10.1364/BOE.7.002565, https://opg.optica.org/boe/abstract.cfm?URI=boe-7-7-2565

3. Azueto, R., Santiago, G., Hernández, G., Hernández, S.: Implementación de un sistema de imagenología infrarroja para la detección vascular del antebrazo y mano. Revista Mexicana de Ingeniería Biomédica. **1**(1), 27–35 (2017). https://www.redalyc.org/articulo.oa?id=61950989005

4. Chen, Y., et al.: VeniBot: towards autonomous venipuncture with semi-supervised vein segmentation from ultrasound images. In: Arxiv, pp. 150–156. arXiv, Berlin (2021)

5. Company, A.: Comparing the accuvein av500 vs veinsight vs500 vs aimvein pro 2.0 (2022). https://aimvein.com/blogs/news/compare-model-av500-vs-vs500-vs-pro-2-0

6. Corzo Gómez, E.G., Gómez Díaz, O.L., Niño Mantilla, M.E., Ramírez Vargas, L.M., Zárate Sierra, L.M.: Distribución de los patrones venosos de la fosa cubital en una muestra de personas nacidas en el departamento de santander, colombia. Int. J. Morphol. 32(1), 221–226 (2014). https://doi.org/10.4067/s0717-95022014000100037

7. Francisco, M.D., et al.: Competitive real-time near infrared (NIR) vein finder imaging device to improve peripheral subcutaneous vein selection in venipuncture for clinical laboratory testing. Micromachines 12(4), 27–35 (2021). https://doi.org/10.3390/mi12040373

8. Fronheiser, M.P., et al.: Real-time optoacoustic monitoring and three-dimensional mapping of a human arm vasculature. J. Biomed. Opt. 15(2), 21305 (2010). https://doi.org/10.1117/1.3370336

9. Isola, P., Zhu, J.Y., Zhou, T., Efros, A.A.: Image-to-image translation with conditional adversarial networks. In: 2017 IEEE Conference on Computer Vision and Pattern Recognition (CVPR) (2017). https://doi.org/10.1109/cvpr.2017.632

10. Kuthiala, A., et al.: U-DAVIS-deep learning based arm venous image segmentation technique for venipuncture. Comput. Intell. Neurosci. 2022, 4559219 (2022). https://doi.org/10.1155/2022/4559219

11. Lee, J., Jeong, I., Kim, K., Cho, J.: Design and implementation of embedded-based vein image processing system with enhanced denoising capabilities. Sensors 22(21), 887 (2022). https://doi.org/10.3390/s22218559

12. Leipheimer, J., Balter, M., Chen, A., Yarmush, M.: Design and evaluation of a handheld robotic device for peripheral catheterization. J. Med. Dev. 16(2), 021015 (2022). https://doi.org/10.1115/1.4053688

13. Li, Y., et al.: A novel method for low-contrast and high-noise vessel segmentation and location in venipuncture. IEEE Trans. Med. Imaging 36(11), 2216–2227 (2017). https://doi.org/10.1109/TMI.2017.2732481

14. Naik, V., Mantha, S.P., Rayani, B.: Vascular access in children. Indian J. Anaesth. 63(9), 737 (2019)

15. Ng, K.W., Furqan, M.S., Gao, Y., Ngiam, K.Y., Khoo, E.T.: Holovein: mixed-reality venipuncture aid via convolutional neural networks and semi-supervised learning. Electronics. 12(2), 292 (2023). https://doi.org/10.3390/electronics12020292, https://www.mdpi.com/2079-9292/12/2/292

16. Rojas, W., Salcedo, E., Sahonero, G.: ADRAS: airborne disease risk assessment system for closed environments. In: Lossio-Ventura, J.A., Valverde-Rebaza, J., Díaz, E., Alatrista-Salas, H. (eds.) Information Management and Big Data, vol. 1837, pp. 96–112. Springer Nature Switzerland, Cham (2023). https://doi.org/10.1007/978-3-031-35445-8_8

17. Shah, Z., et al.: Deep learning-based forearm subcutaneous veins segmentation. IEEE Access 10, 42814–42820 (2022). https://doi.org/10.1109/ACCESS.2022.3167691

18. Shahzad, A., Walter, N., Malik, A.S., Saad, N.M., Meriaudeau, F.: Multispectral venous images analysis for optimum illumination selection. In: 2013 IEEE International Conference on Image Processing, pp. 2383–2387. ICIP, Berlin, September 2013. https://doi.org/10.1109/ICIP.2013.6738491

19. Tang, C., Xia, S., Qian, M., Wang, B.: Deep learning-based vein localization on embedded system. IEEE Access **9**, 27916–27927 (2021). https://doi.org/10.1109/ACCESS.2021.3058014
20. Yildiz, M.Z., Boyraz, Ö.F.: Development of a low-cost microcomputer based vein imaging system. Infrared Phys. Technol. **98**, 27–35 (2019). https://doi.org/10.1016/j.infrared.2019.02.010

Varroa Mite Detection in Honey Bees with Artificial Vision

Apolinar Velarde Martinez$^{(\boxtimes)}$ ⓘ, Gilberto González Rodríguez,
Juan Carlos Estrada Cabral, and Jose Daniel Reyes Moreira

Technological Institute El Llano Aguascalientes, Aguascalientes, Mexico
{apolinar.vm,gilberto.gr,juan.ec,jose.rm}@llano.tecnm.mx

Abstract. The preservation of species is beneficial for the subsistence of life on planet earth. The honey bee, considered a pollinating and food-producing species for humans, faces the attack of the Varroa parasite; Several solutions to detect, exterminate and contain this ectoparasite in bee colonies have been proposed. This paper presents and describes the development of a non-invasive system with artificial vision, which uses Distributed Computing and the Internet of Things to recognize and analyze the thorax and abdomen of honey bees, in images acquired in the entrances of the hives, for the early detection of the Varroa mite. Two techniques have been experimented with for the recognition of the bee at the entrance of the hive, the Support Vector Machine (SVM) and k-Nearest Neighbors (kNN), and with the same two techniques to analyze the Varroa mite in the thorax and neck. bee abdomen. The experiments carried out and the results obtained with each technique are described.

Keywords: Honey Bees · Varroa Mite · Digital Image Processing · Support Vector Machine · k-Nearest Neighbors

1 Introduction

The development of technologies for the care and subsistence of life on planet earth are necessary, because catastrophic environmental events such as forest fires, the growth of urban areas that generate heat islands, pollutant emissions into the atmosphere, the contamination of aquifers and the proliferation of harmful parasites, are causing the massive destruction of plant and animal species. The honey bee is a species used by humans as a pollinator in different tree species and honey and polliniferous crops [1–4]; this species is also used for the production of food for humans, such as honey and propolis [5–7]. Unfortunately, the honey bee has not been immune to catastrophic environmental events and climate change; the loss of habitat and the attack of invasive ectoparasites put its existence and reproduction at high risk in the regions where it is grown.

Scientific and applied research projects have emerged in different areas of science, with the aim of seeking and proposing solutions that reduce the adverse effects of ectoparasites in apiaries and help preserve the honey bee. These

H. Calvo et al. (Eds.): MICAI 2023, LNAI 14392, pp. 315–330, 2024.
https://doi.org/10.1007/978-3-031-47640-2_25

projects have used innovative technologies in their implementation over the years; in [8] a video monitoring system for flight activity at the entrance of the hive is developed; in [9] the use of video surveillance of bee colonies with video analysis for the detection of the arrival of bees with pollen to the colony was addressed; the detection of ectoparasites with the use of video surveillance systems has been very relevant in recent years, with the appearance of miniaturized electronic devices; the objective of these systems is the eradication or reduction of the damages to the honey bee colonies; research that highlights the importance of honey bee survillance systems for the detection of ectoparasites has been presented in [10,11]; in [12] an approach for Varroa Mite detection on honey bee with image analysis is presented; the use of image analysis with monitoring system for early detection of the varroa mite in beehive with deep learning was stated on [13]; in other works image capturing, template matching, color classification, and segmentation filters for the early detection of Varroa mite as well as its early struggle, are used [14]; with the objective of monitoring health state of bee colonies an object detector for the Varroa destructor mite is used in [15].

Varroa is a parasite of global concern, which has a negative impact on beekeeping, so it is important to make an early diagnosis of the infestation levels in the apiary. Currently, this ectoparasite is detected through two visual checks by beekeepers in hives [12,13], according to the Food and Agriculture Organization (FAO) [16]: double sieve sampling and powdered sugar sampling; both verifications are proposed and documented by the Food and Agriculture Organization (FAO); the two verifications imply the opening of the hive, the collection of hundreds of bees that are sacrificed with isopropyl alcohol and then discarded with filters that show the existence or not of the Varroa ectoparasite [12,13]. The disadvantages of these verifications are: the stress that they cause in the colony due to the opening of the hives, the hundreds of bees that are sacrificed from each hive and mainly the effectiveness of the verification, since it is based solely on the periodicity of the verifications. verifications carried out by the beekeeper in the apiary, i.e., if few visual verifications are carried out per year, the risk of attack by the ectoparasite increases.

Therefore, automated visual inspection systems in apiaries are necessary. But, in outdoor environments, different factors influence the images. Factors such as lighting, the area of the real environment and the movement of objects must be considered [6,9]. Lighting is related to environmental conditions. The area of the real environment from which the images are extracted for the analysis of the objects is related to the movement of the objects or if they are static; the objects that are analyzed are inanimate or living beings, inanimate objects in motion are generally moved by a device that regulates their speed, on the other hand, in the case of living beings, the movement is unpredictable, since their positions cannot be controlled. When objects that have movement and different positions in the image are recognized, the distortions that must be treated in the processing are even more complex, and higher processing speeds are required [17].

Considering visual inspections in apiaries and the technologies that contribute to the development of automated visual inspection systems, this paper describes the development of a non-invasive automated visual inspection system for early detection of Varroa in honey bees, Consisting of a hardware system for image acquisition and delivery installed in an apiary, a cluster of servers for image processing, and a software system for detecting bees and then Varroa Mites.

This work is organized as follows: Sect. 2 Research Context, locates the area where the project is carried out, highlights the importance of honey bee cultivation in this area and explains the diagnosis, a description and an analysis of the problem, as well as the proposed solution; in Sect. 3 development of the method, the hardware and software systems are described in detail, as well as the phases that constitute the proposed research project; Sect. 4, justification for the development of the method, describes the reasons why this research is carried out and the contributions it makes in terms of solutions to the problems encountered. The conclusions of this proposal are mentioned in Sect. 5 and future work in Sect. 6.

2   Related Works

With the desire not to be so extensive, in the following paragraphs a list of works, ordered by date of appearance, are referenced. These works show the follow-up of the research works and studies developed for the video surveillance of honey bees in different parts of the world. In each work presented, the different techniques applied to the problem and the importance of the study are highlighted, as well as the results obtained.

In [8] it was considered that flight activity (traffic) along with knowledge of local conditions and prior behavior can indicate if closer inspection or intervention is warranted in the beehive because beekeepers manually inspect hives, beginning with visual observations of flight activity; according to this assumption, in this work a device placed in the hive entrance that consists of up to 32 bidirectional bee-sized tunnels is proposed; device use a digital board camera to acquire color 640×480 video frames at 30 frames/sec. With this device measure flight activity at the hive entrance from video involves detecting bees and tracking their motion through a sequence of frames; they modeled frame to frame changes in bee position and orientation using Gaussian distributions for crawling and flying; According to results they created a manually-annotated dataset of bee video to train motion models and to evaluate the overall systems; the counter detects bees with precision 0.94 and recall 0.97 on the annotated dataset; the counter overcounter arrivals by 2% and undercounted departures by 7% on the annotated dataset. In [9], a system for the detection of honey bees carrying pollen by means of video surveillance obtained at the entrance of the hive is presented; considers the detection of pollen as a previous step to the monitoring of pollination as the final objective; the described system consists of a computational hardware platform for detection and a communication module; the proposed algorithm proceeds as follows: creates a training data set containing honey bee images detected by background subtraction, MOG (Mixture of Gaussians) applied to a training video frame set; each training image is manually checked whether or not it contains a honey bee with pollen; the k-means algorithm groups the pixels of each honey bee image without pollen load, into two groups in color space: blue background and honey bees; the centroid of both groups is calculated based on all the images of honey bees without pollen load; values of mean centroids are used in the Nearest Mean Classifier (NMC) to color segment honey bees in training and testing. In the search for solutions that lead to finding the important factors of colony loss, [10] investigated bee surveillance systems in 27 European countries; they found 25 systems that monitor the causes of colony losses and mortality at the European level; this study determined the general weakness and high variability of most of the surveillance systems in all the investigated systems, for which reason it proposes to reinforce standardization by harmonizing surveillance systems and elaborated a set of recommendations designed to improve the monitoring systems of honey bees at European level. A review of recent examples of surveillance systems with special emphasis on how these efforts have helped to increase understanding of honey bee health is presented in [11]; this study highlights the importance of honey bee video surveillance as a tool to understand and improve honey bee health, identify risk factors associated with colony morbidity and mortality, disease prevention and mitigation, and early detection of threats, discovery and characterization of new diseases and potential pathogens including virulence and distribution; the results of this study consider the need for surveillance systems with designs that guarantee the collection of representative data, coordinate efforts, and standardize approaches. In [12] a novelty approach for Varroa Mite detection on honey bees is presented with three contributions: a foreground detection approach to localize bees on video frames, provides a pipeline system susceptible to be applied to other types of bee parasites and allow to reliably detect Varroa Mites with maximum accuracy over 80%; this research acquire videos of honey beewhen they are entering or leaving the hive; this videos was carried out by a camera system and are used as input to a processing frame by frames; first, the foreground is detected and separated from the background in each single videoframe, and then extract image patches containing individual bees; two different approaches were considered to calculate the background subtraction image: the median image over the complete video as a model for the background and the calculation of the background using Gaussian Mixture Models to model each pixel intensity value as a linear combination of Gaussian Distribution calculated over the histogram of the image; different image classification results was obtained with different combinations of colors models and feature extraction methods; the alternative pipeline provides a maximum accuracy of 0.65 and Fly-measure over 80%.

Research and development of surveillance systems continued until recent years; in [13] a technological solution for detecting bees and then Varroa Mites using cameras inside the broad box, is presented; this system consists of an end node device, the cloud service for the online discovery process, and a hub device serving the online discovery process and a mobile phone application; The system has implemented an intelligent detection algorithm for the early detection of mites. In [14] image capturing, template matching, color classification, and segmentation filters for the early detection of Varroa mite as well as its early struggle, are used; with the objective of monitoring health state of bee colonies an object detector for the Varroa destructor mite is used in [15].

From the previous works described, it is highlighted that video surveillance of hives is an emerging research area that has gained strength in recent years due to its importance in the preservation of species, not only for the detection of diseases, but also for obtaining results of honey bee behavior; A variety of techniques are used in the works described, but in the reviewed literature no work was found that uses the regions of the image for the proposed problem.

3   Research Context

The proposed solution is divided into three main parts. First, the acquisition of the images every minute in the apiary and the transmission of the image from the apiary, every minute, to the data processing center; second, the recognition of the bee in the received image, through techniques of digital image processing and pattern recognition; third, if the bee is recognized in the image, perform analysis of the thorax and abdomen of the bee with digital image processing and pattern recognition techniques.

To execute the three parts mentioned in the previous paragraph, a bee hive modification process was carried out and the electrical power supply system, communication system, data processing center and software system were created. Each one of the systems is explained in the following paragraphs, with the proposed architectural designs and with the images acquired in the real apiary.

3.1   Bee Hive

The bee hive modification process took care not to invade the privacy of the hive and was carried out by a Raspberry Pi camera (Raspi for short), connected to the Raspberry Pi card as an end-node device, with the Raspberry Pi OS operating system; the panel for the generation of solar energy is located in the upper part of the hive. In the design, the bee hive entrance with arches stands out, which was the standard used for this research project. An Arduino Nano device is connected to the Raspi end-node device to detect the temperature of the hive. Figure 1 shows the prototype design of the bee hive.

Each bee hive in the apiary is identified through the record provided by the Secretaria de Desarrollo Rural y Agroempresarial [18]. Figure 2 shows the image acquisition system installed in a bee hive. Because the system is non-invasive, the camera stays outside of the hive, and so does the Raspi. The entrance to the hive was painted white with the aim of highlighting the presence of the bee, at the exit or entrance to the nest. Devices connect to a solar power source.

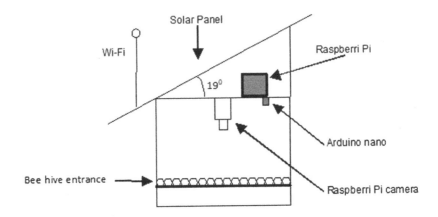

Fig. 1. Bee hive prototype design.

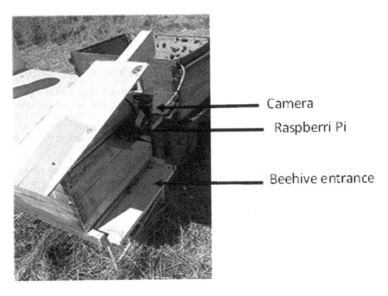

Fig. 2. Beehive prototype installed in the apiary, for the acquisition and transfer of images.

3.2   The Electrical Power Supply System

Because the apiaries where the system works are located in the field, a solar energy system is necessary for the operation of the Arduino devices, Raspberri Pi and the camera. In Fig. 1, the solar panel is shown on top of the bee hive. Solar energy system is constituted by two solar panels connected to a deep-cycle battery to guarantee the supply to the installed hardware. The energy consumption is 20 W per hour; The solar panels manage an energy of 120 W per hour for a cycle of 12 h.

3.3   Communication System

To carry out the transmission of information from the apiary (data and images) to the Data Processing Center (CPD), a communication model consisting of a point-multipoint link was developed and installed, which allows communication standing at a distance of approximately 850 m. An Access Point (AP) installed 52 m from the apiary radiates the signal so that each Raspi installed in the hives can acquire the communication signal.

The communication system works for a period of 8 h during the day; the images are stored and processed by a software agent on the server cluster for further processing. Communication from the apiary is done with the Raspberri Pi board with a Shell program to send the images every minute. In the data processing center, the server receives the images, they are stored and processed with a continuity of one minute. Figure 3 shows the communication prototype that links the apiary to the data processing center.

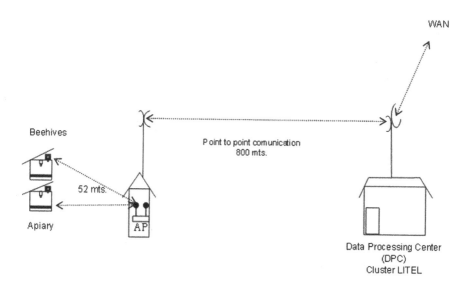

Fig. 3. Communication prototype to link the apiary to the data processing center.

3.4   Data Processing Center

The data processing center is made up of 3 high-end servers with a high speed network. All the hardware cluster is concentrated in a communications rack, located 850 m from the central apiary of the university. Figure 3 shows the position of the DPC in relation to the apiary.

3.5 Software System

The software system performs the image processing in the CPD; with this processing the bees are recognized in the image; Afterwards, the analysis of the thorax and abdomen of the bee is carried out with the digital processing of the images and with the pattern recognition techniques, to verify if the ectoparasite has lodged in any part of the bee. The following paragraphs describe each of the phases of the software system.

Cropping the Image. The cropping is used to removal of distracting content, cuts away areas of an image outside of a selected rectangular region; Cropping is performed mainly to remove unwanted scene content and to improve the overall image composition and find regions of interest [19]. Once the image has been acquired from the apiary and sent to the CPD, cropping is performed. In this case, cropping is used in order to cut the image into partitions, where each partition will be used in the following phases. Figure 4 shows an image acquired from the apiary which is cropped to apply the following phases of digital image processing.

Fig. 4. Image acquired from the apiary.

In each of the generated parts, a honey bee may or may not appear. The following phases do the job of detecting the bee in the image, as well as removing noise that may appear in the scene.

Conversion from RGB Image to Gray. The first process of converting the image is RGB to grayscale. This process is generally used as a preprocessing of the image to prepare it for more complex image processing, and realized to simplify the algorithms and remove complexities related to computational requirements. Figure 5 shows the conversion of each of the parts with the conversion from RGB to gray scale.

Gaussian Blur. To reduce noise and avoid image details Gaussian blur is applied to the image resulting from the previous step. What is sought is a soft blur, to improve the structures of the image at different scales. Figure 6 shows each image after the process of making the conversion to Gaussian blur.

Fig. 5. Image conversion from RGB to gray scale.

Fig. 6. Image with Gaussian Blur applied.

Canny Edge Detector. The Canny edge detector [20, 21] as an operator for edge detection is applied. Figure 7 shows each image after the process of applying the Canny edge detector.

Fig. 7. Image with edge detector applied.

After the four operations of digital image processing, applied to the original image, identification of regions with the coloring algorithm, Characterization of regions in the image using the Freeman Chain Code algorithm, and generation of feature vectors for each region in the image are started. On next paragraphs this process is explained.

Identification of Regions. The identification of regions in the image allows us to identify the object shape. This identification is carried out by segmenting the images into different semantically significant regions [22, 23], to detect the objects and edges in the image [24]. The algorithm de coloring or connected component labeling [22, 25, 26] labels each region with a unique integer. The input to the labeling algorithm is the binary image produced with the contour detection; in the binary image, the background is represented by zero pixels and the objects by values other than zero. The result after labeling is an image with the background represented with zero values and the regions represented with non-zero labels.

In the following paragraphs, the way in which the isolation of the regions in the image is carried out and the generation of the feature vectors [27–29] of each region found is explained, as well as the discrimination noise in the image for object identification

Characterization of the Regions. Each region of the image is characterized and this information is stored in a separate data structure called the feature vectors of the regions. Application of the Freeman Chain Code algorithm. This algorithm string records the movement of tracker during complete tracing of character structure, from which shape primitives, consists of simple line and curve shapes [29]. Once the regions have been identified in the image, the Freeman Chain Code algorithm [20] is executed to identify the features of each region. This algorithm scans the image for the extraction of the features of each region. Characteristics calculated for each region are: perimeter, density and area, which are stored in the vector of characteristics of the region in question. In a second cycle, the algorithm computes the corners, concavities, and moments of each region; in the same way the results of the calculations are stored in the feature vectors.

Recognition of the Object in the Image. The feature vectors of each region created in the previous step are the input to the methods to allow the identification of the honey bee. The identification of the bee is through each of the parts, such as antennae, head, thorax, abdomen and extremities (paws); These parts are represented in the feature vectors through the measurements made.

If the bee is recognized in the image, the next phase to execute is the analysis of the honey bee for the detection of Varroa Mite; in case of not detecting the presence of the bee in the image through the regions, the next phase is not carried out.

Image Analysis for the Detection of Varroa Mite. In the case of this work, the analysis of the image for the detection of Varroa Mite is carried out by characterizing the regions, unlike the techniques applied in [12] where the color in the image is essential for detection. de la Varroa mites, in addition to considering that they are parasites with a button shape and a reddish-brown color and also unlike other techniques that process the image for edge detection and make use of Hough transformations. For the case proposed in this research work, the thorax is the part that identifies the presence or absence of Varroa

Mite; the thorax region is identified by the features calculated in the previous section.

4   Experiments

The experiments of the video surveillance system have been carried out in the apiary of the Instituto Tecnológico del Llano, Aguascalientes, México with 2 hive prototypes, which are registered in the Delegation of Agriculture and installed at the regulatory distance from the campus.

This experimentation was carried out to know the efficiency of each of the SVM and kNN techniques using the feature vectors. The number of images presented to the system was gradually increased by 50 images per experiment to determine the percentage of recognition and detect false positives.

To carry out the experiments with the data processing system, a set of 1550 images was generated, of which 750 images of bees have the Varroa Mite. To the set of images used, no prior digital treatment (improvement) was given to the image obtained from the apiary, that is, the images were not improved or intervened by humans to improve the lighting, position of the bee, increase or decrease of the image; there was no discrimination between cloudy or sunny days. The images are processed in real time. Two types of experiments were carried out using the image set, the recognition of the bees in the image and the recognition of the bees in the image with the Varroa Mite. Each of the experiments is explained in the following paragraphs.

4.1   Recognition of the Bees in the Image

In order to verify the effectiveness of the system, experiments were carried out for the recognition of the bee in the image with the entire set of images. A 61% general assertiveness of the system was obtained with kNN and a 63% general assertiveness of the system was obtained with SVM; both results were compared with other systems in the literature whose assertiveness capacities of the objects oscillate between 60 and 90%. To measure the assertiveness of the system, false positives were not considered.

Comments on the Results Obtained. Due to space constraints, the results obtained with this experiment are briefly discussed. Graph of Fig. 8 shows the recognition percentages with both kNN and SVM techniques, as the number of images proposed to the system were increased; the SVM technique is more oscillating for the recognition process but is more effective, while the kNN technique is maintained with similar results during the execution of the experiments, but its effectiveness percentages are lower. For the recognition of the bee in the image, other extensive experiments have been performed, such as the totality of the set of images, images with noise, processing time per image and the processing time of the total number of images, among others.

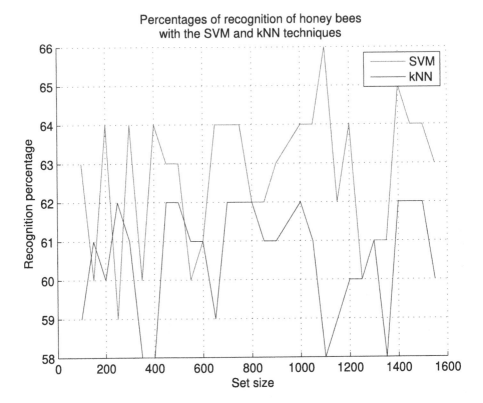

Fig. 8. Recognition percentages of the images with both kNN and SVM techniques.

Although the degree of assertiveness is considered to be regular, we have considered that the results obtained can be improved with the improvement of the techniques proposed in future works that are currently being developed in the server cluster; In addition, as mentioned in previous paragraphs, no discrimination was made between sunny or cloudy days.

4.2   Recognition of the Bees in the Image with the Varroa Mite

For the recognition of the bees with the Varroa Mite, the system must have previously recognized the bee in the image. If the above occurs, the vector of characteristics of the thorax and the vector of characteristics of the abdomen of the bee, with the previous identification of each one of the vectors that each part represents, is classified by the algorithm.

Comments on the Results Obtained. Graph of Fig. 9 shows the recognition percentages with both kNN and SVM techniques, as the number of images proposed to the system were increased. The difficulties for the classification of

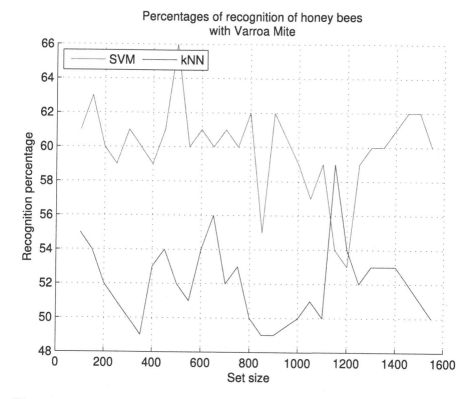

Fig. 9. Recognition percentages of the images with both kNN and SVM techniques when Honey bee has Varrao Mite.

bees with Varroa Mite are several; the system returns many false positives generated by the features obtained in the feature vector. Both the abdomen and the thorax are difficult to identify due to the type of bee analyzed; for example, the Italian honey bee has bands (stripes) on its abdomen that have been difficult to discriminate. These characteristics cause the system to identify the Varroa Mite in a positive way, but in reality they are characteristics of the bee itself.

The results obtained exceed more than 50% recognition, but also a high percentage is discriminated as unrecognized, that is, the system indicates that the bee does not contain Varroa Mite in the thorax or abdomen and the bee is affected by the mite.

Other experiments with other techniques have been carried out to improve the results obtained; for example, the generation of graphs from the image and its analysis using neural network techniques.

5   Conclusions

New technologies focused on the miniaturization of electronic components are important allies for the development of technology that contributes to the solution of problems that beekeeping currently faces. Varroa is a destructive ectoparasite of bee colonies and considered one of the most lethal ectoparasites for bee colonies, which to confront its attacks early requires continuous and invasive observations by humans. In this paper, a non-invasive video surveillance system in hives was presented for the detection of Varroa Mite using Digital Image Processing techniques and techniques for pattern recognition; the results obtained in real environments show us the feasibility of the project, but also the difficulties of developing real-time systems with uncontrolled environments. For the recognition of the objects (honey bees) in the scene, an accuracy of up to 63% was obtained and the recognition of the Varroa Mite reached an accuracy of up to 61%, both results with the SVM technique. Although the results are still limited, new object recognition techniques are currently being explored that are feasible to apply to the classification and recognition of honey bees.

6   Future Works

Because new methods for image recognition have emerged in the literature, a novel image recognition technique based on Graps is currently being experimented with, namely Graph Neural Networks.

References

1. Garratt, M.P.D., et al.: The identity of crop pollinators helps target conservation for improved ecosystem services. Biol. Conserv. **169**, 128–135 (2014). ISSN 0006–3207. https://doi.org/10.1016/j.biocon.2013.11.001, (https://www.sciencedirect.com/science/article/pii/S0006320713003807)
2. Hagler, J.R., Mueller, S., Teuber, L.R., Machtley, S.A., Van Deynze, A.: Foraging range of honey bees, Apis mellifera, in alfalfa seed production fields. J. Insect Sci. **11**, 144 (2011)
3. Smart, M.D., Otto, C.R.V., Carlson, B.L., Roth, C.L.: The influence of spatiotemporally decoupled land use on honey bee colony health and pollination service delivery. Environ. Res. Lett. **13**(8), 084016 (2018). https://doi.org/10.1088/1748-9326/aad4eb
4. Phillips, B.W., Gardiner, M.M.: Use of video surveillance to measure the influences of habitat management and landscape composition on pollinator visitation and pollen deposition in pumpkin (Cucurbita pepo) agroecosystems. PeerJ **3**, e1342 (2015). https://doi.org/10.7717/peerj.1342
5. Ullah, A., Shahzad, M.F., Iqbal, J., Baloch, M.S.: Nutritional effects of supplementary diets on brood development, biological activities and honey production of Apis mellifera L. Saudi J. Biol. Sci. **28**(12), 6861–6868 (2021). ISSN 1319–562X. https://doi.org/10.1016/j.sjbs.2021.07.067, (https://www.sciencedirect.com/science/article/pii/S1319562X21006501)
6. Machado De-Melo, A.A., de Almeida-Muradian, L.B., Teresa Sancho, M., Pascual-Maté, A.: Composition and properties of Apis mellifera honey: a review. J. Apic. Res. (2017). https://doi.org/10.1080/00218839.2017.1338444
7. Soares, S., et al.: Novel diagnostic tools for Asian (Apis cerana) and European (Apis mellifera) honey authentication. Food Res Int. **105**, 686–693 (2018). Epub 2017 Dec 2. PMID: 29433263. https://doi.org/10.1016/j.foodres.2017.11.081

8. Campbell, J., Mummert, L.B., Sukthankar, R.: Video monitoring of honey bee colonies at the hive entrance. In: Conference Proceedings (2008). https://homepages.inf.ed.ac.uk/rbf/VAIB08PAPERS/vaib9_mummert.pdf

9. Babic, Z., Pilipovic, R., Risojevic, V., Mirjanic, G.: Pollen bearing honey bee detection hive entrance video recorded by remote embedded system for pollination monitoring. ISPRS Ann. Photogram., Remote Sens. Spatial Inf. Sci. III7, 51–57 (2016). https://doi.org/10.5194/isprs-annals-III-7-51-2016

10. Hendrikx, P., et al.: Scientific report submitted to EFSA Bee Mortality and Bee Surveillance in Europe. https://efsa.onlinelibrary.wiley.com/doi/pdfdirect/10.2903/sp.efsa.2009.EN-27

11. Lee, K., Steinhauer, N., Travis, D.A., Meixner, M.D., Deen, J., van Engelsdorp, D.: Honey bee surveillance: a tool for understanding and improving honey bee health. Curr. Opinion Insect Sci. 10, 37–44 (2015). ISSN 2214–5745. https://doi.org/10.1016/j.cois.2015.04.009, https://www.sciencedirect.com/science/article/pii/S221457451500070X

12. Schurischuster, S., Remeseiro, B., Radeva, P., Kampel, M.: A preliminary study of image analysis for parasite detection on honey bees. In: Campilho, A., Karray, F., ter Haar Romeny, B. (eds) Image Analysis and Recognition. ICIAR 2018. Lecture Notes in Computer Science, vol. 10882. Springer, Cham (2018). https://doi.org/10.1007/978-3-319-93000-8_52

13. Voudiotis, G., Moraiti, A., Kontogiannis, S.: Deep learning beehive monitoring system for early detection of the varroa mite. Signals 3, 506–523 (2022). https://doi.org/10.3390/signals3030030

14. Sevin, S., Tutun, H., Mutlu, S.: Detection of Varroa mites from honey bee hives by smart technology Var-Gor: a hive monitoring and image processing device. Turk. J. Vet. Anim. Sci. 45, 487–491 (2021)

15. Bilik, S., et al.: Visual diagnosis of the varroa destructor parasitic mite in honeybees using object detector techniques. Sensors 21(8), 2764 (2021). https://doi.org/10.3390/s21082764

16. Método para Determinar Niveles de Varroa en Terreno. Disponible en: https://teca.apps.fao.org/teca/pt/technologies/8663

17. Wu, X., Sahoo, D., Hoy, S.C.H.: Recent advances in deep learning for object detection. Neurocomputing 396, 39–64 (2020). ISSN 0925–2312. https://doi.org/10.1016/j.neucom.2020.01.085.contono

18. Secretaría de Desarrollo Rural y Agroempresarial, Gobierno del Estado de Aguascalientes, México. Fecha de consulta junio de (2023). https://www.aguascalientes.gob.mx/sedrae/

19. Yan, J., Lin, S., Kang, S.B., Tang, X.: Learning the change for automatic image cropping. Open Access Version provided by the Computer Vision Foundation (2013)

20. Vaddi, R., Boggavarapu, L.N.P., Vankayalapati, H.D., Rao Anne, K.: Contour detection using freeman chain code and approximation methods for the real time object detection. Asian J. Comput. Sci. Inf. Technol. 1, 15–17 (2013)

21. Rasche, C.: Rapid contour detection for image classification. IET Image Proc. 12,(2017). https://doi.org/10.1049/iet-ipr.2017.1066

22. Rosenfeld, A., Kak, A.C.: Digital Picture Processing, 2nd edn. Academic Press, New York (1982)

23. Verdoja, F., Grangetto, M.: Efficient representation of segmentation contours using chain codes. In: 2017 IEEE International Conference on Acoustics, Speech and Signal Processing (ICASSP), New Orleans, LA, USA, pp. 1462–1466 (2017). https://doi.org/10.1109/ICASSP.2017.7952399

24. Linares, O.A.C., Botelho, G.M., Rodrigues, F.A., Neto, J.B.: Segmentation of large images based on super-pixels and community detection in graphs. IET Image Process **11**(12), 1219–1228 (2017)

25. Sonka, M., Hlavac, V., Boyle, R.: Image Processing, Analysis, and Machine Vision, Fourth Edition. (2015). Cengage Learning. ISBN-13: 978-1-133-59360-7

26. Appel, K., Haken, W.: Every planar map is four colourable: part I: discharging. Ill. J. Math. **21**, 429–490 (1977)

27. Remias, E., Sheikholeslami, G., Zhang, A.: Block-oriented image decomposition and retrieval in image database systems. In: Proceedings of International Workshop on Multimedia Database Management Systems, Blue Mountain Lake, NY, USA, pp. 85–92 (1996). https://doi.org/10.1109/MMDBMS.1996.541858

28. Azmi, A.N., Nasien, D.: Feature vector of binary image using freeman chain code (FCC) representation based on structural classifier. Int. J. Adv. Soft Comput. Appl. **6**(2) (2014). ISSN 2074–8523

29. Nasien, D., Yulianti, D., Omar, F.S., Adiya, M.H., Desnelita, Y., Chandra, T.: New feature vector from freeman chain code for handwritten roman character recognition. In: 2018 2nd International Conference on Electrical Engineering and Informatics (ICon EEI), Batam, Indonesia, pp. 67–71 (2018). https://doi.org/10.1109/ICon-EEI.2

Author Index

Printed in the United States
by Baker & Taylor Publisher Services